ECONOMIC WELFARE IN THE SOVIET UNION

ECONOMIC WELFARE
IN THE
SOVIET UNION

Poverty, Living Standards, and Inequality

Alastair McAuley

THE UNIVERSITY OF WISCONSIN PRESS

GEORGE ALLEN & UNWIN

Published in the United States and Canada by
The University of Wisconsin Press
Box 1379, Madison, Wisconsin 53701
ISBN 0-299-07640-7

Published in the United Kingdom, Europe, and Australasia by
George Allen & Unwin
Park Lane, Hemel Hempstead, Herts, England
ISBN 0-04-335038-0

First printing 1979
Printed in the United States of America

For Library of Congress and British Library Cataloging in Publication
information, see the colophon

For my mother, who thought that I would never finish this book,

and for my daughter Ellika, who has often wished

that I had never started it

Contents

Charts and Tables

CHARTS

TEXT TABLES

APPENDIX TABLES

Preface

In the writing of any book, I suppose, the author incurs obligations to far more people than he can possibly acknowledge in its preface; that is certainly true of this one. But some of my debts are so substantial that I must make an effort to repay them. My interest in economic welfare and inequality in the USSR (as in so many other aspects of Soviet economics) was first awakened by Peter Wiles. Both his percipience and his occasional wrongheadedness in the conclusions he has drawn from the material have spurred me on to pursue my investigations. But his encouragement has also been of a more practical kind. Frequent invitations to speak at his London School of Economics seminar on the economic problems of the communist world have provided a forum in which the ideas to be found in various parts of this book were first advanced. They have benefited greatly from the sympathetic criticism they received there. I am also grateful to Tony Atkinson, who gave me friendly encouragement both while he was at Essex and after his departure.

Stefan Markowski, another pioneer in the study of Soviet income distribution, gave me the opportunity to express my ideas about wage determination and the role of wage policy in the Soviet approach to welfare and inequality. A paper read to a seminar organized by him at the Centre for Environmental Studies in London forms the basis of chapters 8-10 of this book. Philip Hanson, who worked on consumer problems in the USSR before being lured into the study of more general economic issues, read and suggested material improvements to a set of papers that formed the basis of chapter 2 and chapters 5-7. The latter chapters also benefited from the insight and knowledge of David Granick when they were in a much more advanced stage of completion.

The manuscript itself was written largely during a sabbatical year spent at the University of Wisconsin in Madison. I am grateful to the University and to its Economics Department for the facilities they provided, for the peace in which to work, and for the friendly interest in the book's progress which urged me on to complete it. I am even more grateful to the Political Science Department at the University of Wisconsin and to my wife, who together provided the financial support that enabled me to devote myself full time to writing. Without them, this book would still not have been completed. My own university, the University of Essex, and its Economics Department contributed to the endeavor by allowing me to take the time off to accompany my family to the United States—and thus devote myself to the joys and frustrations of composition.

At a late stage in the proceedings, a grant from the Kennan Institute enabled me to visit Washington, D.C., to enjoy the privilege of working at the Library of Congress, and to improve the treatment of a number of technical topics discussed in the book. In this, the facilities of the Foreign Demographic Analysis Division of the US Department of Commerce were also invaluable. They were generously made available by Murray Feshbach, whose energy and enthusiasm were encouraging in the debilitating conditions of high summer. Murray Feshbach's open-handedness not only contributed to the completion of this work but also broadened my knowledge of topics in the field that I hope to take up in the future.

Further, I should like to express my thanks to Stuart Rees and the staff of the University of Essex Library, and also to Alexander Rollic and his colleagues at the Memorial Library in Madison. The quality of the Soviet collections they maintain greatly facilitated my research; and the zeal and dispatch with which materials not available in these two institutions were obtained from elsewhere did much to allay the irritation that I am sure we all feel when we believe that information exists but cannot be acquired. Also my thanks are due to the Cartographic Laboratory of the University of Wisconsin for their chart drawings, and to the staff of the University of Wisconsin Press and especially Mary Maraniss for having overcome the combined efforts of the British and American postal services to interrupt communication and succeeded in converting turgid English into what I hope is passable American.

Parts of this book have already appeared in one form or another. Most of the statistics in chapter 3 and some of those in chapter 9 were published in my paper "The Distribution of Earnings and Incomes in the Soviet Union" in *Soviet Studies* of April 1977 (although some of the distributions have been revised). I would like to thank the editors for their permission to include them here. Parts of chapters 4 and 11 have been circulated as a discussion paper, *"Anti-Poverty Policy in the USSR,"* by the Institute for Research on Poverty at the University of Wisconsin, Madison, and by the Economics Department at the University of Essex. This paper was also read to the 1977 meetings of both the National Conference on Social Welfare and the midwestern division of the American Association for Slavic

Studies. I am grateful to all of these bodies for providing me with a platform from which to express my views.

Finally, the complete manuscript was read by my wife and by three referees. If I have not always taken account of their suggestions, the comments they made have led me to rethink my position in a number of instances, to argue certain points at greater length, and generally to improve the readability of the book as a whole. It would be wrong to infer that Mary McAuley's role in the production of this monograph has been limited to that of financial provider and referee, however. Throughout the years devoted to its production, her interest and encouragement have been a constant source of support. And if at times I have been rendered speechless by her apparent inability to understand what seem to me to be self-evident propositions, her insistence on logical argument, her willingness to question received dogma, and her concern for the Soviet people, their political and economic conditions, have made me a better scholar and, I believe, have made this a better book. Of course neither she nor any of the others mentioned in this preface is responsible for any of the views advanced here, which are my responsibility alone.

ECONOMIC WELFARE IN THE SOVIET UNION

1

Introduction

INEQUALITY AND SOVIET POLICY

The elimination of inequality between social classes and between different regions of the USSR has been a proclaimed goal of the Soviet government since 1917; indeed, the eradication of differences between town and country, between mental and manual labor is set out as a socialist objective in the writings of Marx, Engels, and Lenin. But there is a distinction between ideologically approved goals and practical policies; there is little to suggest that the Soviet government has been actively concerned about interpersonal or interregional disparities in living standards for much of the period since the revolution. Material welfare and personal consumption did not carry a high priority in the early five-year plans, and Soviet scholars now admit that real wages in 1952 were very little higher than they had been in 1928 (Gordon et al., 1974, p. 59). Until 1960, the plans contained no separate chapter dealing with measures for increasing consumption or improving personal living standards (Karapetyan and Rimashevskaya, 1969, p. 70). And in the early thirties Stalin launched his much-publicized campaign against egalitarian tendencies in the trade union movement and industrial labor force which resulted in greatly increased income differentiation in the short run and, I believe, modified Soviet perceptions of a socialist distribution of income.

There is evidence to suggest, however, that since about 1955 the Soviet government has become more directly interested in the elimination of poverty and in the reduction of inequality in the USSR. This evidence is indirect; it is not possible to point to a new emphasis in the pronouncements of Soviet political leaders, a new preoccupation with the traditional goals of socialism. And, in view of the divorce between rhetoric and action, such an emphasis would be less conclusive than practical measures. But three types of development in Soviet policy making all point to a change in priorities. There has been a substantial expansion in the collection of data that cast light on the standard of living and the extent of inequality, and planning procedures have been modified to highlight these same

3

questions. There has been a significant increase in the amount of official and academic research into poverty, inequality, and wage differentials. There have been extensive changes in the administration of wage and salary policy and a radical reorganization of both pay structures and the various social insurance programs.

In a precomputer society, the collection of data is far from costless. It is unlikely that the family budget survey would have been extended, that wage censuses would have been revived, or that sample surveys of income distribution would have been initiated (for these are the extensions to the data-gathering network mentioned above) unless there was some interest in the information they generated. And interest in information about the distribution of earnings and income surely betokens a concern for poverty and inequality. Also, given the existence of political censorship in the Soviet Union, few books are published that conflict with the current attitudes of the Party and government. The appearance of a series of studies on earnings differentials and the distribution of income during the sixties therefore means that, at least during that period, this was an acceptable topic for academic research, and probably that it was an area of current governmental concern. The other initiatives mentioned emanated more directly from the authorities themselves. They all indicate a new and continuing concern with the problems discussed in this book.

It is interesting to speculate about whether the impetus for this revived interest in poverty and inequality came from the government itself (or from the Party) or whether the authorities were responding to political pressures from below. I do not know if many Soviet citizens feel dissatisfied with their standards of living and whether the proportion has risen or fallen over the past quarter of a century, and I can think of no very adequate way of finding out. This question must, therefore, remain unanswered.

Recent changes in Soviet living standards, the attack on poverty, and attempts to reduce the degree of inequality have not been extensively studied by Western scholars. Janet Chapman's classic study (Chapman, 1963) relates to an earlier period, and the work of others, covering the years since 1960, suffers from a number of weaknesses. Bronson and Severin (Bronson and Severin, 1973; Schroeder and Severin, 1976), for example, concentrate on money income and expenditure; this neglects income in kind, which has been particularly important for certain segments of the population. This is also true of others. And none of this work considers the distribution of income. Wiles and Markowski have attempted to estimate this, but only for a single year (Wiles and Markowski, 1971; Wiles, 1974), and it is possible to improve upon their estimate. Yet the standard of living enjoyed by the Soviet population is a fascinating and important topic not only in its own right but also for what it contributes to the wider study of income distribution and inequality in other societies.

For many, inequality and poverty are the fundamental social and political problems of the second half of the twentieth century. Fifty years ago only a few socialists and radical philosophers like Tawney in England were interested in these topics; today they are studied by sociologists and economists in virtually every industrialized country. Further, in many countries this academic interest either reflects or has generated public concern over existing disparities in income, status, and power. Inequality and poverty are political issues.

The original impetus for this new study of inequality came from sociologists, but the topic has recently been taken up by economists, and they have made a distinctive contribution to the subject. Where sociologists have been concerned with disparities in wealth, status, and power, the degree of coherence between them and their implications for social development, economists have been concerned primarily with the measurement of differences in material well-being and the formulation of detailed policies for modifying the distribution of income. Their work has brought out a number of conceptual problems associated with the measurement of inequality and has demonstrated the dangers in drawing inferences about differences in living standards on inadequate or incomplete information.[1] The results of these economic studies have been incorporated in more recent discussions of social stratification in Western society.

The radical origins of the academic study of inequality and the political opinions of many current scholars have led to the argument that the problems of stratification in industrial society can only be solved by the introduction of socialism. The claim that a socialist society is inherently less unequal than a capitalist one has prompted a number of sociologists to study the nature and extent of stratification in Eastern Europe and the USSR. Both those who believe in the egalitarian nature of socialist society and those who reject it have turned to the experience of the Communist Party-ruled countries of Europe for evidence to support their arguments (Lane, 1971; Matthews, 1972), and this work has influenced the writings of many with no direct interest in specifically Soviet affairs. The absence of more extensive economic studies of living standards and inequality in these societies, however, has resulted in the drawing of a number of mistaken conclusions.

This book, then, has two objectives: first, to gather together the available evidence on recent changes in the standard of living of the Soviet people and on disparities in their material welfare, and to assess the effectiveness of various Soviet policies designed to reduce poverty and inequality; second, to influence the discussion of stratification under state socialism, and indirectly, the study of inequality in other industrial societies.

The material itself is largely statistical. Given the Soviet official attitude towards the publication of economic statistics, the construction of quantitative estimates of personal income and its distribution involves a large amount of detective work and some "guestimation." This is in turn fascinating and frustrating. One experiences a sense of enormous satisfaction after finally teasing out a piece of information that has been concealed or neglected. But one's assumptions can easily be wrong, and it is important to describe sources and methods of estimation in detail to allow the reliability of one's figures to be assessed. I am aware that such descriptions can be boring to those more interested in what the figures show than in how they were obtained, and some effort has been made to confine discussion to the appendices, but the text still contains a great deal.

Inequality, even economic inequality, has many dimensions, and only some of them are considered in this book, but I believe that these are among the most important and are those to which the Soviet authorities have devoted most attention since the mid fifties. The three aspects with which I am concerned are differences between worker and peasant, or rather between the social classes identified in Soviet social theory; differences between the various nationalities that make up the USSR; and differences among Soviet households. Perhaps one should also consider differences between the sexes, but this raises a number of problems about the role of women in the Soviet economy and requires a rather different approach to the analysis of the meager statistical information avaliable. Therefore I have ignored this aspect here, although I intend to explore it at a later date. Similarly, a more explicit treatment of differences in the incomes accruing to occupational groups more closely analogous to the social classes used in Western studies of stratification would be informative, but both the structure of the Soviet economy and the nature of avaliable data make this impossible.

The outline of the book is as follows. Chapter 2 provides estimates of Soviet per capita incomes in a number of postwar years, and these provide an overview of changes in living standards and the way that they have been achieved. It also contains estimates of the incomes of state employees and collective farmers, *kolkhozniki*, separately and a discussion of Soviet attempts to reduce the first type of inequality mentioned above. Chapters 3 and 4 are concerned with disparities in the incomes of individuals and households in the USSR. Chapter 3 contains estimates of the distribution of income for the nonagricultural population of the USSR in 1958 and 1967 and for kolkhozniki in 1965 and 1968, and hypothetical distributions for the population as a whole in 1967-68. Chapter 4 uses these estimates and other material to explore the nature and extent of urban poverty in the USSR in 1958-68 and the way that this has been affected by Soviet welfare policies. Chapters 5-7 are concerned with the character of regional disparities in living standards. Estimates of per capita incomes for both state employees and kolkhozniki in each of the Soviet republics are provided for the three years 1960, 1965, and 1970. These are used to explore the sources of differentiation and the impact of government policy. Chapters 8-10 are concerned with wages and salaries; estimates are provided of the distribution of earnings in the state sector and in industry for a series of years between 1956 and 1970, and an attempt is made to describe changes in Soviet policies on pay, as well as to assess their impact on the distribution of earnings and the extent of earnings differentials. Chapter 11 consists of an analysis of the major welfare programs of the Soviet government and of the impact of the budget as a whole on the distribution of income. The book concludes with a brief chapter that draws together the results from earlier chapters and attempts to set them in a wider perspective. Some of this material has appeared in print already: much of chapter 3 and part of chapter 9 are taken from an earlier paper in *Soviet Studies* (McAuley, 1977); chapter 8 and the rest of chapters 9 and 10 are an expansion of my paper "Wage Determination in Soviet Industry" (McAuley, 1978); a version of chapter 4 was read at the 1977 meeting of the midwestern division of the American Association for Slavic Studies in Ann Arbor and at the National Conference on Social Welfare in Chicago in May of that year. But all of this material has been reworked and particular estimates adjusted in the light of new information.

Before turning to an examination of the evidence on recent changes in the standard of living of the Soviet population, however, I would like to discuss certain methodological problems associated with the measurement of material welfare and inequality. These occupy the remainder of this chapter. How well-off are the citizens of a particular country on the average and how can one determine whether the standard of living has changed between one year and another? How unequal is the distribution of income and how can one measure changes in the degree of inequality? This is the sort of question with which I shall be concerned in this book, but the answers are not necessarily straightforward. Ambiguities in both the concept of the standard of living and the concept of inequality can lead to conflicting conclusions from the same set of statistics. These difficulties arise in all economic systems; there are others peculiar to the Soviet Union. Here I will outline some of the major issues raised by the measurement of economic welfare and inequality and indicate the solutions adopted. Three topics are dealt with: the selection of an appropriate indicator of material well-being, the evaluation of poverty and affluence in the USSR (the problem of international comparisons), and the measurement of economic inequality.

1.2   THE MEASUREMENT OF ECONOMIC WELFARE

Economists have at their disposal a number of statistical measures of economic welfare, the most common being, perhaps, per capita national income and real wages. But there are reasons for supposing that neither of these is an adequate guide to personal well-being in the USSR and the way that it has changed over the past quarter of a century. The first is too broad an aggregate and the second too narrow; neither is appropriate for measuring interpersonal differences.

National income, as defined by Western economists, is a statistical aggregate intended to measure the value of the flow of goods and services that become available to the inhabitants of a particular country for consumption or other uses within a specified period of time—usually a year. Since the Soviet statistical authorities do not compile national income accounts according to the principles used in Western Europe or the USA, the only estimates available are those made by foreign experts. Because the experts lack access to the relevant materials, the estimates are inevitably subject to error. Any other indicator of material welfare is also subject to error, so that this would not matter if national income were clearly the most appropriate indicator of the standard of living. But in the USSR such is not the case.

Where the allocation of resources between consumption and other uses more or less corresponds to the preferences of individual members of society, it can be argued that national income provides a reasonable measure of their material welfare. Subject to certain qualifications about distribution, changes in the value of national income will correspond to individual assessments of changes in living standards. But in the USSR, the state is responsible for approximately half of final expenditure, and there is reason to believe that the preferences of the Party or government do not correspond with those of the population as a whole. It can be argued that the authorities attach a higher value to marginal increments in expenditure on investment, defense, and other public goods than do their citizens. In consequence, the value of these flows as recorded in national income almost certainly overstates the satisfaction derived from them by the private citizen. Changes in the end-use of national income will lead to perceived differences in the standard of living, even if the value of national income remains unchanged. Similarly, the perceived standard of living could remain unchanged when measured national income increases or decreases. Thus per capita national income is an inadequate indicator of material well-being. Further, since much of what follows is concerned with differences in the standard of living of individuals and groups within the Soviet population, and since the imputation to individuals of the satisfaction derived from public expenditure on investment, defense, or administration is largely arbitrary, such flows might as well be excluded from the indicator of material welfare employed.

If per capita national income errs by including too much, the other commonly used indicator of living standards, real wages, is too narrow. As its name implies, this indicator is derived from employment incomes adjusted for changes in the price level. But even in the Soviet Union, households do not derive all of their income from employment. Furthermore, the per capita consumption that can be supported by a given wage will depend upon participation rates—the proportion of household members in employment.

In everyday usage one tends to judge an individual's standard of living by his income, since it is income that generally gives command over goods and services. There is a lot to be said for using a synthetic indicator of material welfare that corresponds reasonably closely to commonsense notions of the standard of living. But although the word may be used frequently in everyday conversations without causing misunderstanding, income is far from a straightforward concept and there have been years of controversy about how it should be measured. Most economists favor the so-called comprehensive or Simons definition: "Personal income may be defined as the sum of (1) the market value of rights exercised in consumption and (2) the change in the value of the store of property rights between the beginning and end of the period" (Simons, 1938, p. 50). This represents an ideal. Available statistics do not usually permit one to estimate income on this definition; in practical work one must be content with a less all-embracing measure.

In this book I shall make use of three concepts of income, that, in principle, approximate more and more closely to the Simons definition. First there is *money income*. This consists of the monetary receipts accruing to a person or group within a particular period, say a year. Soviet statisticians identify four categories of monetary receipt that together constitute the money income of households and individuals. There are payments for labor services; these can be subdivided into earnings from state (or occasionally private) employment and the money payments to kolkhozniki by collective farms. Next, there are monetary receipts from private subsidiary economic activity, the most common probably being the sale of agricultural commodities produced on private plots. Third, there are transfer payments—pensions, stipends, sickness or maternity benefits, and the like. And finally, there are receipts from the financial system— interest on savings deposits, lottery prizes, and so forth. For some individuals and groups this category includes interpersonal transfers, alimony payments, and financial support for family members living apart. (In the aggregate, such flows cancel each other out.) As all these flows are measured in rubles, the calculation of money income involves no problem of valuation; it is therefore the most accurately measured of the concepts used here.

Table 1.1
Income Concepts Used in This Study

A. Money income
   1. Money earnings from employment
      a. in the state sector (excluding holiday pay)
      b. from collective farms
   2. Money receipts from private economic activity
   3. Transfer payments
      a. pensions
      b. other social security benefits (including holiday pay)
      c. stipends
   4. Receipts from the financial system
      a. interest on savings deposits
      b. lottery prizes, etc.
B. Personal income
   1. Money income
   2. Receipts in kind from collective farms
   3. Value of private agricultural output consumed within the producing household
C. Total income
   1. Personal income
   2. State expenditure on
      a. preschool child care
      b. education (excluding stipends)
      c. medical care
      d. custodial care of the old, etc.

The Soviet definition of money income includes the value of loans to the population, net of repayments. These loans are primarily for the purchase of housing. From a strict accounting point of view this is an asset transaction rather than an income flow, but on the Simons definition such transactions should be allowed for. In the estimates of average per capita income given below, I have followed Soviet practice.

The concept of money income excludes the value of benefits received in kind and thus does not fully reflect the individual's command over resources. In the past, such benefits have formed a significant portion of the personal consumption of certain groups in the USSR. They are substantial even today. It is possible to distinguish between two categories of nonmonetary benefit: those that enter fully into the household budget and over whose disposition the household has complete freedom, and those that specified households may consume but cannot make any other use of if they refrain from consuming.

The most important of the benefits that directly enter the household budget in the USSR have been payments for labor services by kolkhozy and that part of the output of private agricultural holdings that is consumed within the producing household. *(Kolkhozy,* collective farms, traditionally paid their members partly in cash and partly in kind; the cash proportion rose significantly during the sixties, but even in 1970, benefits in kind were still important in some areas. This topic is discussed further in chapters 2 and 6.) Estimates of income in kind from kolkhozy and private holdings, together with money income, constitute the second concept which I call *personal income.* Personal income purports to measure the value of resources over which the household or individual exercises control. It ought perhaps to include the imputed rent of owner-occupied housing and perhaps some allowance for certain fringe benefits, but available statistics make this difficult if not impossible. There are three types of owner-occupied housing in the USSR, apartments in housing cooperatives, used primarily by better-off families, *izby* or traditional peasant huts in rural areas, and *dachas.* In principle these are summer residences in resort areas and not permanent accommodation. But they can range from one-room shacks to country mansions used by members of the Politburo, directors of major enterprises, or leading members of the scientific and cultural intellegentsia. Some are lived in throughout the year. Information on the ownership and use of this property is so limited that no attempt has been made to allow for it in the estimates of personal income given below. It has been claimed that approximately one-half of all Soviet families live in private accommodation, so this is a serious omission (Smith, 1976, p. 79; Morton, 1974). But since casual observation suggests that those living in private accommodation are not markedly better housed than those who rent from the state, and since the rents charged for state-owned housing are relatively low, the distortionary effects of this omission should not be too great.

Casual observation and the reports of journalists suggest that fringe benefits are substantial in the USSR—at least for certain groups. Workers in some enterprises or industries may receive protective clothing or have access to subsidized canteens. Reliable or fortunate employees may enjoy subsidized holidays or rest cures at sanitoria on the Black Sea or Baltic coast. Enterprise directors or leading members of the intellegentsia may have access to a chauffeur-driven car or a residence in the country; they may also enjoy the right to purchase some scarce or imported commodities at subsidized prices in special stores. The existence of this network of privilege imposes special problems for the estimation of income and its distribution. Clearly the privileges contribute to the material welfare of those who enjoy them, and so some estimate of their value should be included in income. But rights to them are transferable only to a limited extent if at all. It is doubtful, therefore, how far they should be included in personal income. If a household with access to a rural residence (say in consequence of the husband's position) does not wish to spend its summers in the country but would rather visit the opera more frequently, it is not clear that the household is always at liberty to rent out the property and spend the proceeds on opera tickets. Thus, a rural residence may be different from income in kind from one's private plot, or even from privately owned housing, since that can be rented. On the other hand, access to so-called closed shops may increase the purchasing power of a personal or money income significantly. In any case, discussion of these issues is largely academic. There exist no official statistics on the extent or distribution of such privileges, and I can think of no way of allowing for them in my estimates. Furthermore, the more extreme type of privilege, access to the closed distribution network and so on, is limited to a relatively small elite, perhaps 1 percent or fewer of the country's households (Matthews, 1975; Smith, 1976, pp. 25-53). While failure to allow for privilege will certainly distort my estimates of inequality, this omission will have very little effect on their quality given the other sources of error to which they are subject. In particular, it should not affect the shape of the main body of the distribution, which is all one can hope to obtain at this stage.

Finally, in the USSR as in a number of other countries, the state provides its citizens with a number of services either free of charge or at subsidized prices. To exclude these would understate the standard of living in the USSR, particularly in comparison with other countries. The most important of these services are preschool child care, education, and medical services. The concept of *total income* consists of personal income plus an allowance for the value of these services. It also includes the value of housing subsidies, certain cultural expenditures, and the costs of custodial care for the old.

Both personal and total income are more comprehensive than money income, and although neither includes an estimate of changes in wealth, both come closer to the Simons definition. But both involve the valuation of goods and services for which market prices do not exist; they are therefore likely to contain substantial errors.

Total income suffers from a further weakness. It involves an estimate of the value of services that add to individual income but from which the element of personal control is missing. Such services are included at cost—that is, at the value placed on them by the state. Given the choice, individuals might prefer to devote more resources to the production of food, for example, and rather fewer to the provision of education, or vice versa. In the absence of a market, there is no guarantee that at the margin, individual valuations of such services as health or education correspond to those of the state. Such services should therefore be revalued at prices

reflecting individual preferences. For the Soviet Union such an exercise is impossible.

One may, however, consider total and personal income as two alternative estimates of the same variable. In the first, it is assumed that individuals place the same value as the state on marginal increments of such services as health and education. In the second, it is assumed that individuals place a zero value on increments in such services. Since I suspect that the individual valuation of such services would be positive but less than the state's, the two estimates should bracket the true value of income.

All three concepts of income are used, in this book, to measure economic welfare and the extent of inequality in the Soviet Union. For statistics on the distribution of income and the scale of interpersonal differentiation, money income and to a lesser extent personal income are used. This reflects the impossibility of imputing to individuals or households the value of free services consumed. On the other hand, comparisons of the standards of living of different social groups and the discussion of regional disparity in economic welfare are based on personal and total income. These are the most appropriate indicators, but in any case it has proved impossible to obtain adequate estimates of money income for individual republics or social groups.

There are three further adjustments to be considered before we leave the subject of measuring material welfare: taxes, prices, and the unit of account. First, direct taxes. Insofar as the government uses the revenue from direct taxes to finance the provision of such services as health and education, the relevant sums should be excluded to avoid double counting. Indeed, since individuals have little choice over whether to pay taxes or not, such sums can scarcely be said to be within their control, and an argument could be made for excluding them from personal and money income as well. Where the tax structure is progressive, the post-tax distribution of income surely provides a better measure of inequality in living standards than the pre-tax distribution. There is insufficient information about the incidence of direct taxes in the Soviet Union to permit one to estimate a post-tax distribution of income, but since taxes are small in absolute magnitude and the schedule is almost proportional, this shortcoming should not lead to too great a bias in estimates of inequality.

The second problem is that of price inflation. An increase in nominal incomes that is accompanied by an equal increase in the prices of goods and services does not represent an increase in the standard of living. But if economic welfare is measured by nominal income, it will be recorded as such. To solve this problem, it is customary to deflate estimates of nominal income by a cost-of-living index yielding estimates of real income. This is

the practice followed here. But the measurement of inflation in the Soviet economy raises a number of further problems. The Soviet government does not itself publish a cost-of-living index; it does, however publish a retail price index, and this has been virtually constant since 1955. Many observers argue that this constancy is spurious, a statistical artifact; the real situation, it is suggested, has been one of continuing if modest inflationary pressure. This pressure is of two kinds; there has been some open inflation, and also, the Soviet economy has been characterized by substantial and continuing excess demand—repressed inflation.

The Soviet retail price index is a base-weighted index of the prices of goods sold in Soviet retail trade outlets. By keeping the prices of goods included in the index constant, the Soviet authorities can maintain a stable index, but they are under no obligation to continue to produce and sell these goods. By replacing them with new grades and models carrying a higher price tag, the cost of living can rise, even though the retail price index does not (Bornstein, 1972, pp. 370-75). By carefully comparing value and volume series for a number of commodities that enter retail trade, two Western economists have recently constructed an implicit deflator for personal consumption that does indeed show continuing but modest increases since 1955, accelerating in the seventies (Schroeder and Severin, 1976, p. 652).

Measuring the extent and consequences of repressed inflation is more difficult. Its existence is presumed from the observation that queuing is common and that certain goods are often not available—that is, from basically anecdotal evidence. But until recently no one thought to ask what the impact of repressed inflation would be on the rest of the economy, particularly on labor supply and savings. Since the authorities publish some statistics on these variables, econometric estimates of labor-supply functions or savings functions would permit one to ascertain changes in the severity of repressed inflation, if some relationship existed. This work has now been undertaken, and although only preliminary results have been obtained, they suggest that there has been little change in the extent of repressed inflation in the USSR since the death of Stalin (Portes, 1975, 1976a). Thus one may argue that the queues and shortages that are so common a feature of life in the USSR reflect micro-market disequilibria rather than general excess demand. They should be accompanied by inventory accumulation, but this will not be apparent to the casual observer. If this interpretation is accepted, no further adjustment to estimates of nominal incomes is required to allow for repressed inflation, and none is made here.

Finally there is the question of the unit of account, that is, the definition of the income unit and of the period to which income refers. So far I have assumed implicitly that all individuals receive income, but this is not true.

People marry and have children and—formally at least—children often have no income. Similarly, people grow old and retire. After retirement they may receive a pension, they may live off accumulated savings, or they may live with working children. In these and other cases, the effective standard of living of the individuals concerned may differ from that implied by the income with which they are credited. Differences in family arrangements may not matter too much in the calculation of average income for the population as a whole, but they may affect estimates of the distribution of income significantly and thus the assessment of inequality.

In this book I follow Soviet practice, which has a great deal to recommend it. The income unit is defined as the family, and it is assumed that all the members of one family enjoy the same standard of living. Thus Soviet statisticians eschew all problems associated with intrafamilial distribution. For these purposes, the family is defined as a group of individuals, not necessarily related by blood or marriage, who share a common budget. It is thus closely related to the English concept of a household, and in this book I use the terms interchangeably.

The per capita income of a family or of its members is defined as the total (or personal or money) income accruing to all the members of the family, divided by the number of its members. It is possible to argue, however, that the needs of individuals and therefore their consumption depend upon age and sex. This would imply that families with the same nominal income and the same number of members, but differing in composition, would have different standards of living. There is also the possibility of economies of scale in consumption. That is, while it may not be true that two can live as cheaply as one, it is certainly true that a doubling of family size does not necessarily mean a doubling of all kinds of expenditure. To take a count of these possibilities, statisticians have produced so-called adult equivalent scales. These are intended to allow for differences in the age and sex composition of families and for differences in family size. Their construction raises a number of conceptual problems, and there is little agreement between the scales advocated by different statisticians (Nicholson, 1949; Shvyrkov, 1959 and 1968). In this book, such scales are used only in the analysis of interrepublican differentials.

Lastly, there is the question of the period to which income refers. Here the possibilities are theoretically limitless, but since most national income statistics are collected on an annual, quarterly, or monthly basis, we in practice are limited to these three periods. In fact, most published Soviet statistics are on an annual basis, and that is the period used below for estimates of average incomes. Some of the material used was derived from sample surveys, however, and this usually relates to monthly incomes. For the purpose of estimating average income, it does not matter much whether annual or monthly data are used, but such differences can affect estimates of the extent of inequality. Since the incomes of most families will fluctuate from period to period within certain limits, the shorter the period used, the greater the apparent disparity. In principle, the most appropriate period for analysis will be affected by the extent to which individuals average out their incomes over successive time units. Although in the Soviet Union most forms of income accrue on a monthly or fortnightly basis, it seems plausible to assume that individuals would not regard transitory increases or shortfalls occurring within a given month as necessarily determining consumption in that month. Most families maintain money balances which they draw on in months when income is low and add to when income is high. It seems less plausible to assume that families will behave in this way from year to year, and even less plausible when it is a question of quinquenium to quinquenium. Thus the most appropriate period is probably longer than a month and shorter than five years. It is conventional to use a year, but here again one is in the hands of the Soviet statisticians who collect the primary data. They are faced with a different problem. Since most payments in the USSR accrue on a monthly basis, people are likely to be able to recall what they received in the previous month with some accuracy. In the absence of written records, estimates of income and its components received in the preceding year are likely to be substantially less reliable. Therefore the statistician who collects his information by means of a sample survey must trade off reliability against the possibility of overstating variance and hence inequality. In general, Soviet statisticians have preferred reliability. Distribution data normally refer to monthly incomes and therefore overstate the degree of inequality when compared with annual data. I have no idea how large this bias is (Atkinson, 1975, pp. 36-40).

1.3   THE EVALUATION OF POVERTY AND AFFLUENCE

The indicators of material welfare proposed in the preceding section measure the Soviet standard of living in terms of rubles, but most people who live outside of the USSR have no intuitive feel for the value of a ruble. Therefore the assertion that in a certain year the average per capita income was x rubles conveys no impression of how well or badly off the Soviet population was in that year. To a greater or lesser extent this is a problem for all international studies of living standards. Where the emphasis is on changes in living standards over time or on differences in the level of material welfare enjoyed by particular groups, ruble figures can be regarded as a sort of index; but it is also desirable to provide some measure of absolute achievement both in terms of what has been done elsewhere and in terms of the goals of the Soviet authorities themselves. These points are discussed here.

For purposes of international comparison two methods suggest themselves. Ruble figures can be converted into pounds or dollars at the official rate of exchange, or they can be converted at some purchasing power parity rate. The first has little to recommend it. Given exchange control, the foreign trade monopoly, and fixed exchange rates, there is no reason to suppose that the official rate corresponds to an equilibrium rate. Even if these problems could be overcome, the fact that the structure of personal consumption differs from the pattern of international commodity flows implies that the equilibrium exchange rate is inappropriate for standard-of-living comparisons. It is to take account of these differences that purchasing power parity rates are calculated. For purposes of information, the official rate of exchange was 2.50 rubles to the pound in 1965 ($1.11 to the ruble); in 1976 it stood at 1.35 rubles to the pound ($1.35 to the ruble). More appropriately, Hanson calculated a ppp rate of 3.02-3.48 rubles to the pound in 1965 (Hanson, 1968, p. 56).

The exchange rates of the preceding paragraph can be used to convey a rough idea of Soviet living standards to an international audience. They cannot be used to construct a bench mark for assessing the success of Soviet policy in achieving the government's own objectives. For this I propose to use the Soviet definition of poverty, *maloobespechennost*,[2] and the rest of this section is devoted to a discussion of the Soviet approach to this question.

The measurement of poverty in the USSR is based on the construction of normative budgets. For these a committee of experts determines the quantities of goods and services deemed necessary for a household with a particular composition to achieve a specified standard of living. These goods and services are then valued at ruling prices, to give a ruble value to the poverty standard. Thus the Soviet government and most if not all Soviet economists and sociologists adhere to an absolute definition of poverty. There has been virtually no published discussion of relative approaches. This Soviet work is in the tradition of Rowntree, but the most recent examples have been a great deal more detailed. Not only does the committee of experts determine the composition of food purchases, but it also specifies wardrobes for each member of the household and inventories of household effects. Annual and monthly expenditures are derived by assuming particular depreciation and replacement rates for these "durable" items.

Soviet economists made considerable use of normative budgets in the study of cost-of-living changes in the twenties, but at some time in the thirties all such computations ceased, only to be resumed in 1956. Although absolutist in approach, both Marxist tradition and Soviet practice recognize the relativity of consumer tastes and hence the relativity of the subsistence minimum. It is accepted that the poverty standard will have to be recalculated from time to time, as earnings rise and technological progress generates new consumption possibilities. The first postwar normative budgets were constructed in 1956-58 and may have been used to determine the new minimum wage introduced at that time. Since then there have been a number of subsequent calculations in the course of which the methodology has been improved. For the purposes of this book, the most important version was that compiled in 1965-67.[3]

The 1965 normative budget was designed to assure a minimum of material statisfaction and was described as containing "the volume and structure of necessaries of life required for the reproduction of labor-power among unskilled workers, *rabotniki prostogo truda*" (Sarkisyan and Kuznetsova, 1967, p. 18). It was prepared in two variants, for single workers and for a notional family of four (a married couple, a boy of thirteen, and a girl of seven). This second variant exploits both economies of scale in consumption and the fact that consumption depends upon age and sex. The single-worker budget was compiled separately for nine different regions of the country, and the family-variant for four. Both were restricted to the urban population (Sarkisyan and Kuznetsova, 1967, p. 3).

As reported in 1967, the cost of purchasing the minimum material satisfaction budget (hereafter the MMS budget) was 205.60 rubles a month or 51.40 rubles per capita. Although Sarkisyan and Kuznetsova do not give the adult-equivalent scale they used, coefficients taken from a later paper suggest that in 1965 the cost of the MMS budget for a single worker was some 58.20-59.40 rubles a month.[4]

Fifty-nine percent of the MMS budget for the family of four was spent on food, drink, and tobacco, 27% on clothing, furniture, and other household goods, and the remaining 14% went on rent, utilities, and other services. The MMS budget contains twice as much bread and 34% more potatoes than were consumed on the average in the United Kingdom in 1970; it contains only 58% as much meat, 68% as much milk, and 44% as many eggs. While nutritionally adequate, the prescribed diet is much higher in carbohydrates and lower in protein than that of the average UK citizen (Bush, 1975, p. 57). Food expenditures in total constitute a much higher proportion of the MMS budget than they do in budgets constructed for the United States or many Western European countries. For example, the category food, drink, and tobacco carries almost twice the weight assigned to it in Orshansky's calculations on which the US poverty standard is based. But such comparisons can be misleading; because of differences in economic organization, medical expenses are negligible, rent and transport relatively unimportant, and so on.

In this study I equate the MMS budget standard with the poverty level, or, to be more precise, I assume that in 1965 the Soviet poverty level was equivalent to a per capita personal income of 50 rubles a month. In point

Table 1.2
The Influence of Inflation and Changes in Definition on the Poverty Level, USSR, 1958-68

	Alternative Poverty Levels (R per month per capita)			
	Urlanis	Sarkisyan	Kapustin	Cost-of-living Index
Year	1958	1965	1968	(1960 = 100)
1958	25.0	45.8	54.0	98.3
1965	27.3	50.0	58.9	107.2
1967	28.1	51.5	60.7	110.4
1968	28.7	52.6	61.9	112.7
1975	31.5	57.9	68.2	124.0

Sources: Column 1 is inferred from Urlanis, 1966, pp. 135-46; see chapter 4 for further details. Column 2 is taken from Sarkisyan and Kuznetsova, 1967, p. 67. Column 3 is inferred from Kapustin and Kuznetsova, 1972; see chapter 5 for further details. Column 4 is taken from Schroeder and Severin, 1976, p. 652.

of fact, the published Soviet calculations refer to money income, but the evidence suggests that for urban inhabitants there is little difference between the two concepts. This interpretation of the MMS budget as a poverty level received some confirmation when in 1974 the Soviet government specified 50 rubles per capita per month as the entitlement criterion for its newly introduced family income supplement; it also specified personal and not money income (*Pravda*, 27 Sept. 1974). It may be helpful to know that at the official rate of exchange in 1965, 50 rubles a month was equal to £4.6 a week; at the 1976 rate it was £8.5. Using Hansen's more appropriate purchasing power parity rates, it was equivalent to £3.3-3.8, depending upon whether UK or Soviet consumption weights are used.

The use of any single ruble figure as a poverty standard for a period of twenty or twenty-five years (the period covered by this book) raises problems of its own, and I have not been entirely consistent. Not only has the cost of living changed over this period, but the average income increased by about 50% between 1960 and 1974; between 1955 and 1974-75 it may have doubled. Thus relative to the level of economic welfare enjoyed by the rest of the population, an income of 50 rubles a month (or 44.70 rubles, allowing for inflation) implied a much higher standard of living in 1955 than it did in 1965. Similarly, an income of 50 rubles a month (or even 56.30 rubles) implied greater penury in 1974 than in 1965. The only way of avoiding this conceptual relativism would be to recalculate the MMS budget at yearly intervals or at least relatively frequently, and this apparently has been done by the NIIT.[5]

We know much less about the structure of the normative budgets compiled in 1956-58 than of those for 1965. Indeed, we do not even know the estimated ruble cost of living, but indirect estimates, described more fully in chapter 4, suggest that it amounted to some 25-30 rubles a month per capita. The NIIT apparently also carried out calculations in 1968 leading to an estimated MMS budget cost of 61.9 rubles a month per capita. Again, the ruble figure has been obtained indirectly (the source and methods are described more fully in chapter 5), and as the budget referred to the cost of subsistence in the central provinces of the USSR, this may explain part of the discrepancy. There is also a slight difference in the description of the target living standard. It is not clear whether this conceals a real difference or is merely a matter of writing style.

There are thus three versions of the official poverty standard for the years 1958-68, the highest being amost 247% above the lowest. Over the period, the cost of living increased by about 14.6% and average money income (for the nonagricultural state employee population) by 29-36%. Adjustments in the official definition of poverty are thus much greater than can be explained by either the rate of inflation or the growth of average incomes. This would seem to imply a considerable liberalization of official attitudes. The 1956-58 work on this subject by the NIIT has been criticized for methodological weakness, and it is possible that the 25-ruble limit owes more to a priori beliefs or prejudice than to detailed calculation of the cost of subsistence. After all, the minimum wage was raised to 27-35 rubles a month in September 1956, almost certainly before the results of this work became available, and the new minimum retirement pension for those in urban areas was set at 30 rubles a month at about the same time. Both of these are supposed to be determined with reference to the MMS budget. At the same time, one can argue that the 1968 limit is too high (for the USSR as a whole), and this is probably also true of the 1965 level. From a relativist standpoint, a poverty level that coincides with the fourth decile of the income distribution is rather different from one that corresponds to the first quartile—and its policy implications differ too. Nevertheless, the 50-ruble MMS budget level remains the primary criterion of poverty and affluence used in this study.

1.4   THE MEASUREMENT OF ECONOMIC INEQUALITY

This book deals not only with changes in the average standard of living in the USSR over the past twenty years or so but also with the way that economic inequality has changed over that period. Now, the idea of an equal distribution of income is relatively unambiguous, and it follows logically that if income is not distributed equally, there must be inequality. But faced with two different distributions of income, people may disagree about which is the more unequal. The measurement of inequality is both conceptually and empirically difficult. Problems arise in part because one is trying to reduce a multidimensional construct to a single parameter. As we frequently talk about greater or lesser inequality, such implicit reduction is part of the way we think; difficulties in determining which of two distributions is the more unequal reveal a fundamental ambiguity in our everyday concepts.

Judgments about inequality are frequently called for, not only in the comparison of different societies but also in the assessment of public policy. They have become particularly important in recent years, as the extent of inequality has acquired political significance and as governments have pursued policies designed to reduce it.

The traditional way of displaying the distribution of income is the construction of a Lorenz diagram. This gives the proportion of income recipients on the horizontal axis and the proportion of total income they receive on the vertical axis. Any particular distribution is thus represented as a curve on or below the main diagonal. The main diagonal itself is associated with a perfectly equal distribution of income; the more unequal the distribution the more the Lorenz curv sags away from the diagonal. The numerical measure of inequality associated with the Lorenz curve is the Gini coefficient. This is defined as the ratio of the area between the diagonal and the Lorenz curve to the area beneath the diagonal. It thus varies from a value of zero, for a perfectly equal distribution of income, to unity, when all income is received by a single individual. But a variety of other statistics of concentration and dispersion have also been used to characterize inequality and have thus been used in the assessment of public policy.

Atkinson has shown that these apparently neutral statistical measures imply certain value judgments about the desirability of particular types of redistribution. In particular, he has shown that a necessary and sufficient condition for one distribution to be judged less unequal than another by any quasi-concave utility function is that their Lorenz curves do not intersect. As a corollary, for any two distributions with intersecting Lorenz curves it will always be possible to specify social welfare functions that give divergent rankings. The importance of this result is that differences in the Gini coefficients (or in any other of the commonly used statistical measures of inequality like the log-variance or coefficient of variation) of two distributions do not depend upon whether or not their Lorenz curves intersect. Thus it will be possible to find two distributions with intersecting Lorenz curves and with the Gini coefficient of the first less than that of the second. On this criterion the first will be ranked as less unequal than the second. On some other criterion the ranking will be reversed (Atkinson, 1970).

When one constructs the Lorenz curves relating to the distribution of income in different economies at a specific time or to the same economy at different times, they typically intersect. Thus according to the Atkinson result, one is unable to say which is the more unequal without specifying fairly precisely the sorts of redistribution that are regarded as socially desirable—that is, without specifying a social welfare function. Also, unless there is agreement on the social welfare function, opposing conclusions may be reached from the same set of statistics.

The Atkinson result asserts, however, that if the Lorenz curves of two distributions do not intersect, all measures (and all normal social welfare functions) will show that the distribution associated with the curve lying closer to the main diagonal is less unequal than the other. In empirical work this is of less assistance than might be thought at first, however. Virtually all statistics relating to the distribution of income are presented in grouped form; thus the Lorenz curves can only be constructed with a certain degree of error. Since the Lorenz curves for many actual income distributions are very close to one another, there is a substantial risk of drawing the wrong conclusion from a graphical analysis.

These reservations apply with particular force to Soviet data because of the way that the estimates have been derived. Neither the Lorenz curves nor their associated Gini coefficients can be computed with any accuracy, and I will make no use of these measures. Instead I will rely primarily on two more robust measures of dispersion, for all their limitations. For interrepublican disparities I will use the coefficient of variation, for interpersonal ones the decile ratio. This latter statisic has the advantage of being completely insensitive to errors in the tails of the distribution—regions about which information is particularly weak. It is also insensitive to changes in the body of the distribution, but some attempt will be made to allow for this by using other range-ratios.

In this chapter I have provided definitions of the three indicators of material welfare that will be used in this study to measure changes in Soviet living standards. I have also suggested how these income concepts may be translated for the purposes of international comparisons, and how they may be used to assess the effects of policies designed to reduce or eliminate poverty in the USSR. Finally, I have described some of the difficulties associated with the measurement of inequality, and suggested how they can be resolved (or ignored). I now turn to an examination of the available information on Soviet living standards.

2

Personal Income, 1960–74

THIS CHAPTER will attempt to determine how living standards have changed in the post-Stalin period for the Soviet population as a whole, as well as discussing changes in the relative positions of the basic social groups in the USSR. The figures presented here suggest that the level of material welfare of the Soviet people in 1960 was low, and that in spite of substantial increases over the ensuing decade and a half, the average Soviet household in 1974 had an income that was barely sufficient for the enjoyment of what Soviet sociologists have called "a rational pattern of consumption" but which would more appropriately be called a modest but adequate standard of living. As might be expected, kolkhozniki were substantially worse off than other groups in 1960, and although their income increased the most rapidly of any group in the next ten to fifteen years, they continued to be worse off than state employees in 1974. On the other hand the sixties, in particular, witnessed extensive modernization and monetization of the Soviet economy, reflected in changes in the structure of household income. The figures below suggest, also, that by the end of the period the preeminence, if not the identity, of the Soviet industrial working class had been substantially eroded.

2.1   PER CAPITA INCOMES IN THE USSR
The following estimates of per capita money, personal, and total income have been confined to the years 1960, 1965, 1970, and 1974, because I intend to go behind the All-Union figures and explore both interpersonal and interrepublican differences. Some such limitation was necessary to keep the amount of statistical material within manageable proportions. This decision means that little light will be shed on year-to-year changes in material welfare in the USSR. But such changes have been studied by others (Bronson and Severin, 1973; Schroeder and Severin, 1976), and in any case, I believe that they are of less significance than the longer-term trends which are revealed by the use of benchmark years.

A more complete analysis of living standards in the Soviet Union since the death of Stalin would require estimates of income, in, say, 1955 as well as the years given here. Such estimates could be constructed for the USSR as a whole, but for individual republics or social groups the information is not readily available, if it was ever collected. Since the estimates here are intended to provide marginal control totals for the more detailed figures given later as much as to act as an introductory orientation, no attempt has been made to extend the period covered.

The choice of benchmark years is not as crucial for the Soviet Union as for an economy that suffers from significant cyclical fluctuations. Annual average rates of growth of various indicators will be only slightly altered by small changes in the periods used. The years used here have been chosen partly for numerological reasons and partly for politico-economic ones. Years ending in a five or a zero are seen as more important than the intervening ones—an attitude that bedevils demographers. Because Soviet statisticians are affected by this prejudice, there is somewhat more information available about incomes and living standards in the years chosen than in others. 1974 was selected because it was the latest year for which reasonably complete information was available, when the analysis underlying this chapter was completed. The periodization chosen permits contrasts between the last five years of the Khrushchev period and the first years of Brezhnev and Kosygin.[1]

Most economic statistics in the Soviet Union, as elsewhere, are generated as a by-product of administrative procedures; therefore the concepts and categories used will depend to some extent on the administrative structure that produces them. The very different system of economic administration in the USSR is likely to result in statistics that, even if they bear the same name as Western constructs, differ significantly in coverage or content. Some attempt has been made to identify and explain the content of the main income categories used in the Soviet Union and reproduced here, but doubtless many problems remain. In consequence, comparisons between the structure of income in the USSR and in other market economies should be made with caution.

Estimates of the various components of total income and the way in which they have been derived are given in appendix A. With the exception of the value of agricultural output produced on private plots, all have been taken from official sources. The latter is based on estimates of the value of private production by kolkhozniki, given by Sidorova.[2] These have been grossed up on the assumption that republic by republic, yields per hectare are the same on the private plots of state employees and collective farmers. Since state employees are on the whole better off than kolkhozniki, they may not work their plots so intensively, and consequently the estimates given here may overstate the total value of private agricultural output.[3] Soviet reliance on multiple-pricing systems and the existence of substantial double-counting in the index of gross agricultural output made it impossible to check the adequacy of the estimates from the production side. The fact that the estimates given here correspond closely to those given by other Western scholars, however, suggests that the errors attributable to this source cannot be excessive.

Estimates of per capita money, personal, and total income, together with figures on direct taxation for the four benchmark years used in this chapter, are given in table 2.1. Before they are examined in any depth, some comment on their adequacy is called for. In table 2.2 the figures for

Table 2.1
Per Capita Income, USSR, 1960-74 (rubles per year)

	1960	1965	1970	1974
Total income	510.7	679.0	928.1	1114.9
Personal income	445.6	583.9	798.9	951.5
Money income	382.4	521.8	736.6	910.5
Direct taxes	27.0	34.3	53.8	74.0

Notes and Sources: Derived from appendix tables A1 and A2, and appendix F. Differences between the three income concepts are explained in chapter 1.

Table 2.2
Per Capita Money Income: Alternative Estimates (rubles per year)

Year	Arouca	Bronson-Severin	Karcz	McAuley
1960	na	402.5	425.8	382.4
1965	601.7	538.8	570.8	521.8
1970	845.2	753.7	na	736.6
1974	na	936.4	na	910.5

Sources: Arouca, 1974, table A4.1; Bronson and Severin, 1973, p. 393; Schroeder and Severin, 1976, p. 652; Karcz, 1966, p. 443, table 2.1.

per capita money income are compared with those derived by other scholars. The comparison is confined to money income, since others have restricted themselves to this indicator. At first glance, there are substantial differences between money income as derived here and the estimates given by others. In 1960, for instance, the difference between my figure and that of Bronson and Severin was 5%; for the more recent period it was between 2 and 3%. For both 1965 and 1970 Arouca's estimates are approximately 15% greater than mine. These differences can be explained by the fact that I have excluded items included by both Arouca and Bronson and Severin and as a result of differences in our estimates of the cash component of kolkhoz pay and private agricultural sales. Of these, the first is the most important.

Arouca and Bronson and Severin both include an estimate of the value of military pay and allowances. I omitted this item because I could see no satisfactory way of allocating it between republics. If the Bronson and Severin estimate of this is included in the totals given in appendix A, the revised estimates of per capita money income are (rubles per year):

1960	400.1
1965	536.3
1970	750.6
1974	924.8

These are virtually the same as the figures reported in table 2.2, column 2. Arouca also includes other income categories not given by Bronson and Severin or myself. He does not explain how these figures are derived, and further, it is doubtful whether items like receipts from the sale of private belongings should properly be included as income rather than asset transfers. Consequently, I suggest that his estimates are too high.

The figures in table 2.1 show that between 1960 and 1970 there was a moderate increase in the monetization of the Soviet economy; per capita money income increased from 75% of per capita total income to something more than 79%. In 1974 the relationship between money and total income was virtually the same as in 1970. These changes were a reflection of two developments: a fall in the relative importance of private agricultural activity, which declined from 14% of the total to less than 8%, and an increase in the frequency with which kolkhozy paid their members in cash. As I argue below, these apparently moderate changes in the structure of total income are a consequence of substantial modifications in the position of collective farmers.

Before the figures in table 2.1 can be used to examine the rise in living standards in the USSR, some account must be taken of changes in direct taxation and prices. The relevant information is given in table 2.3, which also contains figures on per capita GNP and average earnings in the state

Table 2.3
Standard of Living Indicators, USSR, 1960-74

Indicator	1960	1965	1970	1974
Personal disposable yearly income (R)	418.6	549.6	745.4	877.5
Cost-of-living index	100.0	107.25	114.42	120.71
Real disposable (personal) income	100.0	122.4	155.6	173.6
Real GNP per capita	100.0	117.6	144.2	163.3
Average monthly earnings (R)	80.6	96.5	122.0	141.1

Sources: For the cost-of-living index, Schroeder and Severin, 1976, p. 652; for real GNP per capita, Greenslade, 1976, p. 269; for monthly earnings, state employees only, NK SSSR '74, p. 562.

sector, for purposes of comparison. Results are given for personal income only, but those who are interested will find it relatively easy to calculate equivalent figures for money income. There is some doubt, however, about how well the cost-of-living index given in the table applies to the series on total income, since the index does not cover "free" services.

Direct taxation has not been very significant in the Soviet Union during the period considered here. In 1960 tax payments amounted to 6% of personal income (8.5% of per capita money income) and in 1974 to 7.8% (8.1%). In view of the possible errors in the estimates given here, one may conclude that at least until 1970, taxes have been proportional to income. Thus the result of the changes in tax structure first introduced by Khrushchev and continued by his successors has been to keep average tax rates constant in the face of rising incomes. The figures in table 2.3 show that the cost of living rose at an average annual rate 1.35% over the fifteen years considered here; not negligible, but substantially less than in most other industrial economies.

Between 1960 and 1974 per capita real personal disposable income increased by 73.6%, that is, at an annual average rate of 4%. The rate of growth was highest in the quinquennium 1965-70, when real incomes grew at 4.9% per annum, but it was also substantial during the last five years of the Khrushchev period (4.1% per annum between 1960 and 1965). On the other hand, after 1970 the rate of growth of real disposable personal income declined to as little as 2.8% per annum. It would seem that neither the difficulties of the late Khrushchev period nor the much-heralded economic reforms of the 1965-68 period had much of an impact on the rise in popular living standards. At the same time, the consequences of the harvest failure of 1972 and of the more general economic problems of the early seventies are clear. But it must be pointed out that a growth rate of 4% per annum in real incomes is a substantial achievement.

Other figures in table 2.3 suggest, moreover, that it is an achievement that cannot be maintained indefinitely. Between 1960 and 1970, personal incomes grew more rapidly than per capita GNP. Although there was a substantial increase in personal saving over the period, the bulk of personal income was consumed, as is usual in the USSR. If incomes grow faster than output in such circumstances, resources must be diverted from investment, defense, or public administration, to provide for increased personal consumption. There are limits to how far such changes in end-use can go. And, since 1970, the rate of growth of disposable income has fallen below that of real GNP.

The rise in living standards in the USSR since 1960 has been impressive, but the absolute level of material welfare attained in 1974 (and even more, that of 1960) was modest. This is true even when the standard of living is assessed in terms of an internally defined criterion like the MMS budget.

Per capita personal income, gross of direct taxes (since tax payments are included in the MMS budget basket) in 1960 was only 79.6% of the 1965 national poverty level adjusted for changes in prices. In 1974 it was some 40% above this level. In the late sixties, a number of Soviet sociologists and economists suggested that an income of 70-75 rubles per month per capita was required to maintain "a rational pattern of consumption" (Gordon and Klopov, 1972, p. 36; Sarkisyan and Kuznetsova, 1967, p. 126); it was not until some time between 1970 and 1974 that this level was attained. Thus after fifteen years of growth in personal incomes, or rather after a quarter of a century, since there is evidence to suggest that incomes grew rapidly after 1952, the Soviet population had achieved only a modest level of economic welfare when judged by their own standards, and certainly when compared with the levels achieved in the other industrialized countries of Europe and North America.

2.2 PEASANT LIVING STANDARDS

The figures in the last section referred to the Soviet population as a whole, but such statistical averages can conceal wide discrepancies in the incomes of both individuals and groups. It is to the analysis of differences between the incomes of collective farmers and of various groups of state employees that the remainder of this chapter is devoted.

In Soviet social theory, the population of the USSR is made up of two nonantagonistic classes and one stratum: the collectivized peasantry, the working class, and the intelligentsia. Formally, these classes are defined in accordance with Marxist theory, by reference to their relationship with the means of production,[4] but they are much more than theoretical constructs. Until at least 1965, the state employed different administrative procedures to regulate almost every aspect of the lives of peasants and workers. (For administrative purposes and often in statistical records, the intelligentsia is included in the working class.)

These differences in legal and social status are reflected in differences in both the standard of living and the structure of incomes of kolkhozniki and state employees. Table 2.4 contains estimates of money, personal, and total income for each of the two Soviet social classes. No account has been taken of changes in the cost of living, for lack of adequate data. The likely consequences of failure to adjust for price changes is problematical. Since consumption patterns for the two groups are unlikely to be the same, one must assume that they have faced different rates of price inflation; it is impossible to guess who has suffered more. Furthermore, I should point out that the estimates of money income for 1960 and 1965 are unreliable. There is reason to believe that the figures given in the table, low as they are, overestimate the money incomes of kolkhozniki in those two years.[5]

Table 2.4

Per Capita Incomes of Kolkhozniki and State Employees, USSR, 1960-74 (rubles per year)

	State Employees				Kolkhozniki			
	1960	1965	1970	1974	1960	1965	1970	1974
Total income	571.9	720.6	969.5	1158.9	378.9	551.2	762.3	900.6
Personal income	499.7	624.3	833.9	984.3	328.9	460.0	659.1	791.5
Money income	(480.3)	(600.4)	790.0	(967.1)	(171.3)	(280.8)	523.2	(634.8)
Direct taxes	39.6	45.5	66.9	89.3	8.3	7.7	9.9	10.8

Notes and Sources: Total and personal income calculated from appendices A, C, and D. Money income in 1970 calculated on the assumption that state employees sell 20% of what they produce on their private plots. (This was the proportion in 1969; see Sarkisyan, 1972, p. 173.) The same ratio was used for other years.

On the basis of the figures in table 2.4 the following conclusions can be drawn. In 1960, the disposable personal per capita income of kolkhozniki was approximately 70% of that of state employees; in 1965, it had risen to almost 80%; and in 1970, it stood at 84.6%. By 1974 kolkhozniki had made further gains: their per capita disposable income amounted to 88.9% of that of state employees. A similar picture emerges if the comparison is made in terms of total incomes, except that, somewhat surprisingly, peasants fail to make relative gains after 1965. In 1974 the per capita total income of kolkhozniki was 76.1% of that of state employees; in 1965 it had been 76.5%.

In 1960, state employees enjoyed a modest enough standard of living, well below that prescribed by the MMS budget, but by 1965 they had surpassed the "poverty level" and in 1970 were approaching a personal income sufficient to permit "rational consumption." In 1960, the personal per capita income of kolkhozniki was little more than half the MMS budget level, and it was only towards the end of the decade that they surpassed it.

The figures in table 2.4, doubtful as they are, also show that even as late as 1960 kolkhozniki were effectively excluded from the modern monetary sector of the Soviet economy. In that year the per capita money income of collective farmers was approximately one-third of that received by state employees. By 1965 it had reached 47%, and in 1970 it was approximately two-thirds of the state employee level. No further gains were made after 1970, but over the decade of the sixties, the peasantry was largely integrated into the money economy.

Both the condition of the collectivized peasantry in 1960 and the relative improvement it experienced in the following ten years can be ascribed to the operation of government policy. Eight years after the death of Stalin, kolkhozniki still suffered from most of those legal, social, and economic disabilities that characterized what may be called the Stalinist development model. Although there is evidence to suggest that peasant earnings, and indeed incomes, had increased dramatically since 1952, that the so-called revolution in farm household incomes was well under way, there had been little change in their social or legal position. The peasantry was still an underprivileged class.

In the fifteen years after 1960 this framework of systematic discrimination started to crumble; in fact, the change of heart on the part of the Soviet government can be pushed back to 1958. One by one, the major sources of legal and social discrimination have been removed (or their repeal has been promised). There are now few remaining administrative distinctions. Changes in policy are reflected in a reduced disparity in living standards between the social classes and in a growing similarity in the structure of incomes received. But as the figures given here show, there is still some way to go.

The differences in treatment meted out to peasants and state employees will be familiar to all those with some knowledge of the Soviet Union, but it may be worth mentioning the aspects of this systematic discrimination that had the greatest effect on living standards in 1960. I will then go on to indicate how far these have been modified in the ensuing period and suggest the ways in which the relaxation has affected peasant incomes. In essence, I believe, the peculiar administrative structure of the USSR has meant that over most of the period considered here, state employees have had greater occupational and geographical mobility than the peasantry, greater access to the social security system, better housing, higher earnings, and greater certainty of payment.

One key to the difference in opportunity between state employees and peasants is that state employees possess internal passports (identity cards). This means that subject to certain limitations (primarily restrictions on living in major cities like Moscow and Leningrad) they can change their jobs and places of residence. Kolkhozniki, on the other hand, do not possess passports, although in 1975 the government promised that they would be issued by 1981 (*Pravda*, 25 December, 1974). Without a passport, the kolkhoznik cannot live in an urban area; he cannot even leave the kolkhoz without the consent of the farm administration. Thus he has little choice of either occupation or place of residence.

The situation is not quite as bleak as this account suggests. Numbers of young kolkhozniki acquire passports on their discharge from the armed forces (after military service), and others obtain them in a variety of accepted but more-or-less unofficial ways. Thus, it seems plausible to assume that the Soviet passport system, although it has been only partially successful in stemming the drift from the land, has helped the authorities keep down agricultural earnings, and therefore peasant incomes, by reducing geographical and occupational choice for kolkhozniki.

The fact that the kolkhozy are legally cooperatives was the cause of another disability suffered by peasants in 1960. State employees are paid their wages once a month (the mid-month pay packet is formally an advance on monthly earnings). Kolkhozniki, in contrast, received no wages until 1966, but instead received a share of the net income of the farm. This share was calculated after all the other obligations of the kolkhoz had been met, including investment. Given the very low prices paid by the state for agricultural products and the frequently inefficient and labor-intensive production methods employed in Soviet agriculture, the share was often extremely small. For doing the same work, state farm employees were usually much better paid.

Nor was low pay the only disability from which kolkhozniki suffered; much of what they received from the collective farm was distributed in kind. In 1960, as much as 38% of total kolkhoz labor payments were distributed *in natura*; in 1965 it was still almost a quarter, but change was rapid after that, and in the seventies it was only 7% or less (Sarkisyan, 1972, p. 173). Also, until the later fifties, kolkhozniki were seldom paid more frequently than once a year. Uncertainty over how much and how often they will be paid has been an important factor in increasing the reliance of kolkhozniki households on private plots.

Finally, until 1965 kolkhozniki were not entitled to state retirement pensions. They were expected to rely upon their plots or upon what their kolkhoz would provide (often little enough), or to remain in employment. When the state pension scheme was extended to collective farms, the benefits provided kolkhozniki were lower and the age of retirement higher than for state employees. In addition, members of collective farms did not receive maternity benefits until 1965 or sickness benefits until 1970. And while a majority of state employees live in heavily subsidized state housing, collective farmers still often live in their own izby. As a result they receive no housing subsidies. These issues are discussed at greater length in chapter 11. The virtual exclusion of the collectivized peasantry from the state social security system until the mid sixties is yet another reason for the kolkhozniki's attachment to his private plot.

Thus the absence of passports, proper wages, and social welfare support contributed to the disability of collective farmers in the USSR in 1960 and indeed to a lesser extent throughout the following fifteen years. Such administrative discrimination has been in addition to the disadvantages normally associated with rural residence—poorer educational and health facilities, inadequate transport and communications, and restricted access to the retail trade network. One should add, too, that geography and climate, the sparsity of population, and the relative backwardness of the country make differences between urban and rural areas more marked in all these respects in the USSR than in most smaller European countries. But in the late fifties the Soviet authorities initiated what appears to have been a concerted attack on the sources of differentiation in the living standards of peasants and workers, I believe they have had a certain measure of success.

There are three major strands to this "new course." First, in the years after 1958, a number of the kolkhozy were converted into state farms. This transformed their members into workers, entitled to be paid wages at sovkhoz rates and eligible for the full range of social security benefits. Almost certainly, an increase in kolkhoznik living standards was not the primary object of the conversion program. Rather, by facilitating the provision of subsidies to agriculture, the authorities hoped to increase agricultural investment significantly and thus bring about a substantial increase in output and efficiency.

The program, however, was operated on quite a large scale and has had a considerable impact upon the structure of the agricultural labor force in the Soviet Union. In 1960, there were 67.3 million kolkhozniki and their dependents in the USSR, 31.7% of the population. By 1965 the share of collective farmers had fallen to 24.7% and by 1970 to 20%; in that year their number had fallen to only 49 million. This relative and absolute decline was primarily the result of the policy of converting kolkhozy into state farms and thus converting peasants into workers, although the drift from the land continued throughout the decade. In 1960, average annual employment in Soviet agriculture was 29.4 million man-years, of which 22.8% were on state farms. In 1965, at the end of the Khrushchev period, the number had fallen to 28 million, while state employment had risen to 32.5% of the total. In 1970 total agricultural employment had fallen still further to 26.8 million, and sovkhoz employment had increased marginally from 9.1 million to 9.8 million, 36.6% of the total (*Narkhoz SSSR '70*, p. 404). And the process has continued.

The conversion program led to increases in wage rates and earnings for peasant members of the converted farms. More generally, a policy of greatly increasing the prices paid by the state for the agricultural commodities it purchases improved the financial position of uncovered kolkhozy. This policy was initiated by Khruschev as early as 1953 and has been continued over the following seventeen years and more. The better financial position of collective farms permitted them to raise the rates at which the labor of their members was remunerated, but the process was impeded by the peculiar legal status of payments for labor under Soviet kolkhoz law before 1966. Since such charges were a residual obligation of the collective farm, any financial difficulty of the farm was immediately and inevitably translated into a cut in the earnings of kolkhozniki. The resultant uncertainty over earnings (and the fact that

on many farms, distributions were still very small) was thought to dis-
courage labor supply. In consequence, the Soviet authorities have introduced a number of measures designed to increase both the level and certainty of kolkhoz pay. These form the second strand of the "new course"
mentioned above.

Dating from the late fifties, a number of regulations were introduced
at first permitting and then requiring kolkhozy to make advances to
their members at more frequent intervals. But still, according to reports,
only 90% of farms in 1968 undertook systematic monthly payments to
their members and a further 5% made such payments at less frequent
intervals (Komarov and Chernyavskii, 1973, p. 49). Of more importance was a decree in May 1966 which made payments for labor a
prior charge on the gross income of the collective farm—that is, made
such payments legally wages. The same decree recommended that kolkhozy should adopt wage scales based on those in force in state agricultural
enterprises. Finally, recognizing that this would increase the costs of some
collective farms substantially, the government authorized the state bank
to extend medium-term credits (up to five years) to cover the additional
wage bill. This was the first time that bank credit had been made available
for wage costs. Clearly the government was hoping for rapid and relatively uniform implementation (*Pravda*, 18 May, 1966). If so, their hopes
were not realized.

Table 2.5
Distribution of Kolkhozy by Pay, 1954-74

Average Earnings as % of Sovkhoz Rate	% of Kolkhozy		
	1954	1962	1974
-10	6	0.3	
10-25	39	8.0	11.3
25-50	30	46.7	
50-75	15	45.0	52.6
75-	10		36.1
Average monthly earnings (R):			
Sovkhozniki	45.6	66.1	122.1
Kolkhozniki	16.4	34.8	90.5

Notes and Sources: Distributions derived from Lagutin, 1965, pp. 29, 34, and Kotov and
Kvachev, 1976, p. 86. Kolkhoz pay in 1974, ibid. Sovkhoz pay 1962, 1974 from *Trud*,
1968, p. 145, and *NK SSSR '74*, p. 562. Kolkhoz pay in 1954, 1962 was calculated from the
fact that pay in 1963 was 2.3 times pay in 1953 (Lagutin, 1965, p. 34); this relationship also
gave sovkhoz pay in 1954. See also Taichinova, 1974, p. 56, for confirmatory calculations.

Some idea of the scale of the difference in earnings between kolkhozniki
and state farm workers can be gained from table 2.5, although, un-

fortunately, the years for which figures are available do not coincide with the periods of substantial policy change. In 1962 more than half of all kolkhozy paid their members at less than half the average sovkhoz rate; in 1954 the proportion was three-quarters, and in 1974, some eight or nine years after the Soviet government passed the decree requiring the collective farms to pay their members wages at sovkhoz rates, 11% of kolkhozy were still in this category. In 1954, the average earnings of state farm workers were approximately 1.85 rubles a day; in 1955 the average monthly earnings of industrial workers were 76.2 rubles, or assuming a six-day week, 2.93 rubles a day. In 1954, then, some 45% of kolkhozy were paying their members less than 46 kopeks a day—less than 16% of the average industrial wage! Certainly the situation has improved immeasurably since Stalin's death, but even in the mid seventies there are problems. In 1968 the Soviet government raised the minimum wage for state employees to 60 rubles a month. In 1973 only 59% of kolkhozy were using pay scales based on this minimum; in a number of republics the minimum wage in force for kolkhozniki was only 40 rubles a month. By 1975 the government had raised the state sector minimum to 70 rubles, and the relative position of collective farmers has apparently deteriorated (Kotov and Kvachev, 1976, p. 87).

Both the conversion program designed to facilitate an increase in investment, and the various price rises and legal reforms mentioned above, which resulted in increases in the level and certainty of earnings, were adopted primarily because of their expected effect upon output and productivity. That they also led to an increase in peasant incomes was perhaps fortuitous. The same cannot be said for the third strand of recent Soviet policy—the gradual elimination of discrimination in the field of socal insurance and social security. The contribution that such policy makes to agricultural efficiency is at best limited. As mentioned above, starting in 1965, the government has gradually extended the major benefits of the Soviet welfare state to the collectivized peasantry. At first, benefit levels were lower and eligibility criteria more stringent than for state employees, but in the years since 1970, even these differences have been whittled away. The subject is discussed at length in chapter 11, and I will not repeat it here. The effects of this policy on peasant incomes is apparent from the figures in table 2.6, and it might be argued that the promised modification to the internal passport system is but a continuation of this approach.

A clearer idea of the impact of the policies pursued by the Soviet government on the incomes of both state employees and collective farmers is conveyed by the figures in table 2.6. In percentage terms, there was little change in the structure of incomes accruing to the first group between 1960 and 1974. Earnings accounted for about three-quarters of income in

Table 2.6
The Structure of Personal Income,
State Employees and Kolkhozniki, USSR, 1960-74 (rubles per year)

Source of Income	State Employees				Kolkhozniki			
	1960	1965	1970	1974	1960	1965	1970	1974
Earnings from								
State	376.1	473.8	623.8	742.3	34.1	36.9	48.0	70.4
Kolkhoz	—	—	—	—	110.3	204.0	310.3	398.2
Private activity	24.2	29.8	41.4	41.3	171.7	194.6	227.2	239.8
Transfers	90.6	111.1	152.5	187.0	4.9	16.2	66.0	69.6
Other	8.8	9.6	16.2	13.7	7.9	8.3	7.6	13.5
Personal income	499.7	624.3	833.9	984.3	328.9	460.0	659.1	791.5

Sources: Appendices A, C, and D.

all of the years for which figures are given, and transfer payments for another 17-18%. The remaining categories of income were relatively unimportant. In contrast, there were substantial changes in the structure of kolkhoznik incomes. In 1960, earnings from the collective farm generated only a third of personal income, and earnings from employment as a whole were responsible for little more than two-fifths of the total. Receipts (income) from private plots accounted for more than half the total, while the contribution of transfer payments was negligible. Between 1960 and 1965 receipts from private plots increased in ruble terms, but their relative importance declined; they were surpassed as a source of income by kolkhoz earnings. In 1965, more than half of the personal income of collective farmers was derived from employment. Although over the same five-year period there was a dramatic relative increase in the value of transfers, in 1965 they were still a negligible proportion of kolkhozniki income. The breakthrough occurred after 1965 with the introduction of pensions for the peasantry.

Over the period as a whole there has been a considerable *rapprochement* in both ruble and percentage terms in the incomes received by the two classes, but significant differences remain. Kolkhozniki still receive less in transfers from the state, although they are on the average less well off, and they still derive a third of their income from private activity. Thus although the Soviet government has made a considerable effort to integrate the collectivized peasantry with the rest of the population, some fourteen million kolkhoznik households were still forced, in 1970, to rely upon tiny plots of land (about half a hectare in size) and small numbers of domestic livestock, to satisfy a third of their needs. They still had to work longer hours for a smaller and less-certain reward than those employed by the state.

2.3   THE INCOMES OF INDUSTRIAL WORKERS

The foregoing analysis has shown that between 1960 and 1974, living standards of the collectivized peasantry grew at a substantially more rapid rate than did those of the rest of the population. But state employees and their dependents form a heterogeneous group of little sociological or ideological significance. In this section I will present estimates of the personal and total per capita income of the industrial working class. Workers, particularly industrial workers, occupy a central position in Soviet ideology and political rhetoric; it was in the name of the working class that the revolution was made, and we are told repeatedly that it is in its interest and through its agency that subsequent achievements have been attained. Yet comparatively little is known about the material welfare of Soviet industrial workers and their families, about the way their living standards have changed over the past quarter of a century, or the extent to which they have been affected by changes in government policies towards wages, taxes, and social welfare expenditures. It is to these questions that this section is addressed.

Identifying such population groups as social classes raises a number of conceptual and empirical questions however, and these, as well as the Soviet authorities' traditional secretiveness about the release of economic statistics, may have contributed to official silence about workers' living standards. These issues are discussed briefly before I present my own income estimates.

In applying the threefold classification of Soviet social structure for practical purposes, statisticians (and presumably administrators) have proceeded in three steps: first, they have identified the head of the family; second, they have assigned him or her to one of the three social groups, primarily on the basis of employment; finally, all members of the family have been assigned to the same social group. There are certain ambiguities involved in this procedure, primarily concerning the definition of a family (or household), the indentification of its head, and the determination of class status for the nonemployed. There are at least three definitions of the head of the family used by Soviet statisticians and sociologists. The 1959 census asked family members to designate a head, and where they could not agree, it was left to the enumerator to do so. The enumerator was instructed to specify the person who contributed most to the family budget, provided he or she resided permanently with the dependents (*Itogi*, 1959 USSR, p. 242). What happened in other cases is not clear. By another system, the head of the family has been defined as the person who contributes most to the family's budget. And a third, used in some surveys, has defined as the head of the family that person in whose name the family's accommodation is registered (*oformlen*). What happens in cases of joint registration is not clear, but perhaps Soviet administrative procedures preclude this (Maslov, 1959a, p. 38).

For census purposes, a family has been defined as a group of two or more people, not necessarily related by blood or marriage, who share a common budget, but most tabulations of family size include only those living in the same place. This leaves a substantial number of persons outside the structure of family classification. Since most of them will either be employed or have been employed, this need not affect estimates of social structure, but it should be borne in mind when dealing with Soviet estimates of the average family size of different social groups.

We should also bear in mind that insofar as social class is determined by employment, the procedure outlined above does not classify persons belonging to families whose head is not employed. If the head of the family receives a pension, one suspects that his last recorded employment is used to determine his class status; if the head is a student, his class status is probably determined by that of his parents. But Soviet sources are silent on these points.

Thus, although this threefold schema suffers from a number of ambiguities, it does recognize that class is a social phenomenon, and therefore it assigns all inhabitants of the USSR (or rather, its permanent population) to one class or another. But insofar as one believes that social class is determined exclusively by occupational status, this results in a certain amount of misclassification. For example, the adult children of a collective farmer who live at home will be classified as kolkhozniki, even if they are employed by the state. Similarly, members of the intellegentsia may be classified as workers, or vice versa, depending upon family relationships. How serious this problem is depends upon the extent of intermarriage and the nature of occupational choice open to different individuals. This in turn depends upon the extent of social mobility and the fineness of one's classification scheme. One would expect more fuzziness in determining the size of the industrial working class than in determining that of the working class as a whole. And the problems of determining the living standards of coal miners, say, or sheet metal workers would be greater than those of determining the standard of living for the working class as a whole. There is substantial intermarriage and intergenerational class mixing even in terms of the simple threefold classification. According to the 1970 census, the first for which this information is given, some 30% of all families contained members in different occupational (and hence social) groups.[6] Although the proportion of mixed-class families was not higher in those republics which were more urbanized, one suspects that the extent of class mixing (on Soviet definitions) has increased since the early fifities.

To cope with this problem, among others, recent Soviet studies of social stratification have abandoned the family-by-family approach in favor of an explicit categorization of the active or gainfully employed population, *samodeyatelnoye naseleniye* (Senyavskii, 1973, pp. 412-45). Such an approach successfully avoids the problem of mixed-class families— but at great cost. Analysis of the social composition of the Soviet population is reduced to an analysis of the structure of the labor force. Taken to its logical conclusion, this approach implies that an individual worker ceases to be a member of the working class as soon as he or she leaves employment. The justification of a class analysis of society, and thus of an interest in changes in the size of particular social groups, rests upon a belief that members of any particular class have fundamental economic and social interest in common. It implies a very narrow and partial conception of interest to assert, as does Senyavskii tacitly, that (for example) a woman who leaves her job to have a baby, *by that action* ceases to possess the interests and aspirations that she shared with her fellows while in employment, or alternatively, to claim that the interests of dependent children are not substantially the same as those of their parents. Further, a stratification procedure that omits 56% of the population (Senyavskii, 1973, p. 425) or on the other hand puts the children of intellectuals and unskilled workers into the same category cannot claim to provide the basis for a class analysis of society. It also makes statements about changes in the living standards of particular social groups essentially meaningless.

For all its limitations, the traditional inclusive classification schema provides a better basis for comparing the living standards of social groups, and it is the one adopted here. Indeed, since this approach underlies the collection of data on family budgets, and since the family budget survey, for all its shortcomings (see chapter 3 below), provides the basic statistical information on the incomes of kolkhozniki and industrial workers, one has little choice in the matter.

The 1970 census figures reveal that some 30% of Soviet families contain employed members from more than one of the three traditional occupational groups: kolkhozniki, workers (*rabochiye*), and clerical staff (*sluzhashchiye*). I would suggest that as one moves from "workers" to "industrial workers," the proportion of mixed households will rise, and that although the figures cited below purport to refer to the standard of living of industrial workers' households, perhaps as many as 40 or 50% of the families covered will contain one or more persons from another occupational group. At the same time, a substantial number of wage earners employed in industry will, in all probability, be excluded from the analysis. This suggests that for the purpose of income comparisons, if not more generally, the industrial working class is not a particularly useful concept. Since families often contain industrial and nonindustrial workers or industrial workers and clerical workers (who may or may not be members of the intelligentsia, but this is another story),[7] one can distinguish only approximately between the standard of living of these groups and the standard of living of kolkhozniki or managerial and technical personnel, for example. Still, in view of the ideological and rhetorical importance of the industrial working class in the USSR it seems worthwhile to make the attempt.

The problem raised here applies to societies other than that of the Soviet Union. It results from an assumption that, in general, there is only one earner per family. This may have been true in the past, but as female participation rates rise and as the birth rate and the age of marriage fall, the assumption becomes less tenable. Or it may be assumed that there is a fundamental similarity in the employment opportunities open to the members of a particular family. In a sense this is probably true, but if, in addition, one ascribes peculiar importance to particular forms of occupation, distinguishing between industrial workers and those employed in a nonmanagerial capacity in shops and offices, for instance, similar problems will arise. But further discussion of these issues and their relevance for a class analysis of society would take us too far afield. I now turn to the problem of estimating the personal and total per capita income accruing to households whose head was an industrial worker during the sixties and the first part of the seventies.

The Soviet authorities publish very little quantitative information about the living standards of their people as a whole or of specific social groups, although recently they released some of the results of the family budget survey. Such material as is made available throws more light on the structure of the incomes of industrial workers than on their level. Consequently, the estimates presented here have been obtained indirectly, on the basis of statistics given by individual Soviet academics.

Komarov and Chernyavskii report that according to family budget survey data, in 1960 the income per family for kolkhozniki was 64.5% of the income of industrial workers, in 1965 it was 72.5%, and in 1969, 75% (Komarov and Chernyavskii, 1975, p. 71). These relationships form the basis of the estimates given here. It is claimed that these figures relate to total income, *sovokupnyi dokhod*, but the same authors state that in 1970, earnings from employment accounted for 86% of the total income of the families of industrial workers (Komarov and Chernyavskii, 1973, p. 70). According to the structure of the incomes of families of industrial workers published by the CSA, in 1970 earnings accounted for 74.4% of total income and 86.4% of what one may call personal income, or *mobilnyi dokhod*.[8] On the assumption that they use terms consistently within the same passage, one may therefore infer that the Komarov and Chernyavskii figures for 1960-69 refer to the latter concept. The data in

Table 2.7
Per Capita Personal Income, Industrial Workers, 1960-74

	1960	1965	1969	1970	1974
Personal income per family, kolkhozniki (R per year)	1380	1815	2168	2218	2479
Personal income per family, industrial workers					
as % of kolkhozniki	155	137.9	133.3	na	na
rubles per year	2140	2504	2891	3001	
Average family size (industrial workers)	3.58	3.49	3.42	3.40	na
Personal income per capita, industrial workers (R per year)	598	717	845	882	1016

Notes and Sources: Row 1, appendix table D1 and appendix table A5; row 2, Komarov and Chernyavskii, 1973, p. 71; row 4, see text; row 5, 1974, calculated on the assumption that earnings per capita equal 51.4% of the average industrial wage; see text for justification. Cf. NK SSSR '74, p. 605.

appendix D may be used to generate estimates of personal income per family for kolkhozniki, and thus one may obtain ruble figures for the personal incomes of industrial worker families. These are given in table 2.7. The figure for 1970 given in the table has been extrapolated from that for 1969; Komarov and Chernyavskii claim that the annual average rate of growth of personal income for industrial worker families in 1961-69 was 3.8% (Komarov and Chernyavskii, 1973, p. 70); it was assumed that the same rate applied to 1969-70.

The figures derived so far refer to income per family, but the families of industrial workers differ in size from those of kolkhozniki, and there is evidence to suggest that their size changed over the period 1960-70. Some account should be taken of these facts in the derivation of indicators of material welfare. According to the census, in 1959 the average size of urban worker families was 3.6 persons; it was 3.88 persons, if allowance is made for those who live apart from their families but contribute to the family budget (Itogi, 1959, USSR, pp. 249-51). I assume that these figures are a reasonable estimate of the size of industrial worker families. The equivalent figures for kolkhozniki in the same year were 3.9 and 4.06 persons, but these refer to families on census definitions. Which corresponds more closely to the concept of family used in the family budget survey? Some Soviet economists have used kolkhoznik households, nalichnye kolkhoznye dvory, the number of which is published each year by the CSA, as equivalent to families in estimates of personal and total income (Sidorova, 1972, pp. 74-75). The data in appendix table A5 imply that in 1959-60 the average size of kolkhoznik household was 3.93 persons. One may therefore assume that the more restrictive concept of the family used in the census corresponds more closely to the concept of kolkhoznik family used in the family budget survey. One may also assume that industrial worker families are treated analogously. (This makes a certain sense: the family budget survey is concerned with patterns of expenditure as much as with levels of income; it would be difficult to obtain consistent data on the expenditures of individuals living apart from their families and to integrate them with the rest of the budget. Rather, I suspect, contributions from such persons will be treated like other transfers—pensions, stipends, and alimony.)

For 1970, the census returns indicate that the average size of pure urban worker families was 3.4 persons, that of pure kolkhoznik families 3.9 persons. The relationship between these two figures corresponds to the claim that on the average, kolkhoznik families were 15% larger than those of industrial workers.[9] Given estimates of the size of industrial worker families in 1959 and 1970, estimates for intervening years may be obtained by interpolation. These estimates are given in table 2.7; in the absence of other information, it was assumed that family size declined at a constant rate over the period 1959-70. These figures permit one to calculate personal income per capita for the years shown. (At this point it should be admitted that there is a certain ambiguity about the figures given in table 2.7. For 1959, kolkhoznik family size as calculated from the census and from the number of households is approximately the same; for 1970, the figures in table A5 imply an average household size of 3.4 persons. If Sarkisyan were using these figures rather than census ones, the implied size of industrial worker families would be 2.93 and not 3.4 persons, which would raise one's estimate of personal income per capita. This alternative was rejected, finally, because Sarkisyan's comment does relate to a census year and because a 5.5% decline in family size over eleven years struck me as inherently more plausible than an 18.6% decline. However, estimates of kolkhoznik income are based on the number of kolkhozniki given in table A.5.)

Komarov and Chernyavskii's figures, together with the assumptions described above, permit one to estimate personal per capita income up to 1970; for 1974 a different approach must be adopted. The one used here has the advantage of simplicity, if not plausibility. Given estimates of per capita personal income, as derived in table 2.7, one may use the data on the structure of income published by the CSA to infer a ruble value of earnings per capita in industrial worker families. This may be compared with the average industrial wage and the resultant relationship may be used to extrapolate per capita earnings to 1974. Data on the structure of income in 1974 may then be used to infer a value of personal income in that year. The relevant figures are given below:[10]

	1960	1965	1970	1974
Earnings per capita (rubles)	502	608	763	879a
Industrial wage (net of holiday pay)	900	1131	1454	1710
Ratio (%)	55.8	53.8	52.4	51.4a

a. Extrapolated.

The figures given above indicate that over the period 1960-70 earnings per capita in the families of industrial workers declined as a percentage of the average industrial wage. This occurred in spite of a modest (assumed) decline in family size and a reported increase in the proportion of workers (employed persons) per family.[11] These relationships suggest that over the decade there was an increase in the proportion of the members of industrial worker families employed in low-wage sectors. Since these sectors or occupations lie for the most part outside those that determine industrial worker or even worker status, this in turn implies that the Soviet industrial working class is becoming less well defined, that an increasing number of the wives and children of industral workers are finding employment in trade or services or as clerical staff in the productive sphere. I have assumed that this trend continued in the 1970-74 period.

The estimates of table 2.7 can be combined with data on the structure of income for industrial worker families to generate estimates of the ruble value of particular income components; this allows certain inferences to be drawn about the impact of government policy on workers' living standards and is dealt with below. They can also be combined with analogous figures for other social groups, to provide information about the relative living standards of workers, state employees, and kolkhozniki at different times in the past fifteen years. Figures on disposable personal income are given in table 2.8; those on disposable total income are given in table 2.9.

Table 2.8
Real Per Capita Disposable Personal Income, Various Social Groups, 1960-74

Group	1960	1965	1970	1974
Total population (1970 rubles per year)	479	586	745	832
As % of total population's income:				
State employees	108.4	103.6	102.9	102.3
Industrial workers	130.7	119.7	107.5	104.5
Kolkhozniki	81.9	88.9	87.1	89.0

Notes and Sources: Personal disposable income calculated from tables 2.1, 2.4, and 2.7, and taxes given in table F4. Series deflated by the Schroeder and Severin index reprinted in appendix table A9.

Table 2.9
Real Per Capita Total Disposable Income, Various Social Groups, 1960-74

Group	1960	1965	1970	1974
Total population (1970 R per year)	553	688	875	986
As % of total population's income:				
State employees	110.8	105.1	103.5	103.0
Industrial workers	127.6	119.9	107.8	103.6
Kolkhozniki	76.6	84.3	86.0	85.5

Notes and Sources: Total disposable income from tables 2.1, 2.4, and 2.10, and taxes as given in appendix F, table 4. Nominal incomes were deflated by the Schroeder and Severin price index reprinted in appendix table A9.

For 1960, the adjustments introduced in this paper make little difference to the relative positions of kolkhozniki and industrial workers. Komarov and Chernyavskii suggested that on a per family basis kolkhoznik incomes were 64.5% of those of industrial workers; the figures in table 2.8 indicate that in terms of personal per capita income collective farmers enjoyed a standard of living that was 62.7% of that of industrial workers, those in table 2.9 suggest that the figure was 60%.

The growth in personal income over the decade 1960-70 has meant that on the average, all social groups can now afford the poverty standard budget. Indeed, the figures in table 2.8 suggest that by 1965 the average per capita income of all state employees was approaching minimum subsistence (600 rubles per year) and that by 1970 the disposable personal income of kolkhozniki had surpassed it. By 1974, the average real per capita disposable income of industrial workers was approaching the level that, in the opinion of some Soviet sociologists, would permit a rational pattern of consumption—72.5 rubles per month, compared with a target of 75 rubles (Gordon and Klopov, 1972, p. 36).

But the figures in tables 2.8 and 2.9 also show that industrial workers and their families suffered a substantial reduction in their standard of living in relation to other groups in the population. In 1960, the standard of living of the Soviet industrial working class, as measured here, was some 28-31% above that of the population as a whole. Over the next decade or decade and a half this preeminence eroded, until in 1970 it was only 8% above the national average and in 1974 as little as 4-5% above it. Although differences are not very large, the relative decline was some-what greater in 1965-70 under Brezhnev than in 1960-65 under Khrushchev. The figures in tables 2.8 and 2.9 record a substantial reduction in class differentiation over the period 1960-70. It is not clear what happened to the living standards of the intelligentsia or of managerial and professional groups during this period, but I would conjecture that they also fell in relation to those of kolkhozniki, and also, probably, in relation to those of industrial workers—at least until 1970. The results given here imply a rather more substantial adjustment to the Komarov-Chernyavskii figures for 1970 than for 1960. According to table 2.8, in 1970 the personal per capita income of kolkhozniki was 84% of that of industrial workers rather than the 75% for 1969 given by the Soviet economists on a per family basis.

The figures given in this section indicate that over the period 1960-74 industrial workers and their dependents made substantial gains in absolute living standards; on the average, they moved from a position barely above the poverty level to one in which they could afford a rational pattern of consumption. At the same time, they have seen their relative affluence eroded;their standard of living is now little better than that of other state employees. In part, this is a consequence of a blurring of class distinctions; it has become almost meaningless to talk of industrial workers as a social class (but not, of course, as an occupational group). But it is also a consequence of the policies pursued by the Soviet authorities in the past quarter of a century.

Since 1972, the CSA has published details of the structure of income received by both industrial workers and kolkhozniki and their families. For purposes of comparison it has also released data relating to a few earlier years. These statistics are based on an analysis of family budgets and should be treated with some circumspection, but in conjunction with the material given above, they provide some evidence of the way that the standards of living of the two groups have changed over the post-Stalin period, of the impact of government policy upon the material welfare of particular classes.

The figures in table 2.6 revealed substantial changes in the structure of kolkhoznik incomes between 1960 and 1974. There were no comparable changes in the structure of income received by industrial workers and their families. The figures in table 2.10 show virtually no change in the relative importance of the various components of personal income during the period considered here. In 1960, earnings from employment accounted for almost 84% of the total, and at the end of the period this share had risen to only 86.5%. Similarly, in 1960 transfers accounted for approximately 11% of the total and in 1974 9.6%. Of course it is possible that there were more substantial changes in subcomponents, in the share of income attributable to the earnings of the head of the household, for example, or in the share made up of individual transfers like pensions and stipends, but the available data do not permit that degree of disaggregation. It is therefore possible that the appearance of policy stagnation is misleading; but one's inferences must be confined to available data.

The apparent stability in the structure of personal income accruing to the families of industrial workers is, at first sight, surprising. Between 1955 and 1974 there were substantial changes in the Soviet government's

Table 2.10
Money, Personal, and Total Income, Industrial Workers, 1960-74

	1960	1965	1970	1974
Personal income (R per year per capita)	598	717	882	1016
of which (%)				
Earnings from employment	83.9	84.8	86.5	86.5
Transfer payments	10.7	10.5	9.5	9.6
Private (agricultural) activity	1.7	2.0	1.5	1.2
Other cash receipts	3.7	2.8	2.5	2.6
Free and subsidized services	11.7	16.0	16.1	15.8
Direct taxes	−8.5	−8.2	−9.2	−9.7
Money income (R per year per capita)	590	706	872	1006

Notes and Sources: Personal income from table 2.7; other entries calculated from *NK SSSR* '72, p. 562, and *NK SSSR* '74, p. 605. Money income calculated on the assumption that industrial workers sell 20% of their private output (see Sarkisyan, 1972, p. 173).

policies on wages and social security; there was also a substantial expansion in the provision of free (or subsidized) services (see below, chapter 8 and 11). One might have expected some of this innovation to be reflected in changes in the structure of income. But the figures in table 2.10 indicate that, so far as industrial workers are concerned, the net effect was one of coordinated growth, whatever the underlying intention. Thus the 50% increase in the minimum wage in 1968 (from 40 to 60 rubles a month), while it led to a 25% increase in earnings per capita between 1965 and 1970, resulted in only a 1.7% increase in the share of earnings in personal income. Similarly, the 50% increase in the minimum pension in 1971 (from 30 to 45 rubles a month) and similar increases in a number of other transfer payments resulted in a barely perceptible 0.1% increase in the share of transfers in personal income.

It is only in the area of free services that there has been any substantial change: between 1960 and 1965, expenditure on these (as a percent of personal income) increased by more than a third. Some part of this increase can be attributed to raises in the salaries of doctors, teachers, and auxiliary personnel in 1964-65, but the figures reflect a considerable expansion in the provision of services as well. Since 1965, however, the rate of growth of this component has been substantially the same as that of personal income as a whole. In 1974, what one may call the social wage amounted to 15.8% of personal income. If, as is sometimes asserted, expenditure on social consumption reflects "communist" distribution principles, and if an increase in the share of income accounted for by these components is interpreted as a progressive phenomenon, the Soviet industrial working class did not move any closer to communism in the first nine years of the Brezhnev period.

Further insight into the impact of Soviet government policy on the living standards of the industrial working class and other groups in the population is given by the figures in table 2.11. These show the annual

Table 2.11
The Growth of Real Per Capita Total Disposable Income, 1960-74

	Average Annual Rate of Growth (%)		
	1960-65	1965-70	1970-74
Total population	4.45	4.92	3.05
State employees	3.34	4.59	2.93
Industrial workers	3.16	2.71	2.03
Kolkhozniki	6.47	5.34	2.89
Real GNP per capita	3.29	4.17	3.17

Sources: Rows 1-4 calculated from table 2.9, row 5 from Greenslade, 1976, p. 271.

average rates of growth of real total disposable income per capita for the three quinquennia into which the period studied here can be divided. The table also contains data on the rate of growth of real per capita GNP over the same period. The figures in the table demonstrate, yet again, the twin features of increases in the absolute standard of living of the industrial working class and declines in its relative preeminence. In all three periods, the rate of growth of the incomes of industrial workers was substantially less than that of any other identified social group, but over the period as a whole, disparities were diminished. In 1960-65, kolkhozniki enjoyed a rate of income growth more than double that of industrial workers; in 1970-74 the disparity was little more than 40%.

For both kolkhozniki and industrial workers, the rate of income growth declined in each successive quinquennium. The decline for kolkhozniki was particularly sharp after 1970. The pattern was different for state employees and consequently for the total population. For these groups, the rate of income growth was higher in 1965-70 than in 1960-65, although there was also a deceleration in the rate at which their material welfare improved after 1970. In fact, growth was lower for all groups in 1970-74 than in 1960-65. These results prompt two observations. First, they show the danger of assuming that the Soviet population consists of collective farmers and industrial workers. This is not something that one does consciously, but it is an error that I believe many Soviet specialists are prone to make, if only subconsciously. Nor can it be argued that in addition to the two classes mentioned above there is only a small elite, the intelligentsia. There are, in fact, substantial numbers of state employees in other sectors—in construction, transport, and agriculture, in trade and in the services—and the experience of these workers and their dependents contributes as much if not more to indicators of average living standards than that of the ideologically more prominent groups. Second, the figures in table 2.11 demonstrate the dangers of relying upon earnings data for particular groups of employees as a proxy for income data pertaining to appropriately specified social groups. The rate of growth of average industrial earnings (wages) differs markedly from that of total real disposable income given in table 2.11. Indeed, the rate of growth of industrial earnings doubled between 1960–65 and 1965–70, according to the CSA series,[12] but such figures ignore changes in family size, family composition, and patterns of employment, and lead to mistaken inferences.

The figures in table 2.11 also permit one to draw another conclusion: as mentioned above, in 1968 the Soviet authorities raised the minimum wage in the state sector from 40 to 60 rubles a month. This was perhaps the most significant single change in earnings in the whole five-year period 1965–70. Because of the way in which the change was introduced, there was little if any increase in the rates of those earnings much above 70 rubles a month in 1967. The rates of growth in incomes given in table 2.11 suggest that the primary beneficiaries of this policy were not industrial workers but rather those employed in other branches of the state economy. It is to this, in all probability, that one can attribute the increase in the rate of growth of state employee incomes in 1965–70. Presumably, industrial workers or at least those who were heads of families were, on the average, earning rather more than 70 rubles a month in 1967. Thus they benefited less from the increase in the minimum wage than did those employed elsewhere.

I would like to say a few words about the overall changes that occurred between 1960 and 1974 and to comment on probable subsequent trends. The figures in tables 2.8 and 2.9 have revealed a substantially reduced differentiation in the living standards of the basic social classes of the USSR over the period considered in this chapter, and the figures in table 2.11 show that this was achieved by allowing the incomes of the least well off to grow more rapidly than the average; there has been a degree of levelling up. But the figures on the rate of growth of GNP show that this was done by allowing personal (or rather total) income to grow more rapidly than total output over the decade 1960–70. Insofar as this difference was not offset by higher saving, it must imply that there was a smaller portion of total output available for other uses in 1970 than there had been at the beginning of the period. Such a policy cannot continue indefinitely; in long-run equilibrium the rate of growth of personal consumption is restricted by the rate of growth of total output. And in 1970–74, rates of growth of total income were less than the rate of growth of GNP. The decline in the latter was accompanied by (and may have been responsible for) the deceleration discussed above. Over the next decade or so, one must expect the growth in personal living standards in the USSR to be conditioned by the growth in output. Given the very low rate of expansion in labor supply expected during this period and given the recent experience with capital output ratios, it is unlikely that the growth of GNP will be as high as in the recent past. Consequently, one can expect a period of slower growth in personal consumption. If there are to be further substantial changes in the extent of inequality, they will have to be brought about more by redistribution than by "levelling up." This is more difficult to achieve and is much more politically divisive. On past performance, it seems unlikely that the present Soviet government will embark upon such a program, but Brezhnev cannot live for ever, and it would be rash to speculate about the political commitments of his successors. Still, on the balance of probabilities, it seems unlikely that the Soviet industrial working class will regain the relative preeminence that it enjoyed in 1960 (and presumably under Stalin). Rather, one would expect the families of industrial workers to continue to merge with other elements of the urban population, both in terms of material welfare and patterns of living. I would suggest that the industrial working class will continue to lose its identity, and hence the concept will continue to decline in analytical value. Perhaps this should be seen as evidence of convergence among industrial societies, but such a conclusion raises a host of other conceptual and empirical problems which are best discussed at another time.

3

The Distribution of Income

IN THIS CHAPTER I shall explore the extent of interpersonal variation in income in the USSR.[1] The material presented is primarily statistical in character: that is, the intention is to describe the extent of inequality rather than to explain it or to consider its economic and political implications, which will be done elsewhere. The emphasis has been dictated by the availability of material, or rather the lack of it.

At present there are no official Soviet statistics published on the distribution of income; in fact, there are no published official statistics on average incomes in the USSR, and it was only in the mid sixties that the authorities resumed publication of a series on average earnings. Since 1960, however, a number of monographs and articles about the distribution of income have appeared in the USSR, and these have contained sufficient indirect information, diagrams, and derived statistics to permit estimates to be constructed.

Among Western economists only Wiles and Markowski have dealt with this topic in any detail (Wiles and Markowski, 1971; Wiles, 1974), but their figures refer only to 1966 and are unsatisfactory in a number of ways. Hence the most important thing at this stage is to collect and collate the available information, and that is done in this chapter; interpretation and analysis are deferred until later. In section 1 the main sources of statistical information on the distribution of income available to Soviet economists are described and their quality assessed. In sections 2-4 I present reconstructions of the distribution of state employees and kolhkozniki by per capita income, and attempt to derive an estimate of the distribution of income for the population as a whole in 1967-68. The chapter ends with a brief discussion of affluence in the USSR; the character and extent of poverty are discussed in chapter 4.

The figures produced in this chapter suggest that the distribution of income in the USSR is moderately unequal but that disparities are less than in a typical market economy. They also show that, as measured here, inequality has declined markedly in the postwar period. Finally, it appears that while inequality is somewhat greater among kolkhozniki than among state employees, the differences are not as great as has been conjectured, for example by Wiles.

3.1 INCOME DISTRIBUTION: SOVIET STATISTICAL SOURCES

The Soviet authorities do not publish statistics relating to the distribution of income in the USSR, but such information is collected and is available to statisticians and economists working on this subject, or at least to those employed in government research establishments. Even if actual statistics are not published, a knowledge of the sources of data is useful for two purposes. It can often aid in the interpretation of specific figures or assertions, and this may be important, since Soviet statisticians and economists are rather casual about questions of definition. It is frequently unclear what is or what is not included in the incomes of particular socio-economic groups, or whether particular categories of the population are included or excluded from specific comparisons.

A knowledge of the probable source of the statistics used can sometimes resolve these problems. Such knowledge can also throw light on the question of the availability of information to the Soviet leadership. It is all too frequently assumed that the Soviet government has at its disposal virtually unlimited information on the state of the economy and society. The failure to publish certain statistics is taken as evidence of the government's obsessive secrecy about economic information, as indicating that the authorities have something to hide. Sometimes this is true, but in a pre-computer society the amount of statistical data that can be handled is strictly limited. The absence of published statistics on a particular subject may only reflect the government's failure to collect them. This is especially likely with the problems of personal welfare and the standard of living, which until recently have not had a high priority in Soviet policy making. Data-collection channels have been primarily concerned with accumulating the information required to monitor plan fulfilment. An awareness of how restricted and partial the information on the distribution of earnings and income available to the Soviet leadership in fact is may also help to explain why the leadership adopts the policies it does and perceives the problems in this area in the way that it does.

There are in fact two official sources of statistical information on the distribution of income in the Soviet Union available to economists and statisticians, and presumably to policy makers. They are the continuing family budget survey and a sequence of specific sample surveys of income distribution. (There are also more frequent censuses of earnings, which are described in chapter 9.) But weaknesses in sample selection procedures and data analysis mean that adequate statistical information on the distribution of income exists for only two, or at most three, postwar years.

FAMILY BUDGET SURVEY

The most extensive source of information on the distribution of earnings and incomes in the USSR is the family budget survey, but unsatisfactory sample selection and data analysis have meant that statistics from this source have been rejected by many, perhaps a majority, of Soviet economists and statisticians as worthless. Still, it remains the only source of information on a number of questions.

The continuous collection of budgetary data in the USSR started in 1929, but a number of sample surveys were conducted in the twenties. The procedures employed were substantially revised in 1951, and there were further modifications in the 1960s. During the 1950s information was collected on the incomes and expenditures of about 50,000 families, and the sample was later expanded to 62,000, or approximately 0.1% of the families in the country. The whole program is administered under the auspices of the Central Statistical Administration. The family budget survey was originally designed to monitor changes in the standard of living of industrial workers (Narrowly defined in Soviet administrative terms as *rabochiye promyshlennosti*, that is, wage earners in manufacturing, mining, and quarrying). In spite of later extensions and modifications, it has not been able to throw off this heritage.[2]

The basic principle used in the selection of households to be included in the survey is the industrial affiliation of wage earners. First, enterprises in specified sectors of the economy are classified into industries and ranked by order of employment. A representative sample of enterprises is chosen, reflecting the industrial mix of the economy as a whole. From selected enterprises a sample of employees is chosen by mechanical means (Levin, 1969, pp. 150-56). These employees and their families are then asked to supply information about their earnings and other incomes and to keep a record of their expenditures.

There are numerous weaknesses in this procedure. First, not all sectors of the economy are included. Until recently the sample of enterprises was confined to industry proper, which by Soviet definition includes mining and quarrying. As a result, the families covered by the survey constituted only a third of all wage and salary earners (Levin, 1969, p. 153). In the 1960s the sample was extended to include enterprises in construction and transport, but those working in distribution and other services are still largely excluded. In rural areas the sample consists almost exclusively of collective farm households; state farm employees are grossly underrepresented, and those whom the Russians call the rural intelligentsia are wholly excluded. Again, there have been changes in sample coverage in the late sixties.

The use of the so-called industrial principle in sample selection results in a number of problems. The sample is both geographically and occupationally unrepresentative of the population as a whole. It is claimed, for example, that there are very few households from Kazakhstan (Levin, 1969, p. 152). More generally, the procedure excludes pure pensioner and pure student households; it also excludes those households all of whose wage and salary earners are employed in trade or in the service industries. These occupations are therefore probably underrepresented. Further, since the probability of selection depends in part on the number of employees in the family, the same will be true of one-worker households. All these categories are among the worst off in the USSR, and as a result, the estimates of average per capita and per family income derived from the family budget survey are biased upwards and those of the distribution of income similarly distorted (Rimashevskaya, 1965, pp. 46-56). The bias in average incomes is reportedly substantial: "A comparison of the budgets of the families of state employees with data drawn from the general survey of incomes, conducted in 1958, showed that budgetary data overestimated family income by some 16-32% and underestimated family size by 6.1%."[3] Thus, in 1958, per capita incomes were overstated by some 24-40%. As a result of changes in sample size and coverage introduced in later years, and perhaps prompted by the scale of error revealed by the 1958 survey, the extent of the bias is likely to be less in later years. If this is true, however, it means that budgetary data will understate the rate of growth of incomes after 1960-61, altogether an unsatisfactory state of affairs. Nevertheless, until 1972, family budget data have remained the only source of information about the level and structure of incomes received by kolkhozniki and their families (Matyukha, 1973, p. 72).

Not only has the method of sample selection meant that the family budget survey yielded biased estimates of the level and distribution of income in the USSR, but weaknesses in data analysis have meant that it has, until recently, provided statisticians, economists, and policy makers with little detailed information about the structure of incomes and expenditures of households with different standards of living. These weaknesses have also impeded comparisons of the material well-being of kolkhozniki and state employees.

Until the late sixties or early seventies the analysis of family budget data was carried out manually in the USSR. Households were classified by income at the local level, and only marginal totals were forwarded to the CSA in Moscow; the detailed returns were retained in the localities. As a result, the central authorities have had at their disposal very little information about the distribution of particular categories of receipts among households with different levels of income or families of different sizes (Rimashevskaya, 1965, pp. 55-56). Further, urban households were classified into eleven income classes according to per capita money income, while kolkhozniki were grouped into twelve classes according to personal income. It is only since 1970 that the same criterion has been used to classify both groups (Komarov and Chernyavskii, 1973, p. 204). These inconsistencies have made it difficult to compare the living standards of peasants and workers.

The absence of detailed information about the structure of income and expenditure in the USSR as a whole may help to explain why so many Soviet monographs on this subject have, in the past, confined themselves to statistical analyses of the position at *oblast* level. Censorship probably explains the failure to identify the *oblasti* used (Korzhenevskii, 1971). Between 1969 and 1972, however, the analysis of family budget data was transferred to the computer. This should greatly increase the information available at the central level, and may also result in the publication of more extensive and more explicit monographs on the living standards of the Soviet population (Mints, 1968, pp. 9-20; Matyukha, 1973, p. 137; Matyukha and Chernisheva, 1975, pp. 15-25).

The family budget survey collects data on both incomes and expenditures. For survey purposes, income is defined as including earnings in cash and kind, pensions, stipends, and other transfers from the government, receipts from the financial system, and an estimate of the value of private agricultural output. Income thus corresponds closely to the concept of personal income used in preceding chapters. There is some confusion in the literature, but it appears that earnings in kind received from collective farms are valued for budget survey purposes at state retail prices. The same may also be true of private agricultural production, or at least that part of it that is domestically consumed.[4]

All these problems make family budget data of questionable value in the analysis of income distribution, and in fact many Soviet analysts have criticized conclusions based upon such statistics. But if the data are rejected, there is no source of information on the distribution of income before 1958, nothing can be said about year-to-year changes in inequality during the postwar period, and nothing about the distribution of income among kolkhozniki until 1972, if not later. For these reasons some Soviet economists still rely upon them. It is, however, as well to be aware of their gross inadequacies when interpreting and assessing the reliability of statements about changes in the level of income or the degree of inequality to be found in the Soviet Union. (For more detail, see McAuley, 1978.)

SURVEYS OF INCOME DISTRIBUTION

Although large quantities of information about the incomes and expenditures of Soviet households are collected each month through the family budget survey, this source has yielded extremely unreliable estimates of the distribution of income. In consequence, many Soviet economists and statisticians prefer to rely upon information provided by a series of specially designed surveys of income distribution undertaken by the CSA. Such surveys have been made in 1958, 1967, and possibly in 1972. It is only for these years that remotely reliable statistical information on the distribution of income in the Soviet Union exists. Even these data are of dubious quality, so one may argue that the Soviet government, like the governments of many Western countries, has no precise idea of the degree of inequality that exists within its society.

Only the 1958 survey has been described in detail, and therefore the account given here applies explicitly to that project only (Zhutkovskaya, 1966; Matyukha, 1960). But there is reason to believe that the two later surveys have been similiar in methodological approach and basic objectives, so these remarks have a more general significance. The aim of the 1958 survey was to collect representative data on housing conditions, incomes, and family composition, and to investigate the possibility of generalizing family budget results to the population as a whole. The subsequent reorganization of this program suggests that the 1958 exercise was unsuccessful in this latter aim. Both the 1958 and 1967 surveys were restricted to the nonagricultural population of the USSR, but the survey which may have been held in 1972 was to have been extended to include kolkhozniki. It also presumably included state farm employees, although there is no mention of this group in the literature (Komarov and Chernyavskii, 1973, p. 205).

In 1958 some 240,000 families were surveyed, in 1967 the sample size was increased to 250,000, and in 1972 it was reportedly 310,000, or approximately 0.4% of the families in the country. In both 1958 and 1967 the sample of families was selected on the basis of industrial affiliation, and presumably a similar procedure was used in 1972. The approach followed in 1958 was in most respects the same as that used to select families for inclusion in the family budget survey, and many of the criticisms leveled at that program also apply to the income distribution surveys. But the fact that all nonagricultural branches of the economy are included in the sample frame and the fact that greater attention was paid to the problem of obtaining a geographically representative sample almost certainly mean that the extent of the bias is less in these specially commissioned investigations.

In 1958, selected enterprises were asked to prepare lists of all those who had worked the full month of April. At this stage apprentices, and presumably part-time workers, were excluded. A random sample was selected mechanically from the lists, and chosen employees were visited in their homes between the tenth and eighteenth of October of that year. These employees were asked to provide information about family composition and housing conditions. All members of their families were asked to supply details of earnings and other sources of income; information about the incomes of those absent from home at the time of the enumerator's visit, however, was provided by other members of the family present at the interview.

For survey purposes, income was defined on an accruals basis—the information recorded refers to the month of September. Zhutkovskaya claims that those who did not work the full month of September were asked to provide data on earnings in the last complete month worked (Zhutkovskaya, 1966, p. 104); there is no mention of this point in Matyukha. Income was defined to include money earnings, pensions, stipends, and other transfers from the government, and financial receipts from other sources. Subsidies, *dotatsiya*, for keeping children in kindergartens, day nurseries, and pioneer camps or for visits to rest homes and sanitoria were excluded, as was other income in kind.[5] Thus income as used in the survey corresponds closely to the concept of money income used in preceding chapters. Family income was defined as the sum of the incomes accruing to members of a family, and per capita income as the family income divided by the number of persons in the family. For the purpose of computing per capita income, no allowance was made for differences in the age and sex composition of families.

In the opinion of most Soviet economists, these periodic income surveys provide the most reliable information available on the distribution of income in the USSR. The data do, however, suffer from serious weaknesses. First, there are all the weaknesses associated with the method of sample selection mentioned above. Second, the survey appears to exclude or at least to underrepresent part-time workers, nor is it clear how fully the secondary earnings of the wholly employed are recorded. Further, because the data refer to a single month, it is to be expected that incomes will show a greater variation and hence imply a larger measure of inequality than if a longer period had been used. This is offset to some extent if those who did not work the full month of September gave earnings information relating to some earlier month. Finally, the income concept employed, because it excludes income in kind and fringe benefits, corresponds only imperfectly to material welfare. The distribution of money income cannot adequately reflect the extent of inequality in the Soviet Union today.

OTHER SOURCES OF DATA

In addition to the official sources of data described so far, there exist a number of unofficial sources. Some academics, primarily sociologists, have conducted private surveys of particular aspects of everyday life in the USSR. The primary research objectives of these surveys have usually not been concerned with the distribution of income, but information on the extent of income differentiation has sometimes been generated as a by-product. In certain cases, the definitions of income and the methods of sample selection are methodologically superior to those used by the CSA. But all these unofficial surveys suffer from one crucial weakness: they relate to sub-populations of the USSR, usually to particular social groups in a specific city or oblast. They cannot, therefore, be used to derive conclusions about the extent and nature of economic inequality in the USSR as a whole (Matthews, 1972, pp. 73-90; Vinokur, 1975).

3.2   INCOME DISTRIBUTION: STATE EMPLOYEES

Only the specially commissioned Income Distribution Surveys described in the preceding section can be regarded as remotely satisfactory, so it is on those that I will concentrate here. In particular, I will give estimates of the distribution of nonagricultural state employees by per capita income in 1958 and 1967, and of the families of these state employees by per capita income in 1967. No information has been found which would permit similar estimates to be presented for 1972. Indeed, it has been suggested that although planned, this survey was cancelled as a result of the economic difficulties the Soviet authorities were having at the time (I. Birman in a private communication).

The preceding section describes data that are available to Soviet statisticians and economists interested in the distribution of income. But there is a distinction between availability to research workers in the USSR and publication. None of the material described so far in this chapter is published. Rather, individual economists and statisticians have reproduced a variety of graphs and diagrams that purport to represent the distribution of income in various years. They also give a number of derived statistics. It is from this at first sight unpromising material that the estimates given in this chapter have been reconstructed. A detailed account of the sources and methods used in these reconstructions is given in appendix G. Here one need only say that the techniques employed are basically those used by Wiles and Markowski in their pioneering study of the subject. Briefly, because the histograms and frequency polygons contained in Soviet academic studies of income distribution are printed without any identifying marks on the axes, reconstruction involves careful measurement of the diagrams and the use of plausible assumptions about the principles upon which they were originally constructed. These assumptions are set out in the appendix.

Estimates of the distribution of nonagricultural state employees by per capita income in 1958 and 1967 are given in table 3.1; table 3.2 contains statistics of location and dispersion derived from these estimates. At the risk of repeating myself, I must emphasize what the figures in tables 3.1 and 3.2 represent: they give the distribution of nonagricultural state em-

Table 3.1
Distribution of the Nonagricultural Population by Per Capita Income, USSR, 1958-67

Income (R per month)	1958[a]	1967	
	% of Individuals	% of Individuals	% of Families with a Per Capita Income
-20	12.92	—	—
20-25	8.76	2.75	1.75
25-30	10.42	4.375	3.5
30-35	10.11	5.7	5.0
35-40	9.2	6.875	5.75
40-45	9.16	8.5	7.5
45-50	9.0	9.5	9.0
50-60	8.33	19.5	19.0
60-70	7.87	15.0	15.5
70-90		15.0	17.5
90-110	14.19	5.0	7.5
110-130		3.0	4.5
130-		4.75	3.5

Sources. 1958: Rimashevskaya, 1965, p. 61. 1967: Rabkina and Rimashevskaya, 1972, p. 120.

a. It is impossible to give more detail about frequencies in the tails of this distribution, as it has been derived from a distribution of earnings using coefficients from Rabkina and Rimashevskaya, 1972, p. 215. See appendix G.

Table 3.2
Soviet Income Distributions: Measures of Location and Dispersion

	1958 Individuals	1967 Individuals	Families
Mean (R)	48.4	62.6	65.7
Median (R)	39.2	56.3	59.2
As % of median:			
1st decile	46.66	57.73	58.70
1st quartile	68.11	76.55	77.36
3rd quartile	140.31	130.90	133.61
9th decile	190.56	179.40	176.86
Decile ratio	4.1	3.1	3.0

ployees and their families by per capita money income in 1958 and 1967; the figures refer to receipts during the month of September of the relevant year, and some of the limitations of the income concept employed have been set out above. Thus although it is difficult to be precise, in view of ambiguities about who is and who is not included in the appropriate parent population, the figures for 1958 refer to about 60% and those for 1967 to about 70% of the Soviet population. The proportions given have differed from the employment shares given in the last chapter, since in this case dependents as well as workers are included.

There is no satisfactory way of determining the reliability of the figures given in table 3.1. The only comparable estimate of the distribution of income in the literature is that given by Wiles for 1966. This is a synthetic distribution, as indeed it must be, since the Soviet authorities did not collect the necessary primary data in that year. Wiles reports a median per capita income of 53.2 rubles a month and a decile ratio of 3.6. The median corresponds fairly closely to that of 56.28 rubles reported in table 3.2 for 1967, but there is a substantial difference in the two estimates of dispersion. Given the indirect nature of Wiles's estimation procedure, I prefer the one given here (Wiles, 1974, pp. 11-25). Wiles's figures, however, correspond more closely to those given by Nemchinova (1965: 3.8, 1970: 3.2), but given the years, hers must have been based on suspect family budget survey data (Nemchinova, 1975, p. 387).

According to the figures contained in tables 3.1 and 3.2, average per capita money incomes increased by 29.3% between 1958 and 1967. This is somewhat less than the increase in average earnings. On the basis of the CSA series, earnings increased by 32.4%[6] over the same period. However, apart from possible errors caused by differences in coverage or differences in methodology of which we may not be aware, the CSA figures include sovkhozniki whose relative position improved between the two years.

Over the same period, the degree of inequality, as measured by the decile ratio, declined by about 24%, reflecting the relatively more rapid increase in incomes in the bottom half of the distribution. Further, the interquartile range remained virtually unchanged between 1958 and 1967 (in the first year it was 28 rubles a month and in the second 31 rubles). This suggests that the bulk of the Soviet population had broadly similar absolute increases in their standards of living. All the same, although the ninth decile declined as a percentage of the median, its increase in ruble terms was larger than that of any lower quantile. This implies that in spite of the reduction in measured inequality, the best-off still enjoyed the largest absolute increases in their standards of living.

From the point of view of material welfare, the figures in table 3.1 make depressing reading. According to the MMS budget, the Soviet poverty line can be set at a per capita money income of 50 rubles a month. According to table 3.1, 37.7% of individuals and 32.5% of families had an income of less than that amount in 1967. In 1958, it was an incredible 69.6%. Allowing for inflation between 1958 and 1965, the poverty standard can be reduced to 45.8 rubles per person per month; on this criterion, the proportion of nonagricultural state employees in need falls to 62.1%. As is shown in the next chapter, however, there is some evidence to suggest that the Soviet authorities at this time considered 25-30 rubles a month the poverty line. On such a definition, some 21.7-32.1% of the nonagricultural population was in poverty in 1958, and thus the extent of deprivation increased between the two survey years.

3.3   INCOME DISTRIBUTION: KOLKHOZNIKI

The statistics relating to the distribution of income among state employees in the Soviet Union may be scanty and inadequate, but they are far more reliable than those relating to kolkhozniki. Figures for years before 1972 can only have been derived from family budget surveys and will thus suffer from all the shortcomings associated with this source. However, since family budget data are collected continuously, distributions should be available for all postwar years. I have only been able to locate sufficient information in Soviet sources to provide estimates for 1965 and 1968.

These estimates are given in table 3.3, while associated statistics of location and dispersion are presented in table 3.4. Since the statistics are based on family budget data, the income referred to is personal income— that is, money income, together with an estimate of the value of kolkhoz

Table 3.3
Distribution of Kolkhozniki and Their Dependents by Per Capita Income, USSR, 1965, 1968

1965		1968	
Personal Income (R per month)	% of kolkhozniki	Personal Income (R per month)	% of kolkhozniki
-10	1.2	-20	2.8
10-15	4.1	20-25	5.2
15-20	8.0	25-30	7.8
20-25	10.1	30-35	9.1
25-30	11.3	35-40	10.0
30-35	11.6	40-45	10.5
35-45	18.9	45-55	17.9
45-55	14.9	55-70	18.9
55-65	8.3	70-90	12.6
65-100	9.3	90-110	3.9
100-120	1.3	110-130	0.9
120-	1.0	130-	0.4

Source: Rabkina and Rimashevskaya, 1972, pp. 122-23.

Table 3.4
Kolkhoznik Income Distributions: Measures of Location and Dispersion

	1965	1968
Mean (R)	41.6	51.4
Median (R)	37.0	47.6
As % of median:		
1st decile	48.4	55.0
1st quartile	69.4	73.5
3rd quartile	139.4	135.1
9th decile	191.9	173.3
Decile ratio	3.97	3.15

pay distributed *in natura* and of the value of privately produced agricultural commodities consumed within the producing household. The figures in table 3.3 have been produced using the same techniques as those in table 3.1; a detailed list of sources is given in appendix G.

How accurate are the figures in table 3.3? This is a difficult question to answer, because nothing similar exists in the literature with which to compare them. As noted in appendix G, there is some uncertainty about the location of the distributions, particularly that for 1965.[7] The one given in the table has been chosen finally because it gives results that are most nearly consistent with those of chapter 2. The ruble intervals used in table 3.3 are not particularly plausible on numerological grounds, however, but the diagram on which the reconstruction is based is badly printed, and those given appear to correspond to those used in the original frequency polygon.

From table 3.4 the average per capita personal income of kolkhozniki in 1965 was 41.6 rubles a month; from table 2.4 one derives an estimate of 38.3 rubles for the same indicator; thus the figures in this chapter appear to overestimate the mean by 8.5%. Since they are based entirely on family budget data and in view of the many uncertainties surrounding the derivation, this is reasonably accurate, particularly in view of the scale of error reported by Shvyrkov for the incomes of state employees. Turning to the 1968 distribution, table 3.3 yields an estimate of mean per capita income of 51.4 rubles a month; from table 2.4 one obtains an estimate of 49.4 rubles. For this year the error is only 4%, which is certainly acceptable in view of the many sources of error involved in the calculations.

The only figures on the dispersion of kolkhoznik incomes that I am aware of relate to the Latvian SSR (Berzkaln, 1971, pp. 64-79). For that republic, the decile ratio of the distribution of kolkhoznik incomes was reported as 3.01 in 1965 and 3.10 in 1968. These are somewhat lower than the figures given in table 3.4 for the USSR as a whole. But Latvia is a small (hence reasonably homogeneous) and relatively affluent republic, and, a priori, I would expect the distribution of income to be more equal here than in the USSR as a whole. Thus there is no necessary conflict between these two sets of figures; if anything, one might wish to suggest that dispersion in 1968 has been understated here. But Berzkaln records a continuous increase in inequality among kolkhozniki in Latvia between 1965 and 1970. Table 3.4 implies that for the USSR as a whole the trend was in the opposite direction, at least for the years 1965-68. On first view this conflict is more disturbing. However, given the array of different policies pursued in the Soviet Union with a view to increasing the incomes of kolkhozniki, particularly those on the poorest farms, I regard a declining trend as more plausible; but an element of doubt remains.

If they are accepted, the figures in table 3.3 demonstrate just how badly off some of the Soviet peasantry were in 1965, even after a decade or more of post-Stalin growth in incomes. In that year, a quarter of the collectivized peasants had incomes of less than half the MMS budget. Now the MMS budget is compiled for urban households (Sarkisyan and Kuznetsova, 1967, p. 8), and a per capita personal income of 50 rubles a month may not correspond precisely to the poverty level in rural areas, but by any conceivable standard, the peasants in this group must have suffered from deprivation. After all, the estimates *include* an allowance for the value of privately produced agricultural goods consumed within the household. Further, the figures suggest that almost three-quarters of the collectivized peasantry had incomes of less than 50 rubles a month in 1965. Poverty was the experience of the overwhelming majority of collective farmers, and only the most affluent could aspire to that "modest but adequate" standard of living that we have conventionally agreed to specify at 70 rubles per capita per month.

Between 1965 and 1968 there was a substantial increase in average per capita kolkhoznik income and a decline in measured inequality. Some of the poorest gained in income; in the latter year only 8% of the peasantry had incomes of less than half the MMS budget level. More than half, however, still had incomes of less than 50 rubles a month. On the other hand affluence, or at least a modest comfort, was more widespread: a fifth of all collective farmers and their dependents lived in families with a per capita income of more than 70 rubles a month. All the same, in spite of real and substantial increases in the incomes of kolkhozniki in the Soviet Union after 1965, it would be correct to conclude that there is widespread rural poverty in the USSR.

3.4 THE DISTRIBUTION OF INCOME IN 1967-68

Not even Soviet statisticians and economists have sufficient information at their disposal to construct reliable and consistent estimates of the distribution of income that apply to the population as a whole, at least for years before 1972. The situation facing the non-Soviet specialist is made more difficult by the official Soviet attitude towards the publication of statistics. The absence of adequate primary information may help to explain the silence of Soviet academics about the distribution of income, but this silence is also in part explained by the low priority assigned to the question by those responsible for policy formation in the USSR.

Yet a knowledge of the distribution of income among the population as a whole would be of some value. The distinction between kolkhozniki and state employees is to a large extent based on the Marxist theory of class; it has little significance to the non-Marxist. For purposes of policy formulation and evaluation there should be no difference between the two groups. Since the Soviet authorities are gradually eliminating the differences in administrative procedures used in dealing with them, it would appear that they share this opinion.

The statistics already presented in this chapter can be combined to generate estimates of the distribution of the population as a whole by per capita income. Given the inconsistencies in the data, the undoubted errors involved in reconstruction, and the doubtfulness of some of the assumptions involved in the integration process, these estimates should be treated with caution. But the resulting distributions do give a better idea than has been available hitherto of the extent of disparity in living standards in the Soviet Union. They also permit more precise comparisons with other countries.

There are three sets of problems that must be resolved before the distributions of tables 3.1 and 3.3 can be combined into a single set of statistics: the income concept, the year to which the resulting distribution is to apply, and the treatment of state farm employees. The estimates in table 3.1 refer to the years 1958 and 1967, while those in table 3.3 relate to 1965 and 1968. Obviously the closest pair of years are 1967 and 1968. However we decide to shift the 1967 distribution of nonagricultural state employees and the 1968 distribution of kolkhozniki, the selection of these two years is likely to involve the least error. Consequently they are the years selected for comparison. Yet as we have seen, during the second half of the sixties both state employees and kolkhozniki enjoyed substantial rates of growth of personal and money income. Some allowance should be made for this. In the estimates given below, I have made use of a technique proposed by Rabkina and Rimashevskaya for predicting shifts in the distribution of earnings to move the distribution of state employees forward to 1968 and the distribution of kolkhozniki back to 1967.

Basically the technique involves assuming that median incomes changed between 1967 and 1968 at a rate equal to the annual average rate of growth of incomes between 1965 and 1970, and that this change was accompanied by a log-linear transformation of the ruble axis of the distribution (Rabkina and Rimashevskaya, 1972, pp. 218-27). The relevant rates of growth were inferred from table 2.4. Both these assumptions are to a certain extent arbitrary. There is no reason to suppose that the distribution of income must have changed in a log-linear manner, but Rabkina and Rimashevskaya claim that this hypothesis is generally satisfactory with Soviet data. Equally, there is no reason to suppose that either personal or money income grew at a constant rate over the period 1965-70, nor that changes in median incomes were equal to those in mean incomes. But in the absence of information on the year-to-year changes in the relevant indicators, this is the best that can be done. A detailed account of the calculations involved is given in the addendum to this chapter.

The second problem to be resolved in this exercise involves the definition of income. The distribution of nonagricultural state employees in table 3.1 relates to money income, while that for kolkhozniki in table 3.3 refers to personal income. Ideally, the two groups should be ranked according to a consistent definition of income, but the necessary information is not available. However, for state employees as a whole, including those employed on state farms, money income amounted to 96% of personal income in 1970 (table 2.4). There is no reason to believe that the percentage in 1967-68 was substantially different. Indeed, for the group excluding sovkhozniki it may have been higher. Of course, arguments about mean incomes convey little information about the distribution of non-cash receipts. It is possible, or even probable, that those with which we are concerned here accrue disproportionately to the lower income groups, since they are most likely to possess and work private agricultural holdings. On this argument, the use of money income is likely to overstate the degree of dispersion among state employees. Alternatively, one could argue that money income is the most appropriate indicator of material welfare for state employees, and that personal income is what should be used for kolkhozniki. This point of view has, I suspect, been advanced by Soviet statisticians in the past; this would explain the use of inconsistent indicators of income in the tabulation of the results of the family budget survey before 1970. If one accepts this point of view, no adjustment is required. For reasons advanced in the first chapter I do not think that this has much merit, but because I have been unable to devise any satisfactory method of adjustment, the distributions given below combine money income for nonagricultural state employees with personal income for kolkhozniki.

Finally, consider the problem of making some allowance for state agricultural employees. As pointed out above, sovkhozniki and their families have been almost wholly excluded from the distributions given in section 3.2. Yet in 1967-68 this group was approximately 8.5% of the population. There are two difficulties to be overcome before they can be included in an estimate of the distribution of the population by income: first, one has to determine how many individuals are involved, and second, decide upon the disparities in income they receive.

The first difficulty has been resolved as follows. In 1967, average annual employment in state agricultural enterprises, those presumably excluded from the sampling frame of the 1967 survey, amounted to 8,836,000 persons (*Narkhoz SSSR '68*, p. 549). Also, it has been reported that in 1970 the average family size for kolkhozniki was 85% of that of sovkhozniki (Sarkisyan, 1972, p. 190); but, from appendix D, the average size of kolkhoznik households in 1970 was 3.36. This implies a family of 3.96 for the average sovkhoznik. It is also reported that the average state employee household contained 1.7-1.8 gainfully employed persons in 1970, yielding a figure of 1.33 dependents per earner (Sarkisyan, 1972, p. 190). I assume that these figures can be applied to sovkhozniki in 1967-68, and consequently derive an estimated total sovkhoz population (employees and dependents) of 20,583,000 in 1967 and 20,738,000 in 1968.

There is no information available on the distribution of sovkhozniki by income, but figures on average earnings and incomes and other general considerations can be used to form some impression of their living standards. On the one hand sovkhozniki are state employees and are therefore covered by the state social security system; they receive regular money wages and possess passports; for administrative purposes they are treated like industrial workers. This might suggest that the distribution of income would be similar to that of nonagricultural state employees. However, sovkhozniki are rural inhabitants and to a large extent share the life style of the collectivized peasantry. The similarities must have been increased by the policy initiated in the late fifties of converting backward kolkhozy into state farms. This would perhaps suggest a distribution of income more like that of kolkhozniki. Rather than construct a distribution that applies explicitly to sovkhozniki, in the estimates given below I have made two alternative assumptions: that the distribution of nonagricultural state employees can be extended to this group, or that the distribution of kolkhozniki can. On the first, referred to as assumption A in the tables, the distributions of table 3.1 and table 3.3 have been combined using the weights 0.78:0.22. These correspond to the Soviet classification of the population by social class (*Narkhoz SSSR '67*, p. 35). On assumption B, the two primary distributions have been combined using the weights 0.69:0.31, which result from transferring the sovkhoz population, as calculated above, to the collectivized peasantry.

Some idea of the relative merits of the two assumptions can be gained by examining the average incomes of state agricultural employees. It has been claimed that the average income of kolkhozniki, per family, was 80% of that of sovkhozniki in 1967. Given differences in family size, this implies a kolkhoznik income, per capita, some 94% of that of sovkhozniki. It has also been stated that, per family, the income of sovkhozniki was 93.6% of that of workers in 1967.[8] But in 1970 the average sovkhoznik family was 35% larger than that of industrial workers, implying an average income, per capita, only 69% that of industrial workers. If differences in averages carry over into other features of the distribution, these calculations suggest that assumption B is the more plausible alternative.

Transformed distributions for kolkhozniki in 1967 and state employees in 1968, together with distributions constructed on assumptions A and B for both 1967 and 1968, are given in table 3.5. The usual measures of location and dispersion are given in table 3.6. As pointed out above, these

Table 3.5
Distribution of Population by Per Capita Income, USSR, 1967-68

Income (R)	Kolkhozniki, 1967	Nonagricultural Sector, 1968	Total Population, 1967		Total Population, 1968	
			A	B	A	B
-20	6.2	—	1.4	1.9	0.6	0.9
20-25	7.3	1.4	3.8	4.2	2.3	2.6
25-30	9.0	3.7	5.4	5.8	4.6	5.0
30-35	10.3	4.5	6.7	7.1	5.5	6.0
35-40	10.1	6.1	7.6	7.9	7.0	7.3
40-45	9.9	7.6	8.8	8.9	8.2	8.5
45-50	7.7	9.0	9.1	8.9	8.9	8.9
50-60	13.1	18.2	18.1	17.5	17.6	17.3
60-70	10.7	16.9	14.0	13.7	16.0	15.6
70-90	11.1	16.4	14.1	13.8	15.6	15.2
90-110	3.3	7.6	4.6	4.5	6.8	6.4
110-130	0.6	3.3	2.5	2.3	2.8	2.6
130-	0.5	5.1	3.8	3.4	4.1	3.6

Notes and Sources: Columns 1 and 2 generated from the distributions in tables 3.1 and 3.3 by the method outlined in the addendum. Columns 3-6 derived by combining distributions that refer to kolkhozniki and nonagricultural state employees with different weights. A (implying that sovkhozniki distributed like other state employees), 0.22:0.78; B (implying that sovkhozniki distributed like kolkhozniki), 0.31:0.69. See text for derivation.

Table 3.6
Distribution of Income, USSR, 1967-68: Measures of Location and Dispersion

	Kolkhozniki, 1967	Nonagricultural Sector, 1968	Total Population, 1967		Total Population, 1968	
			A	B	A	B
Mean (R)	48.0	66.0	59.4	58.0	62.8	61.5
Median (R)	43.6	59.6	54.0	53.0	57.3	56.2
As % of median:						
1st decile	51.8	59.1	54.6	53.6	56.2	55.7
1st quartile	71.8	77.0	74.2	73.2	75.0	74.6
3rd quartile	140.6	132.6	130.0	130.8	131.6	131.3
9th decile	184.2	177.7	174.8	172.1	175.7	174.7
Decile ratio	3.55	3.00	3.20	3.21	3.12	3.14

figures have many shortcomings, but they do give for the first time some impression of the extent of income inequality in the USSR.

They suggest that in 1967-68, average monthly income in the USSR was some 58-62 rubles per capita. This is sufficient to purchase the MMS budget basket but is clearly inadequate when set against the yardstick of rational consumption. The estimate of per capita income derived in this chapter is some 10% higher than that implied by the figures in chapter 2. The difference can be attributed to errors associated with the various assumptions I have made, and also to the upward bias in the sampling procedures used to obtain the primary information. These estimates also yield a value of 3.14-3.21 for the decile coefficient, which implies that there is a moderately unequal distribution of incomes in the USSR. Estimates of this statistic for other East European countries, quoted by Wiles, tend to be lower, but by the same criterion, inequality in the USSR was less than in the United Kingdom and substantially less than in either the USA or Italy.[9]

The distributions presented in this chapter indicate that while affluence is almost exclusively an urban phenomenon in the USSR (or at least is associated with state employment), it is far from untrue that the poor are confined to rural areas. Indeed, the figures suggest that approximately half of those with per capita incomes below the official poverty line are state employees or their dependents. The fact that substantial urban poverty exists,in the USSR has led to a reexamination of Soviet social welfare policy and, more recently, to the introduction of new social security programs. These topics are explored in subsequent chapters. But first I will comment on the other tail of the distribution.

3.5 TOP INCOMES IN THE USSR: A DIGRESSION

The discussion so far in this chapter has concentrated on general features of the distribution of incomes in the Soviet Union and on identifying the poor and the poorest. These are subjects on which sample survey information is likely to be most plentiful and therefore on which one can be most precise. But it can be argued that popular perceptions of inequality are affected by the gap between the incomes of the top 1% (or even less) and the median to a much greater extent than they are by the gap between the median and, say, the lowest decile. That is, dissatisfaction over inequality is motivated more by envy than compassion. Quantitative information about the standard of living of the Soviet elite is completely lacking, but there has been some discussion of these topics in the literature recently and it is to this that I now turn (Matthews, 1975; Wiles, 1975; Smith, 1976, pp. 25-52).

There are a number of reasons why the study of the topic is more difficult in the Soviet Union than in most other countries. The Soviet authorities are notoriously reluctant to publish quantitative information about the salaries received by those in key positions. We have a fair amount of official information about the wage and salary scales of those in rank-and-file jobs, but our knowledge of the salaries paid to political leaders, central Party officials, and the upper echelons of the Soviet bureaucracy is based almost exclusively on the reports of emigres. But even a precise knowledge of the salaries received by the political, cultural, and economic elite in the Soviet Union would not solve the problem of assessing their standards of living.[10] Both Matthews and Smith describe extensive fringe benefits to which these groups are also entitled, some of which it would be virtually impossible to measure in money terms. The benefits include chauffeur-driven automobiles, dachas, a variety of cash bonuses, priority in the purchase of cinema, theater, and concert tickets, and the right to buy imported or scarce high-quality Soviet goods in "closed" retail establishments at reportedly favorable prices.

No mention is made of these privileges in the Soviet literature on living standards and disparity in income, and none is to be found in the Soviet press. It is possible that the Soviet leadership does itself a disservice in being so reticent about its incomes and privileges. In the absence of official information people fall back on rumor, and it is possible that rumor, colored by envy and disaffection, exaggerates the value of benefits received by the Soviet elite.

Be that as it may, Matthews, relying on such sources, has produced an estimate of 450 rubles a month in 1970-72 as the minimum income of a member of his elite, which he suggests consists of about 250,000 people. Very little faith can be placed in either of these numbers, but I would like to suggest that they are not inconsistent with the figures given in this chapter. First, Matthews's figures refer to earnings, rather than income as it has been used in this chapter. Also, his membership figure refers only to adult primary salary earners and not to all family members.

With an average family size, as before, of 2.9 persons, and with 1.75 wage and salary earners per family, one obtains a figure of 538,000 people; with only one salary earner per family, the figure is 725,000, between 0.15% and 0.3% of the population. Now, a number of Soviet economists have suggested that the distribution of incomes in the USSR is approximately log-normal, and one may exploit the regularities of this functional form to compute the hypothetical per capita income received by the top 0.1-0.3% of a distribution with the same mean and variance as that of the Soviet Union in 1967. Since the distributions of most countries deviate substantially from log-normality in the upper tail, this is likely to be an underestimate. Using the distribution applicable to the nonagricultural population, the calculated incomes are 222 rubles and 191 rubles a month. Given the assumptions about family size, these translate into a monthly income of 560-650 rubles. Assuming that top families receive no less in rubles than the average family as nonemployment income, and shifting from 1967 to 1971, one obtains a figure of 425 rubles, or 620 rubles a month, depending on the assumed number of workers per family. This is clearly of the same order of magnitude as Matthews's figure.

The calculations of the preceding paragraph are really no more than playing with numbers. They tell us nothing about the incomes of the Soviet elite. However important this topic may be in the determination of political attitudes toward inequality or in the generation of popular discontent, it must be admitted that there is no published information on it in Soviet sources and it is not therefore amenable to academic study in the West. In view of the Soviet government's reticence, not to say secretiveness, about the topic, I would hazard a guess that it is not a subject of serious study in the Soviet Union either. In conclusion, one might point out that the elite is so small numerically that substantially different assumptions about its income have a barely perceptible impact on average living standards.

In view of all this it is surely better to concentrate on those features of the income distribution about which we have some information. The evidence produced in this chapter suggests that although there has been a noticeable reduction in income disparity in the postwar period, there is still considerable inequality in the Soviet Union. It has also shown, not surprisingly, that kolkhoznik incomes are both lower and more unequally distributed than those of state employees. Further, although there is extensive poverty among collective farmers, deprivation is not exclusively or even mainly a rural phenomenon. Just who the urban poor are and why they should be in need in a society that has an extensive if not particularly munificent welfare system has not yet been established. This topic will be taken up in the next chapter.

A NOTE ON THE DERIVATION OF
HYPOTHETICAL DISTRIBUTIONS FOR 1967 AND 1968

In this note I will describe the method used to generate a distribution of nonagricultural state employees by per capita money income for 1968 from that for 1967 given in table 3.1. The same procedure was used to translate the distribution of kolkhozniki for 1968, given in table 3.3, to 1967.

Without much more information than is in fact available, any such translation is largely arbitrary but the one used here attempts to make use of what little we know, and it is claimed, gives reasonably results using Soviet data (Rabkina and Rimashevskaya, 1972, p. 234). From table 3.2 one can see that between 1958 and 1967, incomes below the median tended to grow faster than those above. A similar pattern is evident, from table 3.4, for kolkhoznik incomes between 1965 and 1968. This feature is reproduced. Also, it is assumed that the rate of growth of median income between 1967 and 1968 was equal to the annual average rate of growth of mean income between 1965 and 1970 derived from table 2.4. Finally, it is assumed that there was no change in the hypothetical upper bound of the open interval between the two years, that is, that there was no increase for those at the very top of the income distribution. This is almost certainly incorrect, but since the upper bound is chosen in an arbitrary way, such an assumption should not be too implausible.

Formally, let $F(x)$ give the proportion of individuals with incomes less than x in 1967 and $G(y)$ give the proportion of individuals with an income less than y in 1968. I postulate the existence of a function $x' = h(x)$ such that for $x_o \leqslant x \leqslant x_n$

$$F(x) = G(x') \text{ for all } x' = h(x)$$

Further, in view of the discussion above, the function $h(x)$ has the following properties:

(a) $x' \geqslant x$ for $x_o \leqslant x \leqslant x_n$
(b) $x'_n = x_n$
(c) $(x^*)' = kx^*$ where $F(x^*) = 0.5$ and k is the growth rate of mean income

The function defined below satisfies these conditions. It is only one of many possibilities, but it has the advantage of lending itself to computation. Rabkina and Rimashevskaya, from whom the technique given here is taken, also claim that it conforms to the changes observed in empirical distributions, or at least to those derived from Soviet data.

Define $x_n = x_o q^n$
and $x^* = x_o q^p$
and consider any x_i such that $x_o \leqslant x_i \leqslant x_n$;
then if $x_i = x_o q^i$,
$$\log (x_i)' = \log x_i + (n-i)/(n-p) \log k \qquad (1)$$
satisfies the conditions a–c above.

In empirical applications, for n sufficiently large (say 12–14, with the data used here) one calculates the sequence $(x_j)^1$ $(j=0....n)$ and notes that the proportion of individuals with incomes between x_{j-1} and x_j in 1967 is the same as the proportion with incomes between $(x_{j-1})^1$ and $(x_j)^1$ in 1968. The original and final distributions used are obtained from that given in table 3.1 by interpolation.

4

Poverty

THE ANALYSIS IN CHAPTER 3 has shown that in spite of substantial increases in living standards since the late fifties, some 35-40% of the Soviet population had per capita incomes below the official poverty level in 1967-68. Further analysis shows that over the decade 1958-68, while the authorities had some success in reducing the numbers with incomes below 25-30 rubles a month, they achieved only a modest reduction in the numbers with incomes below the MMS standard. Since I believe that at this time the Soviet government was committed to a policy of raising living standards and reducing inequality, it is of interest to study these questions in greater detail. That is done in this chapter.

In part, the government's limited success in reducing the numbers with per capita incomes below the 50 rubles a month limit can be explained by the fact that until the end of the period under review, it did not regard them as part of the target population for antipoverty policy. But the lack of success also reflects the absence of an appropriate antipoverty program or indeed of any clear idea of the sources of poverty in their country. Official Soviet approaches to the problem of reducing or eliminating poverty in the USSR in the decade or so after 1955 will be discussed in the following section, where I suggest that while the materials for an empirical analysis of the question have been available since about 1958, little work appears to have been undertaken until ten years later. The rest of the chapter is devoted to an analysis of these materials.

4.1 ANTIPOVERTY POLICY: A MISSED OPPORTUNITY?

In the late 1950s the Soviet government became more concerned with the (apparently low) living standards of the mass of the Soviet people and with the extent of income disparities in the USSR. It was at this time that a number of new data-gathering activities were commissioned and that the authorities initiated changes in planning procedures designed to bring the question of the economic welfare of the population into greater prominence. At the same time, a far-reaching reorganization of pay scales and payment systems was begun, and the law covering social security and social insurance was recodified. But it would seem that the Soviet government did not believe that the existing Soviet welfare system suffered from fundamental shortcomings. Or, alternatively, it felt that the policies necessary to overcome existing weaknesses were obvious. The innovations in planning and the collection of statistical information on incomes and the standard of living have, for the most part, already been described; Soviet policies on wages and salaries and the development of the Soviet social security system will be dealt with in chapters 8-11. But if all these are to be seen as part of a new and vigorous attack on poverty and inequality, they should have been accompanied by complementary actions that appear to have been lacking until the second half of the sixties (from the public record at least).

A consistent and rational antipoverty program involves three prerequisities; two were present in the Soviet Union in 1958 and again in 1967-68. It is not clear whether the third was also there in the late fifties, but it does seem to have emerged by the mid sixties. A rational attack on the problem of want and deprivation requires, first of all, a definition of poverty, an estimate of that income below which, for practical purposes, individuals or families can be considered deprived and in need of assistance. It also requires an estimate of the number of individuals who fall into this category, some assessment of the scale of the problem, and thus some idea of the resources necessary for its solution or alleviation. Finally, it surely requires some analysis of the sources of poverty, of the ways in which poor households and individuals differ from the rest of the population. Supplied with this information, the government can formulate policies or programs designed to compensate the poor for their disadvantages or disabilities in a way consistent with its other objectives. This last may be politically (and economically) difficult; the constraints under which the government is acting may make it impossible to implement the policies it would like; but the exigencies of the economic and political situation do not preclude the formulation of a rational policy. Indeed, the more difficult the circumstances, it might be thought, the greater the justification for careful analysis.

The work on MMS budgets in 1956-58 and again after 1965 provided a working definition of poverty in the USSR. The sample surveys of income, family composition, and housing conditions in 1958 and 1967 provided estimates of the number of households in poverty, at least among nonagricultural state employees. These surveys could also have provided material for an analysis of some of the demographic and social concomitants of poverty. Other work in the late fifties would have shown how far the existing social welfare system (both transfer payments and the broader category of social consumption expenditure) provided support for those in need. But I know of only one published study of the demographic material in the 1958 survey and of none for the later one. And while it is difficult to believe that the Central Statistical Administration would collect data and fail to use it, there is little to suggest that unpublished analyses had any significant impact upon either academic study of this question or official thinking, until the late sixties or early seventies.

The study of the demographic aspects of the 1958 survey was confined to the sub-sample of households living in the Moscow oblast—perhaps a consequence of the primitive computational technology available to those working on social problems at the time (Urlanis, 1966). It was not published until 1966, and I have not come across any reference to it in the literature. Although it was undertaken by an eminent demographer, therefore, it appears to have had little effect upon the development of Soviet attitudes toward poverty and antipoverty policy. Furthermore, although the CSA carried out its second sample survey of the distribution of income in 1967, in a more recent study of inequality, published by two NIIT economists, the discussion of the demographic characteristics of the Soviet poor was based upon a sample of workers "in an industrial centre of the RSFSR" undertaken by the authors themselves (Rabkina and Rimashevskaya, 1972, pp. 46-50). They make no explicit reference to the 1967 survey materials, or for that matter, to any other CSA work on the subject. It is unlikely, although not impossible, that this is a result of either censorship, which might prohibit any reference to unpublished official material, or bureaucratic rivalry between the two institutions, since they do make use of data on the 1967 distribution of income which can only have come from the CSA. All of this suggests that even if analyses of the 1967 demographic material were completed, they were not circulated widely among those responsible for policy formulation and advice. And finally, while a study of the impact of the Soviet welfare state upon the incomes of households at different levels of material well-being, completed by the NIIT in the late fifties, has been published in some detail, in subsequent works its most relevant conclusions have been ignored rather than cited; from the mid sixties, the topic itself appears to have been neglected altogether, or relegated to the private academic sphere (Maslov, 1959a and 1959b; see also section 4.4 below).

Thus, although the building blocks for a rational antipoverty program have been available in the USSR since the late nineteen-fifties, largely as a result of official or semiofficial activity, there is little evidence to suggest that they were used in any fundamental reconsideration of government policy. At least there is no indication of such a reconsideration in the academic literature or in the house journal of the organization most likely to undertake it, the State Committee on Labor and Wages. This impression is reinforced by a consideration of the policies actually pursued in this area until 1968-73. After the reform of the pension law and the rationalization of certain other social insurance benefits in 1955-56 (chapter 11, below), thus antedating the data-gathering activities on which any fundamentally new appraisal could be based, there were no changes in the range of benefits provided, in eligibility criteria, or in formal benefit levels, until after 1968. At least, this was true for state employees; a start was made in extending the system to the collectivized peasantry in 1965. Thus insofar as the Soviet government pursued an active antipoverty policy in the period 1956-68, it must have been through existing programs and through its control over wage rates and salary scales.

The 1958 survey of incomes would have revealed just how low the average standard of living in the Soviet Union was, if the government did not already realize it. It would also have indicated that there were substantial numbers of nonagricultural state employees with incomes significantly below the mean. But the government's subsequent actions imply that it believed there were no peculiar determining factors for this poverty, that there was no significant demographic or social source of deprivation. Certainly for nonagricultural state employees and also to a considerable extent among collective farmers, poverty was thought to be the consequence of low pay. Therefore the primary thrust of official action was toward increasing wages and in particular toward raising the minimum wage. The results of this policy in the kolkhoz sector were described in chapter 2; its impact upon state employees will be dealt with in chapters 8-10. Only the existence of an aging labor force in agriculture appears to have been recognized as generating poverty not alleviated by the social security system; and this was dealt with by the creation of the All-Union Central Pension Fund for Kolkhozy in 1965 and the extension then of limited social insurance to this group.

But the work of data collection and analysis initiated by the authorities in the late fifties, the rebirth of academic economics, and the development of an empirical sociology have gradually revealed that this perception of Soviet society is inadequate. The material showed that in 1958, and even in 1967-68, there was considerable poverty in the USSR. Furthermore, low incomes were not confined to the rural population; on certain definitions a majority of the poor were state employees, possibly nonagricultural state employees. It also suggested that demographically and socially the poor differed from the rest of the population and that the Soviet welfare state failed to provide for their needs. It implied that the strategy of relying primarily on the minimum wage was inadequate and that a more sophisticated, a more complex approach was required.

The remainder of this chapter will attempt to carry out the analysis suggested above. The discussion in chapter 1 has already given a definition of poverty in 1965, and section 4.3 will review some of the indirect evidence of the lower poverty standard suggested for 1958. In section 4.2, the distributions of chapter 3 are used to provide estimates of the numbers in the different social classes with incomes below the official poverty level in these two years. Some attempt is also made to allow for income in kind accruing to state employees, and this provides a lower limit to estimates of the incidence of poverty. Section 4.3 is mainly concerned with an analysis of the distinguishing demographic characteristics of the non-agricultural or urban poor. Section 4.4 contains a review of published Soviet studies of the adequacy of the social security and social welfare systems. This material permits one to form a clearer idea of the nature and extent of the problem facing the Soviet authorities. It also allows one to assess the relevance of the policies pursued by the government after 1956; the policies themselves are discussed in chapters 8-11.

4.2   THE INCIDENCE OF POVERTY

It is sometimes assumed that poverty in the USSR is a rural phenomenon, associated with the legal and social disabilities under which the collectivized peasantry are placed. It is thought that the extensive provisions of the Soviet welfare state should preclude the existence of poverty among state employees and their dependents. It is certainly true that the distributions of the previous chapter show that a higher proportion of kolkhozniki than state employees have incomes below any particular level. But they also show that it is not only the agricultural population that is poor; indeed, figures given below suggest that, on the official definition, a majority of the poor in 1967-68 were nonagricultural state employees and their dependents. This implies that there are significant lacunae in the network of support provided by Soviet social welfare programs. But first let us consider the problem of determining how many people in the USSR may be classified as poor.

The distributions of chapter 3 indicate the proportion of the Soviet population, or of specified social groups, with per capita incomes (variously defined) in different income classes. Given a definition of poverty and a knowledge of the number of persons in the groups to which the distributions refer, it is a matter of simple arithmetic to calculate how many people fall below the poverty line. There are, however, two difficulties to be resolved. In chapter 3, the distribution for nonagricultural state employees (and sovkhozniki on assumption A) referred to money income, while that for kolkhozniki referred to personal income. It can be argued that in estimating the incidence of poverty, some allowance should be made for the value of private agricultural output consumed domestically by state employees. And while the MMS budget yields a precise ruble figure for 1965, there is less information about the poverty level appropriate for 1958.

Table 4.1 gives the number of state employees with a money income

Table 4.1
Numbers in Selected Categories with a Per Capita Money Income
below the Poverty Level, 1958, 1967 (millions)

Money Income (R per month)	Nonagricultural State Employees		Sovkhozniki (1967)	
	1958	1967	A	B
-25.0	27.7	—	—	—
-30.0	41.0	11.5	1.4	4.5
-50.0	88.8	60.8	7.5	12.1
Total population group	127.7	160.7	20.5	

Notes and Sources: The state employee is calculated by subtracting the colectivized peas-antry from the total population. The state agricultural population is estimated by grossing up annual average employment in (state) agriculture by the number of dependents per worker in rural areas, and nonagricultural population by subtracting the result from the total. See *NK SSSR '65*, pp. 42, 558; *NK SSSR '67*, p. 35; *Itogi 1959*, p. 97; *Itogi 1970*, vol. 5, p. 155; and chapter 3 of this book.

Variant A is based on the assumption that sovkhozniki are distributed like other state employees and variant B on the assumption that they are distributed like kolkhozniki.

Table 4.2
Numbers in Selected Categories with Per Capita Personal Income
below the Poverty Level, 1967 (millions)

Personal Income (R per month)	Kolkhozniki	Sovkhozniki		Nonagricultural State Employees	
		A	B	A	B
-25	7.17	—	—	—	—
-30	11.95	0.41	2.21	3.29	3.64
-50	32.13	5.20	10.20	41.94	43.01
Total population group	52.30	20.5		160.7	

Notes and Sources: The numbers of kolkhozniki in each category from chapter 3 and *NK SSSR '67*, pp. 7, 35. The number of state employees in each category is derived by assuming that *all* non-kolkhoznik private agricultural output (5,158 million rubles) accrues to those with a per capita money income of 50 rubles a month or less and that it accrues equally to all in this category. Under variant A this implies the addition of 6.29 rubles per capita per month to income; under variant B, 5.90 rubles. The figures in the table assume that individuals were distributed equally within income classes.

lower than the MMS budget level. In 1958 almost 89 million nonagricul-tural state employees came into this category. In 1967, the number had fallen to 60.8 million, to which should be added a further 7-12 million state farm workers and their dependents (on the basis that even the as-sumption B distribution refers to money income). The figures in table 4.2 indicate that in the same year there were approximately 32 million kolkhozniki with a *personal* income at or below this level. Thus, neglecting the difference in income concept, state employees and their dependents accounted for 68–69% of the Soviet poor in 1967 and nonagricultural state employees for 58-61% in the same year.

Since both agricultural and nonagricultural state employees own and work private plots, the figures given in table 4.1 overestimate the incidence of poverty, if the personal income concept is used. The available data are not sufficient to permit the construction of a distribution of state employees by personal income, but the results of a crude attempt to allow for this factor are given in table 4.2. In particular, the estimates of the number of agricultural and nonagricultural state employees with a per capita personal income of less than 50 rubles a month given there are based on the assumption that only poor state employee households (that is, those with a money income of less than 50 rubles a month) possess private plots, and also that agricultural and nonagricultural state employee households benefit equally from their holdings.

Neither of these assumptions is particularly realistic, but I suggest that if anything, they will overstate the contribution that subsistence agriculture makes to the incomes of the poor, and that therefore the figures in table 4.2 will underestimate the incidence of poverty among state employees. For example, it has been reported that in a sample of industrial workers employed at plants located in large towns in the mid sixties, approximately 39% of households with a per capita money income of less than 50 rubles a month had access to a private plot, *sad i ogorod*. But in the same sample, 30% of households with incomes between 50 and 75 rubles and 20% of those with a per capita income greater than 75 rubles a month also had access to such garden plots. For a sample of worker households in Pavlovskii Posad (a small town in the Moscow oblast) the proportions were 74%, 73%, and 57% for the same three income classes (Gordon and Klopov, 1972, supplement, table 11). Thus, although private plots in urban areas are not confined to the poor, they are somewhat more common among them than among others. Further, as Gordon and Klopov remark, "one must not overestimate the absolute value of income derived from gardens and allotments in an urban worker environment. Even today, in many cases they are not so much a source of income as a form of relaxation, a means of communicating with nature" (Gordon and Klopov, 1972, p. 37). This is surely most true of those with the highest incomes. A number of authors have stated, also, that receipts from private activity are more important to sovkhoznik households than to those of industrial workers, but the statements are too imprecise to permit one to differentiate between the two groups (Sarkisyan, 1972, pp. 170-73; Komarov and Chernyavskii, 1973, p. 70).

There is a further source of error in the adjustment recorded in table 4.2. In that table, the total value of private output accruing to state sector households in 1965 was allocated to those with money incomes below 50 rubles a month in 1967. No attempt was made to estimate private output in 1967 nor to adjust for the value of sales (already included in money income). In 1970, however, such sales accounted for 20% of total production, and there is no reason to believe that the proportion would have been significantly different three years earlier (Sarkisyan, 1972, p. 173). Also, between 1965 and 1970 the value of private agricultural output originating in state sector households increased at an average annual rate of 9.2%. Hence the net effect of those two omissions may have been minor.

Taking the figures in table 4.2 at face value, however, they show that some 42-43 million nonagricultural state employees and their dependents had per capita incomes at or below the MMS budget level and that there were a further 5-10 million state farm workers in the same situation. Thus one may conclude that not less than 50-52% of the poor in 1967 had no connection with agriculture.

The definition of poverty used so far has been based on the MMS budget, worked out in 1967. From the numbers found to be poor, it is possible to suggest that the subsistence standard implicit in this work is rather liberal, particularly from a policy point of view. For this reason, tables 4.1 and 4.2 also contain estimates of the numbers with per capita incomes below 25-30 rubles a month. As indicated below, there is reason to believe that this corresponds more closely to the accepted poverty standard of the late fifties than does the MMS budget; it was approximately equal to the value of a student stipend in 1967.

On this more restrictive definition, there were approximately 11.5 million nonagricultural state employees who, judged by money income, were poor; to these should be added another 1-4 million sovkhozniki. In 1967, some 12 million collective farmers and their dependents had a per capita personal income of less than 30 rubles a month. Thus, neglecting the difference in income concepts, nonagricultural state employees accounted for some 40-45% of the very poor. When allowance is made for domestic consumption of privately produced agricultural commodities, the proportion falls to 20%; but I believe that the figures in table 4.2 relating to this poorest group should be treated with some scepticism.

Finally, the figures given here allow one to trace how the numbers in poverty, at least of nonagricultural state employees, have changed over time. From table 4.1 it can be seen that in the nine-year period 1958-67, the number with a per capita money income of less than 50 rubles a month fell by about 30 million, or a third of the 1958 total. For those with incomes of less than 30 rubles, the fall was only slightly larger in absolute numbers, but substantially larger as a proportion of the 1958 total.[1] These changes would seem to be the result of the relatively equal increments in absolute income enjoyed by a majority of Soviet citizens, mentioned in the previous chapter. In consequence, the Soviet authorities succeeded in substantially reducing, although not eliminating, the most extreme forms of poverty among nonagricultural state employees. In 1967 only 7.1% of this category had a money income below 30 rubles a month. But going by official definitions, in the same year a substantial number were still in want. Also, although precise figures are not available, one may conjecture that the number of kolkhozniki in extreme poverty fell as well. But in 1968, 16% of collective farmers and their families still had personal per capita incomes below 30 rubles a month, and more than half had an income below the MMS budget level. There are no figures relating to the scale of poverty in more recent years, but it has been suggested that during the ninth five-year plan period (1970-75), the number of state employee families with per capita incomes below the MMS budget level was expected to fall by 50%, primarily as a result of increases in wages and modifications of social welfare programs (Mamontova, 1975, p. 299).

4.3   WHO ARE THE SOVIET POOR?

So much for estimates of the incidence of poverty in the USSR, but who are the Soviet poor and in what ways do they differ from the rest of the population? The official sample surveys that provided the data upon which the estimates of section 4.2 were based also contain extensive demographic information that could be used to construct an analysis of the sources of poverty among the nonagricultural population. I know of only one such analysis based on the 1958 data, and this is confined to the sub-sample of households living in the Moscow oblast (Urlanis, 1966). It is, however, probable that other similar studies were undertaken, although I doubt whether they were particularly detailed or sophisticated. On the basis of other work published at this period, it appears that neither analytical techniques nor computational technology was highly developed in the USSR. Also, one can question whether these studies, if they were completed, had any substantial impact upon the ideas and attitudes of those responsible for policy formation or in a position to offer advice. At least in the literature there was no discussion of Urlanis's study or of other unpublished work.

In this section, I will make use of the information provided by Urlanis and of data drawn from two other socioeconomic studies of Soviet industrial workers, in an attempt to identify some of the salient features of the Soviet poor. Because of the nature of the material upon which the analysis is based, the conclusions must be regarded as tentative, but they tend to confirm the inadequacy of the official perception of society outlined at the beginning of the chapter.

Published data on household composition at various levels of income in the USSR and on other social characteristics is extremely limited, but some is available. For 1958, there is the Urlanis study, already mentioned; for the mid sixties there are two or three sample surveys which, although they refer only to industrial workers, *rabochiye promyshlennosti,* also throw some light on the subject. In particular, there is the sample used by Rabkina and Rimashevskaya, mentioned above, and there are two further samples used by Gordon and Klopov (Gordon and Klopov, 1972, supplement, tables 1-11). Data on these were collected primarily for the study of time use, but one may extract some information about the relationship between income and household composition from the sample description statistics. The first of these samples refers to workers employed in industrial enterprises in large urban centers in the European part of the USSR and the second to those employed in Pavlovskii Posad, a small town in the Moscow oblast. There is some reason to believe, however, that the first sample in particular may be representative of the nonagricultural population in the USSR as a whole, at least as far as the distribution of income is concerned (see table 4.3).

In his paper, Urlanis does not explicitly identify the ruble intervals associated with the three income classes into which he subdivides his sample; he simply labels them with the Roman numerals I-III and refers to them as low, middle, and high. But the paper as a whole contains sufficient information to permit one to estimate the relative shares of the three classes in the total sample.[2] It was then assumed that the distribution of income in the Moscow oblast was identical to that in the USSR as a whole, and the computed shares were used to derive the appropriate quantities from the distribution given in table 3.1. These were 23.4 rubles and 68.0 rubles, which were then rounded up to give the class intervals used in table 4.3.[3] Thus the Urlanis study suggests that the poverty level used by the Soviet authorities in 1958 was approximately 25 rubles per month per capita.

Although very little is known about the normative budgets constructed at that time, this identification receives some support from the following considerations. It has been suggested that the budgets constructed were used to determine the new minimum wage adopted during the 1956-65 wage reorganization. Since in 1956 the minimum wage was set at 27-35 rubles a month, since the budget was supposed to specify the cost of attaining a minimum acceptable standard of living, and since the wage might be expected to include some incentive component, one might infer that the Soviet government accepted 25-30 rubles a month as its definition of poverty. On the other hand, the new minimum wage was adopted in 1956, and it is at least probable that the work on normative budget construction was not completed until 1957 or 1958. As I indicate below, the minimum wage was raised, in 1959, to 40-45 rubles a month for those employed in enterprises or industries whose pay scales had been reorganized. But it is unlikely that the upper bound of the lowest income class used by Urlanis is as high as 40 rubles.[4] Rather, one should conclude that until the late fifties the official definition of poverty probably owed as much to preconceptions and prejudice as it did to the empirical analysis of the cost of subsistence.

The Gordon and Klopov samples consisted of 850 workers (500 women and 350 men) drawn from industrial enterprises in four large urban centers in European Russia, and 500 workers (sex ratio unspecified) drawn from plants in Pavlovskii Posad. The four industrial centers were Dnepropetrovsk, Zaporozhe, Kostroma, and Odessa, and the industries included metallurgy, metal fabricating, engineering, and textiles. The large-town sample was derived in two stages: first, "typical" shops at chosen plants were selected, and then the sample was drawn mechanically from persons employed in those shops (Gordon and Klopov, 1972, pp. 19-20). Thus there is reason to believe that the sample is at least quasi-random. Gordon and Klopov report their results (for both samples) for males and females separately. Their data have been used to construct a sample of worker households in the following way. First, it was assumed that each worker represented a separate household; second, that each sub-sample, classified by sex, was itself representative. The male and female sub-samples were then combined with weights 55:45, reflecting the share of the two sexes in worker employment in 1970.[5] The same procedure was followed with the Pavlovskii Posad data.

Gordon and Klopov use this latter sample to contrast the experience of small-town workers with that of workers living in large industrial centers, particularly as concerns the way in which nonworking time is used. It is thus implied that Pavlovskii Posad is typical of small towns in European Russia. This is doubtful, since it is relatively close to Moscow, contains one of the oldest textile plants in the RSFSR, and was once described as one of the leading industrial regions in the country.[6]

The distribution of households by per capita income for the three samples to be used here, together with that taken from table 3.1, is given in table 4.3. In describing their large-town sample, Gordon and Klopov state that "between 5% and 10% of the sample had per capita incomes of less than 35 rubles per month and approximately the same number had incomes in excess of 100 rubles." They also state that the average income for the sample as a whole was "somewhat in excess of 60 rubles per month" (Gordon and Klopov, 1972, p. 35). In deriving the average income reported in table 4.3, I assumed that 10% fell into the lowest category and 5% into the highest. The midpoints of the intervals from this sample were also used to evaluate average income for the Pavlovskii Posad sample.[7]

The figures in table 4.3 suggest that the sample drawn from large towns

Table 4.3
Distribution of Households by Per Capita Money Income:
USSR, Various Samples, 1958, 1965-68

Money Income (R per month)	Non-agricultural State Employees, Moscow Oblast, 1958 (%)	Money Income (R per month)	Non-agricultural State Employees USSR, 1967 (%)	1965-68 (%)	
				Workers, Large Towns	Workers, Pavlovskii Posad
		-35	10.25	5-10	41.0
-25	13.0	35-50	22.25	22-27	
25-70	61.8	50-75	38.90	43	48.3
70-	25.2	75-100	17.10	15-20	10.7
		100-	11.5	5-10	
Average (R)	55.70		65.70	62.80	56.10

Sources: Column 2 derived from Urlanis, 1966; column 4 from chapter 3, table 3.1; columns 5-6 from Gordon and Klopov, 1972, supplement tables 1-6. See text for details of derivation.

corresponds fairly close to the distribution of income for nonagricultural state employees of the USSR as a whole. As one might expect, there are more workers in the middle-income groups and fewer in the tails, but on the whole differences are small. There is some justification, therefore, in assuming that the attributes of this sample can be generalized to the population as a whole. Further, if Pavlovskii Posad is typical of small towns in Russia or the USSR, the figures in the table imply that standards of living there are markedly lower than in larger urban industrial centers. But the size of the income difference between the two samples may only reflect the importance of textiles in this town, since the textile industry is not a high-wage sector of the Soviet economy.

Having described the data samples and made some attempt to assess their representativeness, let us now turn to an examination of differences in the distribution of various household types by per capita income. The relevant figures are given in tables 4.4-4.6. In interpreting these figures one should bear in mind that there are minor differences in the definition of income[8] and that although the Russian descriptions of the various household types are similar, they are not identical, and these terminological distinctions may reflect real differences in coverage.

Turning first to the figures in table 4.4, they show, for example, that although 13% of all households of nonagricultural state employees in the Moscow oblast had a per capita money income of less than 25 rubles a month in 1958—that is, were considered poor at the time—only 4% of single individuals and 5% of childless couples were in this category. On

Table 4.4
Family Composition and Living Standards:
Nonagricultural State Employee Households, Moscow Oblast, 1958

Household Type	% Household Type in Income Class			% Households in Sample
	-25 R	25-70 R	70- R	
Single persons	3.8	52.3	43.8	35.0
Couples without children	5.0	47.3	47.8	9.8
Couples with children	21.1	70.1	8.8	49.1
of which				
Simple families	18.8	72.2	9.0	28.4
Complex families	24.5	69.0	6.5	4.7
Incomplete families	24.2	66.8	9.1	16.0
Other households	13.4	72.9	13.6	6.1
% income class in population	13.0	61.8	25.2	100.0

Source: Calculated from data in Urlanis, 1966, pp. 135-46.

the other hand, some 21% of families with children and almost 25% of incomplete families were living in poverty. To put this another way, families with children were almost four times as likely as childless couples to be poor. Similarly, childless couples and single individuals were between five and six times as likely to be well-off (that is, to have a per capita income of more than 70 rubles a month) as families without children. This suggests that in the absence of an appropriate system of child allowances, the raising of children was associated with a low standard of living in the USSR in the late fifties.

Changes in the definition of poverty, changes in demographic structure, and increases in the minimum or average wage brought about certain changes in the pattern of income distribution among households of different types between 1958 and 1967. The figures in table 4.5 show that in 1965-68, some 32% of worker households were regarded as poor. At the same time, only 15% of single individuals and 3% of young married couples without children were in this category. On the other hand, more than 40% of families with dependent children and two-thirds of incomplete families (those lacking one parent) had a per capita money income of less than 50 rubles a month. Alternatively, one can say that families with children were almost three times as likely as single individuals and fourteen times as likely as childless married couples to be poor. At the other extreme, such couples were seven or eight times as likely to be well off as families with children and were more than thirty times as likely to be well-off as those living in complex families (that is, families including a relative other than parents and their children). These figures show that in the USSR not only the raising of children but also the support of other relatives

Table 4.5
Family Composition and Living Standards,
Workers in Large Towns in European Russia, 1965-68

| Household Type | % Household Type in Income Class | | | % Households in Sample |
	-50 R	50-75 R	75- R	
Young unmarried persons	14.8	28.1	57.1	21.0
Young married persons	2.8	32.8	64.3	7.0
Parents with young children	42.2	48.9	8.9	66.0
of which				
Simple families	32.3	57.3	10.4	44.0
Complex families	60.6	36.5	2.9	17.0
Incomplete families	66.0	18.0	16.0	5.0
Elderly persons	15.0	41.7	43.3	6.0
% income class in population	32.0	43.0	25.0	100.0

Source: Derived from Gordon and Klopov, 1972, supplement tables 2-4.

can result in a reduction in living standards. It suggests that in 1965-68 the Soviet pension system was in need of modification.

Insofar as Pavlovskii Posad can be regarded as typical of small towns in Russia or the USSR, the figures in table 4.6 suggest that poverty is more prevalent in such settlements than in larger industrial centers. In Pavlovskii Posad, some 41% of worker households had a per capita money income of less than 50 rubles a month in 1965-68, and fewer than 11% had incomes of more than 75 rubles. But in this environment, too, the young and childless were better off than those with dependents. Only 16% of young single workers and fewer than 5% of childless couples were classified as poor; in contrast, more than half of all families with young children and

Table 4.6
Family Composition and Living Standards, Workers in Pavlovskii Posad, 1965-68

| Household Type | % Household Type in Income Class | | | % Households in Sample |
	-50 R	50-75 R	75- R	
Young unmarried persons	15.5	61.7	22.8	12.6
Young married persons	4.4	24.1	71.5	5.0
Parents with young children	50.5	48.0	1.5	76.9
of which				
Simple families	52.2	46.8	1.0	53.8
Complex families	39.5	58.8	1.7	17.7
Incomplete families	70.0	24.0	6.0	5.4
Elderly persons	—	43.6	56.4	5.5
% income class in population	41.0	48.3	10.7	100.0

Source: Derived from Gordon and Klopov, 1972, supplement tables 2-4.

as many as 70% of incomplete families were poor. The figures in table 4.6 also imply that young unmarrieds were fifteen times as likely and young marrieds almost forty-eight times as likely as parents with young children to have an income greater than 75 rubles a month. (In this context, young probably means under the age of sixteen, since that is the dividing line used by Urlanis and in some other studies.)

There is one respect in which Pavlovskii Posad appears to differ from the large-town sample and from that based on the Moscow oblast as a whole in 1958. In both the latter, a higher proportion of complex families than of simple families were classified as poor. By contrast, Pavlovskii Posad had a lower proportion of poor complex families. In the former samples, it seems, dependent relatives impose a burden on the family budget; in the latter (and perhaps more generally in small towns, where traditional patterns of life persist or are enforced by the housing situation), it appears that the extended family, by permitting income sharing, contributed to the cost of raising children and thus helped to alleviate poverty.

In interpreting the final category of households in tables 4.4-4.6, the source of the data on which they are based should be remembered. Both the 1958 income survey and the two Gordon and Klopov samples were drawn from persons in employment. Pure pensioner and pure student households are therefore excluded. Elderly (*pozhilye*) households are those where the children have grown up but where the head is still working. Those above working age and the nonemployed young are underrepresented in each of the samples and in all income categories.

The material presented so far permits one to draw certain conclusions about the relationship between household composition and poverty in the USSR and about the way that this changed between 1958 and 1965-68. In table 4.7, the relative shares of households of different types in the in-

Table 4.7
Share of Different Household Types among Poor Families, USSR, 1958-68 (%)

| | 1958 | | 1965-68 | |
| | Moscow | | Large | Pavlovskii |
Household Type	Oblast	Household Type	Towns	Posad
Single persons	10.3	Young unmarrieds	9.7	4.8
Childless couples	3.8	Young marrieds	0.6	0.5
Couples + children	79.6	Parents and young children	87.5	94.7
Simple	41.0	Simple	44.4	68.5
Complex	8.8	Complex	32.8	17.0
Incomplete	29.8	Incomplete	10.3	9.2
Other	6.3	Elderly persons	2.8	—
% of total sample	13.0		32.0	41.0

Source: Derived from tables 4.4-4.6.

come class defined as poor are presented. Once again, in interpreting this table, the changed definition of poverty and the possibility of differences in the classification of households should be borne in mind. But that having been said, the figures suggest that the Soviet authorities have been successful in reducing poverty among those with no dependents. This can be attributed to successive increases in the minimum wage. With a minimum wage of 60 rubles a month, as it was in 1968, only those individuals in part-time employment or those who for some reason or other earned less than the minimum would be in poverty. The same would apply to childless couples, provided both partners worked.[9] On this point, I do not know when precisely during 1965-68 the Gordon and Klopov samples were taken; since the minimum wage was raised at the beginning of January 1968, I would conjecture that the large-town sample relates to an earlier year, while that from Pavlovskii Posad probably covers 1967-68 or even 1968. This would explain the decline in the proportion of young single persons in poverty between the two samples even though Pavlovskii Posad is the lower wage group.

On the other hand, table 4.7 suggests that the Soviet authorities have been less successful at reducing the incidence of poverty among families with children. Neither higher earnings nor the then-existing system of social welfare payments compensated parents for the cost of bringing up children, or the employed for the cost of maintaining dependent relatives. I believe that this remained substantially true even after pensions were raised in 1971. Also, I suspect that the reduction in the importance of incomplete households among the poor between 1958 and 1965-68 is more apparent than real; it probably reflects the more liberal definition of poverty. These families are among the worst off in the USSR, but an increase in the number of households considered poor would tend to reduce their relative weight.[10]

So far, this section has been concerned with the proportions of various household types at different levels of income; but Urlanis's data can also be used to examine the proportion of persons in the different income categories. This is done in table 4.8. The figures imply that while only 13% of employed persons had a per capita income of less than 25 rubles a month in 1958, more than a third of the children under sixteen and almost 37% of nonemployed women were in this category. On the other hand, while 20% of employed persons had per capita incomes of more than 70 rubles a month in 1958, only 7% of nonemployed women and under 4% of children were as well off as this.

As can be seen from the table, about half of those in the lowest income category were nonemployed, whereas fewer than 10% of the highest income group were in that situation. Of dependents in the poor group, the overwhelming majority were children; indeed, children constituted 37%

Table 4.8
Demographic Status and Living Standards, Moscow Oblast, 1958

Demographic Status	% Status Group in Income Class			% Status Group in Sample
	-25 R	25-70 R	70- R	
Employed	49.3	73.4	91.3	71.8
Dependent	50.7	26.6	8.7	28.2
of whom				
Children -16	36.9	19.1	4.8	20.1
Women with children	7.2	3.2	1.6	3.7
Above working age	3.9	2.7	1.2	2.7
Students, etc.	2.7	1.6	1.1	1.7
% income group in sample	18.8	65.4	15.8	100.0
Dependent/worker ratio[a]	1.03	0.36	0.01	0.39
Average family size[b]	4.1	3.2	2.1	3.2

Notes and Sources: Derived from Urlanis, 1966, pp. 138-43.

a. The dependent/worker ratios given here differ significantly from those for the USSR as a whole (urban population 1.2) in 1959 and Moscow Oblast in 1970 (urban and rural population—0.74).

b. Excluding single individuals, average family size was 4.2, 3.5, 2.8, and 3.6, respectively, which corresponds fairly closely to family size for the population as a whole. See *Itogi* 1959.

of the poor. The figures also show that as per capita income fell, the number of dependents per earner rose; average family size also tended to rise.

I have not been able to find similar quantitative data relating to 1967, but Rabkina and Rimashevskaya comment (1972, pp. 47-48):

> On our data, employed persons make up less than one-third of [poor] households; the remainder are more or less equally divided between dependents of the family and those supported by the state (pensioners and students). Among better-off groups participation rates are higher; in the highest group the rate is approximately 90%. . . . According to data from the same survey, poor households consist of about 50% children or old persons, and among those of working age without employment women predominate (basically mothers with young children). . . .
>
> From this one may conclude that large families [*mnogodetnost*, i.e., having many children] are far from the only cause of poverty [*problema obespechennosti*], as economists used to think. Observations in recent years have shown that relatively low incomes are in many cases connected with the maintenance of elderly relatives and the existence of incomplete families (single mothers), and also with the existence of families whose "breadwinner" is either a pensioner or a student.

This analysis is of interest for two reasons. First it suggests that there has been a decline in the proportion of employed among the poor between

1958 and 1967, a decline in the proportion of children (from 37% to about 17%), an increase in the proportion of students and pensioners (from 7% to approximately 33%), and an increase in the proportion of women of working age who remain at home to look after their children (from 7% to about 17%). These changes are striking, but since the sample on which they were based was confined to the RSFSR, they may not reflect changes occurring in Central Asia or the Caucasus; they should be treated with caution.

Second, Rabkina and Rimashevskaya imply that either misleading conclusions were drawn from the analysis of the 1958 survey data or the underlying situation has changed. In any case, they suggest that neither further increases in the minimum wage nor a general program of family allowances would result in the elimination of poverty; rather, they argue for a more differentiated package of measures.

The relative inefficiency of attempting to reduce the incidence of poverty by raising minimum wages is brought out by the figures in table 4.9. These are based on the survey of industrial workers used by Rabkina

Table 4.9
The Relationship between Earnings and Incomes: Industrial Workers, RSFSR, 1967-68

Family Income (R per month)	Wage Class (R per month)			% of Sample in Income Class
	-90	90-160	160-	
-50	15.0	19.0	3.0	37.0
50-75	13.0	23.3	6.7	43.0
75-	3.0	11.2	5.8	20.0
% of sample in wage class	31.0	53.5	15.5	100.0

Source: Derived from data in Rabkina and Rimashevskaya, 1972, p. 50. See text for details.

and Rimashevskaya.[11] They show that, for this sample at least (and perhaps more generally), 37% of households had per capita incomes of less than 50 rubles a month; of these, almost 60% contained workers with monthly earnings of more than 90 rubles. (At this date, average industrial earnings were 109 rubles a month [*Narkhoz SSSR '67*, p. 657].) *Per contra*, more than half of those with wages of less than 90 rubles a month lived in households with a per capita income above the 1965 poverty level. These figures indicate that complexities in family structure were at least as important as low pay in generating deprivation. They also imply that much of the resources devoted to further increases in the minimum wage would go to better-off families.

This section has examined what limited evidence there is on the demographic and social composition of the Soviet urban poor and on the ways in which the poor as a group differ from the rest of society. Such information is essential in formulating effective policies for reducing or eliminating poverty. The analysis has shown that the importance of low pay as a cause of poverty has declined since the late fifties, and that social rather than economic factors have now become the primary determinants of living standards. At least among nonagricultural state employees, the minimum wage is high enough for the vast majority of those with jobs to support themselves, if single, at a standard of living above the poverty level. Deprivation now depends upon whom one marries, whether one's spouse works, the number of children or other relatives that rely upon one for support.

In part this reflects the success of the wage policies pursued by the Soviet government during the sixties, and in part it is the consequence of demographic change. But the new situation calls for a new approach to the problem of poverty, a new analysis of the role of specific welfare programs and of social consumption expenditures as a whole. This in turn requires a knowledge of the part played by these programs in determining the incomes of the poor (and of other sections of society), and it is to this topic that I now turn.

4.4   THE DISTRIBUTION OF SOCIAL WELFARE EXPENDITURES.[12] Evidence about the structure of incomes accruing to households with different levels of material welfare in the USSR is both partial and extremely limited. That which is available to outsiders consists entirely of sample surveys on a relatively small scale, some undertaken officially or semiofficially and others organized by individual economists or sociologists. There is every indication that little more is available to government officials and policy makers. In particular, there is no mention of the data collected through the sample of households on which income distribution statistics are based. Presumably it proved impossible to analyze this material in a meaningful way.

On the basis of a thorough but obviously not exhaustive examination of the literature published since 1956, I have managed to identify three official (or semiofficial) studies and at least two academic ones. The latest refers to 1964, and there are grounds for believing that this is the last until 1972-73, in any case.

The earliest analysis of the contribution that social consumption expenditures make to the incomes of households at different levels of material welfare was conducted by the NIIT in 1956. It is also the study about which most is known and to which reference has been made most frequently by other Soviet economists and sociologists. The results of this study are most fully described in two papers by P. P. Maslov, published in 1959 (Maslov, 1959a and 1959b).

The study itself was based on the family budgets of employees at three large enterprises in Moscow and at ten enterprises in Tbilisi and Erevan (Maslov, 1959a, p. 31). Published results, however, relate to only two enterprises, the Moscow Fish-Processing Kombinat and the Kuskovskii Chemicals Plant.[13] The samples consisted of 1541 employees (managerial and clerical as well as workers) of the Fish-Processing Kombinat and 295 of the Chemicals Plant. These were used to generate a sample of 806-7 households for the Kombinat and 264 households for the Kuskovskii Plant. Although some sources suggest that the published tables refer only to workers, *rabochiye* (Maslov, 1959b, p. 100; Maslov, 1959a, p. 27), an examination of the composition of the samples suggests that both managerial and clerical staff have been included. At the same time, it is likely that junior service personnel have been excluded, or to be more precise, that households whose heads were in this category were not included. Single-person households were also omitted.

Maslov presents analyses of this data classified by the earnings of the "head of the family" and also by per capita money income. The first has been widely quoted,[14] the second is almost never referred to (as an exception, see Rakitskii, 1966, pp. 40-41). It is not clear whether this reflects a weakness in the analysis (of which I am unaware) or should be seen as a consequence of the fact that it does not show what subsequent analysts want to demonstrate. I suspect the latter.

It has been reported that the NIIT undertook a further analysis of a sample of the family budgets of industrial workers in 1964. Only the barest details of this study have been released. For example, it is not known how large the sample was, how it was selected, which groups were covered, and so on, nor have any results from this work been published in tabular form. Our knowledge of it is derived from two sentences in a book by Sarkisyan and Kuznetsova (Sarkisyan and Kuznetsova, 1967, p. 75; it is not clear whether the NIIT was responsible for this work). This study is also referred to by Kunelskii in his 1973 book, without acknowledgement and without indicating that the figures relate to 1964. That Kunelskii is referring to the same data source as Sarkisyan is strongly suggested by the fact that the words he uses are almost identical to those that appear in the 1967 book (Kunelskii, 1973, p. 19). Since Kunelskii is a reasonably authoritative figure in the field of Soviet labor economics (and therefore presumably has access to much official and semiofficial unpublished research in the field), the fact that he is still using 1964 data in a book published almost a decade later is prima facie evidence that little subsequent research on the topic has been completed.

Finally, at some date before 1962, the All-Union Central Council of Trade Unions organized the analysis of some family budgets to investigate the relationship between earnings and receipts from public funds. Not all social consumption expenditures were included, and only the analysis with respect to the earnings of the head of household has been published (Kapustin, 1962, pp. 195-96).

In addition to these official or semiofficial studies, there have been a number of smaller academic investigations of the same problem. There is an analysis of the income structure of 73 families (284 persons) of textile workers employed at the Pavlovskii Posad Worsted Mill in 1960. The study was undertaken by V. A. Vasilieva as part of a comparison of contemporary living standards with those before the revolution (Vasilieva, 1965, pp. 60-80). Her data were used by G. S. Sarkisyan in a more general context (and without acknowledgement [Sarkisyan, 1963, p. 22]). Also, at some date between 1961 and 1965, V. Ya. Lion organized a study of the budgets of 746 families of employees at six industrial enterprises in Ivanovo oblast (Lion, 1965). And, although the published results do not show the dependence of receipts from public funds on per capita money income, N. K. Zemlyanskii reports an analysis of the budgets of a sample of 1464 persons (all categories of industrial personnel) from industrial enterprises in Novokuznetsk and Prokopevsk. The data relate to the period 1961-64 (Agenbegyan et al., 1964, especially pp. 111-49). There have also been references to secondary analyses which show how far inequality is reduced by Soviet social consumption expenditures. But none of these analyses has been published explicitly, and accounts of them are difficult to interpret (Karapetyan and Rimashevskaya, 1969, pp. 160-64).

Thus the published information about the relationship between earnings, incomes, and receipts from public funds is based on a limited number of relatively small samples. I believe that this is also substantially the information on which policy formulation in the USSR has been based. The samples refer almost exclusively to industrial employees (and primarily to workers), but this is a common Soviet weakness. They are also largely confined to the RSFSR and to the period 1956-65—perhaps more serious sources of bias. What do these studies show?

Table 4.10 presents the results of the 1956 NIIT study. In effect, it is the table given by Wiles and Markowski in their pioneering study of Soviet income distribution, but for ease of comparison with other figures in this chapter, I have converted it from old-rubles-per-year to new-rubles-per-month.[15] (This explains the rather peculiar earnings classes for household heads in the food industry.) The figures show that households in the lowest earnings classes, that is, those whose heads earned least, tended to receive most from the state, both absolutely and relatively. But there is no very clear pattern among the other groups; it is not the case that receipts decline as earnings increase. Indeed, as a group, households of employees in heavy industry with earnings of more than 130 rubles a month (in 1956!) received as much, per capita, as did those of employees in the food industry with earnings of less than 50 rubles a month. Further,

Table 4.10
Earnings and Receipts from Public Funds, 1956 (new rubles per month per capita)

Earnings of Head of Household	Earnings		Other Receipts and Services	Total Per Capita Income	% of Households
	Head of Household	Other Members			
Families of Employees in Heavy Industry					
-70	21.9	9.3	14.2	45.4	8
70-80	21.4	11.6	7.1	40.1	8
80-90	22.6	12.4	8.1	43.1	15
90-110	25.6	15.3	6.0	46.9	29
110-130	30.6	13.7	8.3	52.6	22
130-	41.3	18.2	11.1	70.6	18
Average	28.7	14.4	8.4	51.5	100
Families of Employees in Food Industry					
-50	13.5	9.6	11.1	34.2	18
50-83.3	21.4	11.0	7.5	40.0	38
83.3-116.7	26.6	11.0	7.0	44.8	33
116.7-	37.2	12.6	7.8	57.6	11
Average	23.6	10.8	8.1	42.3	100

Source: Maslov, 1959a, pp. 126-27. Maslov gives his data in old rubles per capita per year; for purposes of comparison they have been converted.

the average value of receipts from public funds was slightly higher at the Kuskovskii Chemicals Plant (where the average earnings of household heads were 109 rubles a month) than at the Moscow Fish-Processing Kombinat, where average earnings were only 80.24 rubles a month. The table also shows that the *total* social consumption expenditures (that is, including expenditures on health, education and preschool child care, etc., as well as cash disbursements) on the average amounted to some 25-33% of the earnings of household heads and to 15-20% of total per capita income.

There is some correlation between the earnings of the head of the household and the per capita income of the family and hence the family's standard of living; but the figures in table 4.9 show that substantial numbers of those in the higher earnings group belong to families that are classified as poor, while not all those with low wages come into the same category. In consequence, the analysis of table 4.10 does not cast much light on the relationship between material deprivation and dependence upon social welfare in the Soviet Union. Table 4.11 is somewhat more illuminating. The figures in this table show that, for both the plants considered, there was very little variation in per capita receipts as per capita income increased: the lowest value in either plant was some 12% less than the average (about a ruble per month), and the highest value was only about

Table 4.11
Receipts from Public Funds at Different Levels of Income, 1956 (rubles per month per capita)

Money Income	Money Income			Sample Structure		
Money Income	Earnings (all members)	Other Cash Receipts	Non-Cash Receipts	Households (%)	Individuals (%)	Family Size (persons)
Kuskovskii Chemicals Plant						
10-30	20.7	2.9	5.5	15	20	5.3
30-50	37.5	2.9	4.3	40	43	4.0
50-70	54.1	4.5	4.6	29	24	3.3
70-	70.7	4.6	4.2	16	13	3.3
Average	42.5	3.5	4.6	100	100	3.8
Moscow Fish-Processing Kombinat						
-20	14.6	1.6	6.7	9	12	4.4
20-30	22.6	3.0	6.1	23	26	3.8
30-40	31.4	3.2	5.2	24	24	3.4
40-50	41.1	3.2	4.2	20	19	3.2
50-70	53.8	4.3	4.2	17	14	2.9
70-	78.7	6.1	3.1	7	5	2.4
Average	34.5	3.2	5.2	100	100	3.4

Source: Maslov, 1959a, pp. 131-34.

10-12% above it. Thus, in these samples, receipts from public funds varied by only about two rubles per month per capita as one moved from the poorest households to the most affluent. Also, it was not the poorest who received most, nor was it the best-off who received least. There was much greater variation in the cash received by households at different levels of income. At the Chemicals Plant, the lowest value was 17% below the average, the highest 31% above; in the Moscow Fish-Processing Kombinat, the figures were 50% and 90% respectively. And in both plants, families with the lowest per capita earnings received least, while those with the highest earnings received most.

Table 4.11 also provides a breakdown of receipts from public funds into cash and non-cash components. Given the difficulties of determining usage of various state services and of valuing the services provided in a consistent manner, one would expect the cash component to be more accurately observed. This consists of pensions, stipends and other allowances, sickness benefits, maternity grants, and presumably, although Maslov does not say so explicitly, holiday pay. Many of these are related to earnings, and this relationship is evident in table 4.11. For both samples, there is an unambiguous tendency for cash receipts to rise with income. This is most striking in the Fish-Processing Kombinat sample, where the per capita cash receipts of the top 7% of households are almost four times as large as those of the bottom 9%. But perhaps the bottom tail is exceptional: per capita cash receipts almost double as one moves from the lowest to the next group.

Table 4.12 gives some indication of the structure of non-cash receipts for both samples. The figures show that in the lowest income groups some 50-60% of total benefits were allowances for education and child care. For the most affluent, education accounted for only 11-17% of the total. These differences reflect the variations in family composition at different levels of income that have already been explored. The table also shows that expenditures on medical care accounted for 10-14% of total benefits in the Moscow sample and somewhat less for that from the Chemicals Plant. There is no strong evidence that medical expenditures correlate, either negatively or positively, with income. On the other hand, housing subsidies (for this is what I identify with the residual) do show a marked positive association with income. Since Soviet households pay a flat rent per meter of accommodation, and subsidies are calculated as the cost of maintaining the housing stock less rental income, this result indicates that the more affluent (and smaller) households are better housed (for a fuller discussion of Soviet housing subsidies, see below, chapter 11).

Table 4.12
Structure of Social Consumption Expenditures Received by Families
with Different Levels of Material Welfare, 1956 (%)

Money Income (R per month per capita)	Total Receipts (R)	Non-Cash Receipts					
		Education and Child Care			Medical Care	Other[b]	Cash[c]
		Preschool	School[a]	Further			
Kuskovskii Chemicals Plant							
10-30	8.4	7.1	26.2	17.8	7.1	8.3	34.5
30-50	7.2	8.3	19.4	13.9	11.1	8.3	40.3
50-70	9.1	11.0	12.1	8.8	6.6	11.0	49.4
70-	8.8	4.5	6.8	5.7	8.0	21.6	52.3
Average	8.1	8.6	17.3	12.3	8.6	11.1	43.2
Moscow Fish-Processing Kombinat							
-20	8.3	12.0	28.9	20.5	14.3	3.6	19.3
20-30	9.1	9.9	23.1	18.7	12.1	3.3	33.0
30-40	8.4	8.3	21.4	15.5	9.5	8.3	38.1
40-50	7.4	5.4	16.2	12.2	10.8	10.8	43.2
50-70	8.5	9.4	11.8	8.2	9.4	9.4	50.6
70-	9.2	—	5.4	5.4	10.9	12.0	66.3
Average	8.4	8.3	19.0	14.3	10.7	8.3	38.1

Source: Derived from Maslov, 1959a, pp. 132-33.
   a. Including expenditure on Pioneer camps.
   b. Derived by residual; consists primarily of housing subsidies.
   c. This entry may include receipts from the financial system.

Interesting as are the figures in tables 4.10-12, they are now more than twenty years old. In subsequent tables I will attempt to show how the situation has changed over this period. The figures in table 4.13 refer to a small sample (73 families) of rather affluent textile workers in the Moscow oblast in 1960.[16] They suggest that in the four years since 1956 there had been a substantial increase in the total value of social consumption expenditures per capita. For this sample, the average household member received 13.8 rubles a month as compared with 8-8.5 rubles in 1956. How much of this is a real increase and how much can be attributed to sample variation or to different methods of valuation is not clear; but for the country as a whole, total social consumption expenditure more than doubled between 1950 and 1960.

The figures show that although both cash and non-cash components grew, the bulk of the increase was concentrated on an expansion in the value of free and subsidized services provided. Vasilieva's figures, like Maslov's, also show a tendency for cash receipts to increase absolutely, although not relatively, with money income. But in the Pavlovskii Posad

Table 4.13
Structure of Receipts of Families
with Different Levels of Per Capita Income, 1960 (rubles per month)

Category of Receipt	Per Capita Money Income[a]				
	-35	35-45	45-65	65-	Average
Earnings:					
head of household	13.8	16.0	21.7	37.0	23.1
other members	7.3	13.5	20.0	27.7	19.1
Cash receipts from state[b]	2.5	4.9	3.7	4.4	4.2
Other receipts	2.9	5.4	8.4	12.8	8.3
of which, private activity	1.9	2.0	3.1	1.6	2.4
Money income	26.5	39.9	53.8	82.0	54.6
Subsidized services[c]	2.0	1.8	2.8	5.7	3.1
Free services[d]	7.7	7.2	6.8	4.7	6.5
Total income	36.2	48.9	63.4	92.4	64.2
% of individuals	6.7	30.4	38.9	24.0	100.0
Average family size	4.8	4.8	3.8	3.1	3.9
Family loading[e]	1.66	1.14	0.85	0.5	0.9

Notes and Sources: Derived from Vasilieva, 1965, pp. 66, 67, and 76, on the assumption that per capita receipts have the same ratio, one to another, as expenditures.

a. Income classes inferred; Vasilieva simply labels them I-IV.

b. Holiday pay, pensions, allowances, and stipends.

c. Subsidized visits to sanitoria and rest homes; maintenance of children in preschool child care facilities.

d. Education, medical care, and housing subsidies.

e. Ratio of dependents to employed family members.

sample there is no tendency for non-cash receipts to offset this tendency; thus receipts from public funds increase with income.

Table 4.14 gives the relevant published data from Lion's sample of

Table 4.14
Social Consumption Expenditures and Per Capita Income,
Ivanovo, 1961-65 (rubles per month)

Money Income	Total Social Expenditures	of which		Average Family Size
		Cash	Non-Cash	
-25	14.9	5.2	9.7	4.6
25-35	15.4	6.2	9.2	3.8
35-50	15.9	8.2	7.6	3.4
50-70	19.3	12.2	7.2	2.6
70-	14.1	9.3	4.8	2.1

Source: Lion, 1965, p. 18. Based on a sample of 746 families of employees at six industrial enterprises in Ivanovo oblast. The survey was administered by the author himself, presumably after 1961, since the income classes are given in new rubles.

households in Ivanovo oblast. Lion does not state when the data were collected, but since they are given in new rubles, it is presumed that they refer to some period after 1961. Further, as the author does not indicate the portions of the sample falling into the different income classes, it is not possible to derive explicit estimates of average receipts for the sample as a whole. A priori reasoning suggests that, in total, they amounted to 14-19 rubles per month per capita and thus exceeded the receipts of the Pavlovskii Posad sample. This gives added support to the assignment of the sample to the 1961-65 period.

Lion's data suggest an average cash receipt of 6-9 rubles per month per capita, which is substantially higher than both the 1956 Moscow figure and that for Pavlovskii Posad in 1960. On the other hand, they suggest non-cash receipts of only 6-8 rubles per month; this is higher than in the 1956 sample but less than that for 1960, at least according to the figures in table 4.13. Of course, this may be a consequence of sample bias, of differences in the range of services covered, or in the valuation and imputation methods employed; but it may be interpreted as a consequence of the ongoing wage reorganization. Insofar as cash receipts are related to earnings, an increase in wage scales will raise the value of social security receipts, even if there are no changes in entitlement provisions or in the formulae used to calculate benefits. Finally, Lion's data show that both total and cash benefits from public funds tend to increase with income (with the exception of the most affluent category), but that the cash progression is offset to some extent by non-cash benefits.

In the 1956 samples, cash receipts amounted to 11-12% of money income for the poorest households (those with incomes below 30 rubles a month), and total receipts were approximately 36-38% as large as per capita money income. In 1960, cash receipts accounted for about 10% of the money income of the lowest group, and total receipts had increased to 46% of the value of money income. For the Ivanovo sample, cash receipts were as large as 20-25% of per capita money income, and total benefits were valued at 50-75% of money income (assuming midpoints of 20 rubles and 30 rubles for the two lowest groups). Thus, by the mid sixties, social consumption expenditure programs were making a significant contribution to the standard of living of the poorest state employee households, even though little of it was in the form of cash and much of the effort was directed towards better-off families.

In table 4.15, I give the most recently published statistical information

Table 4.15
The Structure of Personal Income:
State Employee Families at Various Levels of Material Welfare[a] (%)

	Income Class		
Source of Personal Income	Low	Middle	High
Wages and salaries	69	79	83
Personal receipts from public funds (pensions, etc.)	18	11	7
Receipts from private economic activity (evaluated at state retail prices)	13	10	10

Source: Maier, 1967, p. 33.
a. The title of Maier's Table is *Struktura individualnykh dokhodov semei rabochikh i sluzhashchikh s raznym urovnem obespechennosti.*

about the question under discussion. Although Maier gives no indication of the source of his data nor what is meant by his income classes, it is probable that his figures are based on the 1964 NIIT study of family budgets. Writing about the results of this analysis, Sarkisyan and Kuznetsova reported that "according to data from a survey of the budgets of industrial workers in 1964, the share of wages in family money income ranges from 70% for those with minimum per capita income to 85% for families with a per capita income of more than 1200 rubles a year" (Sarkisyan and Kuznetsova, 1967, p. 75). If this identification is correct, the upper limit of the "low" category in table 4.15 is probably 40-50 rubles a month, and the lower limit of the "high" category is probably 75-100 rubles. These figures suggest that Lion's data overstate the value of cash receipts for low-income households.

The figures in tables 4.11-4.15 suggest the following pattern of events over the period 1956-64. First, throughout the period, the ruble value of cash receipts from public funds has tended to increase with per capita income. Second, such receipts have, on the average and for virtually all income groups, grown more rapidly than money earnings. This disparity in growth rates has been most marked for the poorest families. (In all samples, cash receipts for the most affluent groups amounted to some 6-10% of money income.) Thus, at least for state employees and their families, Soviet social security and social insurance programs had a greater equalizing effect in the mid sixties than immediately after Stalin's death. But they contributed towards relative equalization only; at all times, the affluent received larger absolute benefits than the indigent. To some extent, however, at least in the early years, the progressivity in cash receipts was partially offset by a regressivity in the value of non-cash social consumption expenditures. There is some evidence to suggest that this state of affairs persisted into the seventies.[17]

The reason for this is that, at least until 1973-74, almost all Soviet monetary payments (pensions, allowances, and holiday pay) were earnings related. For this and other reasons, a significant part of total social consumption expenditure went to those in families with relatively high per capita incomes. Given the formal structure of entitlement and the Soviet government's apparent suspicion of welfare payments (see below, chapter 8), it has proved both costly and difficult to reach those in need. As Sarkisyan commented in 1974, "shortcomings in the distribution of social consumption funds to some extent hinder the process of reducing differentiation in the living standards of the families of workers [trudyash-chiyesya]" (Sarkisyan, 1974, p. 318).

This chapter has shown that, in spite of relatively rapid increases in living standards since the death of Stalin, there was still substantial poverty in the Soviet Union in 1967-68 by official definition. Nor was this poverty confined to the collective farm population, which had until then been excluded from the support and protection provided by the Soviet welfare state as well as being discriminated against in other ways. Indeed, analysis suggests that a majority of the poor were state employees or even nonagricultural state employees. Although the statistical evidence is inadequate, it seems to suggest that real wages in the USSR, at least until 1968, have been so low that workers have found it difficult to maintain even relatively small numbers of dependents at an adequate standard. In consequence, substantial numbers of children (and the aged) have been condemned to poverty. Breakdowns in marriage, widowhood, and acceptance of responsibility for the support of a wider family group have also, more often than not, led to significant reductions in family living standards.

In a sense this is surprising, since state employees in the Soviet Union benefit from an extensive social welfare system and the authorities provide a range of services free of charge or at subsidized prices. But analysis indicates that rules of entitlement and the formulae used to calculate benefits are inadeqate, in the sense that they result in much of the support going to those who need it least. The reasons for this, and the possibility that the government may be changing the criteria on which social consumption expenditures are allocated, will be discussed below. But first let us turn to an analysis of regional disparities in living standards.

5

Regional Differences
in the Standard of Living, 1960-70

'THE GRADUAL ELIMINATION of socioeconomic differences between social groups [and] between different regions of the country is a characteristic feature of an advanced socialist society" (Kapustin and Kuznetsova, 1972, p. 50). In fact, the reduction of such disparities has been a proclaimed goal not only for advanced socialist societies but of the Soviet government since 1917; and before that, the disappearance of differences between town and country, between mental and manual labor were asserted as socialist objectives in the writings of Marx, Engels, and Lenin. But there is a difference between ideologically approved goals and practical policies, and there is little to suggest that the Soviet government has been concerned at the extent of interpersonal or interregional disparities in living standards for much of the period since the revolution. However, as suggested in chapter 1, there are reasons for believing that its position has now changed, that since the late fifties it has actively sought to reduce the extent of income differentiation not only between state employees and kolkhozniki but also between the different regions of the USSR. The impact of these policies on differences in the living standards of the two fundamental social groups in the Soviet Union was described in chapter 2. In this chapter I will deal with interregional disparities in incomes and in the next, explore differences between "workers" and "peasants" on a republican level.

Figures given later in this chapter suggest that although all republics in the USSR enjoyed substantial increases in per capita incomes, there was little if any reduction in interrepublican variation. If the Soviet government did become more concerned about the extent of regional disparities in the standard of living in the late fifties, and if it actively sought to reduce them, its policies must be adjudged to have failed during the 1960s. The reasons for this are complex. In part, I think it reflects the use of an inadequate indicator of economic welfare and inequality, but also one might suggest that the instruments used by the Soviet government—control over earnings and social welfare expenditures—have not proved particularly effective. This in turn may be explained partly by differences in the social and demographic composition of the populations of individual republics, partly by the other policy objectives of the government, and finally by limitations in the administrative structure of particular welfare programs. These subjects will be explored in greater depth in the next two chapters. Here I will present some evidence of the scale of regional inequality in the Soviet Union in the sixties.

Section 5.1 takes up some of the conceptual problems involved in the measurement of regional inequality and the assessment of the Soviet government's attitudes toward this problem. Section 5.2 contains estimates of per capita personal and total income for each republic for three of the years used in chapter 2. It also contains a preliminary analysis of the impact of differences in demographic structure upon disparities in republican living standards. The analysis of this section shows that, if anything, there was a tendency for interrepublican inequality to increase between 1960 and 1970. It also suggests that demographic factors were not important; or rather, that their effects may have been felt in more subtle ways than could be captured by the methods used in this chapter. Finally, section 5.3 deals with the problem of regional variations in the cost of living—and with those adjustments to earnings and incomes designed to compensate for these variations. The analysis of this section, admittedly rather crude, implies that the elaborate and superficially rather generous system of regional wage supplements may not provide full compensation for regional differences in the cost of living.

5.1   REGIONAL VARIATION IN INCOME:
PROBLEMS OF CONCEPTION AND MEASUREMENT

One of the major instruments used by Soviet planners to monitor living standards is the so-called Balance of Money Incomes and Expenditures of the Population (BMIEP). This is a component of the system of material balances developed by Soviet planners under Stalin. At the All-Union level it has been used since the thirties as the basis for cash emission by the State Bank and also as a check on the existence of some semblance of equiibrium in the market for consumer goods. It is compiled *ex ante* by the planning authorities on the basis of other elements in the plan and *ex post* by the statistical authorities from the accounting records of enterprises and other organizations.[1] It has the form of a sources and uses table; on the sources side it provides estimates of total income (and the main categories of income) accruing to the population of a given area within a specified period of time. The uses side of the table provides estimates of the main categories of personal (household) expenditure. The income categories are wages, money receipts from kolkhozy, receipts from the sale of private agricultural products, pensions and allowances, and stipends and receipts from the financial system. The expenditure categories are purchases of goods in the state cooperative retail trade network, purchases on collective farm markets, payments for services, compulsory and voluntary payments (taxes and subscriptions), and savings. (*Metodicheskiye ukazaniya . . .*, 1969, p. 525).

The BMIEP is the major source of information on the nature and extent of regional disparity in economic welfare available to the Soviet authorities; as such, it suffers from a number of shortcomings. It was not until 1959 that attempts were made to compile a BMIEP separately for each of the fifteen constituent republics of the USSR, and only after 1965 was a consistent methodology worked out and applied in all of them (Karapetyan and Rimashevskaya, 1969, p. 124). Before 1959, the BMIEP was constructed only at the All-Union level, so that before this date the central authorities had no precise idea of the extent of regional variation in income. In fact, the decision to compile the BMIEP for each of the republics should be seen as evidence of increased concern with regional income differences and with the possibility of regional disequilibria in consumer goods markets. Since extensions to the network of plan indicators involve the use of real resources, I do not think that such exercises would be undertaken unless the Soviet government or Gosplan were interested in the information thus provided.

There are certain advantages associated with the use of republican BMIEPs as indicators of the extent of regional disparity in economic welfare, but there are also major shortcomings. To take the advantages first. Since the figures are compiled on a republican basis, they refer to definite administrative units. Any policy measure designed to correct observed inequalities will have a determinate address; it will be possible to identify those responsible for implementation. Further, the data required for compiling the balance is for the most part well understood, and also available, since the appropriate methodology has been worked out over many years at the All-Union level.

In fact, the application of the All-Union methodology to the compilation of republican balances raised a number of problems that were not resolved to the satisfaction of Soviet statisticians until 1966-67. On the incomes side, the various components are estimated from the records of state enterprises and institutions, from kolkhozy, from various ministries and the State Bank. Income figures refer to sums paid out within the territory of the republic. Expenditure estimates are derived from the records of retail trade enterprises, tax authorities, and other official sources. They refer to sums spent within the territory of a given republic. Thus, the income and expenditure totals refer to different populations, and there is no reason why the two totals should be equal. It appears that in republics where "workers go for rest and recuperation" the discrepancy can be quite large.[2]

Formally, the difference between income and expenditure in a republican BMIEP can be identified with interrepublican money flows, an entry that has no counterpart at the All-Union level and one whose measurement has caused Soviet statisticians some problems. Since there may be significant errors and omissions in the estimates of other components and since, anyway, the statisticians want an estimate of the net change in money balances held in the republic, they regard it as desirable to obtain an independent estimate of this component. Information about money transfers through the post office and the banking system are of course available, but there are apparently substantial cash flows about which little information exists. Statisticians have suggested a number of more or less crude methods by which interrepublican money transfers might be measured or estimated, but none has proved wholly satisfactory (Rasulev, 1969, pp. 19, 22; Maier, 1966, pp. 41-42). This component has been ignored in the estimates given below. It is reported, however, that republics like Estonia, Moldavia, and Georgia are net recipients, while Kazakhstan is a net donor (Karapetyan and Rimashevskaya, 1969, p. 124). According to Rasulev's figures, Uzbekistan oscillates between the two states, but the flows are relatively small—about 1-2% of money income (Rasulev, 1969, p. 19).

While the measurement of interrepublican money flows is the topic that has received the most attention from Soviet statisticians, it is possible that published versions of the BMIEP, in some of the republican statistical handbooks at least, suffer from a much more substantial omission. A majority of the republics do not publish estimates of the BMIEP, but those that do include a note stating that transactions between individuals have been omitted. This is understandable, since the primary function of the BMIEP within the framework of Soviet planning is to serve as the basis for the cash-emission plan of the State Bank, and Soviet monetary theory does not consider the income-generating possibilities of household money balances. However, it appears that, at least for Armenia and Azerbaijan, the exclusion of transactions between individuals implies the exclusion, from the income side of the balance, of sales of agricultural products on collective farm markets. The heading "Sales of Agricultural Commodities" in these instances appears to refer solely to the sale of agricultural products to state and cooperative procurement agencies. And it is possible that this exclusion applies more generally to published BMIEP statistics.

Some further support for this conjecture can be derived from a consideration of the sources of information available for compilation of BMIEPs, which for individual republics and for the USSR as a whole are official accounting and other records. It is not clear that there are any such sources of information available about the value of privately produced agricultural commodities sold on collective farm markets. Certainly the market authorities in towns have some idea of the volume and value of sales that takes place, and this is used to provide an estimate of expenditures in such markets. But sales on the market in a particular republic do not correspond to incomes received by the inhabitants of that republic from the sale of goods on such markets. Producers from the other republics may sell in the republic in question, and producers from the republic itself may sell elsewhere; there is no reason to expect these two flows to balance. At the All-Union level, information about the value of output from the private sector and about the value of collective farm market sales is derived from the family budget survey (Matyukha, 1973, p. 72). But weaknesses in sample-selection procedures mean that data from this source exhibit substantial geographic bias. Thus even if republican BMIEPs contain estimates of income derived from the sale of private agricultural output, this component may well be considerably less accurate than other elements.

In spite of these statistical limitations, the use of figures derived from republican BMIEPs as an indicator of regional difference in economic well-being has the advantage of simplicity and administrative determinateness. But one may question how far the differences identified in this way correspond to the differences that gave rise to the political problem which apparently faced the authorities in the late fifties. There are two problems here, one relating to what is being measured and one to the aggregate for which the measurement is undertaken.

It was pointed out in chapter 1 that *money* income is a very imperfect indicator of material welfare or the standard of living. Not only does it exclude goods and services that accrue to individual households in kind, but it also omits benefits derived from the free services provided by the state. There is no reason to suppose that the value of either of these components will be the same for households in all of the fifteen republics, absolutely or relatively. Indeed, on a priori grounds one would suspect that the relative importance of subsistence consumption (possibly the largest component of income in kind) will be greatest in those republics with the lowest standard of living. The same is probably true of expenditures on medical care and education. Thus it might be expected that per capita money income will overstate the extent of regional disparity in living standards when compared with personal or total income. But as monetization proceeds, as the collective farm sector is integrated more and more with the rest of the economy, the use of per capita money income will become more appropriate. Its use over time will therefore suggest that disparities in economic welfare have been reduced to a greater extent than would be implied by either of the other indicators.

It can be argued, also, that differences in per capita money income be-tween the republics do not, of themselves, reflect *regional* differences in economic well-being. There are two points to be made here. First, the USSR is formally a federal state made up of fifteen constituent republics. The republics vary in size, from the RSFSR with a population of 130 million in 1970 (some 53% of the total) down to Estonia with a population of approximately 1.4 million. The republics are administrative units that reflect historical patterns of settlement and previous phases of Soviet nationalities policy. Certainly as administrative units the republics gen-erate statistical data and thus simplify the task of compiling the BMIEP or national income aggregates. Geophysical and economic differences do not wholly coincide with administrative boundaries, however; inter-regional and interrepublican variations are not the same. This is primarily a problem with the RSFSR, which extends from the Baltic to the Pacific, from the Artic Ocean to the Black Sea. But other republics are not always homogenous. Differences in climate and environment may require differing patterns of consumption to ensure a particular standard of living. For example, one might argue that living in the Far North would require one to spend more on housing, heating, clothing, and food to maintain a par-ticular level of economic welfare than living in the more temperate condi-tions of the Black Sea coast or Soviet Central Asia. Further, for retail trade purposes, the USSR has been divided into several price zones; the cost of any given basket of goods tends to rise as one moves north and east. Thus differences in money incomes may overstate differences in *real* incomes.

Under Khrushchev, some attempt was made to introduce a more ra-tional regionalization of the country. It was divided into eighteen eco-nomic regions; ten were in the RSFSR, three in the Ukraine, and ten of the remaining republics were grouped into a further three economic regions—the Baltic, Transcaucasia, and Central Asia. These economic regions showed more internal homogeneity and more external hetero-geneity than do the republics. For a time in the sixties, also, some attempt was made to compile and publish economic statistics by region as well as by republic. But the regions never enjoyed any meaningful administrative existence. Although they were defined in terms of *sovnarkhozy*, there was never any centralized regional administrative organization. With the abolition of the sovnarkhozy in 1965, the publication of economic statis-tics by region was largely abandoned. It must have proved impossible, or more likely irrelevant, to recompute the various statistical indicators on a regional basis. This indicates, I think, the importance attached to administrative determinateness on the part of the Soviet authorities. They see little point in compiling statistical indicators that suggest the need for political initiatives unless they can also identify the political bodies responsible for implementation. It should be pointed out in this context that Arouca describes attempts to construct BMIEPs for individual oblasti and even *raiony* in the latter sixties. Such figures would provide the authorities with a more precise idea of the nature and extent of regional disparity in living standards. But apparently the compilation of such statistics for these areas raises even more intractable problems than for republics; they are still regarded as crude and unreliable (Markovskaya and Voronov, 1971; Mazurenko and Stremskii, 1972).

If differences in republican per capita incomes do not reflect regional disparities in economic well-being, neither do they correspond to differences between the living standards of various national groups within the USSR, the conjectured political stimulus for the collection of this data. Perhaps this should be regarded as an advantage of this indicator. It is true that each of the fifteen republics corresponds to a major language-nationality group in the USSR and that most of the major language groups have their own republics. But it is not true that the individual republics are populated exclusively by the titular nationality or even, necessarily, that members of the titular nationality group live exclusively in their own republic. That is, for example, not all of those who live in Uzbekistan are Uzbeks, and certainly not all Uzbeks live in Uzbekistan. Consequently, average per capita income for the republic of Uzbekistan can provide only a very inaccurate idea of the standard of living enjoyed by Uzbeks. It is impractical if not impossible, however, to collect the data necessary to construct estimates of national income generated by, or personal income accruing to, Uzbeks as a group. As a result, both those who argue for the hypothesis that minority nationality groups in the USSR are economically exploited and those who argue the converse ultimately base their conclusions on territorial statistics—if they use statistics at all.

One could conjecture that such territorially oriented statistics on living standards show less difference among national groups than would ethnically oriented figures if they were available. In most republics, and certainly in Central Asia, members of the titular nationality are primarily rural inhabitants. The urban population is to a large extent made up of Russians, Russified members of the titular nationality, and groups from other republics. Since in almost all cases per capita incomes in urban areas exceed those in rural areas, the use of republican averages may conceal the extent that living standards vary.

The foregoing is largely speculative but plausible. What we do know is that BMIEP-based indicators of income can cast light only on the average standard of living in individual republics. Although from the fifties on, certain Soviet statisticians have suggested that separate balances should be constructed for those with different levels of income, few if any attempts have been made to implement this program (Karapetyan and Rimashevskaya, 1969, pp. 87-90). It would seem that the planners believe, at least, that little benefit would be derived from gathering information about the extent of economic inequality within republics.

Whether or not its interest was provoked by resurgent nationalism among minority populations in the USSR, there is evidence that the Soviet government became more concerned about the extent of regional difference in living standards in the late fifties. Its major source of information about this question has been the BMIEP, which has been compiled on a republican basis since 1959 and more recently for an unspecified number of oblasti also. Since the Soviet authorities have apparently used information about republican differentials to formulate corrective policies and to monitor their success, I shall follow their example in this chapter. But rather than rely upon money income, I present estimates of per capita personal and total income, which provide a better indication of the levels of economic well-being in the various republics. These are given in the next section. Before turning to the estimates themselves, however, I would like to say a few words about the measurement of interrepublican inequality.

The estimates of personal and total income given in appendix B permit one to compute average per capita income in each of the republics. From these it is possible to calculate a number of statistical measures of dispersion, all of which suffer from the shortcomings pointed out by Atkinson and mentioned in chapter 1. Nevertheless, it seems better to use one of these standard measures than to employ some (essentially arbitrary) social welfare function. The simplest such statistic is the range, but this ignores changes in disparities in all but two republics; it is also oversensitive to developments in the richest and poorest areas which may be untypical of the country as a whole. Similarly, with only fifteen republics of very different size, it is problematic what meaning can be attached to modifications of this statistic, like the interquartile range or the quartile ratio. On balance, the variance of republican per capita incomes appears to be the most appropriate measure. Or rather, since ruble incomes increased markedly over the decade, I have used the coefficient of variation (the ratio of the standard deviation to the mean). This is independent of the units used to measure income and of the scale of average incomes; it is also sensitive to changes in disparities at all levels of income.

Once the decision is made to use the coefficient of variation as a measure of the extent of interrepublican inequality in living standards in the USSR, there is a further problem to be resolved. As stated before, the fifteen constituent republics vary in size from the RSFSR with 53% of the population in 1970 down to Estonia with only 0.6%. Since republican incomes differ substantially, the calculated value of the coefficient of variation will depend upon whether one uses population shares as weights in the derivation of the mean and standard deviation of income or whether each republic is treated as a separate and equal observation. The focus of attention is upon *interrepublican* differentials rather than upon the interpersonal ones which were considered in chapter 3, and consequently, primary emphasis is placed upon unweighted coefficients of variation in the analysis that follows.

Finally, since in the calculation of coefficients of variation all republics are treated equally, some attempt is made to supplement the formal measure by more heuristic indicators. That is, from the point of view of policy assessment it is not sufficient to know that measured inequality has or has not changed; one also needs to know how individual republics have fared. Is it the case that incomes in the poorest regions have grown faster than those elsewhere? Or has the growth of living standards in the most affluent areas been held back? And so on. For this reason I also present crude distributions of the republics themselves to show that, by and large, there exists within the USSR a relatively stable hierarchy of regions; that those areas with above-average incomes in 1960 also enjoyed above-average incomes in 1970.

5.2 INTERREPUBLICAN DISPARITIES IN PERSONAL AND TOTAL INCOME

In this section I will show that although there were substantial increases in the standard of living in all the Soviet republics between 1960 and 1970, there was very little reduction in income differentiation. A fuller discussion of the reasons for this is deferred until subsequent chapters.

As suggested above, there is reason to believe that the Soviet government has based its opinions about the extent of regional difference in living standards on differences in average per capita money income in each of the republics. Rather than follow their example, this section contains estimates of per capita personal and total income for each of the republics for the years 1960, 1965, and 1970, according to the definitions used in chapters 1 and 2. The choice has been made for two reasons: first, although information about the proportion of kolkhoz pay distributed in cash and the proportion of privately produced agricultural output sold to the state or on collective farm markets is available for the USSR as a whole (at least for certain years), I have been unable to locate equivalent information for each of the fifteen republics. Thus even if it were desirable to make use of per capita money income (and such figures would make it possible for one to examine the Soviet government's own perception of the problem and its success in dealing with it more precisely), it is not possible to do so with any reliability. However, as pointed out in chapters 1 and 2, personal and total income are more appropriate indicators of economic welfare than is money income, because they include claims on resources that are omitted from the latter.

Estimates of aggregate personal and total income for each of the fifteen republics for the three benchmark years used in this study are given in appendix B. The appendix also contains a detailed list of sources and a description of the estimation procedures used. An extensive discussion of these matters here is therefore unnecessary, but one or two remarks on the reliability of the estimates are in order. First, there is much more information available for some republics than for others; for these latter, many components of income have been derived indirectly. They are therefore less reliable than the remaining entries in the appendix. The republics about which least is published are the Ukraine, Byelorussia, and particularly Turkmenistan. For the last of these almost every entry has been derived indirectly.

Similarly, more information is published about certain components of income than others. The least reliable element is the value of private agricultural production. This has been derived from data on kolkhoznik private output by assuming that yields per hectare on the plots of sovkhozniki and state employees are equal, republic by republic, to those in the collective farm sector. While plausible, the assumption is almost certainly incorrect; therefore both the absolute value of private agricultural output and its allocation among republics is unreliable. Nor is it clear where the most significant biases lie.

The figures used in this section to assess the standard of living attained in the different Soviet republics have not been adjusted for direct taxes or for changes in the price level; they are gross nominal incomes. As shown in chapter 2, direct taxes in the USSR are small, and their inclusion would make very little difference to the results; they are discussed further in chapter 7. Information on difference in the price levels between the republics or on the way in which republican cost-of-living indexes have changed over the decade is not available. The use of the All-Union index would not affect conclusions about the extent of disparity in economic welfare, although it would reduce measured rates of growth of living standards, but since inflation has been relatively modest, no adjustment has been made. These factors should be borne in mind when interpreting the figures given below.

Turning now to the figures themselves. Estimates of personal and total per capita income for each of the republics in each of the benchmark years are given in table 5.1 (as a proportion of the relevant indicator for the USSR as a whole). To recapitulate: personal income consists of receipts accruing to Soviet households, in cash or kind, over whose disposition the household itself exercises a measure of control. The major non-money components of income included in the estimates of table 5.1 are the value of *in natura* payments to collective farmers for labor supplied

Table 5.1
Per Capita Personal and Total Income, USSR and Republics, 1960-70 (USSR = 100)

	Personal Income			Total Income		
	1960	1965	1970	1960	1965	1970
RSFSR	107.8	106.7	108.0	107.5	106.8	107.4
Ukraine	94.5	99.6	97.1	94.0	97.8	96.6
Byelorussia	81.2	88.9	93.8	82.7	89.6	94.6
Uzbekistan	77.4	73.0	74.2	78.0	73.9	75.7
Kazakhstan	95.1	89.8	87.5	95.9	91.7	90.8
Georgia	94.2	87.8	89.4	93.9	87.9	89.4
Azerbaijan	73.0	68.1	66.0	74.5	70.1	68.4
Lithuania	107.8	110.3	117.7	105.7	109.0	116.4
Moldavia	69.9	85.7	86.0	70.9	85.6	87.2
Latvia	124.9	122.7	125.1	124.6	122.2	124.4
Kirgizia	71.8	77.6	72.5	73.8	79.6	75.0
Tadjikistan	66.2	72.7	63.0	68.7	74.5	66.1
Armenia	85.0	83.0	87.1	86.4	84.9	88.2
Turkmenistan	74.0	77.4	78.8	81.2	82.4	80.7
Estonia	129.0	130.0	133.2	129.2	129.9	133.1
USSR (R per year)	446.0	584.0	799.0	511.0	679.0	928.0

to kolkhozy, and an estimate of the value of output produced on private plots but not sold to the state or on collective farm markets. Total income consists of personal income and an estimate of the value of services provided for households free of charge or at subsidized prices by the state. In table 5.1 this consists of expenditure on education, preschool child care, health, and housing subsidies.

As implied by the figures for the USSR as a whole, discussed in chapter 2, per capita personal income in 1960 was very low in a majority of Soviet republics. Only in Latvia and Estonia did it approach the MMS budget level of 50 rubles a month. In the Central Asian republics, in Azerbaijan, Moldavia, and Byelorussia, it was less than 30 rubles a month. Even if one thinks that the MMS budget level is too high to use as a poverty standard in 1960, it must be agreed that these republics suffered from extreme poverty.

Further, in 1960, the inclusion of free services added little to economic welfare. For the USSR as a whole, these components amounted to about 5 rubles per week per capita, and for individual republics their contribution varied from about 4 to about 7 rubles per week. As those republics with the highest personal incomes also spent most, per capita, on free services, disparities in total income were little different from those in personal income. In 1960, for example, per capita personal income in Estonia was 1.94 times that in Tadjikistan; per capita total income was 1.88 times as great.[3]

Between 1960 and 1970, personal income in the USSR as a whole grew at an average rate of 6% per annum. In all but three republics it grew at a rate between 5% and 7% per annum over the same decade; in Byelorussia the rate of growth was 7.5%, in Moldavia 8.4%, and in Azerbaijan only 4.96% per annum. Even though these figures make no allowance for changes in the price level or for direct taxes, they suggest that the populations of all the Soviet republics enjoyed substantial increases in their standards of living over the decade. The growth in total per capita income in virtually all republics corresponded closely to the growth in personal income, but was slightly higher. Expenditure on free services accounted for only a modest proportion of total income, however, even in 1970, although it increased in relation to personal income. The pattern of growth rates is confused; there is little indication that incomes tended to grow faster in the poorer republics than in the more affluent, or vice versa, for that matter. Thus, in crude terms, the pattern of growth rates gives no indication that the Soviet government pursued a purposive policy of reducing interrepublican differentials over the decade.

Whether judged in terms of personal or of total income, the standard of living in a majority of Soviet republics increased more rapidly between 1965 and 1970 than between 1960 and 1965. Rates of growth were also more uniform. In only four republics, Uzbekistan, Moldavia, Kirgizia, and Tadjikistan, did the increase in per capita income in 1960-65 exceed that in 1965-70. It is not clear why the experience of these republics should have differed from that of the rest of the USSR, but perhaps it is worth noting that they were among the poorest in 1960. Perhaps they received preferential treatment under Krushchev.

The rapid rates of growth of personal income meant that by 1970 per capita income in the USSR as a whole and in a majority of the republics was above the MMS budget level. Indeed, in the Baltic republics per capita income was higher than the "modest but adequate" standard denoted by 75 rubles a month. But for the five poorest republics, containing some 10% of the population, per capita income was less than (or barely more than) 50 rubles a month. Thus given the relationship between mean and median, one can assert that in these republics a majority of the people were poor. They were poor relative to the rest of the Soviet Union, and they were poor absolutely, according to the official Soviet poverty standard. The five republics are, however, located for the most part in Central Asia, and their standard of living may have compared favorably with that in the Middle Eastern countries to be found south of the Soviet border.

The ordering of the republics in table 5.1 suggests a great deal of stability, and this is confirmed by correlation analysis. The correlations for the various rankings vary from 0.92 to 0.97. For the most part, changes in position occur within distinct groups, which are shown in table 5.2.

Between 1960 and 1970 there were only three intergroup changes: Moldavia moved from the fifth to the fourth group, Byelorussia from the fourth to the third, and Kazakhstan from the third to the fourth.

Not only was this hierarchy relatively stable, but there was no tendency for the gap between richer and poorer republics to close. This is brought out by the figures in table 5.3. Although the coefficient of variation of both

Table 5.2
Distribution of Republics by Per Capita Personal Income, 1970

Per Capita Income as % of USSR Average	Republics by Groups	% of USSR Population
-80	Turkmenistan, Uzbekistan, Kirgizia, Azerbaijan, Tadjikistan	10.37
80-90	Kazakhstan, Armenia, Moldavia	7.82
90-100	Ukraine, Georgia, Byelorussia	25.16
100-115	RSFSR	53.81
115-	Estonia, Latvia, Lithuania	2.83

Table 5.3
The Variance of Per Capita Incomes, USSR and Republics, 1960-70

	Personal Income			Total Income		
	1960	1965	1970	1960	1965	1970
Mean (rubles)	402.0	535.0	735.0	466.0	627.0	863.0
Standard deviation	85.7	105.2	162.6	93.2	115.7	178.4
Coefficient of variation (%)	21.33	19.67	22.13	20.01	18.44	20.68

Note: The statistics in this table are the unweighted mean and variance of republican incomes.

personal and total income declined somewhat between 1960 and 1965, it increased between 1965 and 1970 and in the latter year was marginally higher than at the beginning of the decade. In deriving the statistics reported in table 5.3, I have treated each republic as a separate and equal observation. No allowance has been made for differences in size, which is appropriate if the focus of interest is on *interrepublican* variations in income. But unweighted statistics overestimate the variance and underestimate the mean of the distribution. (This explains why the mean incomes reported in table 5.3 differ from those in table 5.1.) The conclusion that variations in republican incomes have not been reduced between 1960 and 1970 remains unaltered, however, if allowance is made for variations in the size of the republics. Using population weights, the coefficient of variation for personal income, for example, was 11.22% in 1960 and 12.44 in 1970. Although both figures are lower, they reveal the same trend.

Thus one may conclude that although the Soviet government has been able to ensure substantial increases in living standards for all republics between 1960 and 1970, it has been unable or unwilling to pursue those policies which would have resulted in a reduction in interrepublican differentials. A detailed discussion of the extent to which these disparities in economic welfare can be altered by economic policy and an analysis of the factors determining the variance in personal and total income will be found in chapters 6 and 7. But there is one issue that can be pursued here.

It is sometimes suggested that the differences in living standards revealed by differences in per capita personal income are more apparent than real. It is claimed that difference in demographic structure, the higher birth rate in Central Asia resulting in more children and larger families, means that per capita income fails to measure living standards adequately. It is suggested that the real consumption needs of children are less than those of adults and that, therefore, a given ruble income will denote a higher level of economic welfare if the recipient is a child rather than an adult (or if the recipient is a woman rather than a man). Further, it is suggested that there are economies of scale in consumption, and that any specific ruble income will imply a higher standard of living, say, for a family of three than for three separate individuals.

There is a great deal of merit in these suggestions; the difficulty lies in determining the exact quantitative relationship between the consumption needs of men and women, of adults and children, and in determining the impact of family size upon scale economies. This is the problem that adult equivalent scales are designed to solve. The determination of such scales raises a number of theoretical and empirical problems that cannot be pursued here.[4] But what has been done is to construct a relatively crude set of adult-equivalents based on Soviet calculations and to see how their use affects calculated levels of income and interrepublican disparities in the USSR.

I know of no published Soviet equivalence scales that can be applied to income or the whole of personal expenditure. Kapustin and Kuznetsova, however, in their discussion of the MMS budget, do give weights that can be attached to different notional family members in the calculation of living standards. Shvyrkov gives a more detailed set of weights that can be applied to expenditures on food (Kapustin and Kuznetsova, 1972, p. 49; Shvyrkov, 1968, pp. 324-40). The scale used below is constructed from these two sources.

Details of the construction are given in table 5.4. The expenditure weights given in the first row of the table are those of the MMS budget and probably overstate the importance of food, but alternatives were not readily available. The relationships between adult male consumption of food and clothing and those of other population groups are taken from Kapustin

Table 5.4
An Adult Equivalence Scale for the USSR, 1960-70

	Categories of Final Expenditure			
	Food	Clothing	Other	Total
Weight in MMS budget	0.559	0.209	0.232	
Adult equivalent:				
Adult male	1.0	1.0	1.0	1.0
Adult female	0.85	1.165	1.0	0.95
Juvenile male	0.84	0.6	1.0	0.83
Juvenile female	0.73	0.525	1.0	0.75

Source: Derived from Kapustin and Kuznetsova, 1972, various pages; see text for details.
Juveniles are defined as those under the age of fifteen years.

and Kuznetsova. Where ranges were given in this source, the midpoint has been chosen. Because Kapustin and Kuznetsova give no indication of the assumed needs of women and children for "other expenditures" relative to those of men, it has been assumed that all categories of the population are equal in this respect. Shvyrkov, dealing only with food consumption, identifies nine different population categories; because he suggests that at the age of fourteen or fifteen the food consumption of both boys and girls is equal to that of adult men (and because fifteen is an age point in the census returns), juveniles are defined as those under fifteen years.

The population in each of the republics, broken down into the four age-sex classes indicated above, was taken from the 1959 and 1970 censuses and combined, using the weights given in the last column of table 5.4. The 1959 total was then multiplied by the ratio of the 1960 to the 1959 population; this is the same as assuming that the age-sex structure in 1960 was identical to that in 1959. The adjusted populations were then used to compute the adjusted personal and total per capita incomes for each of the republics given in table 5.5.

As expected, the use of adjusted population raises the estimate of per capita income—and hence, implied living standards—in every republic. But, perhaps surprisingly, it has very little effect on interrepublican differentiation, at least as measured by the coefficient of variation. This suggests that the disparity in economic welfare observed in the different republics of the USSR cannot be explained simply in terms of differences in population structure. It is not a creation of the indicator that has been chosen. Certainly it is true that the adjustment coefficients are crude and that a more sophisticated set might result in a great reduction in measured variance. But given the available information, I believe that any set of equivalence weights must remain to a large extent arbitrary and that little insight is to be gained from further work in this direction. If demographic

Table 5.5
Income Per Capita Adjusted for Demographic Structure,
USSR and Republics, 1960, 1970 (rubles per year)

	Personal Income		Total Income	
	1960	1970	1960	1970
USSR	485	869	556	1009
RSFSR	523	934	598	1079
Ukraine	455	837	520	968
Byelorussia	395	815	461	954
Uzbekistan	381	674	441	799
Kazakhstan	467	763	546	920
Georgia	457	779	522	905
Azerbaijan	359	591	421	711
Lithuania	520	1018	585	1170
Moldavia	342	752	397	886
Latvia	598	1071	683	1237
Kirgizia	354	645	416	776
Tadjikistan	327	567	388	691
Armenia	418	772	487	907
Turkmenistan	365	706	459	840
Estonia	618	1142	714	1325
Coefficient of Variation (%)	20.28	20.58	19.05	19.08

factors affect the scale of regional income differentiation in the USSR, and I believe that they do, their impact should be measured in a more subtle way than by the use of an equivalence scale.

In this respect, I should point out that Clayton, using a different method to allow for variations in population structure, found that this factor accounted for about half of measured inequality in 1965 (Clayton, 1975). In her paper she contrasted total consumption expenditures per capita with expenditures per family in each of the republics. She found that on a weighted basis the coefficient of variation of the latter set was approximately half that of the former. This approach implicitly involves the use of an extreme equivalence scale. It assumes that two families with the same nominal income enjoy the same standard of living, irrespective of differences in their composition; thus the marginal cost of extra family members is zero. Not only can two live as cheaply as one, so can three or four or five! This strikes me as implausible.

Clayton also quoted estimates of regional inequality, as measured by the coefficient of variation in personal consumption, for a number of other countries.[5] By international standards, regional inequality in the USSR is quite modest; it is almost twice that found in such sparsely populated developed countries as Australia or New Zealand, but only about two-thirds of that found in the USA and approximately half of that found in Japan or France. Williamson's figures suggest that regional inequality in the USSR was slightly less than that in the UK. These figures put the Soviet government's problem into perspective; they suggest that, in the absence of an acute political dimension, regional inequality should not be thought of as more serious than differences between social classes or between persons. And if regional differences in income are the source of nationalist resentment, the figures suggest that political prejudice and economic ignorance are important components of that resentment.

5.3 REGIONAL VARIATION IN WAGES AND THE COST OF LIVING
So far this chapter has been concerned with the per capita income received by the population in each of the Soviet republics. It has been assumed that a given ruble income corresponds to the same standard of living irrespective of the republic or region in which it is received. Similarly, it has been assumed that increases in ruble incomes can be equated with increases in living standards. This is clearly an oversimplification, and what follows will consider how the cost of living varies from one part of the country to another and the extent to which nominal incomes are adjusted as a result.

There are two reasons why the cost of living (interpreted as the cost of maintaining a particular standard of living) might vary from one part of the USSR to another. First, for retail trade purposes the country is divided into a number of price zones; in general, the prices charged in state or cooperative stores for any given commodity increase as one moves north and east of Moscow. Thus the cost of any specified basket of goods, for example the one making up the MMS budget, will be higher in Siberia, say, or the Far East, than in the central provinces. The indications are that at least in some areas these price differences are substantial: on Sakhalin, for instance, it is reported that the cost of food was about 21% higher than in the center; in Magadan it was 34% higher (Kapustin and Kuznetsova, 1972, p. 56).

Second, one can argue that the quantities of goods and services necessary for maintaining a particular standard of living will be greater in these inhospitable regions than in the more temperate climate of Central Russia (although from a West European viewpoint the Moscow climate might be considered extreme). To maintain one's living quarters at a given temperature will require more fuel in northern Siberia than in Central Asia, more (or at least different) clothing will be needed, and more food. While it is customary to define the standard of living by referring to a specific "basket" of goods, these considerations suggest that where there are wide differences in external circumstances, such an approach may seriously understate the subjective evaluation of differences in the cost of living.

That is, an income sufficient to purchase a specific basket of goods at the prices ruling in eastern Siberia might well be regarded as entailing a much lower standard of living than the (lower) income necessary to purchase the same basket at the (lower) prices ruling in Moscow or Kiev. Insofar as one can specify a standard of living independently of the goods and services purchased at that standard, these considerations will also affect objective evaluations. Such an approach would seem to involve the specification of ambient temperatures, caloric intake necessary for healthy existence, and so on; it would thus seem analogous to the "attribute" approach to consumer demand (Lancaster, 1971).

Because the RSFSR is the largest republic and the one with the greatest climatic and geophysical variation, both of these sources of difference in the cost of living are largely confined to it. The figures given below suggest that variations from both sources are substantial. The problems we have been discussing should be borne in mind when interpreting data on republican living standards, although I do not think that they undermine the conclusions reached here, since they affect comparatively few people.

These questions have recently been investigated by the NIIT (Kapustin and Kuznetsova, 1972). To take account of the possibility that the real resource cost of maintaining a given standard of living might differ from area to area, the investigators, together with the Soviet Academy of Medical Sciences, constructed a number of normative budgets designed to permit the attainment of a prespecified standard of living in different regions of the USSR. Very little is known about how a standard of living was defined independently of the commodities purchased, so the resultant budget "baskets" must remain to a large extent arbitrary, although it is claimed that both buying habits and the availability of facilities was taken into account. One can have little faith that the baskets would be regarded as equivalent, subjectively or objectively, by consumers in different parts of the country. Also, although it is claimed that the prespecified standard was one that would permit a minimum of material well-being (*minimum materialnoi obespechennosti*), the cost, even in the central provinces, is substantially higher than the 50 rubles per capita per month reported in 1965. In fact, Kapustin and Kuznetsova do not give an explicit ruble figure for the cost of their MMS budget; the one given below has been derived from the various relationships they provide. It is therefore not clear how far the discrepancy can be attributed to differences in the definition of the MMS standard, to errors in the reconstruction, to changes in prices between 1965 and 1968, or to the fact that the Kapustin and Kuznetsova figure applies only to the central provinces, while the Sarkisyan and Kuznetsova figure (for 1965) supposedly refers to the country as a whole. I suspect, however, that differences in the definition of the standard are the most important.

As with the earlier work described in chapter 1, normative budgets were constructed in two variants in 1968: the first applied to a single worker (*rabochii*); the second applied to a notional family of four, consisting of a married couple with two children, a boy aged thirteen, and a girl of seven. Budgets were constructed and costed (or at least results have been published) for the central provinces and for thirteen other regions of the USSR, all but three of them within the RSFSR. My estimates of the total cost of attaining the prescribed standard of living in the central provinces for each version, together with the structure of expenditures, is given in table 5.6. The figures show that the minimum cost of living for a family of four in the central provinces was 248 rubles a month (62 rubles per capita). For a single worker it was substantially higher, 82 rubles a month.

Food accounted for some 47-53% of total expenditure (assuming that only food was bought on collective farm markets), substantially more than in most Western countries. In part this is a reflection of the comparatively low standard of living of the Soviet population, but in part it is a result of the fact that other items of consumers' expenditure take up so little of the budget. For example, in 1968, for the family of four, rents accounted for as little as 1.8% of the budget in the central provinces. Were one to reduce both rents and incomes in the UK (and presumably the availability of accommodation) on a similar scale, the share of food in total

Table 5.6
Estimated Cost of Subsistence, Central Provinces, 1968 (rubles per month)

	Single Worker	Family of Four
Expenditure at state retail prices	68.88	218.40
of which:		
Food	36.20	123.78
Clothing	15.74	51.77
Other	16.94	42.85
Collective farm market supplement	2.10	6.81
Direct taxes	10.96	22.51
Total expenditure	81.94	247.72

Notes and Sources: Derived from Kapustin and Kuznetsova, 1972, tables 1-4. From table 3, food expenditure in the central provinces, allowing for the higher cost of purchases on the CFM, was 81.69 rubles greater than without such an allowance. Table 2 gives indexes of expenditure in each of the regions with and without the CFM supplement. This allows one to make a number of estimates of expenditure on food in the central provinces. The mean of these is 1485.37 rubles a year. But food accounts for 49-54% of the total; taking the midpoint yields the estimate in the table. The derivation of single-worker expenditure was based on the fact that the family of four spent 3.42 times as much on food as a single worker, and that food accounted for 43-48% of total single-worker expenditure. In computing the tax given above, I assumed that both family members worked and that one earned 147 rubles a month and the other earned 100 rubles.

expenditure would rise from 32% to 36%.[6]

In table 5.7 I present estimates of the cost of a minimum standard of living in each of ten eastern and northern regions of the RSFSR, in the Ukraine, in Central Asia, and in Kazakhstan. The table also indicates, for food at least, the extent to which this increased cost is attributable to variations in the basket used and to what extent it is a consequence of higher prices. The ten regions of the RSFSR listed together make up the part of the country in which cost-of-living supplements to wages and salaries are payable. The range of expenditures implied by the table is substantial, the level in Magadan being almost double that in the Ukraine or Central Asia. But variations are greater for single workers than for the notional family of four, largely because workers pay more tax on their higher income than does the average family.

Table 5.7 gives some indication of the extent to which the cost of living varies from one part of the USSR to another. There are also regional variations in incomes which are intended not only to compensate consumers in different parts of the country for differences in prices and in the real cost of subsistence, but also to provide some measure of incentive to move to climatically and culturally less-hospitable regions of the country. In fact, these regional cost-of-living supplements apply only to wages and salaries; no adjustment is made to the value of pensions or other state

Table 5.7
Regional Variations in the Cost of Living, 1968 (Central Provinces = 100)

	Cost of Living		of which		
	Single Worker	Family of Four	Expenditure on Food	Price Effect	Quantity Effect	Wage Rates
Bashkir ASSR	104	100	98	92	106	100
Urals	114	110	113	107	106	101
West Siberia	107	102	98	92	106	102
East Siberia	121	116	114	101	114	122
Far East	130	124	122	111	111	134
Sakhalin	162	149	160	121	139	151
Arkhangelsk	130	126	132	111	120	122
Murmansk	161	146	156	117	139	140
Magadan	183	165	173	134	139	178
Yakut ASSR	174	156	164	125	139	151
Ukraine	94	96	89	87	103	100
Central Asia	94	97	—	—	—	100
Kazakhstan	100	97	94	89	104	100

Sources: Columns 1 and 2 from Kapustin and Kuznetsova, 1972, table 1, after adjustment for differences in expenditures on collective farm markets from table 3. Columns 3-5, ibid., table 4; these figures refer to the single-worker budget. Column 6 from *Spravochnik ekonomista kolkhoza i sovkhoza*, Moscow, 1970, pp. 269-70. See text for details of the calculation.

transfer payments. I now turn to a description of these supplements and attempt to assess their adequacy.

Because one is dealing with subrepublican units of organization, there is very little information available about variations in earnings; the material deals, rather, with differences in wage rates and salary scales. Conclusions will be based on these, and it should be realized that differences in occupational structure or in average levels of skill may well undermine their validity.

The regional differentiation of wage rates has a long history in the USSR, dating back to the first postrevolutionary decrees on wages.[7] But by 1955 the system had become both complex and inconsistent; at that date there were some ninety different regional coefficients in use (Sukharevskii, 1968, p. 302). Different industries, or rather different ministries, had established their own wage-bands (*tarifnye poyasy*), and sanctioned different wage relatives, while in some sectors there was no provision at all for regional supplementation. As a result, workers doing the same job in the same town but in different plants might well receive different regional supplements. It was even possible for workers in the same plant but on different wage scales to receive different regional supplements (Batkaev and Markov, 1964, p. 182). All this was clearly in conflict with the socialist principle of distribution and was thought to result in excessive labor turnover and worker dissatisfacton. So during the wage reorganization of 1956-65 and in subsequent years, the Soviet authorities have attempted to introduce a consistent geographically based system.

Under post-1956 arrangements, regional wage supplements are expressed as a mark-up to the basic rate or *stavka*; workers in all skill-grades receive the same percentage addition to their wages. In principle, the same coefficients are applicable to salaries. Thus, regional wage supplementation will leave intraplant differentials unaltered if they are measured in ratio terms. The supplements introduced in the late fifties ranged from 15-20% for the Urals, southern Siberia, and parts of Central Asia to 100% for parts of the Far North. The areas in which such premium rates are payable are defined in terms of raiony, the smallest administrative units in the USSR, or even in parts of raiony in eastern Siberia where these latter cover vast areas.[8]

In principle, regional supplementation of wages and salaries under the post-1956 scheme was determined by the geographical location of the work place rather than by industrial affiliation. Until 1968, however, regional premia were not paid in agriculture, light industry, food processing, and the nonproductive sphere—that is, in the services sector. In 1968 they were extended to all those employed in these sectors in the North, the Far East, and in East Siberia. During the ninth five-year plan (1970-74) regional supplements were extended to those not previously receiving them in West Siberia, the Urals, Kazakhstan, and some "difficult" areas in Central Asia. At the same time, certain coefficients were increased (Kapustin, 1968, p. 335; Kunelskii, 1972, p. 22; *Gosudarstvennyi* . . . , 1972, p. 288).

In addition to the regional supplements described above, those working in high altitude or in desert areas received a further mark-up. The altitude coefficients increase wages in three stages: 15% for those working between 1,500 and 2,000 meters, 30% for those working between 2,000 and 3,000 meters, and 40% for those working above 3,000 meters (9,842 feet). Regional coefficients may be increased by 10-40% for workers in desert or arid regions, but such increases must be authorized in each specific case by the State Committee on Labor and Wages.

For those working in the Far North there are additional benefits. Individuals receive a 10% increase in wages for each year that they remain in employment. (In some localities, where conditions are particularly adverse, the 10% is paid after each six months' service, in others after every two years.) These supplements are payable on all earnings up to 300 rubles a month but may not, in total, exceed 80% of basic wages. Employees in these areas are also entitled to a variety of other benefits: longer holidays, free travel to the central regions of USSR every three years, subsidized visits to rest homes and sanitoria, earlier retirement, and so on (Batkaev and Markov, 1964, p. 182).

Provisions for the regional supplementation of earnings are elaborate, but they apply to only a small portion of the working population. In the early sixties, the Far North, to which the most generous provisions apply, contained only 1.5% of the country's workers; indeed, the proportion of the employed living in all areas to which regional supplements were applicable was only 10% at the same period (Batkaev and Markov, 1964, p. 186). Further, regional supplements of all kinds accounted for only 4.8% of the total wage and salary bill in 1961 and for 4.1% in 1970 (Kunelskii, 1972, p. 78). Of course they were more important in some industries (17.4% in nonferrous metallurgy, 12.6% in logging), but this was a consequence of the geographical distribution of economic activity (Batkaev and Markov, 1964, p. 221).

As I mentioned above, regional supplements are intended to achieve two objectives: to compensate those employed in inhospitable and underdeveloped regions for the higher prices and higher real costs of subsistence, and to provide an incentive for the settlement of these areas. In the final column of table 5.7 I report the results of an attempt to assess how adequately they fulfill these aims. The figures in this column express the basic wage rates payable in each of the regions listed as a percent of those for the central provinces. The figures are based upon weighted averages of the regional coefficients payable in different areas. Within oblasti, the number of raiony in which particular coefficients were payable (as a proportion of the total number of raiony in the oblast) were used as weights; oblasti themselves were combined, using population weights. No allowance was made for differences in employment structure, differences in skill mix, or other factors.

Although very crude, the figures suggest that in spite of the apparently generous scale of regional wage supplementation, the sums provided are in many cases insufficient to compensate for the higher cost of living, let alone provide positive incentives to permanent settlement. Only in East Siberia, the Far East (and, of course, the Ukraine and Central Asia) were both single workers and families unambiguously better off than in the central provinces. Families might have been better off in Magadan and Sakhalin as well. But it would appear that a move to other parts of the periphery would be associated with a decline in the standard of living. This conclusion is complicated by the fact that, given the average industrial wage, the notional family would be in poverty in the central provinces as well as on the periphery, while the single worker would be modestly affluent everywhere. In 1968, the average industrial wage was 112.7 rubles a month, and with 1.7 workers per family, it is unlikely that transfer payments or other receipts would amount to as much as 56 rubles a month.

Soviet commentators repeatedly point out that higher wages, although perhaps necessary to expand employment in the North and East, are certainly not in themselves enough. Further action by the state in building homes, shops, and cultural facilities, improving the supply of consumer goods, and ensuring a balance of employment opportunities are also necessary. And they cite the difference between gross and net migration flows as evidence that not enough has been done in these directions. For example, it is reported that while 7.8% of the urban population arrived in the Urals in 1959-65, 7.0% departed, leaving a net increase of only 0.8%; for East Siberia the equivalent figures were 10.8% and 9.6% (*Demograficheskiye* . . . , 1969, p. 171). Perhaps these flows can also be explained by the fact that some workers had been misled by apparently high nominal wages and realized only after their arrival that living standards were lower. The fact that the NIIT was studying this problem in 1968-70 and that some regional supplements were raised during the ninth five-year plan suggests that the Soviet authorities are not unaware of the shortcomings of the existing system.

At the beginning of this chapter, I suggested that in the late fifties the Soviet authorities apparently became more concerned than they had been with the extent of regional inequality. If this was the case, and if they have attempted to reduce the inequality, the analysis given here suggests that they have been unsuccessful. While all republics enjoyed substantial rates of growth in living standards between 1960 and 1970, there was no tendency for differences between them to decline. And there is no reason to believe that this conclusion is a consequence only of the indicator chosen to measure inequality.

The analysis of this chapter, then, has shown that there was little change in the extent of regional inequality in the USSR between 1960 and 1970. Thus it may be presumed that the Soviet government was unwilling (or unable) to pursue policies that would reduce interrepublican disparity in income. In fact, I believe that the Soviet authorities have introduced a number of policies that might have been expected to bring about a reduction in regional differences in living standards, but that their efforts have been frustrated by demographic change and by inadequacies in the social security and social welfare systems. These questions are taken up in chapter 7, but first I will turn to an analysis of the level and structure of incomes accruing to state employees and kolkhozniki in individual republics. This material provides additional insight into the sources of variation in republican living standards. It is the subject of chapter 6.

Finally, the material in section 5.3 indicates that there are substantial variations in the cost of living to be found within individual republics, particularly the RSFSR. Thus the assumption that a specific ruble income implies a given standard of living irrespective of the location in which that income is earned is essentially an oversimplification. Further, although the inhabitants of those areas with the higher cost of living generally receive wage supplements, the evidence suggests that these supplements do not fully compensate for higher prices and a higher real cost of subsistence. In consequence, measured average income in the RSFSR may overstate the average standard in that republic. But the supplements apply to relatively few and are not considered a substantial source of bias. In any case, lack of data (and of a meaningful conceptual framework in which any adjustment can be made) mean that this problem is ignored in what follows.

6

Income Variation among Republics: Kolkhozniki and State Employees

THIS CHAPTER CONTAINS estimates of personal and total per capita income accruing to kolkhozniki in each of the fifteen constituent republics of the USSR for a number of years between 1960 and 1970. Together with the estimates of personal and total income given in the last chapter, these figures make it possible to derive estimates of per capita personal and total income received by state employees in each of the republics in the three benchmark years. The figures, for all their limitations, are of interest for two reasons. First, they shed light on the standards of living of the two social classes in different parts of the Soviet Union. Second, they may help to explain the extent of the interrepublican disparity in income described in the previous chapter. As I have shown, in 1960 and even in 1970 collective farmers were the major disadvantaged group in the USSR, discriminated against in terms of job opportunities, civil liberties, and access to social services. Differences in the proportion of kolkhozniki in republican populations may go far in explaining the extent of disparity in economic welfare between republics. On the other hand, it may be that differences in kolkhoznik incomes account for a significant portion of the variance in republican living standards. In either case, the estimates presented here should help resolve the issue.

Also, since the death of Stalin, there have been substantial increases in the labor payments to kolkhozniki. They have been well studied at the All-Union level, but their impact on earnings and income in individual republics has received much less attention. The material in this chapter helps to correct this deficiency. At the same time, it shows how misleading it is to draw inferences about changes in the standard of living of kolkhozniki from information on earnings alone.

6.1 PERSONAL AND TOTAL INCOMES OF KOLKHOZNIKI, 1960-70
The Soviet government publishes very little official information about the level and structure of kolkhoznik incomes, and, contrary to a widespread belief in the West, I am convinced that it collects very little.

Silence reflects official ignorance and possibly indifference rather than secretiveness or embarrassment. The estimates given in this chapter are based on the work of Soviet academics and are therefore less reliable than if they had been derived from official sources; but there is no alternative.

Before going on to describe the way in which the figures given here have been obtained, it is worth spending a little time on the official but unpublished sources of statistical information available in the USSR. A knowledge of such sources can help in the assessment of Soviet policy towards the collective farm sector and can also throw some light on the reliability of particular income components derived from secondary material. There are basically two sources of information on kolkhoznik incomes available to Soviet officials: the accounting records of kolkhozy, collected by the Central Statistical Administration in the process of monitoring plan fulfillment, and the family budget survey. In addition, there may be data from the sample survey of income, family composition, and housing conditions undertaken in 1972. These sources have been described in some detail in chapters 3 and 5. It will be recalled that the family budget survey suffers from significant bias because of faulty sample-selection methods and provides less information than might be expected because of weaknesses in data analysis. The sample survey, of course, provides information for at most one year.

Further, the accounting records of kolkhozy can provide figures on only some of the components of kolkhoznik household income. These are used in the construction of the BMIEP (Balance of Money Incomes and Expenditures of the Population), which is compiled separately for kolkhozniki and the rest of the population. With all its shortcomings, the BMIEP is the primary source of information about interrepublican differentials in kolkhoznik incomes available to Soviet officials. For it, data on the earnings of collective farmers from their primary employment is derived from the accounting records of kolkhozy. These records, together with those of the relevant state organizations, also provide details of the transfer payments received by collective farm households. The family budget survey is used to obtain information about income from the sale of privately produced agricultural output. But although the survey also contains information on the earnings of members of kolkhoznik households employed by the state, the statisticians who compile the BMIEP prefer to estimate this component from other sources—an indication of their opinion of the reliability of family budget data (*Metodicheskiye ukazaniya . . .* , 1969, p. 542). Thus the statistical information on the standard of living of kolkhozniki used by the Soviet government is based on doubtful original data. It also excludes significant components of personal consumption—*in natura* payments by collective farms and subsistence from private plots. Finally, BMIEP data provide information only about average living standards in individual republics; on the distribution of income within them it is silent.

For these reasons, either personal or total income as defined in chapter 1 provides a better indicator of living standards than does money income, and only they will be considered here. As a result of the way in which the estimates have been obtained, the figures on total income are probably more reliable than those on personal income. But given the low level of personal income in certain republics and given the importance of free services received by the average household, the problem of the value ascribed to the services by kolkhozniki becomes particularly acute. Individual households cannot divert the resources used to produce such services as education and medical care into the production of other things that they may prefer. They may therefore attach a much lower value to free services than the cost of provision. For this reason the personal income data, for all their limitations, are important.

The estimates of total (and therefore of personal) income given in this chapter have been derived from figures published by M. I. Sidorova.[1] As far as possible, Sidorova bases her estimates on the accounting records of collective farms, but family budget survey material has been used to provide information on the value of private agricultural activity and possibly also on the value of earnings from the socialist sector. Estimates of the value of transfer payments and other social welfare expenditures are her own, and she says little about the methods used to derive them.

Total income in this chapter corresponds to the magnitude described by Sidorova in 1969 as *polnyi sovokupnyi dokhod* (full gross income) and as *fond vosproizvodstva rabochei sily* (fund for the reproduction of labor power) in 1972. Although the labels differ in the two books, a comparison of the statistics themselves shows that the two aggregates are the same.

The estimates given here have been derived almost exclusively from Sidorova's work, but they have been transformed in various ways. Sidorova's figures are given for the most part on a per-family basis: they are also usually expressed as percentages of the relevant USSR magnitude. To make the estimates given in this chapter consistent with those to be found elsewhere in the book, Sidorova's figures have been converted to rubles per capita. With one exception, I am confident that these conversions give estimates that correspond closely to those used by Sidorova herself.

The basis of the conversion is as follows. Sidorova suggests two ways in which the average labor receipts per kolkhoznik family may be obtained, other than by using family budget data (Sidorova, 1972, p. 74). She suggests that one can either multiply average annual earnings by the average number of able-bodied adult family members (*vzroslye trudosposobnye chleny semya*), or one can divide total payments to labor by the number of kolkhoznik families. She herself expresses a preference for the second method and explicitly identifies the number of kolkhoznik families with kolkhoznik households (*chislo nalichnykh dvorov*). Since both total payments to labor and the number of kolkhoznik households are published in the statistical handbooks (at least for the USSR and for some republics), one can obtain the ruble figure used by Sidorova correct to within one or two decimal places. Given ruble estimates of kolkhoznik family earnings, virtually all other components follow. With ruble estimates of income per kolkhoznik family, estimates of total income can be derived using the number of families (households) in each republic. Details of the methods used and of the sources of particular figures are given in appendix D.

The procedures outlined above give reasonably consistent estimates of total income and of most income components, but they reveal significant inconsistencies in Sidorova's estimates of social welfare expenditures, particularly those from state funds. Given the correct ruble value for categories of kolkhoznik family income and given the correct number of families in each republic, the sum of the amounts accruing in each of the fifteen republics should equal the amount assigned for the USSR as a whole. From the figures in table 6.1 it can be seen that for the five years for which Sidorova gives full information, this condition is approximately satisfied for most of the income components identified. With the exception of state (and hence total) social welfare expenditures, the entries virtually all lie within 5% of the USSR figures; most are a good deal closer. But state social welfare expenditures allocated to individual republics

Table 6.1
Total Kolkhoznik Incomes: Analysis of Errors, 1960-70

| | | Social Welfare Expenditure | | | | | | |
Year	Kolkhoz Labor Payments	Total	from State	from Kolkhozy	Private Subsidiary Activity	Earnings in Socialist Sector	Other	Total
1960	97.87	76.39	72.92	102.53	100.58	108.48		97.16
1963	104.32	74.17	65.20	133.72	98.08	96.46		95.88
1965	99.56	75.56	69.95	100.36	100.89	101.30	105.58	95.56
1966	100.91	74.13	67.76	99.62	101.77	101.11	109.85	96.11
1970	99.42	74.38	65.99	102.50	101.72	102.82		94.80

Note: Entries in the table express the sum of amounts allocated to individual republics on the first round reconstruction as a percent of the allocation to the USSR as a whole. See text for further explanation.

account for little more than two-thirds of the total allocated to kolkhozniki for the USSR as a whole.

Sidorova's own work makes no mention of this fact (which would not be apparent from the format in which she presents her statistics) and suggests no explanation of the source of the shortfall. Since from her descriptions of the way in which the estimates were produced I presume that the figure for the USSR as a whole is the more reliable (or rather is closer to the figure that would have been used by the CSA), I have replaced Sidorova's estimates of social welfare expenditures with my own, both here and in appendix D. Mine were derived as follows. Entries for total income and for each of the income components other than state social welfare expenditures were adjusted proportionately to sum to the USSR totals.[2] State social welfare expenditures were then obtained as the residual. This means that on the average, estimates given in this chapter exceed those given by Sidorova by about a third. Consequently, social welfare expenditures accruing to state employees and their dependents in the various republics will be lower than implied by Sidorova's work. Since I do not know in fact why this apparent inconsistency exists in Sidorova's work, it must be recognized that the proportionate adjustments made here are essentially arbitrary. But in the absence of any other plausible explanation of the difference, they seem the most appropriate corrections to make.

From material given by Sidorova, it is possible to derive estimates of the components of total kolkhoznik income for five of the eleven years 1960-70 and estimates of total income alone for another two. They are presented in appendix D. However, since I have calculated total and personal income for the USSR as a whole and for each of the republics for only the three years 1960, 1965, and 1970, I will concentrate on these for the rest of the chapter.

Estimates of per capita personal and total income of kolkhozniki in each of these years are given in table 6.2. Since Sidorova does not publish any information about personal income, the estimates given here have been derived from other sources. Details of the assumptions used in their construction are given in appendix tables D10-D12. It should be pointed out that the figures for 1970, in particular, are subject to considerable uncertainty; and as indicators of the change in kolkhoznik living standards, the figures in the table suffer from a number of familiar weaknesses that I have made no attempt to correct. They take no account of direct taxes, and they are not adjusted for regional differences in the cost of living nor for changes in the price level over time. These adjustments have been neglected for lack of data. Also, no attempt has been made to allow for demographic differences in the various republics. Again, lack of information about the age and sex composition of the kolkhoznik population would preclude precise adjustments, but some allowance could have

Table 6.2
Total and Personal Per Capita Income:
Kolkhozniki, USSR and Republics, 1960-70 (rubles per year)

	Total Income			Personal Income		
	1960	1965	1970	1960	1965	1970
USSR	379	551	762	329	460	659
RSFSR	410	607	877	341	475	716
Ukraine	362	551	744	327	484	676
Byelorussia	358	517	759	325	456	688
Uzbekistan	377	428	555	328	374	499
Kazakhstan	381	630	889	321	412	624
Georgia	401	494	758	365	434	696
Azerbaijan	264	302	471	236	254	424
Lithuania	544	887	1205	504	793	1069
Moldavia	271	476	674	249	431	606
Latvia	729	975	1309	646	819	1123
Kirgizia	290	461	544	254	390	473
Tadjikistan	218	358	440	193	316	396
Armenia	303	430	612	226	355	516
Turkmenistan	268	497	724	239	438	645
Estonia	642	1158	1644	551	933	1333

been made. In the light of the results obtained in the last chapter, however, it did not seem worthwhile to do the extra work.

As might have been expected from the discussion in chapters 2, 4, and 5, the figures in table 6.2 show just how badly off kolkhozniki were in most Soviet republics, especially in 1960. For the USSR as a whole, personal income per capita was only 27.42 rubles a month in that year, barely more than half the 1965 MMS budget standard. In the six poorest republics it scarcely exceeded 20 rubles a month, and in Tadjikistan it was as low as 16 rubles, which is less than a third of the official 1965 poverty level and about half of the implicit poverty standard used in 1958. Nor does the picture change radically if one considers total per capital income. The six poorest republics all had average incomes of 25 rubles or less; in Tadjikistan it was less than 20 rubles. Only in the three Baltic republics do personal incomes exceed 40 rubles a month. Furthermore, not only are the incomes of kolkhozniki relatively low, but also there are significant differences in the standard of living of collective farmers in different parts of the country; total per capita income in Latvia in 1960 was 3.34 times that in Tadjikistan.

Between 1960 and 1970 both personal and total per capita incomes of kolkhozniki in the USSR as a whole grew rapidly; their average rates of growth were 7.2% per annum. Even when allowance is made for the possible effects of direct taxes and changes in the cost of living, such figures suggest that living standards rose markedly over the decade. But the rates of growth of income differed markedly between the republics. In only seven was the rate of growth of total income within one percentage point of that for the USSR as a whole; in five it was greater and in three less. It was greatest in Turkmenistan, at 10.4% per annum, but Estonia recorded 9.9%. It was least in Uzbekistan, with a rate of 3.9%, but Latvia recorded a rate of only 6.0%. Thus there is no very clear pattern in the growth rate of total (or for that matter, personal) income.

For the USSR as a whole and for a majority of republics, total per capita income grew more rapidly in the first half of the decade than it did between 1965 and 1970. But again, the experience of six republics diverged; in Byelorussia, Uzbekistan, Georgia, Azerbaijan, Latvia, and Armenia, gains were greatest in the latter part of the period. The experience with personal income was the opposite; for the USSR as a whole, growth was more rapid after 1965. This may reflect the impact of the extension of state-financed retirement pensions to the collective farm population after 1965 or may only be a consequence of my having overestimated personal income in 1970. Again, however, the experience of eight republics differed from that of the remainder: in the Ukraine, Lithuania, Moldavia, Kirgizia, Tadjikistan, Armenia, Turkmenistan, and Estonia, personal incomes grew more rapidly between 1960 and 1965 than in the rest of the decade. This variety in the growth experience of the different republics suggests that no coordinated policies to reduce interrepublican income differentials among kolkhozniki have been pursued by the Soviet government—or that such policies have been unsuccessful.

The rapid rates of growth of personal and total per capita income recorded in most Soviet republics meant that the standard of living of kolkhozniki increased markedly between 1960 and 1970. In the latter year, their average per capita personal income in the USSR as a whole was 54.9 rubles a month, well above the 1965 MMS budget standard. However, in five republics of Central Asia and Transcaucasia it was still less than 50 rubles a month, and in Azerbaijan and Tadjikistan it was less than 40 rubles. In these republics certainly, and possibly also in Turkmenistan and Moldavia, where personal per capita income barely exceeded the MMS budget level, a majority of the collective farm population was still living in poverty.

The figures in table 6.2 also suggest that there is a great deal of stability in the ranking of the different republics by per capita personal or total kolkhoznik income. For the various orderings derived from the table, the Spearman's rank correlation coefficient varies from 0.764 (personal income in 1960 and 1965) to 0.973 (personal and total income in 1960). This suggests that, as with the republics as a whole, one can construct an income hierarchy for kolkhozniki in different parts of the country. One version of this is given in table 6.3. Again, although the figures refer to

Table 6.3
Distribution of Republics by Per Capita Personal Income of Kolkhozniki, 1970

% of USSR Average	Republics, in Ascending Order by Income	% of all Kolkhozniki
–85	Armenia, Uzbekistan, Kirgizia, Azerbaijan, Tadjikistan	18.3
85–150	RSFSR, Georgia, Byelorussia, Ukraine, Turkmenistan,	
	Kazakhstan, Moldavia	79.3
150–	Estonia, Latvia, Lithuania	2.4

1970, the fact that changes in position are largely confined within the groups identified means that a distribution for 1965 or 1960, or one using total rather than personal income, would differ little. In fact, intergroup movement was confined to Uzbekistan (down from second to third), Moldavia and Turkmenistan (up from third to second). The distribution in table 6.3 has a lot in common with that in table 5.2; it also shows that the five poorest republics contained almost a fifth of all kolkhozniki in the Soviet Union.

Not only was the ranking of republics by per capita kolkhoznik income relatively stable over the decade 1960-70, but there was no tendency for the gap between the richer and the poorer to narrow in relative, let alone absolute, terms. As pointed out above, kolkhozniki in the best-off republic in 1960 had an average total income 3.34 times that in the poorest. In 1970, kolkhoznik incomes in Estonia, the most affluent republic, were 3.74 times those in Tadjikistan. Table 6.4 shows that this was not only a feature of extremes. The figures there indicate that the coefficient of variation of both personal and total income increased somewhat over the decade.[3] Thus, one may conclude that although kolkhozniki in most republics enjoyed substantial increases in living standards, the so-called revolution in farm household incomes did not bring about any significant changes in the relative position of collective farmers in different parts of the country during the sixties, nor did it result in a reduction in interrepublican disparities in economic welfare.

The figures in appendix D can be used to shed light not only on differ-

Table 6.4
The Variance of Per Capita Kolkhoznik Incomes, USSR and Republics, 1960-70

	Total Income			Personal Income		
	1960	1965	1970	1960	1965	1970
Mean (rubles)	388	585	814	343	491	699
Standard deviation	140.6	231.6	323.9	123.8	189.9	261.9
Coefficient of variation (%)	36.25	39.61	39.80	36.09	38.68	37.47

Note: The figures in this table are the unweighted mean and standard deviation of republican per capita kolkhoznik total and personal income.

ences in per capita personal and total incomes of kolkhozniki in the various republics of the USSR but also on differences in the structure of income received, on the relative importance of different sources of income. From Sidorova's figures it is possible to identify four or five categories of income: receipts for labor services supplied to collective farms, the value of private subsidiary agricultural activity, the earnings of family members employed by state organizations or enterprises, transfer payments (that is, stipends, pensions, and allowances, where paid), and finally, miscellaneous receipts such as interest on savings deposits, insurance benefits, loans, and remittances from relatives living elsewhere in the USSR. Since it is not always possible to distinguish between earnings from the socialist sector and miscellaneous receipts, these two categories have been grouped together in tables 6.5-6.7.

Table 6.5 gives the proportion of personal income that accrued to kolkhozniki and their dependents in the form of each of these income

Table 6.5
The Structure of Kolkhoznik Incomes, USSR and Republics, 1960 (% of personal income)

	Kolkhoz Labor Payments	Private Subsidiary Activity	Earnings in Socialist Sector, etc.	Transfer Payments	Personal Income	Non-Cash Social Welfare Expenditure
USSR	33.5	52.5	12.8	1.5	100.0	15.2
RSFSR	34.4	49.7	14.3	1.6	100.0	20.3
Ukraine	30.6	55.4	12.5	1.6	100.0	10.6
Byelorussia	21.6	64.8	12.8	0.8	100.0	10.2
Uzbekistan	52.4	37.7	8.3	1.6	100.0	15.0
Kazakhstan	54.6	37.3	6.3	1.7	100.0	18.7
Georgia	19.3	66.0	13.7	0.9	100.0	9.9
Azerbaijan	38.5	48.8	11.4	1.3	100.0	11.6
Lithuania	17.1	75.6	6.5	0.7	100.0	7.8
Moldavia	27.2	55.4	15.7	1.7	100.0	9.2
Latvia	27.1	65.3	6.9	0.6	100.0	12.9
Kirgizia	46.9	37.9	12.8	2.4	100.0	14.2
Tadjikistan	42.2	43.0	12.2	2.6	100.0	12.6
Armenia	35.9	39.0	23.8	1.3	100.0	13.8
Turkmenistan	52.8	34.2	10.6	2.5	100.0	12.1
Estonia	32.9	59.6	6.2	1.4	100.0	16.4

categories in each of the republics in 1960. Tables 6.6 and 6.7 give similar figures for 1965 and 1970. The tables also show the relationship between personal income and the value of free services (or subsidies) provided by the state in each of the years studied. The most striking feature of table 6.5 is the relative unimportance of kolkhoz labor payments, supposedly the primary source of income, in determining the standard of living of collective farm households in a majority of Soviet republics. In twelve of the fifteen they accounted for less than half of personal income,

Table 6.6
The Structure of Kolkhoznik Incomes, USSR and Republics, 1965 (% of personal income)

	Kolkhoz Labor Payments	Private Subsidiary Activity	Earnings in Socialist Sector, etc.	Transfer Payments	Personal Income	Non-Cash Social Welfare Expenditure
USSR	44.3	42.3	9.8	3.5	100.0	19.8
RSFSR	45.1	41.1	10.0	3.8	100.0	27.7
Ukraine	44.2	42.3	9.9	3.6	100.0	13.8
Byelorussia	35.4	51.8	10.3	2.4	100.0	13.6
Uzbekistan	53.1	35.2	7.5	4.2	100.0	14.3
Kazakhstan	60.2	29.0	6.0	4.8	100.0	52.8
Georgia	23.1	60.0	15.2	1.7	100.0	13.8
Azerbaijan	45.1	37.0	14.2	3.7	100.0	18.8
Lithuania	30.4	62.4	5.3	1.9	100.0	11.8
Moldavia	46.1	41.3	9.0	3.6	100.0	10.6
Latvia	36.9	53.2	7.7	2.2	100.0	19.1
Kirgizia	56.3	30.7	8.5	4.4	100.0	18.4
Tadjikistan	52.0	36.9	7.2	3.8	100.0	13.2
Armenia	46.8	29.7	20.3	3.2	100.0	21.2
Turkmenistan	60.6	27.4	8.8	3.2	100.0	13.5
Estonia	39.2	51.6	5.9	3.3	100.0	24.2

Table 6.7
The Structure of Kolkhoznik Incomes, USSR and Republics, 1970 (% of personal income)

	Kolkhoz Labor Payments	Private Subsidiary Activity	Earnings in Socialist Sector	Transfer Payments	Personal Income	Non-Cash Social Welfare Expenditure
USSR	47.1	34.5	8.4	10.0	100.0	15.7
RSFSR	51.8	29.4	7.5	11.3	100.0	22.5
Ukraine	43.8	36.7	9.6	9.9	100.0	10.1
Byelorussia	41.1	42.9	5.2	10.8	100.0	10.3
Uzbekistan	49.4	35.0	7.6	8.0	100.0	11.3
Kazakhstan	59.6	23.4	4.8	12.2	100.0	42.5
Georgia	23.4	54.5	14.5	7.8	100.0	8.9
Azerbaijan	42.9	33.4	13.1	10.6	100.0	11.0
Lithuania	40.7	46.9	3.8	8.6	100.0	12.7
Moldavia	45.0	41.0	7.4	6.6	100.0	11.2
Latvia	45.4	38.8	6.7	9.1	100.0	16.6
Kirgizia	53.2	29.4	7.2	10.2	100.0	14.9
Tadjikistan	43.2	32.3	15.9	8.6	100.0	11.2
Armenia	46.7	27.0	17.8	8.5	100.0	18.5
Turkmenistan	64.1	24.1	7.1	4.7	100.0	12.3
Estonia	52.4	34.6	4.5	8.5	100.0	23.3

and in seven for less than a third. In Georgia and Lithuania they were responsible for less than a fifth of personal income. *Per contra,* so-called private subsidiary agricultural activity was responsible for more than half of per capita personal income of kolkhozniki in the USSR as a whole and in a majority of the Union republics. In five—Byelorussia, Georgia, Latvia, Lithuania, and Estonia—the private plot and associated activities were responsible for 60% or more of personal income. The fact that the private sector was more important than the kolkhoz as a source of income in 1960 will come as no surprise to those with any knowledge of the Soviet Union, but a quantitative measure of the disparity in certain republics is new and I think astonishing. Kolkhozniki in the five republics listed, if not all those where private activity accounts for more than half of personal income, might more properly be called peasants with a subsidiary interest in the collective farm.

Perhaps equally striking—certainly as well known to Soviet specialists in qualitative terms, and a condemnation of the Soviet system as it existed in 1960—are the trivial amounts received by collective farm households as transfer payments from all sources. On the average, these amounted to less than 5 rubles per person per year, and in Byleorussia to about half of that. Amounts of this magnitude mean that kolkhozniki were effectively without support from the state or cooperative in sickness, old age, or adversity. Either they were supported by relatives or, presumably, most were left to suffer on their own. And it must be realized that by 1960 there had been significant increases in the prices paid by the state for agricultural products since the death of Stalin. Consequently, the financial position of the farms was much improved; in 1960 they were in a position to pay their members more for their labor as well as to make greater provision for those in difficulty. Conditions under Stalin must have been extremely bad.

By 1965, increases in the day rates paid by collective farms meant that for the USSR as a whole a larger proportion of kolkhoznik personal per capita income was derived from kolkhoz work than from private agricutural activity. Kolkhoz pay still accounted for less than half of the total, however, in ten of the fifteen republics. Only in Kazakhstan and the four Central Asian republics did kolkhozniki derive more than 50% of their incomes from their primary employment. In five republics—the Baltic area, Byleorussia, and Georgia—more than half of personal income still came from the private plot and associated activities. Transfer payments still amounted to less than 5% of personal income; on the average, this represented some 16 rubles a year, a threefold increase over the five years but still only enough to support an individual at the poverty level for about ten days. Around this average there were substantial variations; in Estonia, the average peasant household received some 30 rubles per capita (per year), while in Georgia it got little more than 7 rubles per person.

There were further substantial changes in the structure of per capita kolkhoznik income between 1965 and 1970. The continued increase in day rates paid by collective farms meant that at the end of the decade, although kolkhoz pay did not account for more than half of personal income in most republics, it was a more important source of income than the private plot in all but three—Byelorussia, Georgia, and Lithuania. In Georgia, it should be noted, more than half of personal income was still generated by so-called subsidiary activities. For the rest of the country, the private plot generated between 20 and 40% of personal per capita income. More striking was the change in the importance of transfer payments. Largely as a result of the extension of state retirement pensions to the collective farm population, the share of transfers in personal income tripled to about 10%.

One further feature of the figures in tables 6.5-6.7 merits comment at this stage: between 1960 and 1965 the value of non-cash social welfare expenditures per capita (state and kolkhoz expenditure on education, medical care, etc.) increased both absolutely and relative to personal income, in almost all republics. Only in Uzbekistan did it fall from 15% of personal income to 14.3%, but this fall implies a small increase in ruble expenditure. However, between 1965 and 1970, the relative value of non-cash social welfare expenditure declined in virtually all republics, and in two republics this decline represented an absolute fall in the value of such expenditure. In part, this may be a consequence of my having overestimated the value of transfer payments (that is, pensions) received by kolkhozniki in 1970. But it also suggests that collective farm sector pensions were financed at the expense of other forms of social consumption.

Both the discussion of chapter 2 and the estimates presented here indicate that the Soviet government has pursued an active policy of increasing kolkhoznik incomes. The figures in tables 6.5-6.7 suggest that collective farmers in all republics have felt the effects of these policies, but the figures in tables 6.4 demonstrate that official policy has been unsuccessful at reducing interrepublican disparity in living standards. This result must have been disappointing to the Soviet authorities, and it is somewhat paradoxical. It is a consequence of demographic change and the increasing coherence of the Soviet economy—or possibly, the Soviet labor market. Its resolution will be dealt with in chapter 7, but first I will present estimates of personal and total per capita income for state employees in each of the Soviet republics for the three years considered in this study.

6.2 PERSONAL AND TOTAL INCOMES
OF STATE EMPLOYEES, 1960-70

The estimates of kolkhoznik incomes given in the last section can be combined with those for republican per capita incomes from chapter 5 to provide figures on the personal and total incomes of state employees.

These are of interest both for the information they provide about the living standards of this particular group in the various Soviet republics and because a knowledge of the incomes of state employees and kolkhozniki separately permits a more detailed analysis of the sources of variation in republican incomes. This latter topic will be taken up in chapter 7; here I concentrate on the extent of disparity between state employee incomes and on the improvement in the economic welfare of state employees during the sixties.

It is tempting to think of state employees as synonymous with the urban working class in the Soviet Union, or even as synonymous with urban workers, but this is mistaken. First it must be remembered that the categories *state employees* and *kolkhozniki*, as used in this and previous chapters, include the dependents of those employed in state organizations and enterprises and of members of collective farms. Second, state employees as a group include those who work in state agricultural enterprises—sovkhozy, etc. The relative importance of this group increased during the sixties and by 1970 accounted for approximately 10% of all those employed by the state. And there are others who work in rural areas. Lastly, the category "state employees" includes clerical, managerial, and supervisory staff and those who work in service occupations. More precisely, the two groups are defined as follows: heads of households are classified as either kolkhozniki or state employees, depending upon occupation; all members of the family of a kolkhoznik are classified as kolkhozniki, others are defined as state employees. The head of a household who does not work but has been a member of a collective farm or maintains some link with one—living on its territory, working a private plot, and so on—is classified as a kolkhoznik; otherwise he or she is a state employee. Thus it might be more accurate to refer to the two groups as "kolkhozniki and their dependents" and "the remainder of the population," but I shall retain the Soviet terms.

Estimates of per capita personal and total income for state employees in each of the Soviet republics are given in table 6.9. Before examining in detail the evidence they provide about disparities in living standards in the three benchmark years, however, there is a question of reliability that must be resolved. A comparison of the figures in tables 6.2 and 6.9 will show that in all three Baltic republics in 1965 and 1970 and in Lithuania and Latvia in 1960, per capita incomes of kolkhozniki exceeded those of state employees. Such a result was unexpected, and it conflicts with the preconceptions of most Soviet specialists. It is therefore worth examining the data for these three republics in greater detail to show that, however implausible, the result is correct.

Ruble values for the components of total per capita income for each of the two social classes in each of the years 1960, 1965, and 1970 for all three Baltic republics are shown in table 6.8. From the table it is clear that the gap exists, that it is substantial in some years, and that in Latvia and Lithuania it widened between 1960 and 1965 and narrowed between 1965 and 1970. The Estonian experience is somewhat different.

The reason why many Soviet specialists may find this result hard to accept is that they are used to forming implicit judgements about living standards or differences in economic welfare on the basis of earnings data.

Table 6.8
The Structure of Total Per Capita Income, Baltic Republics, 1960-70 (rubles per year)

	Earnings from Employment	Earnings per Employee	of which Proportion of Population in Employment	Social Welfare Expenditure	Other Sources	Total Income
1960						
Lithuania						
State employees	319	801	0.398	129	90	538
Kolkhozniki	86	231	0.373	43	415	544
Latvia						
State employees	399	892	0.447	166	43	608
Kolkhozniki	175	387	0.452	88	466	729
Estonia						
State employees	454	945	0.480	179	37	670
Kolkhozniki	181	527	0.343	98	363	642
1965						
Lithuania						
State employees	438	1008	0.435	176	71	685
Kolkhozniki	241	596	0.405	109	537	887
Latvia						
State employees	532	1070	0.497	227	39	798
Kolkhozniki	302	659	0.458	174	499	975
Estonia						
State employees	571	1147	0.498	235	35	841
Kolkhozniki	366	811	0.451	256	536	1158
1970						
Lithuania						
State employees	660	1369	0.482	267	117	1044
Kolkhozniki	435	1003	0.434	227	543	1205
Latvia						
State employees	721	1417	0.509	325	84	1130
Kolkhozniki	511	1097	0.466	288	510	1309
Estonia						
State employees	777	1551	0.501	348	66	1191
Kolkhozniki	697	1508	0.462	424	523	1644

An examination of the first two columns of the table shows that in terms of earnings per capita or per person employed, state employees received more than kolkhozniki in all years in all three republics; usually they received substantially more.[4] Because a larger proportion of the dependents of state employees were gainfully employed than those of kolkhozniki, the gap in earnings per capita was larger than that in earnings per employee. Differences in participation rates can be explained by the fact that, generally, the birth rate is higher in rural areas than in urban areas (and more kolkhozniki live in the countryside than state employees), and also, that kolkhozniki spend more of their time working on private plots. The impact of the rapid growth in kolkhoz wage rates can also be seen. Although in Latvia, for example, per capita earnings of state employees increased by some 80% over the decade, the growth in the per capita earnings of kolkhozniki was so rapid that they increased from some 44% of the state sector level in 1960 to more than 70% in 1970. The pattern in the other republics was similar.

Table 6.8 also brings out the difference in the value of social welfare benefits received by the two classes (that is, expenditures on health, education, etc., and transfers like pensions and allowances). In Lithuania, for example, in 1960, welfare expenditures per capita for state employees were more than three times those for kolkhozniki. The increasing affluence of the collective farm sector, and perhaps more important, the extension of the state system to kolkhozniki resulted in a substantial reduction in the relative advantage of state employees with respect to this component of economic well-being. By 1970, per capita social consumption expenditures on state employees in Lithuania exceeded those on kolkhozniki by less than 18%. The experience in Latvia was similar, and in Estonia in 1970 peasants actually received 20% more than state employees from this source.

Finally, table 6.8 brings out the importance of the private plot in determining the relative living standards of the two classes in these republics. It is, ultimately, because the Baltic peasantry were able to produce so much on their private plots and associated livestock holdings that they were able to compensate for lower employment earnings and for comparatively lower benefits from social consumption expenditures and were able to procure for themselves the relatively high standards of living indicated by the table. It should be remembered, however, in interpreting the figures in table 6.8, that for kolkhozniki, "other sources of income" includes both the earnings of family members in state employment and receipts from the financial system. All the same, this component has proved vital. In Lithuania, for example, in 1960, on a per capita basis, it was more than four times as important to kolkhozniki as to state employees, in Latvia in the same year almost ten times, and over the decade has tended in general to increase in value.

This analysis has, I hope, made the apparently counterintuitive conclusion that kolkhozniki in the Baltic states have a higher standard of
living than state employees more plausible. The conclusion reached here
finds partial confirmation in some recent Soviet work. It has been reported that the real incomes of kolkhozniki in Latvia in 1970 were some
6.3% greater than those of state employees.[5] The numerical magnitude
differs from that in table 6.8, but the direction is the same.

As I have suggested, the reason why so many Soviet specialists find
this result surprising is that they have become used to making inferences about the standard of living on the basis of earnings data. The discussion has shown, perhaps, how important it is to use a more comprehensive concept like total income. In this connection, by the way, it is
possible that the Soviet government, which, I have suggested, makes use
of money income figures in forming its ideas about living standards, may
until recently also have been unaware of the relative levels of economic
welfare enjoyed by kolkhozniki and state employees in the Baltic republics.
Without information on the proportion of kolkhoz pay distributed in
cash in each of the republics, and knowledge of the proportion of private
output that is sold rather than consumed within the household, it is
impossible to derive adequate estimates of per capita money incomes.
But using USSR average rates for these categories, it turns out that, except
for Estonia in 1970, the hypothetical money incomes of state employees
exceed those of kolkhozniki in all cases. Thus the government may have
been misled by its own indicator.

When we turn to the figures in table 6.9, they show, as expected, that
state employees were better off than collective farmers in the USSR as a
whole and in most republics. In no republic did per capita personal income fall below 30 rubles a month in 1960. In the RSFSR, the Ukraine,
Moldavia, and Armenia, as well as in two of the three Baltic republics,
it was higher than 40 rubles a month. With the inclusion of social consumption, only in Uzbekistan, Kirgizia, and Byelorussia did it fall below
this level, and in the RSFSR and some of the smaller republics and possibly
in the Ukraine, it approached or exceeded 50 rubles a month. Furthermore, disparities in living standards, whether judged by personal or total
income, were less marked among state employees than among kolkhozniki; average personal income in the best-off republic was only some
60-65% higher than that in the worst-off.

Between 1960 and 1970 per capita total income for state employees in
the USSR as a whole grew at an average rate of 5.4% a year. Per capita
personal income grew at the slightly lower rate of 5.2%. This is certainly
lower than the rate of growth of kolkhoznik incomes, but even when it
is recognized that these figures make no allowance for changes in direct

Table 6.9
Per Capita Total and Personal Income, State Employees,
USSR and Republics, 1960-70 (rubles per year)

	Total Income			Personal Income		
	1960	1965	1970	1960	1965	1970
USSR	572	721	970	500	624	834
RSFSR	590	748	1013	522	652	884
Ukraine	575	732	965	496	640	821
Byelorussia	471	659	923	389	555	773
Uzbekistan	417	554	798	360	463	654
Kazakhstan	518	625	840	450	537	704
Georgia	561	670	863	477	570	723
Azerbaijan	500	581	699	416	484	568
Lithuania	538	685	1044	466	588	903
Moldavia	688	778	940	538	622	772
Latvia	608	798	1130	530	695	979
Kirgizia	432	577	759	363	482	622
Tadjikistan	537	675	764	438	548	597
Armenia	566	637	876	481	538	746
Turkmenistan	581	605	784	433	463	618
Estonia	670	841	1191	582	733	1035

taxes or the cost of living, they imply that state employees enjoyed a respectable increase in living standards. In seven of the fifteen republics, however, the annual average rate of growth of total income diverged by more than one percentage point from that of the USSR as a whole. In Byelorussia, for example, it was almost 7%, and in Moldavia little more than 3%.

For the USSR as a whole, both total and personal per capita income of state employees grew more rapidly in the period 1965-70 than in the first half of the decade. This was also true of most of the republics, as far as total income is concerned; only in Tadjikistan did total per capita income grow more rapidly under Krushchev than under his successors. There were more deviants for personal income. In the Ukraine and Byelorussia, in Kirgizia and in Tadjikistan, personal per capita income grew at a faster rate in 1960-65 than under Brezhnev and Kosygin. It is not clear why there should have been a difference among republics. Certainly the growth rate figures do not suggest that the poorest improved their relative status under either government.

The substantial rates of growth during the sixties together with the generally higher level of income in 1960 mean that by 1970 per capita personal income for state employees exceeded the MMS budget level in all but two republics. Only in Tadjikistan and Azerbaijan did the average fall below 50 rubles a month. In Latvia and Estonia average personal income exceeded 75 rubles a month, and in Lithuania and the RSFSR it was above 70 rubles. Thus in all these republics one may conclude that "rational consumption patterns" were being approached or had been achieved. Even if disparities in living standards were not as great as among kolkhozniki, however, the gap between the richest and the poorest republics widened between 1960 and 1970. In the latter year it was between 70 and 80%.

The ranking of republics in terms of per capita personal or total income of state employees between 1960 and 1970 shows somewhat less stability than that for kolkhoznik incomes. Still, the two hierarchies share certain features: in 1960 only Byelorussia and Azerbaijan rank lower than the Central Asian republics, and by 1970 these latter, together with Azerbaijan, have emerged as the worst-off areas in the USSR. More generally, by 1970, in terms of personal, and to a lesser extent total, income, the republics fall into three or four distinct groups, as depicted in table 6.10. Best off,

Table 6.10

Distribution of Republics by Personal Per Capita State Employee Income, 1970

% of USSR Average	Republics, in Ascending Order by Income	% of State Employees
–85	Uzbekistan, Kirgizia, Turkmenistan, Tadjikistan, Azerbaijan	8.21
85–100	Ukraine, Byelorussia, Moldavia, Armenia, Georgia, Kazakhstan	29.90
100–107.5	RSFSR	58.96
107.5–	Estonia, Latvia, Lithuania	2.93

as usual, are the Baltic states; next, the RSFSR; then the other Slav republics, Moldavia, Georgia, Armenia, and Kazakhstan; finally, there are the four Central Asian republics and Azerbaijan. This distribution should be compared with the one given in table 6.3.

In terms of total income, there was very little correspondence between the rankings of republics by kolkhozniki and state employees in 1960 (Spearman's rank correlation coefficient was 0.257), but by the end of the decade there was a much greater measure of consistency. The correlation coefficient between the two rankings had risen to 0.825; for personal income it was even higher, 0.928, but this may be affected by errors in the allocation of pensions between the two classes. The meaning that I believe should be ascribed to this increased coherence will be dealt with in the next chapter.

The figures in table 6.11 show that not only did the range of disparity in per capita state employee income increase over the period but that there was also some increase in the coefficient of variation. This is true for both the income concepts used in this chapter. Once again it should be pointed out that the figures in table 6.11 refer to the unweighted mean

Table 6.11
The Variance of Per Capita State Employee Incomes, USSR and Republics, 1960-70

	Total Income			Personal Income		
	1960	1965	1970	1960	1965	1970
Mean (rubles)	550.0	678.0	904.0	463.0	572.0	760.0
Standard deviation	73.9	83.3	139.4	62.9	81.3	137.1
Coefficient of variation (%)	13.44	12.30	15.40	13.59	14.22	18.04

Note: The figures in this table are the unweighted mean and standard deviation of republican per capita state employee incomes.

and standard deviation of per capita incomes. The same trend, however, is displayed by weighted means and variances, although at a lower level. For instance, using state employee population weights, the coefficient of variation of total income was 5.06% in 1960; in 1970 it was 6.34%.

Tables 6.12 and 6.13 provide details of the structure of personal and total income in each of the republics in 1960 and 1970. The pattern in

Table 6.12
The Structure of State Employee Incomes, USSR and Republics, 1960 (% of personal income)

	Earnings from Employment	Private Economic Activity, etc.	Transfer Payments	Personal Income	Non-Cash Social Welfare Expenditure
USSR	77.0	4.8	18.1	100.0	14.4
RSFSR	77.5	4.0	18.5	100.0	13.2
Ukraine	77.0	4.4	18.6	100.0	16.0
Byelorussia	69.6	15.4	15.0	100.0	21.0
Uzbekistan	73.7	9.0	17.2	100.0	16.0
Kazakhstan	79.2	5.9	14.9	100.0	15.0
Georgia	74.9	5.3	19.8	100.0	17.6
Azerbaijan	80.0	—	20.0	100.0	20.2
Lithuania	68.4	19.4	12.2	100.0	15.5
Moldavia	73.8	5.8	20.5	100.0	28.0
Latvia	75.3	8.0	16.6	100.0	14.8
Kirgizia	74.7	8.4	16.9	100.0	19.2
Tadjikistan	72.0	13.2	14.8	100.0	22.6
Armenia	70.6	9.8	19.6	100.0	17.8
Turkmenistan	85.2	—	14.8	100.0	34.3
Estonia	78.0	6.4	15.7	100.0	15.1

1965, not given here, is essentially identical. The absence of recorded private receipts for Azerbaijan or Turkmenistan is a consequence of the methods used to estimate this component. Because, apparently, state employees in these republics occupied less than ten thousand hectares in 1960 (and in Turkmenistan in 1970), the statistical handbook records a zero holding. This results in zero receipts, since state employee receipts depend upon the area held.

Table 6.13
The Structure of State Employee Incomes, USSR and Republics, 1970 (% of personal income)

	Earnings from Employment	Private Economic Activity	Transfer Payments	Personal Income	Non-Cash Social Welfare Expenditure
USSR	76.7	5.0	18.3	100.0	16.3
RSFSR	77.1	4.1	18.8	100.0	14.7
Ukraine	77.3	3.5	19.2	100.0	17.7
Byelorussia	73.5	11.8	14.7	100.0	19.4
Uzbekistan	70.6	12.8	16.6	100.0	22.1
Kazakhstan	78.7	5.1	16.2	100.0	19.2
Georgia	73.5	10.2	16.3	100.0	19.4
Azerbaijan	73.0	9.8	17.2	100.0	23.0
Lithuania	73.0	13.0	14.0	100.0	15.6
Moldavia	77.5	7.3	15.2	100.0	23.4
Latvia	73.6	8.5	17.9	100.0	15.3
Kirgizia	75.9	6.8	17.3	100.0	22.0
Tadjikistan	77.9	6.1	16.9	100.0	28.0
Armenia	78.0	5.2	16.8	100.0	17.3
Turkmenistan	84.5	—	15.5	100.0	23.9
Estonia	75.1	6.4	18.5	100.0	15.1

The pattern of incomes received in 1970 is, in most fundamentals, the same as that in 1960. Also, the structure of state employee income in all republics is much more alike than that of kolkhozniki. Neglecting Azerbaijan and Turkmenistan, in 1960 earnings accounted for between two-thirds and four-fifths of income in all republics. Transfers accounted for a further 15-20%. Except in Byelorussia, Lithuania, and Tadjikistan, private activities were relatively unimportant on a per capita basis. In 1970, little had changed other than a small increase in the relative importance of non-cash social welfare expenditure. For state employees, this now accounted for almost a fifth of personal income on the average, and in some of the poorer republics for more than a quarter. This contrasts with the position of kolkhozniki. Bearing in mind the problems with the allocation of pensions between collective farmers in the different republics, non-cash social consumption expenditures amounted on the average to about 10% of kolkhoznik personal income, and further, were highest in those republics where personal income was highest.

The developments outlined in this chapter are a consequence of interactions between government policy on the one hand and demographic and social change on the other. The effects of these upon the variance of republican incomes and the extent to which they may have frustrated the Soviet authorities' attempts to reduce interrepublican disparity in living standards are the subjects of the next chapter.

7

Sources of Income Variation among Republics

THE DISCUSSION OF THE PRECEDING CHAPTERS has shown that there was substantial disparity in per capita income between the constituent republics of the USSR in 1960. I have suggested that in the late fifties the Soviet government became more concerned with the question of inequality and economic welfare, and one would therefore have expected that a reduction in regional differentiation would have received some priority in the formulation and implementation of economic policy. But the figures given in chapter 6 suggest that there was no reduction in interrepublican income differences in the ten years after 1960. Indeed, if one measures differentiation by the coefficient of variation (CV), table 5.3 indicates that it increased by some 3 or 4% over the decade. In point of fact, the table shows that the unweighted CV of per capita total income declined by 7.8% between 1960 and 1965 and rose by 12.5% in the next five years. The picture implied by per capita personal income is virtually identical. This suggests that the Soviet government may have had some success in reducing regional inequality under Khrushchev but that the gains were lost under Brezhnev and Kosygin.

The analysis of chapter 6 shows that there were substantial differences in the per capita incomes received by state employees and kolkhozniki in the various republics when these two social classes are considered separately, and that the extent of difference increased between 1960 and 1970. In fact, for state employees the unweighted CV of total per capita income increased by 14.6% over the decade, and that for kolkhozniki by 9.8%.

These results are a little surprising. While most Soviet specialists would expect there to be substantial income differences between the Soviet republics, they would also expect that these differences would have declined during the 1960s. There are three reasons for this. The basic social cleavage in the USSR is between kolkhozniki and state employees. Over the decade, the proportion of kolkhozniki in the population as a whole and in each republic declined, and the earnings of kolkhozniki increased relative to those of state employees. These developments made the popu-

143

lation of each republic more homogeneous and might have been expected to reduce interrepublican differentials.

Second, over the decade as a whole, and particularly after 1965, there was a substantial increase in ruble expenditure on social consumption. At the same time, state retirement pensions and some other social security benefits were extended to the collective farm population. These developments contributed to reducing the difference between the two social classes and so might have been expected to reduce interrepublican differences in the standard of living.

Finally, the wage reform of 1956-65 and subsequent increases in the minimum wage led to a reduction in the inequality of earnings among state employees. Again, this might have been expected to reduce the differences between state employee incomes in the various republics.

All three of these conjectures suffer from similiar weaknesses. They concentrate on individual components of income rather than on income as a whole, and they fail to consider interactions between the various income components. Now, in chapters 5 and 6, the coefficient of variation has been used to measure the extent of interrepublican differentiation in incomes; an increase in the CV has been taken to imply an increase in inequality, and vice versa.[1] But the CV is defined as the quotient of the standard deviation and the mean of a distribution, and thus its value depends *inter alia* upon the variance of the distribution. Changes in the variance will be reflected in changes in the CV. Personal or total income can be expressed as the sum of a number of components, and therefore the variance of income will depend upon the variances of these components *and upon their covariances.* It is this latter point that the conjectures suggested above appear to neglect. As will be shown below, the conjectured developments are for the most part correct, but interactions between them have resulted in the failure of interrepublican income differentials to decline.

In the next section I describe the determination of personal income in the USSR and show how it is related to measured variance. In this way the policy instruments at the government's disposal are identified. In sections 2 and 3 this framework is applied in the analysis of income differentiation among state employees and kolkhozniki. Section 4 deals with the problems posed by the population as a whole and includes a discussion of the effects of the decline in the number of collective farmers. The chapter concludes with an analysis of the impact of direct and indirect taxation on the republican distribution of income.

7.1   THE VARIANCE IN REPUBLICAN INCOMES: A FRAMEWORK

By definition, per capita total (or personal) income is made up of per capita earnings and other sources of income. Consequently the variance in republican per capita income, and hence the coefficient of variation, can be explained in terms of the variances of these two components and the covariance between them. (Perhaps *expressed* would be a better word than *explained*, since the relationship described is algebraic, but *explained* conforms to statistical usage.) Policies which successfully reduce interrepublican disparities in economic welfare must either reduce the variance of these components or reduce the relationship between them. Factors which militate against reductions in the variance of earnings or other sources of income or which increase the correlation between them will, *ceteris paribus*, frustrate attempts at reducing regional inequality.[2]

Now, earnings per capita depend upon earnings per person employed and on the proportion of the population in employment. In the Soviet Union, the government has a measure of direct control over wage rates, salary scales, and the rates of pay on collective farms; it can therefore exert considerable influence over earnings per person employed. But while it can attempt to maintain more or less full employment among the working-age populations of the different republics, its influence over more general features of demographic structure—over the balance of the sexes, birth and death rates, and life expectancy—is limited. Indeed, in the short run, these are largely independent of government policy. Consequently the variance in per capita earnings in the Soviet Union is not completely controlled by the government; adverse changes in population structure may nullify the beneficial effects of wage policy upon income differentials.

It should be remembered, also, that the elimination of disparity in republican incomes, or even a reduction in interpersonal differentials, is not the major objective of those who determine wage and salary scales. It might be claimed that distributional considerations are of secondary importance and that the primary aim is to ensure an efficient allocation of labor (or at least a certain measure of equilibrium in the labor market). Such considerations impose further restrictions upon the ability of the Soviet government to eliminate regional disparity in per capita earnings.

The Soviet government's control over other sources of household income—state social welfare expenditures and private subsidiary economic activity—is also less than total. The government can exert some influence over private agricultural production through its control of the size of holdings, through the prices it pays for their produce, through the taxes it levies on private incomes, and perhaps by influencing prices on collective farm markets. But agricultural shortages have plagued the Soviet government for much of the period since the revolution. During the sixties it was unable to ensure sufficient output from the state-collective sector to satisfy demand at ruling prices. It has not been completely free to use the instruments at its disposal to restrict private agricultural activity in order to reduce regional inequality.

To put it another way, it seems unlikely that the Soviet government would be willing, in present circumstances, to trade off reductions in regional income disparity against an overall reduction in economic welfare that would result from substantial further restrictions on private agricultural activity. In any case, it is not the scale of private activity per se that gives rise to interrepublican inequality but the differences in level in different parts of the country. These in turn reflect differences in climate, in soil conditions, in productivity, and in the balance of net advantage between private and collective agriculture. An effective reduction in interrepublican differentials would require discriminatory measures against the most efficient production units. Given the state of Soviet agriculture and the burden it imposes upon the balance of payments, such measures would be economically ill advised. They would also be politically unpopular, although that has not deterred the Soviet government in the past.

So much for private activity; but it cannot even be claimed that a reduction in regional disparity in the standard of living is the primary aim of the state's social welfare programs. In any case, administrative inertia, the unwillingness to change radically the relative importance of ongoing programs or to rewrite their entitlement rules, means that the scope for a substantial modification in the republican distribution of income through social consumption expenditures is limited.

Thus the Soviet government has at its disposal two broad sets of instruments with which to influence interrepublican differentials in income, control over wages and salaries and control over social welfare expenditures (and taxation). In this context, the conversion of kolkhozy into state farms, because it permits the payment of wages at sovkhoz rates and because it facilitates the subsidization of economically weak collective farms, should perhaps be thought of as part of the first set of instruments. However, these policy instruments have to be used for other purposes as well: they affect interpersonal (or interfamily) differences in economic welfare and they affect the operation of the labor market and the more general allocation of resources in the Soviet economy. It is a commonplace of the theory of economic policy that the successful realization of economic objectives requires an instrument for every target. It is thus possible that in spite of the extensive powers exercised by the Soviet government, it does not possess sufficient control over the Soviet economy to realize its goals in the area of regional equality.

The preceding paragraphs have sketched in the outlines of a theory of the determination of personal income in the USSR and the role played by government policy. It is possible to identify the various elements with components in a decomposition of the variance in personal or total incomes. By examining changes in these components over the period 1960-70, one can determine which factors have been responsible for the Soviet government's apparent failure to reduce disparity in the standard of living between the constituent republics of the USSR.

Formally, one may express the relationship between per capita income and its components in the following equations:

$$y_i = w_i + z_i \quad (i = 1 \ldots 15)$$
$$w_i = w^*_i \cdot p_i \quad (i = 1 \ldots 15) \tag{1}$$
$$z_i = q_i + e_i \quad (i = 1 \ldots 15)$$

where y_i is per capita total income in the ith republic;

w_i is per capita earnings in the ith republic;

z_i are other sources of income, per capita in the ith republic;

w^*_i is earnings per person employed in the ith republic;

p_i is the proportion of the population in employment in the ith republic;

q_i is per capita receipts from private activity in the ith republic; and

e_i is per capita social welfare expenditure in the ith republic.

Making use of standard statistical formulae, one may express the variances of the LHS of equations (1) as (Goodman, 1960, pp. 708-13):

$$Var(y) = Var(w) + Var(z) + 2Cov(w,z)$$
$$Var(z) = Var(q) + Var(e) + 2Cov(q,e) \tag{2}$$
$$Var(w) = \bar{p}^2 Var(w^*) + (\bar{w}^*)^2 Var(p) + \text{``interaction''}$$

By substituting the second and third equations of (2) into the first, one obtains an expression for the variance of total per capita income in terms of the factors identified in the preceding discussion. For example, $\bar{p}^2 Var(w^*)$ indicates how much of the variance in total income can be attributed directly to the variance in earnings per person employed. By examining how this changed over the decade 1960-70, one can see how far, if at all, Soviet wage policy contributed to a reduction in republican income differentials. The other terms in (2) can be explained in a similar fashion.

The discussion of the preceding paragraphs suggests that the Soviet government exercises a measure of direct control over the elements w^*_i and e_i; a purposeful policy of reducing republican differentials should result in a reduction of the variance in these components. It also suggests that the elements q_i and p_i are to a considerable extent outside the government's control; one would therefore expect less change in these components. But income generation takes place within the context of a labor market, and one might expect a relationship between w_i and p_i reflecting the household

Table 7.1

Variance in Per Capita Total Income: State Employees, USSR and Republics, 1960-70

	Earnings per Capita	of which			Income from Other Sources	of which			Interaction, Wages, etc.
		Earnings per Employee	Participation Rate	Inter-action		Social Welfare	Private, etc.	Inter-action	
1960									
Mean (rubles)	348.8	817.7	0.431	—	201.3	166.5	34.8	—	—
CV (%)	15.2	12.0	18.1	—	16.7	20.8	63.9	—	—
% variance explained	51.1	32.9	74.6	−56.4	20.7	21.9	9.0	−10.2	28.2
1965									
Mean (rubles)	436.1	1016.2	0.431	—	241.5	201.3	40.1	—	—
CV (%)	15.0	8.7	15.1	—	11.2	11.4	47.9	—	—
% variance explained	61.4	20.9	63.2	−22.7	10.6	7.6	5.3	−2.3	28.0
1970									
Mean (rubles)	575.9	1304.9	0.441	—	329.4	273.1	56.3	—	—
CV (%)	17.5	9.3	13.9	—	14.2	11.8	51.2	—	—
% variance explained	52.3	14.6	32.8	4.8	11.2	5.4	4.3	1.6	36.5

Note: Entries in the table were calculated by means of the formulae given in text equations (2); rows may not add to totals because of rounding.

labor supply function. The sign and magnitude of $Cov(w,z)$ or $Cov(w+q,e)$ will indicate the extent to which the Soviet welfare state "corrects" the initial distribution of income, the extent to which social consumption expenditure redistributes income from rich to poor republics, or vice versa.

In the next two sections I make use of equations (2) to explore changes in the structure of incomes of state employees and kolkhozniki in the constituent republics of the USSR and their impact on interrepublican differentiation.

7.2   THE VARIANCE IN REPUBLICAN INCOMES: STATE EMPLOYEES[3]

Between 1960 and 1970 state employees in all republics of the USSR enjoyed substantial increases in per capita incomes, but as the analysis of chapter 6 has shown, interrepublican inequality was not diminished. The coefficient of variation of total per capita income, in fact, rose by almost 15%. Actually it fell by 8.5% between 1960 and 1965 and rose by 25.2% in the next five years; thus there was some reduction in differentials under Khrushchev which was reversed under his successors.

The framework of the preceding section permits one to explore the influence of changes in the variance of particular components of income on the variance of income as a whole. The analysis of this section suggests that while the Soviet government was successful in reducing the variance of the elements under its direct control, changes in other factors and the way in which policies were implemented led to a general failure in reducing disparity.

Values for the various components of equations (2), expressed as percentages of the variance in total per capita income, are given in table 7.1 for the years 1960, 1965, and 1970. The table also includes figures on variations in the individual components of per capita state employee income for each of these years. As with the estimates in chapters 5 and 6, those in table 7.1 are of the *unweighted* means and coefficients of variation of income and its components. Also, because of the way in which the data were derived, earnings per capita and earnings per employee both include per capita receipts from the financial system. Finally, participation rates are derived as the quotient of average annual employment in the state sector and the state employee population as given in appendix A. They thus include those members of kolkhoznik households employed by state enterprises and organizations.

The figures in table 7.1 show that in 1960 approximately half the variance in total income could be attributed to the variance in per capita earnings; a further 20% was the result of variance in other sources of income. Somewhat more than a quarter of the total could be ascribed to the interaction of these two components, that is, to the tendency for other sources of income to be high when earnings were high, and vice versa. In 1965, earnings accounted for as much as three-fifths of the variance in total incomes, other sources for about a tenth, and inter-actions for about the same proportion as in 1960. In 1970, earnings were again responsible for about half the variance in total income, other sources for about a tenth, and interactions for more than a third.

Over the decade there was little change in what one may call the inherent variability of the two components; the CV of per capita earnings increased slightly from 15% to 17.5%, while that of other sources fell from 16.7% to 14.2%. Nor was there any substantial change in the relative magnitude of the two components: on average, "other sources" was equal to 55-57% of per capita earnings in all three years. But there was an increase in what one may call the coherence of the two components: the correlation coefficient between per capita earnings and other sources of income increased from 0.433 in 1960 to 0.753 in 1970. The decline in the CV of total per capita income under Khrushchev would seem to be attributable to a fall in the variance of other sources of income, its increase under Brezhnev and Kosygin to an increase in the variance of this component and to an increase in correlation between the different sources of income. Thus it seems unlikely that either the wage reorganization of 1956-65 or the so-called economic reform of 1965-70 had any substantial impact on regional disparity in state employee incomes.

The apparent stability in the structure of state employee incomes con-ceals substantial changes within the individual components. The figures in table 7.1 suggest that there were marked changes within the labor market, as it were, and also changes in the role of social welfare expendi-ture. But in interpreting the figures in the table, it is well to recall how they were derived. Because of the nonlinear relationship between earnings per person employed and participation rates, the contribution of the variance in earnings per person employed to the variance in total income is affected by participation rates, and vice versa.

From table 7.1 it can be seen that the variance in earnings per person employed as defined in equations (2)—that is, $\bar{p}^2 Var(w^*)$—was responsible for about a third of the variance in total income in 1960. This proportion had fallen to about a fifth in 1965 and by 1970 to less than 15%. There were equally dramatic reductions in the proportion of the variance in total income attributable to variations in participation rates. These declines were accompanied by reductions in the inherent vari-ability of the components in question; the CVs of both components declined by about a quarter. But these developments were accompanied by changes in the relationship between earnings and participation rates which tended to offset the effects of Soviet wage policy on the variance of per capita earnings. Because the interaction term in the third relation of equations (2) is complex, it cannot be equated with a correlation coefficient. But if the correlation coefficient between earnings per person employed and the proportion of the population employed is calculated, it indicates the existence of a negative relationship between the two variables in 1960 ($r = -0.451$); the relationship is still negative in 1965 but somewhat weaker ($r = -0.328$); by 1970, no linear relationship appears to exist ($r = 0.095$).

These results suggest that in 1960, and possibly in 1965, households in the state sector of the Soviet economy possessed a backward-bending labor supply curve. They consumed part of any increase in real wages in the form of greater leisure. *Per contra*, reductions in real wages would lead to increases in the proportion of women seeking employment and to reductions in the proportion of young people continuing their education. By the end of the decade this relationship had disappeared. The inference to be drawn from these figures is that participation rates within the state sector are now largely determined outside the labor market, that demographic factors are now of more importance than purely economic ones.

Turning to the other components of income analyzed in table 7.1, it can be seen that although private receipts were inherently the most variable source of income, at no time in the sixties did they account for more than 10% of the variance in total incomes; by 1970, they accounted for less than 5%. This can be explained by their relative unimportance in the incomes of state employees.

There was a fall in the proportion of the variance in total income that could be ascribed to variations in social welfare expenditures between 1960 and 1970; there was also a decline in the inherent variability of this component. Thus, although per capita social welfare expenditures increased, on average, by about two-thirds over the decade, in 1970 they were directly responsible for only 5% of the variance in total income, whereas in 1960 they had accounted for more than a fifth.

These changes appear to have had some undesirable consequences. In 1960, social welfare expenditures compensated, in some sense, for variations in private receipts; or perhaps one should state the relationship in an inverse form: private receipts appear to have compensated for variations in social consumption expenditures between republics. At any rate, there was a negative relationship between them ($r = -0.363$). By 1965, this relationship had weakened ($r = -0.182$), and by 1970 it may have been replaced by a positive relationship ($r = 0.169$). Thus a policy of increasing social welfare expenditures and of reducing interrepublican disparities was partly offset by the way in which these expenditures related to private receipts.

Table 7.2

Variance in Per Capita Total Income: Kolkhozniki, USSR and Republics, 1960-70

	Kolkhoz Pay per Capita	of which			Income from Other Sources	of which			
		Pay per Employee	Participation Rate	Interaction		Social Welfare	Private, etc.	Interaction	Interaction, Pay, etc.
1960									
Mean (rubles)	115.2	394.3	0.299	—	272.5	49.5	233.0	—	—
CV (%)	34.9	34.3	21.8	—	45.1	42.9	49.1	—	—
% variance explained	8.2	8.3	3.4	-3.4	76.4	2.3	60.7	13.4	15.4
1965									
Mean (rubles)	211.5	696.1	0.308	—	371.5	107.8	263.7	—	—
CV (%)	31.4	21.7	28.0	—	48.6	57.7	53.7	—	—
% variance explained	8.2	4.0	6.7	-2.5	60.7	7.2	37.4	16.1	31.1
1970									
Mean (rubles)	326.9	1024.8	0.318	—	486.8	177.5	309.3	—	—
CV (%)	42.6	25.0	30.4	—	41.4	56.5	42.7	—	—
% variance explained	18.5	6.3	9.4	2.8	38.8	9.6	16.6	12.6	42.7

Note: Entries in the table were derived by applying the formulae in text equations (2); rows may not sum to totals because of rounding.

In fact, even in 1960, this negative relationship between social consumption and private receipts was outweighed by the positive relationship between earnings and social welfare expenditures. It is possible to classify total per capita income into primary income (earnings from employment and receipts from private activity and the financial system) and social consumption. The former reflects the distribution generated by the production side of the economy; the latter reflects the impact of any redistribution brought about by the Soviet welfare state. If, in fact, this leads to a reduction in interrepublican differentials, if it operates to redistribute income from richer to poorer republics, the two components will be negatively correlated; social consumption expenditures will be high in those republics in which primary income per capita is low, and vice versa. During the 1960s the two variables were positively correlated and the strength of the relationship increased between 1960 and 1970; in 1960, $r = 0.469$, in 1965, $r = 0.681$, and in 1970 $r = 0.843$. Thus one may conclude that the Soviet welfare state operated to accentuate rather than to attenuate regional disparity in the average incomes of state employees and consequently in their standards of living. Of course, this conclusion neglects the impact of direct taxation, but the rate structure and average levels of tax are such that it is unlikely to have had any substantial impact. The question is dealt with at greater length later in the chapter.

In conclusion, then, the analysis of this section suggests that although the Soviet government was successful in the 1960s in reducing regional disparity in earnings per person employed, changes in the labor market and in demographic structure meant that these reductions did not carry over into earnings per capita. They therefore failed to bring about any reduction in the variance of total income. Secondly, although regional differences in social consumption expenditure were reduced, the particular programs selected, the definitions of entitlement, and other administrative features meant that, rather than leading to a reduction in differences in living standards between republics, the operation of the Soviet welfare state has tended to increase regional inequality, at least for state employees.

7.3   THE VARIANCE IN REPUBLICAN INCOMES: KOLKHOZNIKI

The analysis of chapter 6 showed that the per capita incomes of kolkhozniki as well as state employees increased substantially in all republics between 1960 and 1970. It also demonstrated that there was some increase in interrepublican variation in kolkhoznik incomes over the decade. Between 1960 and 1970, the unweighted CV of total per capita income increased by almost 10%. Virtually all of this increase occurred between 1960 and 1965. In this section I will apply the framework of section 7.1 to identify the factors responsible for this increase. The relevant figures are given in table 7.2. In the table, earnings refer to receipts from kolkhozy for labor supplied; earnings of dependents from state employment are included in other sources of income, along with receipts from the financial system and the imputed value of private agricultural activity.

In contrast to the position of state employees, the variance in kolkhoznik earnings accounted for less than 10% of the variance in total per capita income in both 1960 and 1965, and for almost 20% in 1970. At the beginning of the decade, more than three-quarters of the variance in total income could be attributed to the variance in other sources of income. This had declined to 60% in 1965 and to less than two-fifths in 1970. Over the decade, the proportion of the variance attributable to the inter-action between earnings and other sources of income increased from 15% to more than 40%.

The changes in the proportion of the variance in total incomes attribut-able to the different components of income can be explained by changes in their relative magnitude and in their inherent variability. Between 1960 and 1970, per capita earnings increased from less than one-half of other sources, on the average, to more than three-quarters. Over the same period, the CV of per capita earnings increased by about 20%, while that of "other sources" declined by about 15%. At the same time, there was a marked increase in the coherence of the two variables, in the tendency for other sources of income to be large where earnings per capita were high, and vice versa. In 1960, the simple correlation coefficient between per capita earnings and other sources of income for kolkhozniki was 0.307, in 1965 it was 0.695, and in 1970 it was 0.797.

Table 7.2 suggests that there were changes in the kolkhoz labor market that in some ways paralleled those for state employees. There was a decline in the CV of earnings per person employed, in spite of increases in average earnings. This resulted in a decline in the proportion of the variance in total income attributable to this factor, from 8.3% in 1960 to 6.3% in 1970. (However, both the inherent variability of earnings and the proportion of the variance in total income explained by them in-creased after 1965.) There was also some evidence of a negative relation-ship between earnings per person employed and participation rates in 1960 and 1965, although it was weaker than for state employees. (In 1960, the simple correlation coefficient between these two variables was -0.323, in 1965 it was -0.238, but by 1970 it had dropped to 0.033.) One may conjecture that for kolkhozniki as well as for state employees, demo-graphic factors had become more important than economic ones in deter-mining participation. On the other hand, it should be pointed out that the behavior of kolkhoznik participation rates differs from that of state employees. Over the decade as a whole they show some tendency to increase and also to become inherently more variable. As a result, the proportion of the variance in total income attributable to them increases—although even in 1970 this factor was not as important in explaining the variance in kolkhoznik incomes as it was in explaining the variance in state employee incomes.

There were much greater variations in kolkhoznik earnings per person employed during the sixties than in state employee earnings. Further, although there were substantial reductions in interrepublican differentials in 1960-65, there was some tendency for these to increase again in the second half of the decade. This suggests that even in narrowly conceived terms, any Soviet government policy aimed at reducing earnings disparity in the collective farm sector was only partially successful. When allowance is made for increases in the variability in participation rates and the disappearance of any significant relationship between earnings and participation, it must be concluded that wage policy failed to bring about any reduction in interrepublican differentiation in kolkhoznik incomes, but, rather, tended to increase it.

In 1960, variations in the private nonemployment incomes of kolkhozniki accounted for 60% of the variance in total per capita incomes. By 1970, they accounted for less than 17%. Since there was only a moderate decline in the inherent variability of this item, its declining importance must be ascribed to the decline in its relative magnitude. Also, in 1960, variations in per capita social welfare expenditures were responsible for little more than 2% of the variance in total income; by 1970, they accounted for almost 10%. This can be explained by the dramatic increase in the value of these expenditures and an increase in their variability. It should also be noted that, for kolkhozniki, there was no tendency for variation in social welfare expenditure to offset variation in private receipts; in 1960, the correlation between these two variables was 0.570, and in 1970 it was 0.498. Throughout the decade, there was a tendency for kolkhozniki in republics with the highest private receipts to also be those receiving the largest benefits from the state.

This relationship is strengthened by the inclusion of earnings from collective farm employment. In 1960, the simple correlation coefficient between primary per capita income, as defined in the last section, and social welfare expenditures was 0.762; in 1965 it was 0.648 and in 1970 0.770. Thus, the substantial increases in state social consumption expenditures, although they have led to increases in per capita income, have also resulted in increases in the differentiation of kolkhoznik incomes. In part, this may have been a consequence of the application of rigid sets of rules in the face of a changing demographic and social structure, but, if the intention of the state's social welfare program was to reduce disparity in interrepublican incomes for kolkhozniki, it must be adjudged to have failed.

7.4   THE VARIANCE IN REPUBLICAN INCOMES:
SOCIAL COMPOSITION

The fact that the sources of variance in the incomes of state employees and of kolkhozniki appear to have differed during the sixties, and the fact that the experience of the two social classes also differed over the decade, suggests that differences in the social composition of republican populations might go some way towards explaining the disparity in republican living standards revealed in chapter 5. That is, it seems reasonable to suppose that living standards will be lowest in those republics where the share of kolkhozniki in the population is highest, and that a reduction in the disparity between the incomes of the two groups as well as reductions in the overall weight of the collective farm sector will have led to a reduction in regional inequality. This question will be explored at greater length here.

The conjecture offered above seems plausible, and it is one to which, I suspect, many Soviet specialists would subscribe—at least initially. But since the variance in republican incomes did not fall between 1960 and 1970 (although both the share of kolkhozniki and the average disparity in per capita incomes declined), it must be inadequate. What is lacking is an explanation of the way in which income differences affect the social composition of republican populations. Again, one finds that interactions have been omitted.

Perhaps a formal statement of the relationships involved would clarify the issue. One may express republican per capita income in terms of the incomes of kolkhozniki and state employees and of the social composition of the population as follows:

$$y_i = a_i y_{ki} + (1-a_i) y_{si} \quad (i = 1 \ldots 15)$$
$$= y_{si} + a_i(y_{ki} - y_{si}) \tag{3}$$

where y_i is per capita income in the ith republic;

y_{ki} is per capita income of kolkhozniki in the ith republic;

y_{si} is per capita income of state employees in the ith republic;

a_i is the share of kolkhozniki in the population of the ith republic.

Thus from (3) it follows that republican per capita income depends not only upon the social composition of the population but also upon the size of the income differential between the two social classes, and that the dependence is multiplicative. This complicates the calculation of variances and their decomposition. Employing the standard formulae, and making use of the relationship underlying (2), one can write the variance of (3) as

$$Var(y) = Var(y_s) + Var[a(y_k - y_s)] + 2Cov[y_s, a(y_k - y_s)]$$
$$Var[a(y_k - y_s)] = a^2 Var(y_k - y_s) + \overline{(y_k - y_s)}^2 Var(a) \tag{4}$$
$$+ \text{``interaction''}$$

The variance of republican income will be affected by any relationship between y_s and $a(y_k - y_s)$, through the covariance term, and also by relationships between a and $(y_k - y_s)$ through the "interaction" component in the second equation of (4).

The conjecture outlined at the beginning of this section can be interpreted as implying that both $Var(y_s)$ and the covariance term are small relative to $Var[a(y_k - y_s)]$, and possibly also that $\overline{(y_k - y_s)}^2 Var(a)$ is large relative to the other terms in the second equation of (4). It is in this sense that it can be said that variations in republican living standards will depend upon the social composition of the population. More generally, the decomposition of the variance in republican incomes, given in (4), will permit a further assessment of the impact of certain aspects of government policy on regional inequality. For example, one can examine the importance of the variability in state sector living standards relative to other factors, the consequences of the conversion program, the upgrading of kolkhozniki in relation to the rest of the population, and the interactions between them. Each of these can be identified with a particular term in (4). Let us call the variance component associated with $a(y_k - y_s)$ the social composition effect in its broad definition and that associated with a the social composition effect in its narrow definition. Let us also call the variance component associated with $(y_k - y_s)$ the income differential effect.

The relevant figures are given in table 7.3. Once again, two caveats are in order. First, the variances on which the table is based are unweighted—each republic is treated as a separate and equal observation. Second, figures are given for both total and personal income, but some doubt attaches to the estimates of personal income for the two social classes, especially in 1970. Thus, when the two indicators give rise to

Table 7.3
The Variance in Republican Income: Effects of Social Composition, 1960-70

	Total Income			Personal Income		
	1960	1965	1970	1960	1965	1970
Total variance (%)	100.0	100.0	100.0	100.0	100.0	100.0
State employee income	62.9	51.9	61.1	53.1	59.8	71.1
Relative difference	89.3	34.5	9.7	54.0	22.0	5.6
of which						
Share of kolkhozniki	7.1	1.4	2.0	4.5	1.3	0.2
Income difference	38.4	27.4	10.4	27.3	19.5	6.4
Interaction	43.8	5.7	−2.7	22.2	1.2	−1.1
Interaction between state employee income and difference	−52.3	13.6	29.2	−7.1	18.2	23.3

Note: Entries in table were derived by applying the formulae of equations (4) to data on republican incomes. Columns may not sum to totals because of rounding.

divergent explanations, one should regard that implied by total income as the more plausible.

The figures in table 7.3 demonstrate that the conjecture with which I began this section is incorrect, or at least grossly inadequate. While it is true that in 1960, social composition in the broad sense was the largest component in the decomposition of variance, $Var(y_s)$ was also substantial. By 1970, the proportion of the variance ascribable to differences in social composition had fallen to less than 10% of the total. Further, the proportion of the variance ascribable to social composition in the narrow sense was small in all three years and by the end of the decade was negligible. Finally, the figures suggest that interactions of one sort or another were important, particularly in 1960. Clearly, the relationship between disparity in living standards and social composition is a great deal more complex than indicated by my initial hypothesis.

Table 7.3 shows that in all three years, the variance in state employee incomes accounted for more than half the variance in republican incomes. The figures on personal income suggest that the contribution of this component increased throughout the decade; those for total income suggest that some gains were made up until 1965 but that the situation deteriorated thereafter. As indicated above, the latter explanation is more plausible. Thus, many of the sources of regional income differentiation in the USSR are to be found within the state sector.

The table also suggests that the nature of the relationship between social composition and state sector variations in income changed between 1960 and 1970. This is brought out by the sign and size of the covariance term in (4). It is worth spelling out what this interrelationship was, since because of the negativity of $(y_k - y_s)$, the interpretation of correlation coefficients can be confusing. In 1960, the figures suggest that there was a tendency for state sector incomes to be highest in those republics where either the share of kolkhozniki was high or the difference between kolkhoznik and state employee incomes was large, or both. In 1970, in contrast, state sector incomes were highest, in general, in those republics where $a(y_k - y_s)$ was small and negative, or even positive. A more precise idea of the strength of this relationship can be gained by converting the covariance into a correlation coefficient. The relevant figures are given in table 7.4. Thus in 1960 there was probably some significant negative relationship between the two variables; in 1965 they were apparently uncorrelated, and by 1970 there was almost certainly a significant positive correlation between them. (These relationships are inferred from the total income series.)

The negative relationship in 1960 is consistent with a situation in which the authorities concentrated on ensuring that a limited number of privileged workers in a modern sector enjoyed an adequate standard of living at

Table 7.4

Correlations between the Components of Republican Income, 1960-70

Correlation Coefficient between	Total Income			Personal Income		
	1960	1965	1970	1960	1965	1970
y_s and $a(y_k - y_s)$	−0.349	0.161	0.601	−0.066	0.251	0.665
a and $(y_k - y_s)$	−0.738	−0.714	−0.657	−0.614	−0.478	−0.507

Note: See text for an explanation of terms.

the expense of the mass of underprivileged and impoverished peasantry. The smaller the modern sector (the larger a) and the greater the disparity in living standards (the larger, negatively $y_k - y_s$), the higher the standard of living enjoyed by the urban working class (the higher y_s). Of course there are difficulties with this explanation (for instance, the identification of state employees with urban workers), but it is possible to suggest that it characterizes the Soviet system under Stalin. At least in the thirties and forties, legal, social, and economic controls were used to keep down real wages in agriculture and to retain an agricultural labor force of a sufficient size. At the same time, while urban living standards were very low, substantial monetary incentives were provided to encourage the acquisition of those skills deemed necessary for the state's industrialization program. Hence, some of those employed in heavy industry received high wages or salaries and thus enjoyed a relatively high standard of living. If this analysis is accepted, the figures in tables 7.3 and 7.4 suggest that the Stalinist relationships still existed in 1960. They also show that the fact that, in general, the modern sector was smallest in those republics where it was relatively best off implied that the variance in republican incomes was less than might have been inferred from the variances of the two components taken separately.

By 1970, apparently, the situation had changed. In that year state sector incomes were highest in those republics where the share of kolkhozniki was lowest, or where the incomes of kolkhozniki were closest to (or greater than) those of state employees. No longer, apparently, does the modern sector benefit at the expense of the peasantry; rather, the living standards of both classes move together. This is consistent with a situation in which the incomes of one class, say state employees, are determined by productivity and those of the other by the existence of a unified labor market. That is, where state employee income is high, income in agriculture (or at least in collectivized agriculture) is also high, since the transfer earnings of the peasants are high. But if transfer earnings are high, the proportion of the population engaged in agriculture (or, rather, the proportion belonging to collective farms) is low. In all of this, high and low should be interpreted as meaning high or low relative to the incomes of the other social class in the same republic. Thus according to this explanation, developments in the Soviet economy in the sixties led to the emergence of a unified labor market in each republic—although possibly not a general market for the country as a whole. While the connections are not spelled out explicitly, the most important of these developments was probably the conversion program, which removed the legal restrictions on the mobility of some of those with the lowest incomes.

The figures in table 7.3 suggest that, while increasing the efficiency of labor force allocation, this development contributed to an increase in interrepublican disparity in living standards. That is, in 1970, the variance in incomes was higher than it would have been if y_s and $a(y_k - y_s)$ were negatively correlated. In fact, some 30% of the variance in total incomes can be attributed to this interaction.

So far, the discussion has concentrated on the role of social composition in its broad sense in the determination of interrepublican income differentials. But the formal analysis showed that interactions between a and $(y_k - y_s)$ would also affect the extent of regional inequality. Table 7.3 shows that the contribution of both social composition, narrowly defined, and income differences declined over the decade. Thus the various Soviet republics apparently became more alike in social composition; there was a corresponding decline in the relative importance of class income differences. The first of these effects should be attributed to the conversion program and to the continuing shift from agricultural to nonagricultural occupations. The second was a consequence of the relative improvement in the situation of collective farmers, as well as of the conversion program.

These policy-induced changes in the relative deprivation of collective farmers appear to have been accompanied by internal changes in the relationship between the income differential and social composition. At least, the figures in table 7.3 record a substantial decline in the relative importance of the interaction between them. Because these two components enter republican income variance multiplicatively, the interaction term is not a simple covariance and cannot be used to derive a correlation coefficient. Indeed, there seems to be little connection between the sign and value of the interaction term and the appropriate correlation coefficient. This latter is given in table 7.4. From the table it is clear that in all three years a and $(y_k - y_s)$ were negatively correlated and that the correlation was substantial. The figures imply that the gap between kolkhoznik and state employee living standards was greatest in those republics where the share of collective farmers in the population was highest. They also indicate that there was very little change in the strength of this relationship over the decade. Whatever the interpretation placed upon this (and it might be thought to imply that the Stalinist development model was still valid), table 7.3 shows that by 1970 interactions between a and $(y_k - y_s)$ contributed little to the variance in republican incomes.

The figures in table 5.3 showed that between 1960 and 1970 there was virtually no change in the extent of regional inequality in the USSR, at least as measured by the coefficient of variation in per capita incomes. The analysis of this section shows that this apparent stability conceals significant changes in the nature of the underlying relationships. In 1960, the proportion of the variance attributable to variations in social composition, broadly defined, was substantial, but the relationship between state sector income and that of kolkhozniki, as modified by the share of kolkhozniki in the population, acted to mitigate its effects on regional inequality. In 1970, the inherent variability due to social composition was much less, but it was reinforced by a positive correlation with variations in state sector incomes. These developments are consistent with, if not a consequence of, the replacement of Stalinist dualism by a unified labor market. Thus it would seem that the modernization of the Soviet economy, increased monetization, and the elimination (or reduction) of artificial barriers on labor mobility have contributed to an increase in regional inequality. Or rather, that regional disparities in living standards were higher in 1970 than they would have been, given the average values of individual components, had the 1960 relationships between them persisted. This is something of a paradox, since these same policies appear to have led to a reduction in the differences between the standards of living of kolkhozniki and state employees and to a decline in interpersonal differentials.

7.5   THE VARIANCE IN REPUBLICAN INCOMES: DEMOGRAPHIC FACTORS

The analysis of the preceding section has shown that variations in the social composition of the population in the USSR can no longer explain the variation in republican incomes, if they ever could. The analysis of sections 7.2 and 7.3 showed that by and large the Soviet government succeeded in reducing disparity in earnings per person employed, and also that it had some success in reducing differences in per capita social consumption expenditures. But changes in the relationship between earnings and participation and the way in which social welfare programs were administered meant that the variance in per capita incomes increased in spite of these achievements. I conjectured that demographic factors may have been partly responsible for this failure. In this section I consider them in more detail.

The analysis of sections 7.2-7.4 was based largely on estimates   of

Table 7.5

The Variance of Per Capita Personal Income, Total Population, 1960-70

	Earnings per Capita	of which			Income from Other Sources	of which			
		Earnings per Employee	Participation Rate	Interaction		Transfers	Private, etc.	Interaction	Interaction, Wages, etc.
1960									
Mean (R)	256.0	700.3	0.364	—	145.5	53.5	92.1	—	—
CV (%)	24.3	16.8	13.2	—	30.6	31.9	45.8	—	—
% variance explained	52.0	24.8	15.2	12.0	26.6	3.9	23.9	-1.2	21.4
1965									
Mean (R)	366.5	957.4	0.383	—	168.0	76.9	91.1	—	—
CV (%)	20.8	10.4	16.6	—	26.8	31.0	44.3	—	—
% variance explained	52.5	13.3	33.6	5.6	18.3	5.2	14.7	-1.6	29.2
1970									
Mean (R)	507.1	1257.3	0.402	—	227.5	121.6	105.9	—	—
CV (%)	22.8	11.4	17.6	—	27.2	31.4	43.4	—	—
% variance explained	50.6	12.6	30.0	8.1	14.5	5.5	8.0	1.0	34.9

Note: Entries in the table were calculated by means of the formulae given in equations (2). Rows may not sum to totals because of rounding.

total per capita income. But for the population as a whole there exist reliable estimates of personal income, and since there are grounds for arguing that, because of valuation problems, total income is inferior to personal income as an indicator of republican living standards as perceived by the population, the analysis of this section is based on the latter. The relevant figures are given in table 7.5. In this table, earnings consist of payments for labor by collective farms and receipts from state employment; receipts from the financial system are included with those from other private activities. Transfer payments conform to the definitions of the preceding chapters, and participation rates are derived as the quotient of average annual employment in the state and cooperative sectors and republican populations as given in appendix A.

Before considering the impact of demographic factors on the variance of republican incomes explicitly, it is worth examining the implications of the analytical framework set out in section 7.1 for the explanation of the variance in republican standards of living. The figures in table 7.5 suggest that, in 1960, approximately half the variance in per capita personal income could be attributed to variations in per capita earnings. A further quarter was explained by the variance in other sources of income, and the balance by interactions between these two variables. This is similar to the picture shown in table 7.1. There was little change in the proportion of the variance in per capita personal income due to the variance in per capita earnings in 1965 or 1970; but the relative importance of "other sources" declined, while that of interactions increased. In this, too, the position was similar to that of state employees considered separately.

It should be noted, however, that in table 7.5, variations in participation rates in all three years were positively related to variations in earnings per person employed, although the relationship was never strong. Also, there was some decline in the inherent variability of earnings per person employed, and consequently in the proportion of the variance in personal income attributable to this source. And although on the average, per capita transfer payments more than doubled, the CV of this variable remained virtually constant. Thus the figures of table 7.5 confirm the analysis of tables 7.1 and 7.2; they indicate that the factors responsible for existing variations in republican living standards are variations in participation rates and the way in which the Soviet welfare state is administered.

In 1970, variations in participation rates were the largest single source of variations in per capita income. At the same time, it can be shown that there was no significant relationship between variations in these rates and variations in earnings per person employed; the simple correlation coefficient between these two variables in 1970 was 0.127

(in 1960, $r = 0.168$). If there is no relationship between earnings and employment, one can then ask on what participation depends.

In table 7.6 I give estimates of the proportion of the working age popu-

Table 7.6
Percent of Working Age Population in Employment, USSR and Republics, 1959, 1970

	1959	1970		1959	1970
USSR	82.8	88.3	Lithuania	88.1	91.2
RSFSR	81.9	88.8	Moldavia	97.7	94.2
Ukraine	83.8	88.8	Latvia	88.7	94.6
Byelorussia	93.5	90.2	Kirgizia	81.2	84.8
Uzbekistan	82.0	85.1	Tadjikistan	83.3	82.1
Kazakhstan	74.8	84.7	Armenia	76.2	81.5
Georgia	82.0	85.2	Turkmenistan	78.4	84.5
Azerbaijan	80.3	79.1	Estonia	89.4	94.8

Sources and Note: *Itogi*, 1970, vol. 2, table 3, and vol. 5, tables 4 and 10. The above figures are calculated as the quotient of the population in employment, *zanyatoye naseleniye*, and the population of working age, *naseleniye v trudosposobnom vozraste*. They therefore include those who, although not of working age, are employed, but they exclude those primarily engaged in subsidiary agriculture. This may explain the surprisingly high figures for republics like Byelorussia or Moldavia.

lation in employment for each of the Soviet republics for 1959 and for 1970, the two most recent census years. The figures are uniformly high, and there is little variation from republic to republic, particularly in 1970. Broken down by sex, it can be seen that most of the existing variation can be attributed to differences in female employment. In turn, it can be shown that there is a significant degree of correlation between female participation rates and the birth rate. (In 1970, the correlation between columns 5 and 8 of table 7.7 was 0.730, and that between columns 7 and 8 was 0.707.) Thus one may conjecture that high birth rates keep women out of the labor force, and that low participation rates are more a consequence of a large proportion of the population being too young to work (or being engaged in looking after these children) than of the fact that, at existing levels of wages, leisure appears more attractive than employment.

The figures in table 7.5 indicate that, in 1970, relatively little of the variance in personal income could be attributed directly to the variance in earnings per person employed or in transfer payments per capita, the elements most explicitly under the government's control. Rather, the major sources of variation were differences in participation rates and the correlation between earnings and other sources of income. Each of these contributes about a third of the total. One would suspect, therefore, that a further equalization in republican earnings or further increases in the

Table 7.7

Occupational Classification of the Female Population of Working Age, USSR and Republics, 1959, 1970 (%)

	1959				1970			
	Employed/ Stipend	Subsidiary Agriculture	Other	Birth Rate[a]	Employed/ Stipend	Subsidiary Agriculture	Other	Birth Rate[a]
USSR	74.9	7.4	17.7	24.9	89.1	2.5	8.4	17.4
RSFSR	76.1	7.1	16.8	23.2	90.7	1.7	7.6	14.6
Ukraine	74.9	7.3	17.8	20.5	89.2	3.5	7.3	15.2
Byelorussia	80.9	7.5	11.6	24.4	92.0	3.0	5.0	16.2
Uzbekistan	71.3	6.5	22.2	39.9	83.6	1.9	14.5	33.5
Kazakhstan	61.8	13.1	25.1	37.1	82.5	3.0	14.5	23.3
Georgia	66.7	10.2	23.1	24.7	81.9	4.2	13.9	19.2
Azerbaijan	67.3	6.2	26.5	42.6	72.3	4.9	22.8	29.2
Lithuania	72.6	8.8	18.6	22.5	90.4	6.4	3.2	17.6
Moldavia	84.7	4.6	10.7	29.3	95.6	3.1	1.3	19.4
Latvia	75.7	6.0	18.3	16.7	96.7	3.4	0.1	14.5
Kirgizia	70.7	8.9	20.4	36.9	83.7	2.8	13.5	30.5
Tadjikistan	70.3	11.3	18.4	33.5	75.7	10.5	13.8	34.7
Armenia	64.8	8.5	26.7	40.1	77.8	3.2	19.0	22.1
Turkmenistan	66.3	8.9	24.8	42.4	80.8	2.8	16.4	35.2
Estonia	76.9	2.4	20.7	16.6	97.7	2.1	0.2	15.8

Sources and Note: *Itogi, 1959*, USSR vol., table 32; *Itogi, 1970*, vol. 2, table 3; ibid, vol. 5, tables 4 and 11; *NK SSSR '70*, p. 51. As with the preceding table, it is possible that some of the women in employment are above working age; this seems probable in Latvia and Estonia at least.

a. Birth rates are measured in live births per thousand of the population.

value of transfer payments, with no change in the way that the social security system is administered, would result in little further reduction in regional inequality. Since the Soviet government cannot control the birth rate directly, what is required is the adoption of social welfare programs that provide more adequate compensation for the cost of bringing up children.

7.6   THE IMPACT OF THE SOVIET WELFARE STATE

So far in this chapter I have ignored the impact of direct taxation upon the living standards of the people of the various Soviet republics. In chapter 2 I showed that such taxes were, on the average, only a modest burden on the budget of the typical Soviet household. It is possible, though, that they affect families in the various republics differentially, that those in the better-off regions pay a disproportionate share of the tax bill. Certainly, if one is concerned with the redistributive impact of the Soviet budget, with the extent to which those in the less-developed parts of the country receive transfers (or free services) from the central authorities and thus enjoy a higher standard of living than they would without help, then it is necessary to consider costs as well as benefits. Although available data are not sufficient to permit the imputation of taxes to the two social classes separately in each of the republics, it is possible to estimate total direct (and indirect) tax receipts from individual republics and thus compute per capita tax payments. The relevant figures for the three benchmark years used in this study, together with an account of the assumptions used, are given in appendix F.

This tax data can be combined with the figures in appendix B to provide estimates of per capita disposable personal and total income for the years 1960, 1965, and 1970. As I have shown, average per capita tax payments in the USSR were modest in 1960 and remained more or less constant, relative to income, in the following decade. This was also true for individual republics. The use of disposable rather than nominal income does not change in any material way the analysis of rates of growth of republican living standards given above; it only entails a modest reduction in the levels attained in particular years. There is therefore no point in supplementing table 5.1 with a table showing the pattern of per capita disposable incomes in the various republics.

But the tax data do permit one to assess the impact of the Soviet budget upon the regional distribution of income more precisely, and it is with this issue that I shall be concerned here. To do this, one can start with the distribution of primary income defined earlier in the chapter. Primary income, as used here, is personal income net of transfer payments. It is the distribution generated by the production sector of the economy (including incomes from the supply of those services which Soviet statisticians assign to the nonproductive sphere). This can be thought of as the raw distribution of income that the Soviet authorities may wish to modify through budgetary transactions. In particular, they may wish to supplement the incomes of the disadvantaged (either persons or regions) through the provision of transfer payments or free services; and they may wish to finance a part or all of these transactions through taxes on the more affluent (again, either persons or regions). So long as it remains impossible to compile the BMIEP for different income classes, it is difficult to explore the redistributive impact of the budget on persons. But the tax and social expenditure data that are available permit one to study its regional (or rather its republican) impact.

In point of fact, one can compute three phases of redistribution. First, one can examine the effects of direct taxes and transfers, that is, one can compare the variance in primary income with the variance in disposable personal income. Second, one can include the contribution of free and subsidized services, the so-called social wage. Here one contrasts the variance of primary income with that of disposable total income. Finally, one can adjust for republican differences in the incidence of indirect taxes—explicitly, the turnover tax.

It is unusual to include indirect taxes in the study of income distribution. But the reason why they are normally excluded is that in most cases there is no information about the amounts paid by persons with different levels of income. This, of course, does not apply to the study of regional income distribution. Further, the Soviet government has traditionally raised a significant proportion of its budgetary revenue through the turnover tax, and its exclusion would therefore lead to a substantial bias in one's conclusions.

But the turnover tax is not precisely analogous to the sales taxes levied by governments in market economies. One function of the tax is to divorce the set of enterprise wholesale prices (those received by manufacturers) from industrial wholesale and retail prices (paid by retail trade establishments and the consuming public). In this way, Soviet planners partially insulate producers from the pressure of supply and demand. As a result, tax schedules are very detailed, listing specific ruble taxes for thousands of individual commodities; in certain cases, the same commodity, produced by different enterprises, carries different rates of tax. Soviet economists argue that the turnover tax is not a tax like that levied in capitalist economies, but a vehicle through which a socialist government collects and redistributes part of the surplus product produced in the economy. And while one need not accept the Marxist analytical framework, it is true that the turnover tax serves to collect some of the economic rents accruing, for example, to enterprises in favored locations. At the same time, it is possible (or even probable) that tax rates on better-quality goods or on commodities more commonly bought by the relatively affluent are higher than those on staples or utilitarian lines. This has not always been the case; under Stalin, for example, the tax on bread was particularly heavy. At the present time, however, the structure of tax rates may contain some built-in redistributive effect. In any case, I show the consequences of including turnover taxes in the figures given below, but in the light of these comments, the results should be interpreted with caution.

If the Soviet budget acts to redistribute income from the more affluent to the less affluent republics, then one would observe that net receipts from social consumption expenditure (that is, for example, transfer payments less direct taxes), are negatively correlated with primary income. The larger per capita primary income, the lower should be net receipts; indeed, it is possible that above a certain income, net receipts will be negative. Further, if the system is progressive, one would expect the relationship to be nonlinear.

To test for the redistributive effect of the budget, the three concepts of net receipts described above were calculated on a per capita basis for each of the Soviet republics for the years 1960, 1965, and 1970 and were then regressed against per capita primary income. The results are given in table 7.8. To repeat, if the budget has a positive redistributive effect, the coefficient on primary income should be negative. It will be seen that only when turnover taxes are included is this the case. Also, on the basis of the scatter diagrams, it is possible that this relationship was nonlinear, particularly in 1970 and perhaps in 1965. But only a linear functional form was tried.

The fit is not particularly good, but the results in table 7.8 suggest the existence of a definite relationship between net social benefits, however defined, and primary income. Further, when only direct taxes are considered, the relationship is such that those with the highest primary incomes tend to receive most from the state budget; that is, far from redistributing income from rich to poor republics, the budget redistributes from the poorer to the richer. If anything, then, the net effect of the Soviet welfare state, as conventionally defined, is to accentuate regional inequality.

It is only when one takes account of indirect taxation, when one includes the turnover tax with income tax and local taxes, that the budget exhibits positive redistributional effects. (This conclusion ignores the regional impact of budgetary expenditure on investment and productive activities.) The results in table 7.8 also suggest that the redistributional system became more liberal between 1960 and 1970. From the figures, it can be calculated that in 1960 net total income, allowing for indirect taxes, would be lower than primary income in any republic with a per capita primary

Table 7.8
The Impact of the Soviet Budget: Regression Results

Dependent Variable	Intercept	Slope	R^2
1960			
Net transfers	−1.2615	+0.0768	0.3836
(cash transfers less direct taxes)	(0.12)	(2.73)	
Net social welfare benefits	29.3746	+0.1711	0.5484
(social consumption less direct taxes)	(1.81)	(3.82)	
Net benefits less turnover tax	23.1669	−0.1736	0.4827
	(1.23)	(3.34)	
1965			
Net transfers	−3.2032	+0.0979	0.4604
	(0.22)	(3.20)	
Net social welfare benefits	37.1840	+0.2104	0.6271
	(1.68)	(4.50)	
Net benefits less turnover tax	88.1956	−0.2205	0.6435
	(3.93)	(4.66)	
1970			
Net transfers	−6.9245	+0.1168	0.6203
	(0.41)	(4.42)	
Net social welfare benefits	48.8469	+0.2322	0.7753
	(2.12)	(6.43)	
Net benefits less turnover tax	97.0163	−0.1422	0.4288
	(3.20)	(3.00)	

Note: T-statistics in parentheses.

income of 133.4 rubles a year or more. This is only 34.7% of per capita primary income for the USSR as a whole in that year, and in fact, there were no republics with a primary income as low as this. Thus the net effect of the Soviet budget was to lower incomes in all republics, including the poorest, although, of course, those with the highest incomes contributed most.

Similar calculations show that in 1965, net receipts were negative in all republics with a per capita primary income of more than 400 rubles a year, 80.6% of the USSR average.[4] This is certainly more liberal than the position in 1960, but it should be realized that according to the first equation for 1965 in the table, a primary income of 400 rubles a year was associated with a net personal income of only 36 rubles a month, about 70% of the official poverty line. Thus in 1965 even poor republics were still making a net contribution to the Soviet budget.

In 1970, the minimum per capita primary income at which the net impact of budgetary transactions became negative, according to the regression equation, was 682.25 rubles a year, or 102.7% of average per capita primary income in the USSR as a whole. According to calculations, this is equivalent to a net personal income of 63 rubles a month. Thus only by 1970 did a majority of the Soviet republics (and possibly their populations, too) receive more from the Soviet budget than they contributed. It is only at the end of the period under study that the system appears to have developed a positive distributional stance.

In previous chapters I have used the coefficient of variation to measure the extent of regional inequality, or rather the extent of interrepublican disparity, in income in the USSR. In table 7.9 I give estimates of the value of this coefficient for primary income and for each of the disposable income

Table 7.9
Regional Inequality and the Budget: Coefficients of Variation (%)

	Unweighted			Weighted		
	1960	1965	1970	1960	1965	1970
Primary income	20.7	18.9	21.2	11.1	9.9	11.4
Net personal income	20.9	19.1	21.5	12.9	10.3	12.7
Net total income	19.5	17.8	20.0	10.8	9.9	12.0
Net total income less T-tax	19.5	15.9	18.3	9.8	9.1	10.6

concepts described above, in both weighted and unweighted form, for all three years under review. The weights used are the population shares of the individual republics. Although the unweighted coefficients are uniformly higher than the weighted ones (by a factor of two), the differences between individual components in each series are very similar.

The figures show three things that should have become familiar from the previous discussion. First, they show that in all three years, disparities in disposable personal income were at least as great as those in primary income. This was the conclusion reached above on the basis of the gross estimates. They also show that disparities in disposable total income were marginally less than those in personal income; the difference was most significant in 1965 and in that year amounted to some 4 to 6%. This again was shown by the gross figures. In fact, the coefficient of variation in total disposable income was very similar to that of primary income, and thus one again reaches the conclusion that the measures normally included in a government's fiscal armory did not reduce regional income inequality in the USSR. Finally, table 7.9 shows that measured inequality declined between 1960 and 1965, only to increase to its former level by

1970. Since this decline also occurred in primary income, it cannot be attributed to the operation of the Soviet welfare state. Previous evidence suggests it was not caused by the operation of the government's wages policy either. It is not clear to what it can be attributed.

Table 7.9 also provides a measure of the impact of the state budget, including turnover tax, on the scale of regional inequality. In this respect, the results are a little surprising. Using the weighted series, one can calculate that the Soviet budget reduced inequality (or rather the coefficient of variation) by some 12% in 1960, by 8% in 1965, and by the same amount or a little less in 1970. Thus the more liberal system described above does not seem to have been more effective in reducing disparity in living standards than the one in force at the beginning of the sixties. The conclusion to be drawn from the unweighted series is slightly different. In 1960 the budget reduced measured inequality by about 6%, in 1965 by almost 15%, and in 1970 by 14%. On this basis, there was some definite improvement between 1960 and 1965, but more recent developments have not been effective.

7.7   CONCLUSION

The discussion of regional disparity in living standards in this and the preceding two chapters started from the presumption that in the late fifties the Soviet authorities believed that interrepublican income differentials were excessive and that in the subsequent ten or fifteen years (up to 1970) they tried to reduce them. The figures presented here suggest that income differences in 1960 were substantial, but they also suggest that there has been no reduction in inequality since then. This is true, irrespective of the income concept used, and is as true of state employees as it is of kolkhozniki. The analysis has shown that while all republics and both social classes have enjoyed substantial increases in income, there appears to exist a relatively stable hierarchy of republics, and the government has been unable, or unwilling, to close the gaps between them.

The period since 1960 has, however, been marked by a number of significant changes in policy, some of which have already been described and others which will be discussed in subsequent chapters, and these have had a considerable impact on the structure of personal and total income in the different republics. Even if these policies were not introduced primarily to bring about a reduction in regional inequality, it is the case that the apparent stagnation described above is accidental and perhaps unfortunate. One might have expected that wage reorganization, the conversion of kolkhozy into state farms, the continuing decline in agricultural employment, the extension of the social security system to the collectivized peasantry, and so on would have had some impact upon regional income disparity. And, in fact, they did. The analysis presented here suggests that the sources of regional inequality have changed over the decade.

In 1960, interrepublican differentials could be attributed to differences in earnings per person employed in both the collective farm and state sectors, to differences in social composition, and to differences in entitlement to various social insurance and social welfare benefits. But because of the way in which the system was articulated, perhaps because it still conformed to a Stalinist development model, overall disparity was not as great as implied by the variances in individual components. There was some measure of compensation in the system; republics scoring highly on one indicator scored low on another.

Over the decade the Soviet government reduced the variance in earnings per person employed in both sectors, reduced the difference between the earnings of kolkhozniki and state employees, and increased the average value of social welfare benefits. By 1970, differences in social composition had little direct influence on the extent of regional inequality. Also, the figures suggest that there is little scope for a further reduction in the variance in republican earnings per person employed. Thus one may conclude that wage policy has been reasonably successful.

But this success has been bought at a cost. Perhaps as a consequence of the introduction of a unified labor market for collective farmers and state employees, there is now greater coherence between different types of earnings and between earnings and private sources of income. Further, because the Soviet social insurance system as it developed under Stalin was tied so closely to wages, the rise in the average value of benefits and the extension of the system to more and more of the population (either through the conversion program or to kolkhozniki directly) has tended to reinforce the distribution of income generated in the production sector. The structure of direct taxes has not offset this. This conclusion applies explicitly only to interrepublican differences in income, but I would suspect that the net impact of the Soviet budget upon interpersonal differences is similar, at least for those in employment and their dependents.

Differences in demographic structure, the very high birth rates in Central Asia, and possibly the absence of adequate preschool child care facilities in these republics have meant that the variance in earnings per capita is much greater than in earnings per person employed. In the last analysis, it is differences in participation rates that, together with the coherence described in the previous paragraph, are responsible for maintaining regional inequality in the USSR at the levels of 1960.

Since the Soviet government cannot exercise substantial control over the birth rate in the short run, this implies that reductions in regional inequality will require modification of the existing social welfare system, a partial divorce of benefits from employment or wages, and perhaps a change in the priorities attached to individual programs. It also suggests the need for a reform of the tax system. In this respect, the analysis of regional inequality agrees with the discussion of interpersonal differentials and poverty in chapters 3 and 4. There, too, the support of dependents, particularly children, was shown to be associated with deprivation, and the system of social welfare benefits was found to be inadequate.

There is some indication that the Soviet government also realizes this, and in the seventies it has embarked upon a program of reform. There is, however, no indication that it has decided to adopt any new approach to the structure of direct taxes. These questions will be explored further in chapter 11, after I have described how the Soviet authorities have succeeded in modifying the structure of earnings differentials through their wage policies.

8

Wage Determination in the Soviet Union

THE EVIDENCE PRODUCED in earlier chapters permits certain conclusions about changes in the level and distribution of economic welfare of the Soviet population in the last quarter-century. It shows that average per capita income has risen substantially since the death of Stalin and that this rise has been accompanied by some reduction in inequality. The analysis of chapter 2 shows that differences in the standard of living of kolkhozniki and state employees were less marked in 1970 than in 1960—and, *a fortiori*, much less marked than in 1953. There was also a decline in interpersonal income differentials between 1958 and 1967, at least as measured by the decile coefficient. And if the analysis of chapters 5-7 does not reveal any decline in interrepublican disparity in living standards, it does suggest that the sources of disparity changed between 1960 and 1970, that the evolution of Soviet society had a considerable impact upon the way in which republican incomes were generated.

Consideration of the powers possessed by the Soviet government, the role it plays in the organization of economic activity, suggests that it has at its disposal two broad sets of instruments with which to influence, if not determine, popular living standards. First, there is its control over wages and salaries, which derives at least in part from its position as major employer. It is important to realize that the government can specify only wage rates and salary scales (directly); the determination of earnings and hence of income will depend upon the wage rates specified, but also upon the allocation of labor between industries and occupations and the scale and incidence of bonus payments over which the central government exercises at best only partial control.

The second set of instruments at the government's disposal includes the social security system, the pattern and level of social consumption expenditure, and direct taxation. Here again, while the central authorities can and do exercise fairly detailed control over conditions of entitlement, formulae for calculating benefits and liabilities, and the specific programs adopted, levels of total expenditure and hence impact upon the distribution of income are also affected by the characteristics of the population and the way that these change. (And, presumably, by the extent to which various benefits are taken up; but on this there is no information. If Western experience is anything to go by, however, variation between programs may be substantial.)

There are other sources of income for many Soviet households and therefore a third set of instruments that the Soviet authorities can use to influence average living standards and the degree of inequality. That is, many households derive income from private subsidiary economic activity and the financial system. Incomes from these sources are largest in peasant households, and thus the scope for using such instruments to influence state employee incomes is limited. Of course, in a sense, the fact that nonemployment incomes form so small a part of the disposable income of Soviet state employee households is a consequence of the fact that the authorities have already adopted policies under this heading. The decision to nationalize the means of production and to prohibit the private ownership of (large accumulations of) private capital must have had a not insignificant impact upon the distribution of income.

It is not yet possible to model formally the connection between the distribution of incomes and the distribution of earnings, but earnings are a substantial part of the incomes of Soviet households—especially those of state employees—and it seems reasonable to assume that changes in the level and structure of earnings will have a significant impact upon disparity in living standards. Indeed, the analysis of chapters 2 and 6 implies that between 1960 and 1970, most of the growth in the incomes of state employees can be attributed to the growth in earnings. The analysis of chapter 6 also suggests that over the same period there was a decline in the variance of earnings per person employed (or its coefficient of variation), and thus in one sort of economic inequality. Thus an analysis of Soviet policy towards wages and salaries and their distribution may be particularly important in an investigation of how the relative inequality in living standards in the USSR has changed.

There is a further reason for studying the administration of wage policy and the institutions for wage determination in the Soviet Union. Figures produced below show that between 1956 and 1973 average earnings in the state sector increased by about 84%; over the same period there was a 30% reduction in inequality as measured by the decile ratio. This represents substantial change in the level and distribution of earnings, and the implied changes in occupational differentials appear to have been achieved without significant overt inflation. The Schroeder and Severin cost-of-living index increased at an average annual rate of only 1.2% over the period—far less than in most other industrialized countries.[1] What is suggested by this is that the Soviet institutional framework and post-

Stalin wage and salary policies have been relatively successful at reconciling the conflicts between the allocative and distributive functions of wages. Since that is a conflict that has caused problems for the governments of many industrial nations in recent years, a study of the Soviet experience in formulating and administering wage and salary policy may be of value not only to those concerned with changes in living standards and inequality in the USSR but also to many who have no direct interest in Soviet affairs.

Since 1955-57 the Soviet government has pursued a more active policy on wages and salaries than in the preceding quarter-century, or at least it has pursued a policy in which central control and coordination are more evident. But Soviet views on the proper role and objectives of wage policy, Soviet theories of occupational differentials, and the specific policy measures introduced are difficult to reconcile with the record of Soviet achievement in the area of earnings growth and inequality. It is not clear how far success in these fields can be ascribed to policy; it is at least possible that the growth of earnings and the reduction of differences in earnings can be attributed to the evolution of the Soviet labor market and the way in which the population of working age has changed since the death of Stalin.

In the analysis here I will first concentrate on Soviet views of wage policy, theories of wage differentiation, and policies adopted. In chapters 9 and 10 I will consider a variety of statistical evidence about the level and structure of earnings. The purpose of this organization is two-fold. First, pay scales in the USSR have a number of features not found in those of other (market) economies. The discussion of policy and evidences of inequality is made simpler if one has some idea of these special characteristics. Since they derive, at least in principle, from the Soviet (Marxist) theory of occupational differentials, an account of Soviet theorizing is required. Certain features of the institutional control of wage policy in the USSR also derive from these theories, an added justification for an account of recent Soviet work. Second, the basic objective of this study is to ascertain the extent to which the growth of earnings (and reductions in earnings inequality) can be ascribed to the operation of Soviet policy. At the risk of committing *post-hoc-ergo-propter-hoc* fallacies, it will be assumed that changes in average earnings or their dispersion that follow the introduction of specific policy measures can be attributed to the effects of those measures. It is therefore desirable to have a chronological account of policy against which the statistical evidence can be compared.

Before embarking on this account of Soviet views of the role of wage policy, Soviet theories of wages and wage differentials, and the history of wage policy since about 1955, it is desirable to have some framework of analysis against which to assess the adequacy of Soviet formulations and in terms of which the complexity of wage determination can be made apparent. This is provided in section 8.1. Section 8.2 contains a description of recent Soviet views on the same topic; it shows that, for all the difference in ideology and in the analytical concepts used in the two approaches, there is substantial agreement on the nature of the problems to be solved by wage policy and on the constraints under which it must be formulated. Section 8.3 provides a brief account of current Soviet theories on occupational differentials and shows how these can be used to explain (if they do not determine) specific features of Soviet wage structures, at least in industry. And finally, section 8.4 gives a historical account of major innovations in the administration of wages in the USSR since 1955, showing how far it can be regarded as a consistent attempt to realize the theoretical principles set out in preceding sections, or on the contrary, the extent to which individual measures can be attributed to other factors.

8.1   THE ECONOMIC FUNCTIONS OF WAGES[2]

The role of wages is much the same in a market economy and in a planned economy of the Soviet type, that is, a planned economy with relatively free markets for labor and consumer goods. In both, earnings differentials are used to allocate labor between occupations and industries, and in both, earnings differentials influence the distribution of income between households and thus affect differences between individual living standards. It is this dual function of wages that creates the need for a government wage policy and at the same time generates constraints on government policy.

When a choice must be made between techniques to use with a limited supply of primary resources, decisions to employ factors in particular combinations to produce specific commodities impose a cost on society, a cost equal to the value of the commodities that might have been produced if the resources had been otherwise employed. From this set of so-called opportunity costs, economists generate shadow prices of resources. In a decentralized (market) system, it is argued that these shadow prices should be paid by those who make production decisions. In the absence of such signals, the efficient allocation of resources will be, if not impossible, at least only fortuitous. The calculation of shadow prices can also provide a valuable aid in the determination of efficient allocations of resources in a centralized decision-making system. But if there exists an alternative allocational mechanism, it will be possible to divorce the rewards distributed to the owners of particular resources from this set of shadow prices.

Where a relatively free labor market exists, it is assumed that the individual's decision about whether to work, where to work, and what to do are affected by wages. Unless the supply of labor to particular occupations or industries can be fixed or otherwise controlled, changes in relative wages will affect their supply of labor. But people do not seek money for its own sake; they are interested in what can be bought in the form of goods and services. Wages are no more than a synthetic indicator of the real consumption possibilities associated with a job, and it is ultimately these possibilities that determine occupational choice. It is this link between wages and consumption that restricts the divorcing of allocation from distribution. People are induced to undertake particular activities by the belief that the consumption possibilities associated with the wages they will receive will more than compensate them for the disutility of the job itself. Thus "brownie points" will not do. The existence of a free labor market implies that it is not possible to use the shadow price system to influence the decisions of producing enterprises (by having them pay notional wages to the state, for example) while distributing income to individuals on some other principle—according to need, for instance.[3]

The fact that wages determine consumption and wage differentials determine the allocation of labor imposes the first set of constraints upon the administration of wage policy. To avoid inflationary pressure, the total value of wages paid out (together with the receipts accruing to the owners of other factors) must correspond to the value of goods and services available for consumption, after allowing for savings decisions. Yet the possibility of changes in technology or tastes implies that there should be a certain degree of flexibility in occupational differentials. It is the task of government policy or the institutional framework to reconcile the requirements of a responsive wage determination system with those of macroeconomic equilibrium. (And it is to be suspected that rigidities in the systems that exist in such countries as Britain are responsible for some of the very high rates of inflation in recent years.)

But as pointed out above, wage differentials determine not only the allocation of labor but also, in large measure, the distribution of income. Government policy must therefore also take into account popular ideas of social justice. Differentials should not only generate an appropriate allocation of labor, but should also be seen to be fair. In principle, this consideration does not impose further constraints on wages policy. If differentials are just sufficient to compensate for the unpleasantness of the labor associated with certain activities, they should also be "fair." But in practice, a person's opinions about the relative attractiveness of various jobs and the "justice" of particular earnings differentials may be inconsistent, and furthermore, people may disagree among themselves. All of this means that the reconciliation of economic efficiency with ethical considerations is likely to be one of the most difficult tasks in the administration of wage policy.

The argument outlined above suggests that *some* set of earnings differentials will be necessary in both a planned and a market economy, to achieve an efficient allocation of resources, unless recourse is made to the outright direction of labor. To deny it would involve asserting that occupational choices are made independently of relative wages. But the argument does not suggest that the *same* set of differentials will be required in all economic systems. Nor does it suggest that existing differentials are either right or necessary. No reason has yet been advanced for claiming that the set of differentials that exists in Britain today, for example, or that which existed in the USSR in the mid fifties, is either equitable or conducive to economic efficiency.

Differences in the disutility of the labor associated with particular occupations or industries are only one source of earnings disparity in any existing system. Wage differentials may also be the result of differences in training costs, restrictions on entry into the occupation imposed by trade unions or professional associations, or prejudice in the educational system and job-selection procedures. This whole complex of factors is usually described by economists as giving rise to noncompeting groups in the labor market. A different set of social and political institutions, differences in political ideology and social mores, may well result in a different structure of noncompeting groups and hence in differences in the structure of earnings. It is also the case that abilities, tastes, and preferences may be affected by cultural traditions, and these in turn influence the disutility of labor associated with particular activities. Thus, a priori, one would expect that "efficient" sets of occupational differentials might differ between market and planned economies, between countries, and between periods. What is appropriate for Britain or the USA may well not suit the USSR; what is right in the thirties may be inadequate today.

Would one expect the scale of disparities in earnings to be greater under capitalism or socialism, in a planned or a market economy? Bergson refers to an argument, often used by socialists, that suggests there would be less inequality under socialism. Pecuniary reward is not the only determinant of occupational choice; power, prestige, and social obligation are not negligible motives under capitalism, and it is claimed that they will play a greater role under socialism:

> The common ownership of the means of production, the knowledge that every value created by the worker "ultimately redounds to the benefit of himself, his own kind and class" has been presented specifically as the basis for far-reaching changes in the worker's attitude towards labor. This view assumes, perhaps, a greater plasticity in human nature than is justified, but to the extent that workers can be stimulated by non-pecuniary incentives, the pecuniary differentials prevailing under socialism may be reduced (Bergson, 1944, p. 16).

On the other hand, two Soviet labor economists have recently argued the opposite. Under socialism, they suggest, wage differentials are determined by productivity differences; under capitalism they are the result of differences in the costs of reproducing labor of different skills. Because of exploitation, cost differences are less than productivity differences. Therefore, *ceteris paribus*, one would expect occupational differentials to be greater in a socialist system (Rabkina and Rimashevskaya, 1972, pp. 26-30). I suspect that no clear-cut answer to the question exists on theoretical grounds. Neither theory nor comparison can provide standards against which the adequacy of existing Soviet differentials can be judged.

The objectives of wage policy, then, are threefold: to maintain sufficient control over the growth of wages to ensure macroeconomic equilibrium, to permit or encourage changes in differentials that are needed to bring about an efficient allocation of labor, and to break down those restrictions on the supply of labor that give rise to noncompeting groups and "unjustified" disparities in earnings. It is widely believed that such restrictions exert a considerable influence upon the distribution of earnings in many countries, and that if the political authorities were willing and able to mount a concerted attack upon them, it would be possible to bring about a considerable reduction in earnings inequality—and hence in the inequality of incomes—without affecting the allocation of labor between occupations. A belief that wage policy was being used to increase social justice would make the government's control over wages politically more acceptable.

These three aspects of wage policy are relevant in all economies in which a relatively free labor market exists; thus they should apply to the Soviet Union. In the next section I will explore the extent to which they have influenced Soviet attitudes towards wages and the proper scope of government policy.

8.2 WAGE POLICY IN A PLANNED ECONOMY: SOVIET VIEWS

It is sometimes assumed in the West that socialism is about equality, and it is true that indignation with extreme differences in wealth and income and the belief that these are caused by exploitation based on the private ownership of productive capital can go far in explaining the growth of the socialist movement in the past century. But the persistence of earnings inequality under socialism is well-established Marxist doctrine.

Marx himself distinguished between socialism and communism, although he did not use those terms.[4] Under communism there is an abundance of material goods, and individuals are willing to work irrespective of material rewards. Only under communism will it be possible for "society to inscribe upon its banners: From each according to his ability, to each according to his need." Only under communism will true equality be possible. Under socialism, material goods are still scarce, and people work to acquire the wherewithal for consumption. Under socialism, Marx argued, wages should be proportional to labor. Soviet economists refer to this as the socialist distribution principle: From each according to his ability, to each according to his labor.

The socialist distribution principle implies the persistence of earnings differentials, because although nationalization of the means of production puts an end to exploitation and imposes upon all the same obligation to work, it does not, of itself, bring about an equalization of labor. Individuals are still endowed with different abilities and skills, and Marx makes it clear that they should be taken into account in determining relative wages.

These ideas from Marxist thought form the basis of all Soviet theorizing about wages and wage differentials, but as policies have changed, so have they been reinterpreted. They were used by Stalin, after a fashion, to justify his attack on egalitarianism in the trade unions in the early thirties. They have also been used to support the new approach to wage determination that has emerged since the mid fifties. Although the terms and concepts may sound strange to Western economists, the problems and ideas involved are like those set out in the last section. First, it is argued that the problem of macro-balance, the problem of determining the appropriate size for the "wage fund" and ensuring that it corresponds to the "volume of goods essential for the reproduction of labor power," is resolved by the plan. The function of wage policy is the "establishment of the proportions in which the fund designated by society for personal consumption is divided among all those who participate in production. . . . Given the wage fund, the shares of individual producers are determined by the law of distribution according to labor and only by that law" (Rabkina and Rimashevskaya, 1972, p. 15).

Thus the socialist distribution principle has been used to delineate a sphere for wages and to separate questions of wage determination from those of income distribution. Wage determination, it is asserted, should be governed primarily by the needs of labor allocation rather than by more general considerations of poverty and equality. Several authors quote with approval a comment by Lenin that "wages should be connected only with production and that all that bears the stamp [nosit kharakter] of social security should in no way be connected with wages" (Sukharevskii, 1968, p. 271; Rabkina and Rimashevskaya, 1972, p. 28; these comments are significant because Sukharevskii's occurs in an official publication of the State Committee on Labor and Wages and because Rimashevskaya is employed at NIIT). The implication is that if the pattern of differentials required to achieve a particular allocation of labor results in a distribution of income that is unsatisfactory in one way or another, the situation should be alleviated, if at all, by the social security system and not by adjustment of wage differentials. The citation of Lenin here should be seen as an attempt to gain authority for this particular view. Lenin's authority has also been used to support the existence of a certain degree of differentiation. The following passage from an early decree on wages, signed by Lenin, has been quoted or referred to on several occasions: ". . . in determining wage scales for workers with different skills, for clerical staff, for technical and higher administrative personnel, all thought of equalization [*uravnitelnost*] must be rejected" (Kapustin, 1974, p. 249; Sukharevskii, 1974, p. 204; the passage is taken from the Basic Decree on the Tariff Question (1921), *Sobraniye ukazov RSFSR* 1921, no. 67, p. 513).

Soviet authors, particularly those associated with NIIT, not only argue that wage policy should be concerned primarily with the allocative function of wages, but they also stress the state's restricted freedom of action: ". . . wage differentials in the broadest sense of the term are the result of the structure of labor at the disposal of a socialist society. At any given time, their scale is objectively determined" (Rabkina and Rimashevskaya, 1972, p. 18; Kapustin, 1968, p. 309). They are critical of the fact that

> some economists, both theoretical and applied, still have the deeply mistaken belief that it is possible to regulate wage differentiation arbitrarily [*proizvolno*; and here they mean earnings, and not only wage rates or salary scales]. In spite of the facts and contemporary views about the objective character of economic laws, they claim that the state, or the planners, can give to the distribution of earnings any form they choose, determining its parameters at their own discretion. Such a view of things has been and remains the cause of many errors in the construction of models or the making of forecasts (Rabkina and Rimashevskaya, 1972, p. 208).

Of course in an economy like that of the USSR, where wage rates and salary scales are centrally determined, the authorities are *able* to impose any rate structure they please, and surely economists like Kapustin, Rabkina, and Rimashevskaya realize this. But in emphasizing the objective determinants of wages, they are asserting that government policy is not made in a vacuum, that it is constrained by the real economic system and by interaction with other economic agents. If the government selects the "right" set of differentials, it will facilitate the rational use of labor and encourage the acquisition of appropriate skills. If it chooses a "wrong" set, it will affect labor productivity adversely and may reduce the quality of output. Wrong differentials will encourage labor turnover, result in shortages of particular skills, and lead to violations of the state's wage policy as enterprise managers attempt to attract the labor they require. This is the sense in which differentials are objectively determined.

The objective determination of the distribution of earnings does not imply, however, that there is no scope for an active wage policy. Soviet economists argue that the government must identify changes in the structure of the labor force and adjust wage scales accordingly; it may also design pay scales that will encourage the acquisition of particular skills, or otherwise seek to influence changes in the structure of the labor force. But it does mean that wage differentials should not be arbitrarily increased or reduced, that the distribution of earnings cannot be specified at will in the pursuit of some arbitrarily chosen standard of social justice.

The views of Soviet labor economists on the role and scope of wage policy, as outlined so far, appear somewhat conservative. It is suggested that the government possesses only limited freedom to affect differentials, and that the primary aim of policies in this area should be to establish those differentials that will secure an efficient allocation of labor and provide adequate incentives for the further acquisition of skills. But it has also been suggested that the differentials built into the wage and salary scales of the thirties were excessive in the conditions of the fifties and sixties. Technological progress, increased mechanization, and a better-educated labor force have resulted in greater uniformity in skill; this change should be reflected in a contraction of occupational differentials. The particular arguments used in developing this point depend upon the Marxist definition of skilled labor and its relationship to unskilled or simple labor; but the proposition itself has served to justify a reduction in earnings differentials in the economy as a whole and in industry in particular (Batkaev and Markov, 1964, pp. 32 ff.; Kirsch, 1972, pp. 98 ff.).

These general views about the status of wage policy in a planned economy have been complemented by more explicit ideas about desirable features of wage and salary structures. The socialist distribution principle has been interpreted to imply "equal pay for equal work" (Sukharevskii, 1968, p. 284). This, and more particularly its contrary, "unequal pay for unequal work," have been used as an ethical justification for the existence of occupational differentials, although very little attempt has been made to explain the justice of specific disparities in earnings. Rather, allusion is made in general terms to Marxist principles of measuring differences in the complexity of labor and to Marx's assertion that wages should correspond to the quantity and quality of labor supplied.

More important, "equal pay for equal work" has been held to justify the extensive rationalization of wage scales within industries and plants and also the extensive use of the principle of comparability and job evaluation in the determination of wage relativities. It is asserted implicitly that an efficient allocation of labor requires that equal quantities of work should be paid the same, irrespective of the industry or region in which the work is undertaken. It is thus necessary to devise methods for measuring work that can be applied generally and also to ensure that such work is paid at the same rate throughout the economy. The first of these requirements is provided by Soviet wage theory and the second by the existence of a centralized body responsible for wage administration.

This discussion indicates, I believe, that Soviet labor economists are aware of the constraints on wage policy set out in the previous section. It also suggests, perhaps, that since the mid fifties, policy has been dominated by a desire to improve the efficiency of the Soviet labor market, that allocative considerations have been more important than distributional ones. But I will argue below that this interpretation is too simple, that an examination of the measures adopted reveals that on some occasions wage policy has been used to mitigate poverty at the expense of labor market efficiency. Finally, the above discussion suggests that Soviet wage policy has been affected by a desire to eliminate irrational and unjustified differentials. Again, empirical analysis raises questions about the vigor with which the Soviet government has been prepared to attack the vested interests of certain groups of workers, but on a formal level at least, policy appears to have been directed toward an increased equity in earnings distribution.

The Soviet theory of wage differentials clearly occupies a central position in the administration of wage policy. It also explains certain peculiar features of the pay scales used in the USSR. This theory is set out in the next section, before we turn to a review of wage policy since 1955.

8.3   THE SOVIET THEORY OF OCCUPATIONAL DIFFERENTIALS

In Soviet theory, the formulation of an efficient and equitable wage structure involves two steps: first, the determination of the amount of labor involved in specific occupations or jobs, and second, the specification of appropriate money differentials that correspond to differences in the amount of labor supplied. Since the mid fifties, numerous theoretical and empirical studies on wage determination have been published in the USSR. As might be expected, there are frequent disagreements about the applicability and definition of certain concepts or about the relevance and applicability of particular pieces of empirical information. No attempt is made here to reflect these differences of opinion, to take sides in these disputes, or to comment on the consistency of specific formulations. Rather, the intention has been to provide a summary of widely held opinions, a synthesis of Soviet views on occupational differentials. In attempting to reflect the views of many Soviet economists, one runs the risk of representing none adequately, but that is a risk that will have to be taken.

The Soviet approach to the first of the questions outlined above is derived from Marx's version of the labor theory of value. According to this, the values of particular commodities are determined by the quantities of socially necessary labor needed to produce them. Since the activities of workers differ in their specific content, the postulate that labor constitutes a measure of value implies the possibility of converting different sorts of work to a common denominator. This is the principle of the reduction of labor; as Marx expressed it, "relatively complex labor is only simple labor raised to some power, or rather, multiplied" (Marx and Engels, *Collected Works*, Russian ed., vol. 23, p. 53). Much of the content of the Soviet theory of occupational differentials consists of specifying ways in which the complexity of labor may be measured.

In their recent writings on the subject, Soviet labor economists identify five or six dimensions to labor which jointly determine its quantity and quality. Quantitative differences in the amount of labor supplied by different individuals are determined by the length of time worked, and thus pose no problems of measurement. Theoretical discussion and disagreement concentrate on the remaining four or five dimensions which supposedly determine the quality or complexity of labor. They are the conditions under which the labor is performed, the skill that is involved, and the region, industry, and enterprise where it takes place. Of these, the most fundamental is the skill component; it is to this that Soviet labor economists devote most attention, both theoretical and in a sense empirical, and it is the skill factor that determines the ruble value of payments for other components.

Each of the components mentioned above is identified with a separate element of Soviet pay scales, and thus these factors jointly determine the extent and structure of occupational differentials in the USSR. The theory and its associated pay scales are most fully worked out for industrial workers (wage earners). Wages and salaries for other categories of state employee are set, to a considerable extent, by comparison with earnings in industry. It is not clear how new this particular approach really is. The various components of pay scales with which individual theoretical components are linked have existed in something like their present form for up to half a century. Perhaps all that is new is the conscious attempt at unification, at rationalization, at making the system as a whole internally consistent. Soviet economists themselves tend to play down the novelty of their practical, and even more their theoretical, innovations. Instead, they suggest that the policy of the fifties and sixties represents a return to Leninist norms and socialist principles after an unfortunate interlude. But such an attitude should be treated with circumspection.

Soviet economists and others refer to the pay scales that supposedly reflect the different dimensions of labor quality as the tariff system. In the narrow sense, this consists of four elements: a set of basic rates, *stavki*, differentiated by industry and payable to the least-skilled workers in any branch. These stavki are specified in rubles and are supposed to reflect differences in the economic significance of different branches. Then there are a set of skill scales, *tarifnye setki*, one or more for each industry, which indicates how much more is paid for skilled labor than unskilled in individual sectors. These scales are expressed relative to the base rates payed in each branch. In certain industries, in addition, there are coefficients that raise the rates payable for piecework or for work undertaken in hot, arduous, or otherwise harmful circumstances. Finally, there are further coefficients that raise the wages paid in enterprises or plants located in particular geographical areas. The interenterprise differential referred to above is reflected in differences in the bonuses or other premiums paid out of the so-called Enterprise Fund or the Fund for Material Incentives.

The structure outlined in the previous paragraph applies most specifically to the pay scales of industrial workers, but the pay scales of manual workers in transport, construction, and other branches of what the Russians call material production are, to all intents and purposes, identical. Employees in other sectors like health or local services, the clerical staff in all sectors, and managerial, supervisory, technical, and professional staff are paid salaries. There are a variety of salary scales in use, to some extent differentiated by industry, but the theoretical justification of their structure is much less developed. In principle, it is argued, salaries depend upon the qualifications and experience of their recipient. But an examination of particular scales suggests that rewards for responsibility and the hierarchical principle exert a significant influence. The various components of industrial wage scales are examined in greater detail in the remainder of this section.

THE SKILL DIFFERENTIAL

It is a feature of the "new" Soviet theory of wages that the various dimensions of labor quality are independent. This implies that skill can be measured, or at least conceived, independently of the industry or occupation in which it is exercised. Thus it is possible to construct skill scales and therefore wage scales that are not industry-specific. Indeed, the doctrine of equal pay for equal work implies the existence of a single scale. Much progress has been made toward realizing this goal in the Soviet Union. In 1955, there were approximately nineteen hundred skill scales in use in Soviet industry; by 1960-61, the number had been reduced to ten or twelve; and it was claimed that after the post-1972 wage round had been completed, there would be only three in operation (Sukharevskii, 1974, p. 241).

The measurement of skill and the construction of skill scales involves three processes: one must determine the relationship between the extreme elements of the scale—that is, by how much the rate paid to the most-skilled should exceed that paid to the unskilled; one must determine how many intermediate steps to include in the scale and what rate relativities to specify; and finally, all the diverse occupations and activities in the industry or industries to which the scale is to apply must be categorized by one or more of the skill grades of the scale. It is this detailed work of job classification and job evaluation that for the most part constitutes the administration of wage policy in the USSR.

Discussions published in the Soviet Union are of little help in deciding how the first of these steps is carried out in practice, what determines the maximum spread of skill differentials in specific industries. As far as the 1956-61 reorganization of industrial wages is concerned, this was probably determined by the constraints under which the reform was carried out. It was supposed to be completed without reducing the earnings of any substantial group of workers. Given the scale of differentiation that existed in 1955, particularly in heavy industry, it would have cost a great deal to have reduced differentials to a level comparable to those found in light industry, for example.[5] As a result, a number of different scales were retained and the *diapazon*, or maximum spread, of those used in heavy industry and also in extractive industry was substantially greater than the diapazon of those used in other sectors. It should also be pointed out that the reform of wage scales in heavy and extractive industry was substantially complete before the unified six-point scale (which was used in much of the rest of industry) was developed; it was probably thought undesirable to introduce this scale into industries that had been subjected to a major reorganization of wage scales and payment structures only a year or so previously. The fact that a six-point scale was used in many heavy industrial branches in the 1972 round of rate revisions suggests that such considerations were more important than the claim that the range of skill involved in an industry like ferrous metallurgy is objectively greater than that in textiles, for example.[6]

One economist has suggested that the diapazon of particular skill scales can and should be determined by the length of time it takes to acquire the highest skill grade and the length of time the average worker can expect to remain in employment.[7] This rather crude version of human capital theory indicates a much smaller spread of wage rates than that in any of the scales introduced either in 1956-61 or after 1972. Initially, Maier's proposals met with opposition from the NIIT and presumably from the State Committee on Labor and Wages itself. More recently, they appear to have won a measure of acceptance from theoreticians, but it is doubtful whether they have had much influence upon the determination of actual wage scales (Kapustin, 1974, pp. 252-53).

Given the diapazon, the next step is to determine the number of intermediate points on the scale, and on this the Soviet literature is more explicit. First, it is argued that unless increments are of a sufficient size they will fail to elicit a response from the worker. Further, it is suggested that individual decisions depend upon relative rather than absolute increments; that is, a 10-ruble increment is supposed to be worth less to a worker earning 150 rubles a month than to one earning only 75. More precisely, it is suggested that equal percentage increments will be equally effective at all levels of income. Although no grounds are given, it is usually suggested that the minimum perceived increment is about 10%. Finally, it is claimed that increases in skill at the lower end of the scale involve little more than the acquisition of experience and good working habits; at the top end, they involve the learning of substantially new skills. Since more is involved at the top, it is argued, increments should be larger. These considerations effectively determine the number of grades on a scale, once its diapazon has been fixed. They also explain why the scales introduced in 1956-61 as well as those used after 1972 all display increasing absolute and relative differentials (Batkaev and Markov, 1964, pp. 50-64; Rabkina and Rimashevskaya, 1972, p. 83; Sukharevskii, 1968, p. 292. For examples, see table 8.1 below).

While the propositions outlined in the last paragraph may explain how Soviet skill scales are determined, they do not constitute a theory, and certainly not a Marxist theory. Also, the argument is circular in at least one place. Whether or not increases in skill at the lower end of the scale involve "little more than the acquisition of experience and good work habits" depends upon the definition of the competence necessary to acquire these grades. A different definition of grade II or grade III status might involve the acquisition of more substantive skills and therefore merit

Table 8.1
Skill Differentials in Soviet Industry: Selected Tariff Scales

Skill Grade	Extractive Industry		Machine Building		Light Industry	
	1958-68	1972-	1959-68	1972-	1959-68	1972-
I	1.0	1.0	1.0	1.0	1.0	1.0
II	1.13	1.11	1.13	1.09	1.11	n.a.
III	1.50	1.22	1.29	1.20	1.25	n.a.
IV	1.67	1.38	1.48	1.33	1.41	n.a.
V	2.50	1.58	1.72	1.50	1.59	n.a.
VI	3.13	1.86	2.00	1.71	1.80	1.58
VII	3.33	—	—	—	—	—
VIII	3.75	—	—	—	—	—

Sources. Extractive Industry, 1958: Maier, 1963, p. 147; the scale refers to underground coal-mining. 1972: Batkaev and Safronov, 1974, p. 379. Machine Building, 1959: Batkaev and Markov, 1964, p. 65. 1972: Batkaev and Safronov, 1974, p. 383. Light Industry, 1959: Batkaev and Markov, 1964, p. 65. 1972: table 9.4.

larger increments. It might be a good personnel management practice to provide for almost automatic increments early in a worker's career— but it is not inherent in the structure of nature. On the other hand, the relatively high pay granted to skilled workers might be a consequence of the power possessed by this particular group, but, again, it does not follow from the Marxist concept of skill.

⎣Given skill scales derived as above, the final step in the implementation of a wage structure involves the classification and evaluation of the hundreds or thousands of jobs to be found in industry. It is this industry-wide and interindustrial job evaluation scheme that provides the basis for realizing the objective of equal pay for equal work. During the wage reorganization of 1956-61, State Committee experts and experts from various industrial committees undertook the enormous task of reclassifying and evaluating virtually all the specific occupations to be found in Soviet industry. The results of this work are to be found in the so-called *Edinyi tarifno-kvalifikatsionnyi spravochnik skvoznykh professii* and in *spravochniki* for particular industries. The first of these deals with those occupations to be found in more than one industry, and for each, specifies what the worker must be able to do and what he should know before being assigned to a particular skill grade. It also gives examples of the skill job classification of particular occupations or activities.[8] As a result, at least in principle, the classification of, say, maintenance and repair work will be common to the whole of Soviet industry, as will the assignment of skill grades (but not wages, since there are other factors to be taken into account.) The *spravochniki* for particular industries deal with jobs and occupations to be found only in those industries. It has been claimed that by the early sixties, some 60% of all industrial workers were covered by the *Edinyi spravochnik*, but there are reasons to doubt this claim (Kirsch, 1972, pp. 80-81). Work on job evaluation continued throughout the sixties, and the 1972 wage round apparently involved further steps in the rationalization of skill grading in industry.

For the most part, this program of job evaluation has made use of the so-called analytical method. In this, certain abstract characteristics of all occupations are identified (those used in the USSR include accounting, preparation of the work place, the work itself, control and maintenance of machinery, and responsibility), the content of the jobs is assessed in each of these dimensions, and the assessments are combined according to a particular formula to give a final score. A comparison of this score with benchmarks on a scale indicates the skill grade to which the job in question should be assigned (*Metodicheskiye ukazaniya po sostavleniyu tarifno-kvalifikatsionnykh spravochnikov*, Moscow, 1957; Batkaev and Markov, 1964, pp. 40-60; Loznevaya, 1969). Although this analytical method has been used extensively in the Soviet job evaluation program, there is a suggestion that, recently, it may have been supplemented by the use of training time (Kapustin, 1974, p. 253). ⊃

Much of the discussion here has been based on the assumption that it is primarily *workers* who are assigned to particular skill grades, but this is not strictly correct. In accordance with the socialist principle of distribution, it is argued that wages "should correspond to the quantity and quality of labor actually expended, rather than to the abilities of the individual who undertakes the work. For this reason, wages are related to the skills necessary for a particular job and not to the qualifications of the worker who undertakes it."[9] Thus it is first and foremost the *jobs* that are classified into skill grades. Nevertheless, the efficient allocation of resources and the demands of management require that workers be assigned to jobs of a complexity they are capable of achieving, and consequently most of the Soviet industrial labor force is classified into skill grades according to criteria set out in one or the other of the tariff qualification handbooks described above.

⌊The reorganization of skill scales and the job evaluation program they involve has cost the Soviet authorities a good deal of effort, and it has resulted in a more logical structure of wages. But in part at least because it is administered centrally, the new system is very rigid; it is also not clear whether it is more efficient in allocating labor than the system that went before.⌋

Tables 8.1 and 8.4 convey some idea of the impact of successive re-organizations upon the scale of intra-industrial differentials in basic wage rates—or, rather, that part of them attributable to variations in skill. In 1955, the highest reported diapazon was 4.1:1 in ferrous metallurgy, although it is possible that there was a larger spread in underground mining (Batkaev and Markov, 1964, p. 67). (At least, the maximum differential in mining after 1961 was greater than in ferrous metallurgy.) Before the 1956-61 reorganization, differentiation was least in some part of milk and meat processing, where it was only 1.25:1. The reorganization greatly decreased the number of scales and rationalized their use; on balance it led to a modest reduction in *diapazony* in heavy industry (the maximum declined from 4.1 to 3.2:1, again in ferrous metallurgy). In light industry, engineering, and food processing it resulted in some increase in differentials for those on the tightest scale, but for most workers it is supposed to have led to some reduction. The introduction of the 60-ruble minimum wage and the promulgation of new scales in 1972 have resulted in a further narrowing of formal skill differentials which in heavy industry at least has been substantial. The figures indicate that in little more than fifteen years the maximum diapazon in Soviet industry has been reduced by more than half.

These figures should be treated with some caution, however, as they refer to formal differences in basic rates; they do not refer to earnings, nor do they take account of the fact that in many industries in the mid fifties the lowest points on the skill scales were not used. But the fact that the Soviet authorities have been able to make such drastic changes in the structure of wage rates apparently without affecting the allocation of labor adversely suggests that in 1955, or even in 1961-68, differentials were excessive. This is supported by the empirical evidence, such as it is. A number of Soviet studies carried out in the early sixties reported that it was impossible to distinguish between workers in grades V-VI and those in grade IV (and possibly grade III) on any grounds except for *stazh*, the length of time they had been employed in their enterprises. In terms of education, training, experience, and other measures of skill, they were identical. This is interpreted to mean that the then-existing differentials were more than sufficient to generate an adequate supply of workers both willing and able to undertake the most highly skilled jobs. Since wage rates are centrally determined, they cannot fall, relatively, to equate supply and demand; available jobs are therefore allocated on a seniority basis. There is job rationing.[10] Whether this is the correct interpretation or not, the fact that diapazony in all sectors were lower after the completion of the 1972 wage round than they were in 1962 (although in some they were higher than in 1968-72) suggests that those responsible for wage determination in the USSR believed them to be excessive even after the 1956-61 reorganization.

INTERINDUSTRIAL DIFFERENTIALS IN BASE RATES

The skill scales described above are supposed to be independent of industrial characteristics. In principle, the same scale can be used in a number of industries; some of the ten or twelve scales developed during the 1956-61 wage reorganization were confined to a single industry, but others were more widely used. All three of those employed after 1972 apply to more than one industrial sector. Skill scales, then, determine (or partly determine) intra-industrial differentials; interindustrial differentials are generated by specifying different base rates for different branches. Formally, it is claimed that the existence of varying base rates reflects differences in the economic significance of particular industries. In principle, these stavki could be used to generate incentives for labor to move into expanding industries and out of contracting ones. And the relevance of supply and demand considerations has not escaped all Soviet economists. In this context, one of them remarked that "one must not forget the balance of skilled workers, bearing in mind the demands of the law of planned (proportional) development upon the size of wages" (Sukharevskii, 1968, p. 291). But in practice, this source of potential flexibility seems to have been little used. Both before and after the 1956-61 wage reorganization in industry and even in the 1970s, the spectrum of base rates appears to have remained very much the same. The highest rates are in extractive industry, then come the heavy industrial branches, and finally, light and food industries. Over the period, absolute differences have contracted somewhat, but this has been the result of increases in the minimum wage more than of selective responses to labor market conditions (for data on base rates see Chapman, 1970, and Kirsch, 1972). And since Soviet economists do not explain what they understand by "economic significance" in discussions of wage determination, it is difficult to ascertain the principles employed in the specification of these stavki. One suspects that they reflect custom, tradition, and the prejudices of Soviet leaders.

DIFFERENTIALS FOR WORKING CONDITIONS

There are two sorts of wage supplement included under this heading. First, in most Soviet industries, pieceworkers are paid at higher rates than time workers. This is supposed to compensate them for both the added tension under which they work and the risks of earnings-loss resulting from organizational disruption. On the average, rates for pieceworkers are some 5 to 15% higher than those for time workers, and again, the highest supplements are payable in heavy industry. This differentiation of rates appears to have been introduced in the late twenties or early thirties when the use of piecework-payment systems was greatly expanded. As such, it was an ad hoc attempt to gain workers' acceptance for the new system. It has been retained, probably in response to the pressure of vested interests, but there is little discussion of it in theoretical terms.[11]

Second, in certain industries, the wages of those doing heavy work or of those working in hot and unhealthy conditions are higher than the wages of those working in normal circumstances. In formal terms, Soviet labor economists justify these wage supplements by arguing that wages must permit the worker to recoup energy, and that arduous work or work in hot and harmful conditions involves the use of more energy than normal. But since the payments are related to base pay (those engaged on hot or heavy work receive a percentage mark-up over their normal rate) rather than being a fixed addition to wages irrespective of skill grade, it would seem that the supplements are determined more by some idea of what must be paid to attract the necessary labor (that is, by primitive supply and demand considerations) than by any objective measure of the extra energy expended. This conjecture is given added weight by the fact that Soviet economists have recently added unattractiveness, *neprivlekatelnost*, to the list of factors meriting wage supplements.[12] It is also supported by the general provision of a 14-25% supplement for "the inconvenience and arduousness, *tyazhest*, of work during the hours of darkness" in the ninth five-year plan (*Gosudarstvennyi* . . . , 1972, p. 288).

Soviet ideas about compensation for unpleasant working conditions are not well worked out. Even after the 1956-61 wage reorganization, it is claimed, there were three separate methods of allowing for such circumstances (Kapustin, 1968, pp. 332-33). In extractive industry, where the basic factor was thought to be the location of the work place, there were separate scales for underground and surface work. Since there is no reason to believe that underground work is essentially hotter, heavier, or more harmful than the *same* work performed on the surface, although it may be more unpleasant and it is almost certainly more dangerous, that was already a move away from the presumed source of this differential in Soviet theory. The retention of separate scales for underground miners, especially coal miners, reflects the existence of a vested interest that the Soviet government was either unwilling or unable to eliminate.

In many branches of manufacturing industry, adverse working conditions are allowed for by the use of one, or sometimes two, supplemental coefficients. In these branches, those working in hot, heavy, or harmful conditions have their wages raised by a given percentage. The coefficients are industry-specific and tend to be higher in heavy industry than in light. There has been some tendency to expand the number sectors in which coefficients are employed, and as can be seen from table 8.2,

Table 8.2
Scale of Wage Supplementation for Work in Hot, Heavy, or Unpleasant Conditions, USSR, 1960-72 (%)

	1961-62	1972-
Hot-heavy premium	8-17	10-12
Extra hot-heavy premium	22-32	16-24
Underground work	14-33	22-37

Sources. 1961-62: Sukharevskii, 1968, p. 292. 1972: rows 1 and 2, Kapustin, 1974, p. 271; row 3, Sukharevskii, 1974, p. 222.

some attempt has been made to make them more uniform across industries. but this component of Soviet industrial wage structure still appears to be very much an ad hoc adjustment. It is the responsibility of the State Committee on Labor and Wages to decide the circumstances under which such supplements should be paid. This it does by issuing lists of typical work environments, *tipovye perechni rabot,* or classes of worker, entitled to higher wages (Volkov, 1974, p. 22; Batkaev and Markov, 1964, p. 64).

In some industries, no provision was made for paying working condition supplements. In these, it is claimed, managements of the enterprises attract the labor they require for unpleasant or heavy jobs by reducing labor norms, illicitly upgrading workers, and otherwise contravening the state's wage regulations.

In the early sixties, differences in the mark-up paid for hot, heavy, or harmful work in various branches were substantial. In the clothing industry, for example, it was only 8%; in some branches of heavy industry it was more than double, the maximum rate being 17%. In fact, of course, disparities were even greater: as pointed out above, some industries made no provision at all, others recognized two categories of adverse conditions, "hot and heavy" and "extremely hot and heavy"; for the latter category the premium was 22-32%; thus the overall range of adjustment for adverse conditions was about a third.

The empirical evidence suggests that these premia were, in general, insufficient. Throughout the sixties there were reports of shortages of workers willing to undertake certain unpleasant jobs, and the rates of labor turnover were markedly higher for such work than for work in normal conditions. Furthermore, a number of studies reported that the differences in earnings between those working in adverse conditions and those in normal shops were greater than formal differences in rates. This has been interpreted to imply that enterprises were reducing norms to provide additional unofficial incentives to workers in such jobs.

All of this suggests that in quantitative terms at least, the allowance for varying conditions of work was not well thought out in the 1956-61 wage reorganization. And given the general impression of inadequacy, it is perhaps surprising that the first impression created by the figures in table 8.2 is that the scale of supplementation was reduced after 1972. This is misleading, however; at the same time, supplements for hot and heavy conditions were introduced in a number of sectors that did not previously use them and the three-tier structure was extended to certain branches of light industry.[13] As a result, it is possible that the effective contribution of this adjustment was increased. All the same, the record does not convey the impression that those responsible for wage rate determination have been working according to scientific principles.

REGIONAL DIFFERENTIALS

Regional differentials were described in some detail in chapter 5, and the description will not be repeated here. The earlier discussion indicated that although in principle regional wage supplements were based on purely geographical considerations, there were marked differences between sectors until the mid seventies. It also suggested that, on balance, the regional coefficients built into the 1956-61 wage reorganization were insufficient to compensate workers for the higher cost of living in the Far North and Far East. Again, the evidence suggests that at a micro-level, wage rate determination did not pay sufficient attention to labor market conditions.

INTERENTERPRISE DIFFERENTIALS

The four components described so far are the only ones explicitly recognized in the structure of wage rates. In the late fifties and early sixties Soviet labor economists denied the existence of a pure interenterprise differential. That is, they explained the existence of differences in average wages between plants either in terms of the interaction between the factors considered so far or as a consequence of shortcomings in the administration of the government's wages policy. Interenterprise differentials, it was suggested, would conflict with the principle of equal pay for equal work and therefore could not be derived from Marxist conceptions of differences in the quality of labor. But the so-called economic reform of 1965 stressed the desirability of relating earnings to enterprise performance and in certain recent discussions of wage determination, interenterprise differentials have been recognized as legitimate: ". . . in evaluating the labor of a particular worker, the production results of the enterprise at which he is employed should tell [dolzhny skazatsya] on his earnings" (Sukharevskii, 1974, p. 218). In fact, this type of assertion adds nothing to the foregoing theory and should be recognized as a rather specious form of ex-post justification of government policy that is still distressingly common in Soviet academic writing.

As a positive theory of wages, the ideas set out in the preceding paragraphs leave something to be desired. In spite of Soviet claims to the contrary, in a planned economy of the Soviet type, wages are still a price, and Western economists are accustomed to thinking of price determination in the context of a market. An adequate theory will identify the factors affecting supply and demand schedules separately and analyze the ways in which they interact. The demand side of the labor market is almost completely absent from the Soviet theory. This may be partly explained by the Marxist argument that under socialism labor ceases to be a commodity, that its price is no longer market-determined. But as pointed out above, actual wage determination recognizes the relevance of supply and demand considerations. On the other hand, it may reflect the assumption that the demand for labor is not price-determined but is derived from the plan; that individual enterprise managers have little scope for varying their demand for labor or the wages they are prepared to pay. Soviet economists, too, may be unwilling to conceptualize the state as acting in a more general economic environment, constrained by the decisions of other economic agents. This unwillingness is probably a hangover from the past, from Stalinism and from the so-called teleological theory of planning that prevailed during the thirties. But as pointed out above, some economists have overcome this reluctance to think abstractly about the state as part of an economic model. Further, it is widely recognized that in practice, individual enterprises are fairly autonomous in determining wages. Perhaps, in time, this will lead to the development of a more market-oriented theory of wage determination.

Because they are unwilling to speculate about wages in a market context, there is very little discussion by Soviet economists of wages as an allocative mechanism, of wage adjustments as a means of reducing the supply of labor in particular occupations or regions—or rather, there is very little theoretical discussion of this topic. In practical policy discussions, the most commonly proposed solutions for apparent shortages of labor (for example, in the north and east of the country) are an increase in regional wage supplements and an improvement in the supply of goods and services in these regions. Similar solutions are often proposed, *mutatis mutandis*, for shortages of particular skills. In this context there is little recognition, however, of the potential effects of wage increases on production costs, on the profitability of industry, and thus on the location of industrial activity and the demand for labor.

The Soviet theory of wage differentials, set out above, places great stress upon the incentive effects of wages. It is to preserve these that Soviet economists argue that wage adjustments should not be used to bring about an equitable distribution of income. But these incentive effects seem to be largely restricted to encouraging the acquisition of new and desirable skills, to increasing the participation rate, and to eliciting a greater supply of effort from those already on the job. This last is produced by the use of piecework payment systems and the provision of various bonuses. Increases in average earnings or possibly in the minimum wage supposedly increase the supply of labor to the state sector, and various skill differentials are expected to make workers more willing to undertake further training. In all of this, the incentive effects of wage differentials on the allocation and reallocation of labor between industries is neglected.

On empirical grounds, there are reasons to doubt that the effects of wage differentials are restricted in this way. Historically, at least, it would seem that the Soviet government was able to recruit a high proportion of women into the labor force, thus increasing participation rates, by driving down the real wage. And there are some indications that at the present time Soviet households would rather take potential increases in real wages in the form of more leisure than as higher earnings or increased consumption. Although the issue will not be discussed here, there are reasons to doubt, also, that Soviet incentive systems have always been effective.[14] And the evidence above suggests that skill differentials have, in general, been more than sufficient to ensure an adequate supply of qualified manpower.

The role of wage differentials in allocating labor between industries may have been neglected by Soviet economists because there is very little such movement or because interindustrial mobility is determined by the plan rather than by market forces. It is known, for example, that Soviet industrial training is extremely specialized, and it may be that once a worker has been employed in a particular industry he will remain within that industry or occupation, although he may move from enterprise to enterprise. On this, available evidence is inadequate, but what there is tends to refute the hypothesis. There is apparently substantial interindustrial mobility, and nearly all of it takes place through decentralized channels. At least in the sixties, the recruitment of workers devolved overwhelmingly upon the enterprise rather than the central organization. Figures published in an NIIT study indicate that individual enterprises recruited between 85% and 89% of all workers taken on in Soviet industry from 1963 to 1970. Orgnabor, the state's labor allocation body, was responsible for only 2.3-3.9% (Danilov, 1973, p. 39). Thus, almost all hiring decisions and job-search activities are decentralized. This does not demonstrate that wage differentials play a key role in employment decisions, but at least it is consistent with such a situation.

Furthermore, in a sample of 10,700 workers who left jobs and were hired by Leningrad enterprises in the fifteen months preceding April 1963, only 45% kept their old occupations in their new places of employment. The variation of proportion among occupations ranged from 73% for fitters, *slesari*, down to 34.6% for textile workers, *tekstilshchiki*.[15] If such results can be generalized to the whole of Soviet industry, they suggest that there is considerable occupational mobility. Again, wage differentials may be important in determining the direction and scale of particular flows. Soviet silence on their role is unfortunate.

These reflections suggest that the Soviet theory of wage differentials fails as a positive theory of the operation of a labor market in a planned economy. But the Soviet theory has a certain ethical content, even if discussion of distributive justice is limited and rather superficial. The principle of equal pay for equal work has great intuitive appeal that is certainly not limited to socialist ideology. The theory has provided for wage-setters a coherent view of their responsibilities, a justification for their work; this intellectual unity may possibly have contributed as much as the existence of a centralized bureaucracy to the Soviet government's ability to carry through a far-reaching reform of wage and payment systems since 1955. The structure of the bureaucracy and an account of the reorganization of wages will be described in the next section.

8.4 SOVIET WAGE POLICY 1955-75: A HISTORY

The history of Soviet wage policy since the mid fifties is largely an account of the actions of the State Committee on Labor and Wages (Volkov,

1974, pp. 3-52; Kirsch, 1972, pp. 1-10). This organization was established in 1955 (as a sort of Ministry of Labor) to exercise a measure of centralized control over wage-determination and labor policy and to coordinate the activities of republican ministries of social security. The latter function appears to have assumed greater importance in recent years, and in 1976 the State Committee's title was changed to The State Committee on Labor and Social Questions (*Ekonomika selskogo khozyaistvo,* 1976, no. 12, p. 119). Its terms of reference were presumably changed at the same time.

The first chairman of the State Committee was Lazar Kaganovich, a senior party official of the Stalin period. In 1956 he was replaced by A. P. Volkov, who retained his position for the rest of the period considered here. Given the timing of the changeover, it is unlikely to have been connected with the so-called Anti-Party Group affair in which Kaganovich was disgraced. The committee's terms of reference were specified as the drafting of laws and statutes on labor and wages, participation in the preparation of current and long-term plans, particularly those aspects relating to labor and wages, and the promulgation of regulations on the basis of existing legislation. It was also empowered to prepare proposals for improving the state's pension system and empowered to coordinate the activities of republican ministries of social security. Specifically in the area of wages, the committee is responsible for the preparation of draft wage scales, for intersectoral and interregional rationalization of wages, and for the general administration of the state's wage policy (Volkov, 1974, p. 22).

The founding of the State Committee was accompanied by a renaissance of Soviet labor economics. Since the mid fifties, a large number of monographs and academic papers have been published on various aspects of wage determination and the functioning of the Soviet labor market. There have also been many official and private empirical studies of particular topics in this area, a development that the State Committee itself has done much to foster, through the work of its research organization, NIIT, and by disseminating the results of academic work in its various publications. Some of the ideas appearing in this work have already been described in sections 8.2 and 8.3. It is not clear how far these ideas and principles reflect only the views of the State Committee or whether they may be used to infer the policy intentions of the Soviet government and Party leadership as well.

On the one hand, it is to be expected that a bureaucracy, any bureaucracy, vested with extensive administrative authority will develop a set of principles, a guide to action, in terms of which its behavior can be shown to be rational. And there is certainly an element of *post-hoc* rationalization in the ideas outlined above. This would suggest that the "new"

Soviet theory of wages and reflections on the role of wage policy in a planned economy represent only the attitudes of those most directly concerned with these questions; they may be at variance with the objectives of government (or Party) policy. There is certainly some suggestion of conflicting policy objectives, a matter that will be explored in greater detail below. However, the State Committee was set up in the same year that the Soviet government abandoned Stalin's postwar policy of annual price reductions and just before various administrative restrictions on labor mobility were formally repealed. This may be a coincidence, but it would seem plausible to assume that the establishment of the State Committee was an early indication of a new and more sophisticated approach to questions of economic welfare and inequality on the part of the Soviet government; it may also reflect an official desire to improve the operation of the Soviet labor market. In this case, the new views about wages and wage policy may well command a wider acceptance. On balance, it is probably the case that while the Soviet party and government wanted to move in a new direction in 1955, their ideas about what was desirable were ill thought out and perhaps inconsistent. The opinions and theories described above would then represent a subsequent elaboration of the early intentions, an elaboration that may, in certain respects, conflict with the opinions of the central leadership that started the process (and their successors).

When the State Committee was first established, there was considerable confusion about the division of responsibility for wages between itself and the industrial ministries. As might be expected, there were complaints in the press of departmentalism and bureaucratic obstruction. The bureaucratic problems are probably more important than the personal and political shortcomings of its first chairman in explaining why the committee achieved little in its first eighteen months. The State Committee on Labor and Wages, however, did not suffer the fate of so many Soviet institutions that have tried to exercise control over those ministries. Fortuitously, as a result of intra-Party conflict, the ministries were replaced, in 1957, by sovnarkhozy, regional economic councils, and were reestablished only in 1965. Therefore, for its first nine or ten formative years, the committee faced little or no coordinated bureaucratic opposition to its policies. The reactions of individual enterprises, managers, and groups of workers were economic rather than political; they constrained rather than challenged the formulation of Soviet policy. When industrial ministries were reintroduced in 1965, the competence and authority of the committee on questions of wages were firmly established, and they have not been seriously questioned since.

The actions of the State Committee since 1955 bring out certain features of the way in which the formal ideas described above have been realized, and they cast some light on the economic constraints under which wage policy has developed in the USSR. It is to this that I now turn. A chronology of major measures affecting wages in the period 1955-75 is given in table 8.3. Soviet labor economists usually identify three phases in the government's wage policy in this period, and although this ascribes greater coherence and consistency to policy than is warranted, it is convenient to organize discussion around these phases.

Table 8.3
Soviet Wage Policy: A Chronology

Date	Measures Implemented	Source
May 1955	State Committee on Labor and Wages established; L. Kaganovich appointed chairman	Kirsch, 1972, p. 4
June 1956	A. P. Volkov appointed chairman of State Committee on Labor and Wages	Fearn, 1963, p. 13
	Minimum wage set at 27-35 R a month	Livshits, 1972, p. 230
Sept. 1958	Wage reform complete in coal mining, ferrous and nonferrous metallurgy, chemicals, cement	Chapman, 1970, p. 19; Kirsch, p. 6
Feb. 1959	Minimum wage set at 40-45 R in converted branches	Fearn, p. 17
Sept. 1959	Geographical principle of reorganization adopted	Kirsch, p. 6
Dec. 1959	Approx. 13 million workers on new pay scales, mainly in heavy industry	Chapman, p. 20
1960	Approx. 30 million workers on new pay scales, almost all industry, construction and some other sectors	Chapman, p. 24
	Tax liability removed for those earning less than 60 rubles a month	Volkov, 1968, p. 24
1956-60	Conversion to 7-hour day (6-hour day underground)	Volkov, 1974, p. 24
	Conversion to 41-hour standard work week	Kirsch, p. 6
1961	More than 40 million workers on new pay scales, all those in productive sphere and in scientific work	Chapman, p. 20
1964	Revision of pay scale for underground miners	Chapman, p. 20
May 1964	New wage scales in nonproductive sphere: average increase—education, 26%; health, 24%; trade and local services, 19%	Kunelskii, 1968a, p. 82; Matyukha, 1973, p. 32; Maier, 1968, p. 100
Sept. 1965	Elimination of urban-rural differential in health and education	

1967	Introduction of 5-day week	Volkov, 1968, p. 38
	Minimum holiday raised from 12 to 15 days	Volkov, 1968, p. 38
Jan. 1968	Minimum wage raised to 60 R a month	Kunelskii, 1968b, p. 18
	Rural-urban differential abolished. Grade I rates raised in all sectors except underground mining	Kunelskii, 1968a, p. 86
	Extension of regional supplements to those in light industry and services in certain areas; modifications to regional coefficients	Chapman, p. 126; Kunelskii, 1968a, p. 88
	Wage scales for machine tool operators raised by 15%	Chapman, p. 132
	Some modifications to clerical salaries	Kunelskii, 1968a, p. 86
	Tax liability reduced for those earning from 61-80 R a month	Chapman, p. 132
1969	Revised wage scale in construction, average increase 25%; conditions of work premia introduced	Kapustin, 1974, p. 266
	New pay scale in construction materials, average increase 23%; conditions of work premia introduced	Kapustin, p. 266
1965-70	Modification and extension of regional coefficients	Kunelskii, 1972, p. 22
1971	70-ruble minimum introduced in transport and agriculture; new wage scales	*Gosudarstvennyi . . .* , p. 286
Jan. 1972	Regional coefficients extended to all not receiving them in Siberia; regional coefficients introduced in TuSSR and European North	*Gosudarstvennyi*, p. 286; Kapustin, p. 268
Sept. 1972	Increased salaries in health, education (20%), preschool child care (29%), all regions	Kapustin, p. 268
	70-ruble minimum and new pay scales for productive sector employees in North and East	*Gosudarstvennyi*, p. 286
1973	70-ruble minimum and new pay scales for productive sector employees in Kazakhstan, Central Asia, and parts of Central Russia	*Gosudarstvennyi*, p. 286
1974-75	70-ruble minimum and new pay scales for rest of labor force	*Gosudarstvennyi*, p. 286

Note: Measures cited from *Gosudarstvennyi* were planned to go into effect at the time indicated, but their implementation may have been delayed.

THE WAGE REORGANIZATION OF 1956-65

The State Committee assumed as its first task the reorganization of Soviet wage and salary structures after their degeneration during the last fifteen or twenty years of Stalin's lifetime. From the abolition of Narkomtrud

(The People's Commissariat of Labor) until the establishment of the committee itself, there was no body below the Council of Ministers empowered to make general regulations on questions of wages. Each ministry was responsible for wages and working conditions at plants under its jurisdiction. Since plants producing similar products were frequently subordinated to different ministries, there were often many different wage scales for workers doing the same or similar jobs.[16] The absence of a centralized administrative authority also meant that, although earnings had more than doubled between 1940 and 1955, there had been very little change in the level of basic rates since before the Second World War (Volkov, 1974, p. 21). All that had happened was that the Council of Ministers had introduced a series of *ad hoc* modifications to the pay scales of particular workers with little or no regard for their impact upon the general structure of wages. By 1955, these developments had eroded much of the logic initially possessed by the wages system developed in the thirties (Kirsch, 1972, pp. 2ff.). This chaotic situation was made worse by official ignorance about wages and salaries. Since the late thirties, no statistics on wages, not even average earnings, had been published, and one may seriously question the reliability of the figures used by planners. No data were collected about the distribution of earnings, the scale of earnings disparities, between the thirties and 1956 (with the possible exception of 1946; see below, p. 219). And this too, can be attributed to the absence of a central administrative authority.

Some idea of the complexity, of the irrationality, of the situation with which the State Committee was faced in 1955 can be gained from table 8.4. In 1955 there were several thousand basic rates, stavki, in use in Soviet industry, approximately nineteen hundred skill scales, and ninety regional coefficients. If all permutations had been possible, there would have been more pay scales than industrial workers!

Table 8.4
Effects of Wage Policy on Industrial Wage Structures, 1955-75

	Before Wage Reorganization, 1957-61	After Wage Reorganization, 1961-68	After 1968 Wage Hike	After 1972 Wage Round
Tariff scales	approx. 1900	10	25	3
Grades per scale	5-15	6-10	6-10	6-8
Range (highest/lowest rate)	1.25; 4.1	1.8; 3.2	1.2; 2.3	1.58; 2.1
Base rates, normal conditions	several thousands	50	40	17
Salary scales	700+	150	150	75
Regional coefficients	90	10	10	10

Source: Sukharevskii, 1974, p. 241.

The chairman of the State Committee has claimed that the 1956-65 wage reorganization was designed to bring about a radical simplification of the system, to raise the earnings[17] of the low-paid relative to the high-paid, and to increase the incentive effect of the rate structure while at the same time ensuring, so far as possible, that no workers suffered a reduction in wages. A study of the measures adopted between 1956 and 1965 suggests that, while the program did not have the coherence and consistency ascribed to it by Volkov (perhaps with the benefit of hindsight), these objectives, by and large, were achieved.

The program involved the following related measures. First, the number of skill scales and the number of base rates used in industry were sharply reduced. After 1961, when the reorganization was completed in the productive sector, there were no more than ten or twelve skill scales and fifty base rates in use. This reduction was achieved by an application of the industrial principle: the same wage scale (or occasionally scales) was applied in all plants and enterprises classified as belonging to a particular industry. The fact that, at the time, industry was organized on territorial lines under sovnarkhozy made this much simpler. The regional economic councils had no vested interest in particular wage structures. Reorganization was undertaken first in mining, in ferrous and nonferrous metallurgy, and in the chemicals and cement industries, and completed in them by the end of 1958 (Chapman, 1970, p. 19). Apparently, this industry-by-industry approach led to disruption, to an increase in labor turnover, as workers sought to move between converted and unconverted industries.[18] In any case, in September 1959 a modified geographical approach was adopted in which between 1959 and 1961 the remaining branches of industry and the rest of the productive sphere were reorganized simultaneously, area by area. At this stage, some attempt was made to apply the six-point scale uniformly throughout all remaining sectors, thus giving form to the idea that skill could be conceived of in a non-industry-specific way. At the same time as skill scales were reformed, an attempt was made to introduce a degree of consistency into the payment of regional cost-of-living supplements and premium rates for unhealthy or unpleasant working conditions.

Second, in September 1956 the minimum wage was set at 27-35 rubles a month, the minimum determined by branch of industry and by enterprise location. It was set at 33-35 rubles for heavy industry and construction, at 32-33 rubles for light industry and food processing, at 30 rubles for plants located in rural areas, and at 27 rubles for unmechanized work in state agriculture and in certain other "nonproductive" occupations (Livshits, 1972, p. 230). Before 1956 it had been approximately 22 rubles a month, with some urban-rural differentiation (Kunelskii, 1968b, p. 15).

The minimum wage was raised to 40-45 rubles a month in February 1959 for those industries, sectors, or enterprises whose wage systems had been reorganized (Fearn, 1963, p. 17; Livshits, 1973, p. 230, states that the minimum wage was not raised to 40-45 rubles a month until 1965, but this is a legalism—it was not until 1965 that the final sectors of the economy underwent reorganization).

The final measure in the program was the reorganization, in 1964-65, of wages and salaries in the so-called nonproductive sphere—in health, education, and other such services (Kunelskii, 1968a, p. 82).

The wage reform of 1956-65 is generally regarded as a success. It is represented by Soviet economists as the implementation of a consistent and coherent policy on wages and salaries, designed to increase the productive efficiency of the Soviet economy while at the same time making the distribution of earnings more equitable. It is certainly true that the reorganization led to a marked increase in the coherence of the Soviet wage and salary system, particularly in industry. But the above account suggests that many of the measures were taken on an *ad hoc* basis, and there are doubts about the extent to which some of its goals were reached.

Virtually all Soviet commentators claim that the 1956-61 wage reform resulted in a reduction of both intra-industrial and interindustrial differentials, and it is true that the scales introduced at the time of the reform exhibit a lower degree of overall differentiation, a smaller diapazon, than those in force previously. But Soviet economists also frequently comment on the fact that just before the reform, very few workers were classified in the lowest skill grades. Galenson has pointed out that if these grades are omitted, post-reform scales show greater differentiation than those used previously. Thus the reform appears to have resulted in an increase in the effective differentiation of wage rates (Galenson, 1963, p. 307). Kirsch has pointed out, however, that before the reform, differentiation of earnings exceeded that of rates; that the reform was accompanied by the introduction of tighter labor norms, especially for the higher skill grades; and that, therefore, an increase in effective rate differentiation is consistent with a reduction in earnings differentials (Kirsch, 1972, pp. 94 ff.).

Figures produced in the next chapter tend to confirm Kirsch's hypothesis. They show that interpersonal earnings differentials for the state sector as a whole fell after 1957, and that interpersonal earnings differentials in industry were smaller than those in the state sector in both 1961 and 1964—at least as measured by the decile coefficient. This suggests that interpersonal differentials in industry as a whole probably fell after 1957. On the other hand, interindustrial differentials apparently increased— at least when measured by the coefficient of variation of average branch earnings. Since interpersonal differentials are determined by interindustrial and intra-industrial disparities in earnings, these two results suggest that intra-industrial earnings differentials fell after 1955-57, whatever happened to the spread of effective rates.

The Soviet theory of wage differentials implies that there should be only one skill scale in use in Soviet industry. Certainly, the 1956-61 reform was a major step towards this goal, and further progress was made after 1972. But the retention of ten or more scales in 1956-61 and the fact that those used for heavy and extraction industry showed greater differentiation than those used in the rest of the economy suggest that the reform was tempered by caution, that either the Soviet government or the State Committee was unwilling to antagonize workers in these sectors by imposing upon them cuts in take-home pay (even if that was what was prescribed by their policy principles).

Further, I have seen no satisfactory explanation of the three-year delay between the completion of reorganization in the productive sector and its extension to the rest of the economy. Perhaps it was a consequence of the economic difficulties that arose during the final years of the Khrushchev period; perhaps the original intention was to confine the reform to industry or to the productive sectors, and only recruitment problems or the new priority for services resulted in the 1964-65 raises. In any case, the delay must have sorely tried the patience of those who waited three years, as well as raising doubts about the equity of the reform.

Finally, there is the question of the minimum wage. Soviet economists argue that this should be related to the costs of subsistence for the worker and his dependents. Now, there was virtually no change in the official retail price index between 1956 and 1959, and the increase in the cost of living implied by the Schroeder and Severin index was only 2.6%. Thus if 40-45 rubles represents an acceptable minimum in 1959, the minimum in 1956 should have been 39-44 rubles a month rather than 27-35 rubles.

It is possible that the 1959 minimum wage is a consequence of the adoption in that year of a new and more liberal definition of poverty. That is, it may represent the first effects of the program of normative budget construction, revived in 1956 after a long intermission. In that case, the 27-35 ruble minimum of 1956 can only have been a shot in the dark, a guess at the cost of subsistence, based on little or no empirical evidence. Yet this minimum wage was retained in some sectors until 1965. Soviet wage policy is not infused with a great sense of urgency!

On the other hand, it is possible that even in 1956 the authorities realized that the cost of subsistence justified a minimum wage of 40-45 rubles a month—perhaps because the normative budget calculations did not take long to complete—but thought that a doubling of the minimum wage was impossible, both politically and economically.

It is also possible that the fact that the new minimum applied initially only to "reorganized" branches of industry might imply that revised skill scales and other adjustments would have resulted in a reduction in the take-home pay of substantial groups of workers, especially when applied in low-wage sectors like textiles. There are a number of possible explanations, but they are all speculative. Soviet economists do not dwell upon the problem. It must be admitted, however, that the introduction of two minimum wages in the short span of three years is hardly the hallmark of a consistent and well-thought-out policy.

THE 1968 MINIMUM WAGE HIKE

After the completion of the wage reorganization in May 1965, there were no further developments in Soviet wage policy for almost three years. Attention was centered, rather, on the more general Kosygin economic reform. Between 1965 and 1968, however, there was a changeover to the five-day week, and the minimum holiday entitlement was raised from twelve to fifteen days (Volkov, 1974, p. 38). Thus policy at the center emphasized increases in leisure rather than increases in money wages. Presumably it was thought that as a consequence of the economic reform, wage increases would be generated by individual enterprises.

Then in January 1968, with little prior warning, the minimum wage for all state employees was raised from 40-45 to 60 rubles a month. At the same time, the urban-rural differential was eliminated in those industries or occupations that still retained it.[19] When the new minimum was introduced, new base rates, stavki, were specified for all sectors except underground mining (Kunelskii, 1968a, p. 86). But, these new stavki were not used to permit increases in earnings for those with wages much above 70 rubles a month. In effect, skill scales in all industries were contracted, in some cases dramatically (Kunelskii, 1968a, p. 87).

The introduction of the 60-ruble minimum wage led to substantial increases in earnings for certain categories of state employee, but also, because of the way it was introduced, it resulted in a marked reduction in both interindustrial and intra-industrial differentials. In certain branches of industry, the basic wages of the highest-paid workers were no more than 20% above those of the lowest-paid; in state agriculture the differential was as low as 16% (10 rubles) (see table 8.4 and Kapustin, 1974, p. 269). If in Soviet terms the pre-existing differentials corresponded to the quality and quantity of labor involved in particular industries and occupations, after 1968 those with higher skills were underpaid relative to the unskilled. More generally, it is to be expected that such a significant and rapid reduction in differentials would adversely affect the supply of labor to particular occupations. It is therefore interesting to speculate about the reasons for adopting such a policy.

At the time, three arguments were put forward for concentrating so large a proportion of available resources upon the low-paid. None of them are wholly convincing. First, it was suggested that to raise the minimum wage to 60 rubles and to allow other rates to rise to levels implied by the tariff structure would have cost more than the state could afford (Kunelskii, 1968a, p. 87). By itself, this does not preclude the selection of some other lower minimum wage and the retention of existing differentials. There must, therefore, have been some additional reason for selecting the 60-ruble minimum. Although the connection is not made explicit, there is some reference to the MMS budget work described in chapter 1 in this context (Kunelskii, 1968b, p. 20). The budget showed that the cost of subsistence for a notional family of four was 50 rubles a month, and implicitly, it suggested that the cost of subsistence for a single worker was 55-57 rubles. Thus, before the 1968 hike, the minimum wage was substantially below the poverty level. It is possible, therefore, that the decision to concentrate resources on the low-paid at the expense of differentials reflected a desire to reduce poverty.

It was also suggested in 1968 that labor turnover was highest among the low-skill grades and that "an improvement in the conditions of paying for their labor would facilitate the retention of such labor on the job [*zakrepleniye kadrov na proizvodstve*]" (Kunelskii, 1968a, p. 86). There is, however, some reason to doubt that this could have been a strong motive for the 1968 wage hike. It is true that in the NIIT study of labor turnover, conducted in 1967-68, there was a higher proportion of low-skill workers (grades I-II) among those who quit than in the labor force as a whole, in the four sectors for which results were given.[20] But this figure includes quits for all reasons. In another study of workers in Leningrad, carried out in 1962-63, only 25.4% of grade I workers who quit gave dissatisfaction with pay as their reason. The proportion for grade II was 21.8%, for grade V, 23%, and for grade VI, 20.3%. The most common reason for quitting given by grade I workers was "dissatisfaction with housing conditions, etc."; this was cited by 38% of all those who left their jobs (Blyakhman et al., 1965, pp. 57, 64). It was also the most frequently quoted reason among workers of all other grades. These figures suggest that the low-paid were not substantially more dissatisfied over pay than other state employees. The figures, of course, relate to Leningrad in 1962-63, and the situation may have been different in the USSR as a whole in 1968, but this is doubtful. The authors of the NIIT study comment that dissatisfaction over wages was most common among those leaving enterprises in the instrument-making, coke ovens, and ferrous alloys branches, none of which are low-paying. They also claim that fitters and electricians were among those most likely to be dissatisfied over pay— again, not the least-skilled.[21]

Finally, it was claimed that the introduction of the 60-ruble minimum wage would substantially increase the earnings of many workers in the services sector—sales staff and cashiers in retail trade, library staff, typists, and those employed in preschool child-care facilities; it was claimed that this would create "more favorable conditions for attracting [such personnel] into employment, which is particularly important, considering the difficulties currently experienced by enterprises and organizations in recruiting [komplektovaniye] them" (Kunelskii, 1968a, p. 86). These occupations are largely staffed by women, and as shown in chapter 7, there was an increase in women's participation rates between 1959 and 1970. But how far this can be ascribed to increases in the minimum wage has yet to be determined. In any case, there is little evidence of a significant increase in the growth of female employment after 1968.

The three arguments considered so far suggest that the 1968 minimum wage hike was a special response to particular circumstances. There is another, much more speculative interpretation. As suggested above, there is some evidence to suggest that the occupational differentials that emerged from the 1956-65 wage reform were excessive. This implies that, on purely efficiency grounds, there was scope for further wage equalization. Further, at least one Soviet economist has suggested that the appropriate skill differential in modern conditions is no greater than 24%, rather than the 100% or more that existed at the time (Maier, 1963, as quoted by Kirsch, 1972, pp. 112-17). The actual figures may be crude, but Maier argued strongly that there was further scope for narrowing differentials. His arguments were challenged by Kapustin and other NIIT economists, and it is possible that this academic dispute concealed a wider political disagreement about the desirability of a more or less egalitarian distribution of wages. If this is the case, perhaps the 1968 wage hike should be seen as a victory for the extreme egalitarians. But (as will become clear below) such a victory, if victory it was, has been short-lived.

The explanation suggested in the preceding paragraph is largely speculation; I can think of no developments in the wider political field that would make it more plausible. Therefore I think one must reject the hypothesis that there exists a radical egalitarian minority either inside the State Committee on Labor and Wages or elsewhere in the policy-making hierarchy.

The suggestion that the 1968 wage hike was a response to new information on the cost of living, however, reveals another possible split among policy makers. As has been pointed out, it is part of the dominant State Committee philosophy that the spheres of wages and social security should be kept separate and that wage relativities should not be reduced for distributional purposes. Attempts are made to invest this doctrine with the imprimatur of Lenin. Yet this is exactly what the 1968 wage hike involved, although, as official State Committee spokesmen are keen to point out, the distortion of differentials was only temporary.[22] Further, there is at least a suggestion that an extension of the social security system was considered at this time but ultimately rejected in favor of the wage hike (Kunelskii, 1968b, p. 16).

The reasons for this rejection are intriguing. Kunelskii states that the use of social security—that is, presumably, the payment of income supplements to the low-paid (or nonemployed)—would undermine labor discipline, while the use of the wage system would constitute a material incentive. He seems to imply, when this rather cryptic remark is spelled out, that an increase in the minimum wage would increase the opportunity cost of leisure (or rather, domestic activity) for those not employed, and thus lead to an increase in the labor supply. For the employed, it would encourage labor productivity, since the minimum is paid only to those "who conscientiously fulfill their obligations" (Livshits, 1972, p. 228). It would also increase the cost to the worker of changing his job. In the USSR there is no unemployment pay, and the 1967-68 NIIT survey of labor turnover reported that the average period spent between jobs was thirty-three days; for women it was as high as forty-seven days. Thus the 1968 wage hike would have added something like 15-20 rubles to the average opportunity cost of a job change for the lowest paid, or possibly even more, since women predominate in this category (Rabkina and Rimashevskaya, 1972, p. 47). Thus the 1968 wage hike might reduce labor turnover among the unskilled.

Table 8.5
Average Period Spent between Jobs, USSR, 1967-68 (days)

Age Group	All Workers	Female Workers
Workers of All Ages	33	47
-20	41	49
21-29	33	56
30-39	28	37
40-	27	33

Source: Danilov, 1973, p. 205.

These comments by Kunelskii are at variance with the attitude and approach of the State Committee outlined at the beginning of the chapter, and it is my belief that they should be read as a grudging justification for a policy that was imposed upon it from the outside, most probably by the Party. The suggestion that the new minimum wage was to commemorate the fiftieth anniversary of the Revolution can be discounted; no mention of this fact was made in the propaganda of the period (Sukharevskii, 1974, p. 242). More likely, faced with new evidence about the extent of poverty in the USSR, the central Party and State authorities decided to override the advice of those responsible for wage administration and to subvert the existing system of occupational differentials rather than extend the social security system. If this is the case, it is interesting to speculate about how the economic and political situation changed sufficiently between 1968 and 1974 to make the family income supplement acceptable in the latter year.

THE 1972-76 WAGE ROUND

Although many Soviet commentators date the third phase of wage policy from 1972, it can be said to have started as early as 1969. In that year, new wage scales were introduced for construction and the construction materials industry, and the rates paid to certain categories of machine tool operator were increased by 15%. In 1971, a start was made at introducing both the 70-ruble minimum wage and new skill scales in industry. The ninth five-year plan contained a timetable for the reorganization of wages and salaries in all sectors of the economy between 1971 and 1975. Completion of this program was delayed by economic difficulties, but it was finished by 1976 (*Gosudarstvennyi* . . . , 1972, pp. 286-87; Kapustin, 1974, pp. 268-70; Sukharevskii, 1974, p. 241).

The measures included in the 1972-76 wage round suggest a return to the policies of 1956-65 after the 1968 interlude. Further progress has been made towards the goal of a single skill scale for the whole of industry. At the same time, while increasing occupational differentials in such low-pay industries as clothing and food processing, the new scales indicate that, formally at least, the range of differentiation in extractive and heavy industry should fall. The 1972-76 wage round also included a rationalization of salary scales and an increase in the salaries paid to managerial, technical, and supervisory personnel. The earnings of these groups have increased relative to those of production workers. In the early sixties it was argued that there should be a narrowing of differentials between management and shop-floor workers: it is not clear whether the developments of the 1968-72 period led to recruitment difficulties, particularly for foremen, or whether there has been a change of heart over the desirability of status differentials.

There is also some doubt about how one should interpret the decision to initiate the move to the 70-ruble minimum wage barely two years after the adoption of the 60-ruble level. It may be that the new minimum should be seen as compensation to the low-paid for the raises given to the more highly skilled, a sugar coating to the pill of greater inequality, as it were. On the other hand, it may reflect yet another instance of belated recognition that the cost of living has increased, or possibly be an attempt to eliminate particular pockets of poverty. In this connection, the Schroeder and Severin index implies that the cost of living rose by 1.3% per annum between 1965 and 1970; this would mean a poverty level of 58 rubles a month in the latter year. In 1968, the minimum wage was set at 20% above the 1965 poverty level; a 20% mark-up on the implied cost of subsistence in 1970 yields a figure of 69.56 rubles.

This survey of Soviet wage administration between the years 1955 and 1975 and of the principles upon which it has been based has shown that wage policy has been neither as coherent nor as consistent as the accounts of Soviet commentators would have us believe. Many decisions appear to have been taken on an *ad hoc* basis, some have been reversed after a comparatively short time, and there appears also to have been disagreements about the basic objectives of policy and about the best means of attaining these objectives. Nevertheless, on balance it is a record of substantial success, but one that gives rise to certain questions.

The central authorities are now much better informed about the state of the labor market than they were in 1955; they have a much clearer idea of the way in which the features of their system operate and interact. They also, perhaps, have a better idea of the significance of particular institutions. All this can be attributed to the work of Soviet labor economists, industrial sociologists, and the State Committee on Labor and Wages.

Further, thanks to the work of the same people, the Soviet economy now has an industrial wage structure with an apparent logic. It may not give rise to a pattern of wages that will bring about a rational allocation of labor, that will generate equilibrium in the labor market, but it is surely more coherent and more appropriate than the structure that prevailed in 1955.

There is a conflict between allocational and distributional considerations, between equity (or, rather, equality) and efficiency, that is inherent in the dual function of wages. It cannot be avoided even in a planned (socialist) economy unless recourse is had to the direction of labor. Current Soviet views on wage determination recognize this contradiction explicitly, and if formal theorizing about policy places undue stress upon efficiency, practical implementation has certainly been influenced by equity. The fact that existing differentials can be explained in terms of a rational theoretical system that embodies a widely accepted principle of equity like equal pay for equal work may make them both socially and politically acceptable. In practice, one suspects, this acceptability owes a lot to the extensive program of job evaluation that has been undertaken in the past twenty years or so.

Actually, one has very little idea about how widespread dissatisfaction over wages is in the Soviet Union. In a system that discourages, if it does not prohibit, strikes and other manifestations of workers' discontent, one must be careful not to confuse passive or grudging acceptance of the status quo with active and wholehearted approval of the system and the benefits it provides. The work of dissenters, made available through *samizdat* or foreign publication, sheds little light on this question. In part, this is because most such authors are intellectuals and their preoccupations are different, but even the work of self-confessed socialists conveys little about attitudes within the Soviet working class. The channels of communication within Soviet society are not good enough for this. And, I believe, one should not place too great an emphasis upon accounts of such special incidents as the response to increases in the price of foodstuffs in 1962, however important they may be for explaining subsequent official immobility on this question.[23] It does not seem plausible to assume that Soviet industry is staffed by a labor force seething with discontent over low living standards and resentment about the scale of inequality. On the one hand, sociological investigations of reasons for changing jobs and the statistical data on labor turnover, such as it is, do not support such an interpretation. It is plausible to assume, too, that Soviet workers, like their counterparts in other countries, will suffer from enough money illusion to have been assuaged by the relatively rapid increases in earnings and incomes that have come over the past twenty or twenty-five years. If and when the rate of growth of earnings slows down—and the figures in table 2.3 suggest that this has already happened—the situation may change. But at present I would conjecture that the Soviet industrial labor force is reasonably contented. Dissatisfaction will be most acute, I suspect, among the most highly skilled and highly paid workers and among those managerial and clerical personnel who have seen their relative affluence eroded by successive increases in the minimum wage coupled with rate restraint in the top half of the wage scale. But this discontent will not be general.

Whatever the attitudes of Soviet workers, Soviet wage policy in the past twenty years or so has been associated with a substantial increase in average earnings and a marked reduction in inequality. Just how great these changes have been will be the subject of the next chapter. But this record is, to a certain extent, paradoxical. As interpreted by Soviet officials, the theory of occupational differentials set out in section 8.3 requires, or at least justifies, the centralized, bureaucratic determination of wage rates. Given the scale of the economy, this implies a rigid and inflexible system in which increases in earnings accrue discontinuously. As there have been only three general rounds of rate revision since 1956, one would expect most Soviet workers to have had only three substantial increases over the same period. In fact, the evidence suggests that average earnings increase on much the same scale from year to year. This implies the intermediation of some other factor or factors in the earnings determination process. And this, in turn, raises the question of the extent to which increases in earnings can properly be attributed to the operation of government policy. Second, if factors other than central decisions on wage rates and salary scales are important, how has the government been able to ensure that the requirements for macroeconomic equilibrium have been maintained? Or has it?

I have suggested that since 1955 there has been a marked reduction in earnings inequality in the Soviet Union. Soviet economists ascribe this to the reduction in the diapazony of skill scales introduced in the course of successive rate revisions. There are at least prima facie grounds for questioning how substantial these reductions were in practice. But if the decline in inequality is not to be attributed to this source, how has it been achieved?

Throughout the book so far I have maintained that the Soviet authorities became more concerned with the questions of popular welfare and inequality in the second half of the fifties. I have shown that the pursuit of an active, interventionist central wage policy dates from 1955. But, at least *ex-post*, the primary objectives of this policy were said to be an improvement in the allocative efficiency of the labor market rather than an attempt to attain greater distributional justice or to ensure a more rapid rise in living standards. What evidence is there about the impact of post-1955 policy upon living standards or inequality? These are the questions I shall seek to answer in chapters 9 and 10.

9

The Distribution of Earnings, 1956-72

THE LAST CHAPTER documented the extensive changes in the administration of wages and salaries that took place in the USSR after 1955. These innovations gave rise to a number of questions about the effectiveness of Soviet policy in this area, about the contribution it has made to the growth of earnings and the reduction of inequality. An attempt will be made to answer these questions in chapters 9 and 10. First, I will take up the question of earnings inequality. Estimates of the distribution of state employees by per capita earnings will be provided for a number of years, together with data for some other groups. The material indicates that between 1956 and 1972 there was a substantial decline in earnings differentiation; the decline was even greater between 1956 and 1968. Other evidence suggests that little of this can be attributed to a reduction in intersectoral or interindustrial differentials introduced during the wage reorganization of the late fifties. It therefore tends to confirm Kirsch's analysis mentioned in the previous chapter. The wage reform, or certain aspects of it, must have led to a contraction in intraindustrial differences in earnings, whatever its impact upon effective wage rates. At the same time, the material casts doubt upon the assertion that the reduction in inequality in the USSR between 1956 and 1972 can be attributed wholly to the impact of government policy. It appears that the evolution of the Societ economy and market forces also played a role.

In section 9.4 I will attempt to go behind the more general figures on the distribution of earnings in the Soviet economy or in Soviet industry. Most of the material up to this point has been concerned with the wage rates and earnings of manual workers. In that I will discuss the level of salaries in the USSR and try to trace changes in what one may call status differentials. The material presented casts some further light on the extent of inequality within industrial enterprises, and also on differences in the earnings of such groups as workers on the one hand and teachers or doctors on the other. While the differences in the USSR are not as extreme as those in a country like the USA, the analysis does reveal substantial differ-

214

ences in earnings. It also shows that considerations like responsibility and authority are of some importance in the determination of basic salary levels.

This chapter, then, contains an empirical analysis of wage and salary differentials in the USSR; the problem of reconciling the growth in earnings with the administration of Soviet wage policy is deferred until chapter 10. But before such an analysis can be undertaken, there are several difficulties that must be resolved, some specific to the Soviet Union, others reflecting possible confusions about the way in which we think about disparity in pay. These are discussed in section 9.1.

9.1   THE CONCEPT AND MEASUREMENT OF EARNINGS INEQUALITY

In this chapter, an attempt is made to assess the extent of earnings inequality among state employees in the USSR and to determine how this has changed since, say, 1955. Statisticians have developed a number of related concepts that emphasize particular aspects of employment-related income, and analyses in terms of one may not always give the same results as analyses in terms of another. It is desirable, therefore, to be clear about which indicators are being used, what they represent, and why they are relevant. The basic dichotomy is between wage rates (or salary scales) and earnings, or take-home pay—that is, earnings less deductions. Between these extremes there are a number of intermediate concepts such as that of basic wages (which attempts to capture differences in normal working hours), and a variety of adjusted or normalized earnings series designed to eliminate the influence of particular variations in conditions of work. Either gross or net earnings (take-home pay) are the most relevant for assessing disparities in living standards, but wage rates or basic wages are probably more important in determining occupational choice. Certainly these are closer to the variables used in theory, and in most contexts, the individual is more likely to have information on the wage rates associated with particular jobs or positions than on the gross (or net) earnings of their present occupants. Because the emphasis of this study is on the standard of living, I will concentrate on earnings in this chapter—and because Soviet statistics do not provide information about deductions, I will use gross rather than net earnings.

There is also a distinction between wages and salaries, each of which can be defined in a variety of ways. To a large extent, the distinction is administrative rather than economic, reflecting forms of payment and the way in which the labor force is classified. But insofar as this classification reflects differences in economic function or social position, differences in the earnings of manual workers and of managerial or supervisory staff can reveal changes in the underlying economic or social structure.

Finally, there is the problem of the sources of differentiation. Formally, it is possible to ascribe interpersonal differences in earnings to interindustrial sources and intraindustrial ones. The first can be measured relatively unambiguously by differences in average earnings between branches of industry or sectors of the economy. It is not clear what empirical meaning can be ascribed to the latter; presumably they refer to the spread of earnings within particular plants or within a specific sector. On this, for the Soviet Union, there is very little information; what data there is refers to rates rather than earnings.

Because the analysis in this chapter relies upon Soviet statistical sources, it is subject to certain limitations that derive from the Soviet classification of the labor force. Until 1966, as pointed out in an earlier chapter, only the employment incomes of state employees were legally regarded as wages or salaries in the USSR. Indeed, available statistics are still confined to this group. Since the share of state employees in total employment has changed since 1950, the analysis given here applies to a varying proportion of the population. An idea of the distortion caused by this method of classification can be gained from an examination of the structure of employment in the Soviet Union and the way it has changed since the war. The relevant figures are given in table 9.1.

Table 9.1
The Structure of Employment, USSR, 1950-70

	1950	1955	1960	1965	1970
Total occupied population ('000)	79,567	81,585	94,274	102,828	112,592
of which (%)					
State employees[a]	50.8	59.3	65.8	74.8	80.1
including wage-earners	34.8	44.0	47.1	52.5	55.1
Industrial workers	16.6	20.1	20.6	22.5	22.8
Agricultural workers	2.8	3.3	6.4	7.9	6.2
Kolkhozniki: collective work	34.3	32.1	23.0	18.1	14.8
Private activity	14.9	8.6	11.1	7.1	5.1
State employee families	5.2	3.6	4.2	4.7	4.2
Kolkhoznik families	9.7	5.0	6.9	2.4	0.9

Notes and Sources: Total occupied population derived by grossing up the annual average number of state employees by their share in the total occupied population. Number of state employees: *Trud*, 1968, pp. 24-25; *NK SSSR* '70, p. 510. Structure of employment: *Trud*, 1968, p. 21; *NK SSSR* '70, p. 508. Total wage earners: *NK SSSR* '70, p. 509. Industrial workers: *Trud*, 1968, p. 81; *NK SSSR* '74, p. 188. Agricultural workers: *Trud*, 1968, p. 126; *NK SSSR* '74, p. 443. Kolkhozniki: annual average employment of kolkhozniki engaged in collective work, *NK SSSR* '60, p. 523; *NK SSSR* '70, p. 405. Private activity: sum of the following two entries. State employee families: *Trud*, 1968, p. 21; *NK SSSR* '70, p. 508; includes "other population," single peasants, etc. Kolkhoznik families derived as the difference between kolkhozniki engaged on collective and private work (*Trud*, 1968, p. 21; *NK SSSR* '70, p. 508) and those engaged only in collective work.

a. Includes cooperative artisans.

The category "total occupied population" used in the table corresponds to the Soviet concept *naseleniye imeyushcheye zanyatiya*. The figures have been derived from Soviet series on annual average employment in particular categories; in the derivation of these series, individuals are weighted by the proportion of the year that they spend in particular types of employment. They therefore give lower totals than figures derived from population censuses. In 1970, for example, the total occupied population amounted to 114.8 million persons, according to the census, 1.95% higher than the figure in table 9.1. In 1970, also, the occupied population, on census definitions, amounted to approximately 88% of the population of working age (90% for males and almost 86% for females). The nonemployed, or rather the nonoccupied, are those in full-time education, those who have retired early, those who through injury or disability are incapable of working, and some married women with or without small children.[1]

Soviet statisticians recognize three categories of occupation, only one of which generates wages or salaries: state employment, participation in the collective work of kolkhozy, and private subsidiary (mainly agricultural) activity. The figures in table 9.1 show that in 1950 only half the occupied population was employed by the state, and thus only half earned wages or salaries. The proportion has risen in the following twenty years, and by 1970, state employment accounted for about four-fifths of the total. Over the same period, collective farm activity declined by more than 50%, from about a third of the total to less than 15%. There was an even more dramatic decline in the relative importance of the recorded private sector.[2]

In 1950, manual workers accounted for little more than a third of total employment, about the same as collective farmers, and it was not until 1965 that they made up more than half the total. The table also shows what impact the program of converting collective farms into sovkhozy had upon the structure of employment. Further, in 1950, industrial workers,[3] who occupy such an important place in Soviet ideology and in the writings of Soviet labor economists, accounted for only 16.6% of the occupied population—very little more than the private sector! By the 1960s, however, industrial workers made up between a fifth and a quarter of the total.

Although not strictly relevant to the topic of this chapter, the figures on the structure of the private sector are interesting, but possibly misleading. They indicate that over the twenty-year period covered by the table, the share of kolkhozniki and their families in the private sector declined from about two-thirds to under a fifth, and that the share of private activity in total kolkhoznik employment declined from about a fifth to about 5%. But given the way in which the numbers have been derived,

they may understate the importance of private-plot work in total kolkhoznik activity. The figures in the table are based on two series on annual
average employment; they are thus based on some concept of an average
working year. They presumably exclude the amount of what may be
called "free time" that kolkhozniki spend on their holdings. They also
exclude the free time spent by workers and their families in similar occupations. It is to be expected that kolkhozniki spend much more of their
notional leisure on their holdings than do state employees. These changes
in the structure of the labor force should be borne in mind when assessing
the significance of the results given below.

9.2   THE DISTRIBUTION OF EARNINGS, 1956-72

Published statistics on the distribution of earnings in the Soviet Union
are almost nonexistent, but the figures that I have managed to find show
that dispersion, as measured by the decile ratio, declined by about a
third between 1956 and 1970. Between 1956 and 1968 the fall was closer
to 40%. This section will describe the sources of the statistics quoted
above, present estimates of the distribution of state employees by money
earnings for a number of postwar years, and explore the impact of wage
policy upon the scale of interindustrial differentiation. The material
shows the importance of central policy in determining the scale of earnings differentials, particularly increases in the minimum wage, but it also
suggests strongly that other factors have been at work.

The basic source of statistical information about the distribution of
earnings in the USSR has been the March wage census, *otchet*, which has
been held every two or three years since 1956. Very few figures and none
of the distributions compiled on the basis of these *otchety* have been
published. Rather, as with data on the distribution of income, individual
academics have reproduced some more or less inadequate histograms or
frequency polygons, and it is with these that one must work. What follow
are reconstructions of the distribution of earnings for eight out of the ten
or eleven years in which, apparently, censuses have been held. For the
most part, these have been obtained by methods analogous to those used
in deriving the income distributions of chapter 3; further details on
methods and sources are given in appendix F.

The first of the current series of wage censuses was held in 1956, although similar enquiries had been held in the thirties and one may have
been conducted in 1946. Since 1956, otchety have been organized every
two or three years. There were censuses almost certainly in 1956, 1959,
1961, 1964, and 1966, and probably also in 1957, 1968, 1970, and 1972.
This gives a total of nine postwar years for which earnings distributions
exist, to which one may add, with some reservations, 1946. One or more
censuses might have been organized since 1972.[4] Soviet economists have

used the distribution of earnings in 1946 as a benchmark against which postwar developments can be assessed, but it is not clear that a census was held in that year; the sources quoted in the last footnote suggest that the 1956 census was the first since before the war. On the other hand, if there was no 1946 census, it is not clear where the estimated distribution of earnings was obtained. A possible source is the family budget survey (which is also the probable source of all statistics on the distribution of earnings in non-census years). In view of the manifold weaknesses of this source, especially as early as 1946, the purported distribution of earnings for this year should be treated with suspicion. I have not given figures relating to 1946 in tables 9.2-9.4, but estimates of the distribution used by Soviet labor economists may be found in Wiles and Markowski, p. 503, and Chapman, 1974, p. 20.

A brief description of the census methodology will help in assessing the meaning to be ascribed to the statistics presented later in the chapter. For census purposes, all enterprises, organizations, and institutions in the state sector are required to provide information on numbers employed and total wages paid out and to give distributions of employees both by wage rate (salary scale), *tarifnye stavki ili dolzhnostnye oklady*, and by gross earnings, *nachislennaya zarabotnaya plata* (Rimashevskaya, 1965, p. 46). So far as I know, published Soviet sources give no information about the first of these distributions; the figures given below relate to gross earnings. More precisely, they cover all state employees who worked a full month, usually March or April, in the census year, and gross earnings consist of wages, salaries, and all incentive payments from the wage fund and other sources. Loans from enterprise funds and the reimbursement of expenses are excluded (Matyukha, 1973, p. 77). It is not clear how multiple job-holding or part-time work are dealt with. I presume that part-time workers are excluded and that those individuals, usually professionals, who hold more than one position, *sovmestitelstvo*, are counted only at their primary place of work. If they hold more than one position in the same organization, however, their full earnings are included. Thus, the figures given below relate to the distribution of full-time state employees by monetary receipts in a single month of the relevant year. One might therefore expect dispersion to be somewhat less than had all employees been included; on the other hand, dispersion will probably be increased by confining observations to so short a period. It is not known how far these two effects offset each other.

In at least two years, the census has been accompanied by a sample survey designed to investigate the structure of earnings for particular groups of employees. Such a survey has also been held in at least one year when there was no census (Labok, 1966, pp. 270-80; Rimashevskaya, 1965, p. 47). The surveys covered the earnings of all employed at selected enterprises. In the three years for which there is explicit information, these enterprises have been restricted to industry and construction. Their primary purpose has been to investigate the structure of earnings, the relative importance of basic wages, various bonuses, and plus-rates in connection with wage reorganization; but they may also have been used to generate more comprehensive statistical information about the distribution of earnings, at least in the sectors covered.

Estimates of the distribution of earnings for a selection of postwar years are given in table 9.2, and some attempt is made to assess their reliability in table 9.3. In this latter table, certain statistical measures of dispersion, calculated from the distributions of table 9.2, are compared with their analogues given in the Soviet literature. The overall impression is that the figures given here are reasonably reliable but that one should have certain reservations about the distributions for 1956 and 1964. That for 1956 appears to overstate disparity in earnings (by about 10%, according to the decile ratio), while that for 1964 understates the disparity by about 10 or 15%, depending on the measure used. The errors arise out of the reconstruction process and are in addition to any bias resulting from the methodology used in conducting the census itself. They imply that for these two years in particular, the numbers for classes at the extremes of the income scale are likely to be unreliable.[5]

Table 9.2
The Distribution of State Employees by Monthly Earnings, USSR, 1956-70 (%)

Earnings (rubles per month)	1956	1957	1959	1961	1964	1966	1968	1970
-25	9.7	8.2	} 4.4		} 2.2		} 3.0	} 5.1
25-30	6.0	6.0		} 15.0		} 2.2		
30-35	5.0	5.6	8.0		} 5.3			
35-40	5.2	4.8	4.8					
40-50	11.5	10.1	12.0	11.2	6.2	7.1		
50-60	10.5	9.6	11.3	11.4	9.9	11.3	5.4	5.2
60-70	9.5	9.1	9.2	12.2	10.5	11.9	8.3	} 17.2
70-80	7.8	8.1	8.4	9.4	11.1	10.4	10.2	
80-90	7.3	7.3	7.8	8.2	10.4	9.6	11.2	} 21.6
90-100	6.7	6.6	7.1	7.2	9.3	8.5	10.5	
100-120	9.2	9.6	10.3	8.0	13.6	13.3	17.6	12.8
120-140	5.3	6.1	7.1	6.9	9.4	8.7	12.5	} 21.1
140-160	3.1	3.8	4.6	4.0	5.7	5.8	8.3	
160-200	2.5	4.1	4.0	} 6.4	5.0	6.8	7.4	10.4
200-	0.6	0.7	1.0		1.4	4.4	5.5	6.6

Notes and Sources: The years 1956-59, 1964, Shvyrkov and Aidina, 1968, p. 234. 1961, 1970 derived from Chapman, 1974, p. 20; Chapman's estimates are based on fitting a lognormal distribution with parameters derived from the equation in Rabkina and Rimashevskaya, 1972, p. 250; the 1961 distribution has been extended by using data from McAuley, 1977. 1966 and 1968 from Rabkina and Rimashevskaya, 1972, p. 194.

Table 9.3
The Distribution of Earnings, 1956–70: Reliability

	1956	1957	1959	1961	1964	1966	1968	1970
As reported:								
d_9/d_1	4.4	n.a	4.2	n.a	3.7	3.2	2.7	3.2
$\bar{x}/d_1$	n.a	n.a	n.a	2.5	2.4	n.a	n.a	1.8
As calculated:								
d_9/d_1	4.9	5.1	4.2	4.3	3.3	3.3	2.8	3.1
$\bar{x}/d_1$	2.6	2.8	2.4	2.5	2.0	2.0	1.8	1.9

Sources: Rows 1 and 2, excluding 1959, from Sarkisyan, 1972, pp. 124, 126; 132-33; 1959 quoted in Chapman, 1974, p. 20. Rows 3 and 4 calculated from table 9.2.

There is a further puzzle arising out of the estimates of table 9.2. They imply figures for average earnings that, in 1956-57, differ significantly from those published by the Central Statistical Administration. From table 9.2, average money earnings in 1956 were estimated as 69.0 rubles a month; for 1957 the figure was 73.9 rubles. The corresponding figures from the published series were 73.40 rubles and 76.20 rubles a month for 1956 and 1957 respectively. It is unlikely that this error can be attributed to the reconstruction. Shvyrkov states that between 1956 and 1964 average earnings increased by 29.3%, and that they increased by 6.2% between 1956 and 1957. The growth rates implied by the CSA's series are 22.75% and 3.8% respectively. It is difficult to see that Shvyrkov's figures could be the result of a printing error. Consequently, the March census series yields either lower estimates of average earnings in 1956 or a higher esti- mate for 1964. Since the growth rates for the periods 1959-61 and 1961-64 are substantially the same in both sources, the first alternative seems more plausible (Shvyrkov and Aidina, 1968, p. 233). This receives indi- rect support from another source. Rabkina and Rimashevskaya give an equation for average earnings as a function of time, which they claim has a maximum error of 2.9 rubles and which was estimated on the basis of census data. Substituting into this equation for 1956 yields a figure of 69.58 rubles for average earnings in that year. From their remark about the size of the error component, this makes an estimate of 69.0 rubles a month for the census value of average earnings in 1956 more plausible than one of 73.4 rubles (Rabkina and Rimashevskaya, 1972, p. 250).

It is difficult to conceive of a plausible explanation for an error of 4.4 rubles in average earnings (approximately 6.4%), particularly since only two years are affected. Most probably it reflects a weakness in the initial census methodology, since the two years affected are the first in the cur- rent series. Perhaps certain categories of income were excluded or some group of highly paid state employees omitted. At all events, the two series move closely together after 1959.[6]

Estimates of a number of statistical measures of location and dispersion derived from the distributions in table 9.2 are given in table 9.4. The figures in these two tables provide a great deal of information about the nature and extent of the earnings revolution in the USSR in the fourteen years after Khrushchev's secret speech. They permit inferences to be drawn about the impact of the 1956-65 wage and salary reorganization, and about the effects of successive increases in the minimum wage on both the level of earnings and the extent of inequality in the Soviet Union. (But it should be remembered that the figures in tables 9.2 and 9.4 refer to nominal and not real earnings.)

Table 9.4
The Distribution of Earnings, 1956-70: Measures of Location and Dispersion

	1956	1957	1959	1961	1964	1966	1968	1970
Mean (rubles)	69.6	73.9	79.2	83.1	91.0	98.9	110.9	115.5
Median (rubles)	62.2	66.3	70.4	70.2	84.0	87.4	101.3	101.4
as % of median:								
1st decile	40.7	40.0	47.6	47.4	53.6	57.9	61.0	58.6
1st quartile	62.9	60.9	66.0	69.6	73.1	72.9	77.0	76.0
3rd quartile	150.6	150.2	147.7	143.8	136.8	139.1	132.3	142.8
9th decile	200.0	202.1	201.1	203.0	177.1	190.8	169.8	184.3
d_9/d_1	4.9	5.1	4.2	4.3	3.3	3.3	2.8	3.1
q_3/q_1	2.4	2.5	2.2	2.1	1.9	1.9	1.7	1.9
Average earnings (rubles)	73.4	76.2	79.0	83.4	90.1	99.2	112.7	122.0

Sources: Last row taken from *Trud*, 1968, p. 137; *NK SSSR za 1922-72*, p. 350.

The figures given in table 9.4 suggest that average monthly earnings grew by 66% between 1956 and 1970. (Fortuitously, the same increase is implied by the CSA.) Over the same period, inequality decreased by about 30%, as measured by the decile coefficient. If one considers only the period 1956-68, the decline in inequality, on the same measure, was 42.8%. (Using the Soviet estimate of the decile coefficient in 1956, the decline was 36.4%.)

This was achieved by a substantial increase in the earnings of the low-paid, accompanied by some restriction in the growth of earnings at the top. Between 1956 and 1970 the first decile of the earnings distribution increased by 135%, the ninth by 50%. In ruble terms, increases were similar at all levels of income, particularly up to 1968. In 1956, the interquartile range was 54.55 rubles, twelve years later it was 55.94 rubles; over the same period the interdecile range $(d_9 - d_1)$ increased from 99.10 rubles to 110.20 rubles. Looked at in this way, one can say that differentials in the Soviet Union have remained more or less constant in ruble terms; the whole distribution has been shifted bodily to the right. Thus the consequence of the so-called earnings revolution has been to give the vast majority of state employees more or less the same increment in money earnings. It is this that has produced the marked fall in inequality.

The figures in table 9.4 show that reductions in inequality, like increases in average earnings, did not occur smoothly over the period. Further, significant changes in the dispersion of earnings seem to coincide with the major innovations of state wage policy. The initial phase of wage reorganization, that in the productive sector, brought about some reduction in the decile coefficient, about 5% if one accepts the Soviet figure for K_d in 1956 (and 14% if one uses the figure in table 9.4). Completion of the reorganization in 1964-65 and the associated dissemination of the 40- to 45-ruble minimum wage to the nonproductive sphere led to a further reduction in inequality of between 12 and 20% depending on the figures used. Finally, the 1968 minimum wage hike resulted in another decline of 15%. The initial phases of the post-1972 wage round, which I suggested in chapter 8 could be dated to 1969, have been associated with an 11-18% increase in inequality. This suggests, I think, that changes in earnings differentials in the Soviet Union can be attributed, at least in part, to the operation of central government policy. To be more precise, evidence given later suggests that changes in the pressure of demand may have affected the scale of interindustrial differentials but that these changes are not sufficient to explain the reduction in inequality documented in tables 9.2 and 9.4.

Finally, I should point out that, according to the figures in table 9.4, the first decile of the earnings distribution throughout the period coincided approximately with the legal minimum wage. Since part-time workers are apparently excluded from the wage censuses and since apprentices make up only 1-2% of the labor force, this implies that substantial numbers of Soviet workers are paid at rates below the minimum wage. A recent legal monograph defined the latter as "that limit below which the remuneration of an employee who conscientiously fulfills his obligations cannot fall" (Livshits, 1972, p. 208). It is possible that managers in fact exercise their implied authority to penalize financially those who do not fulfill their output targets, but figures given below suggest that few of the poorly paid are to be found in industry. Given the increases in average earnings in state agriculture, it has become less plausible to assume that they are to be found in that sector. But workers in the lowest-wage sectors, like health, do not operate under a system of output targets, norm-fulfillment bonuses, and productivity growth. Thus the identity of these very low-paid groups remains a minor statistical puzzle.

The figures discussed so far have referred to state employees as a whole, and these figures are the most relevant for assessing the impact of wages and salaries policy on the distribution of earnings and disparities in living standards. However, there is some limited information available about the distribution of earnings within particular sub-sectors of the Soviet economy and for certain sub-groups of the Soviet labor force. Although the distributions refer only to one or two isolated years, these data can both add to one's understanding of the general distribution of earnings and cast light on the operation of the policies described in the previous chapter. The available figures are given in tables 9.5 and 9.6. Once again, the distributions have been reconstructed from histograms or frequency polygons by what one may call the Wiles-Markowski method; further details on their derivation and a list of sources are given in appendix F. (Soviet sources also contain details of the distribution of earnings in specific industries, but these are too few in number to allow any very meaningful conclusions to be drawn from them.)

Table 9.5
The Distribution of Earnings, Selected Groups, 1961-68

Earnings (rubles per month)	Industry				Other State Employees	
	All Employees		Workers			
	1961	1964	1961	1968	1961	1964
-30	} 4.8	1.2	2.2	} 3.0	} 20.6	2.7
30-40		2.6	3.5			6.7
40-50	7.3	5.1	6.4		13.3	6.9
50-60	8.0	7.6	8.1		13.3	11.2
60-70	10.4	9.9	10.5	6.0	13.2	10.9
70-80	11.8	11.2	11.9	9.5	8.1	11.0
80-90	11.6	11.5	11.5	11.6	6.3	9.8
90-100	10.2	10.5	10.2	11.4	5.5	8.6
100-120	14.8	15.9	15.7	19.8	4.3	12.3
120-140	8.6	9.9	9.0	14.4	6.0	9.1
140-160	5.2	5.8	5.0	9.4	3.3	5.6
160-200	4.7	5.2	4.5	8.9	} 6.1	} 5.2
200-	2.4	3.5	1.4	6.1		

Source: Rabkina and Rimashevskaya, 1972, pp. 79, 198, and 202, and 79; table 9.2. For details, see appendix F.

There is very little independent information upon which the reliability of the distributions of table 9.5 can be judged; most of what is available was used in the reconstruction. But a comparison of the mean of the distribution for nonindustrial employees with the estimate of average earnings implied by the CSA's annual series on earnings in the state sector reveals certain discrepancies, particularly in 1964. In that year, calculated mean earnings were some 6.5% less than reported average earnings. Thus this distribution at least contains a downward bias that should be borne in mind.

If one accepts the figures at their face value, however, they indicate

Table 9.6
The Distribution of Earnings, Selected Groups, 1961-68:
Measures of Location and Dispersion

	Industry				Other State Employees	
	All Employees		Workers			
	1961	1964	1961	1968	1961	1964
Mean (rubles)	94.3	99.6	92.3	118.2	76.2	89.8
Median (rubles)	86.5	90.9	86.3	107.9	62.1	80.6
as % of median:						
1st decile	54.4	56.7	54.0	65.9	47.8	50.7
1st quartile	74.7	75.5	74.7	79.4	69.7	71.7
3rd quartile	131.5	131.4	131.4	128.9	145.5	138.6
9th decile	172.0	171.3	166.4	165.5	222.1	177.2
95th percentile	205.4	207.5	194.4	202.0	297.8	203.9
d_9/d_1	3.2	3.0	3.1	2.5	4.6	3.5
q_3/q_1	1.8	1.7	1.8	1.6	2.1	1.9
Average earnings (rubles)					77.25	84.4

Sources: Calculated from table 9.5; last row from *Trud*, 1968, pp. 137, 139.

that in 1961 industrial earnings were substantially higher than those in the rest of the state sector and that inequality was much less. This is not surprising, particularly if one believes that the wage reform led to reductions in the differentiation of earnings. By 1961, wage reorganization had been completed in industry, while in the nonproductive sector it had barely begun. By 1964, when the wage reform had made substantial progress in the services sector,[7] earnings inequality among nonindustrial state employees was much lower. But even in 1964 there were greater disparities in earnings among nonindustrial state employees than within industry; and this is to be expected, given the heterogeneity of the former group, which ranges from health-sector employees to state administrators and scientific research workers.

Tables 9.5 and 9.6 also contain estimates of the distribution of industrial workers by money earnings in 1961 and 1968. The fact that manual workers make up approximately 85% of all industrial employees explains why there is so little difference between the two industry distributions in 1961. It is only in the upper tail that any substantial divergences occur. The distribution that in fact results if workers are netted out is a combination of the distribution for clerical staff and that for managerial, technical, and supervisory staff. It proved impossible to unscramble these two, with the information available.

In 1961, the first decile of the distribution of industrial workers was 46.6 rubles. At this date, the minimum wage in industry was 40-45 rubles a month, depending upon the location and industrial affiliation of the employing enterprise. Only 5-6% of workers had earnings of less than 40 rubles a month. In 1968, when the minimum wage was raised to 60 rubles, as few as 3% of workers fell below this level. Thus the poorly paid tenth of the work force mentioned above are not to be found, for the most part, among Soviet industrial workers.

According to the account of Soviet wage policy given in section 8.4 there were no substantial modifications in wage rates or salary scales in Soviet industry between 1961 and 1964; yet the figures in table 9.6 indicate that, as measured by the decile coefficient, earnings inequality declined by about 6% over this period. Also, in view of the timing of the wage censuses and the introduction of new salary structures in the services sector, it is doubtful whether all of the recorded decline in inequality of 23.9% can be ascribed to the effects of government policy. It may be that at this time there were other factors operating in the Soviet labor market that tended to reduce the scale of earnings differentials. I shall return to this point below.

Table 9.6 shows that between 1961 and 1968 there was a substantial reduction in earnings disparity among Soviet workers as measured by the decile coefficient; the decline was not as marked when measured by the quartile ratio. But changes were less regular than for the state sector as a whole. In percentage terms, the largest increases came to those who were worst off: all deciles below the median recorded relative gains, while those above the median saw their relative superiority eroded. In absolute terms, however, the largest gains were recorded at the top of the distribution.

In this context, the behavior of the ninety-fifth percentile should be mentioned. Relative to the median, it increased both for industrial employees as a whole between 1961 and 1964 and for industrial workers between 1961 and 1968. The implication is that while the bulk of managerial, technical, and supervisory personnel and skilled workers saw their earnings fall relative to the median, those with the highest pay experienced a small relative increase. Some part of this may be attributed to the introduction of new pay scales for underground miners (already one of the highest-paid groups in Soviet industry) in 1964; but since coal mining, both opencast and underground, accounted for only 5.2% of industrial employment in 1960 and for 3.9% in 1968, and since only some 16-30% of the labor force was in the top two or three skill grades, other factors were clearly at work (statistics from *Vestnik Statistiki*, no. 10, 1970, no. 4, 1971, and no. 11, 1973). Although the estimates that can be derived from the distributions in table 9.2 are not particularly reliable, they suggest that for the state sector as a whole, the ninety-fifth percentile declined relative to the median over most of the period; increases were registered in 1957, 1966, and 1970. Unfortunately, the value of this statistic in 1961, as derived from table 9.2, is very inaccurate; but for all plausible assumptions about the distribution of observations in the highest two income classes, the figures imply that between 1961 and 1968, for the state sector as a whole, the ninety-fifth percentile declined relative to the median.[8]

One is tempted to conjecture that these results mean that the scope for increases in the earnings of managers and professionals under the post-1965 system of economic administration was greater in industry than in the rest of the economy, and that industrial managers took full advantage of their opportunities. There is some evidence to suggest that this was the case, but it cannot be inferred from these figures. First, such a conjecture does not explain the increases that occurred in 1961-64, before the new system of administration was adopted. Second, it does not deal with the increases received by the most highly paid industrial workers between 1961 and 1968.

These results call into question the conclusion that reductions in earnings disparities can be attributed to the operation of the government's central control over the determination of wage rates and salary scales. Certainly, if the dispersion statistics given in tables 9.3 or 9.4 are plotted against time, the impression created is that significant changes in inequality have coincided with the introduction of specific policy measures. At the risk of committing a *post-hoc-ergo-propter-hoc* fallacy, one may ascribe these changes to the operation of central policy. But the impression created by such a comparison is misleading. The years for which there are statistics on the distribution of earnings have tended to coincide with the years in which there have been significant policy changes. There is little information available about the way that differentials have changed in intercensal years, and there is little hope of finding comparable statistics that would throw light on this question. An analysis of the distribution of earnings in industry does suggest that other factors have been at work, however.

9.3   EARNINGS DIFFERENTIALS: THE IMPACT OF POLICY

There is one method that might help to identify the way in which earnings disparities have changed in intercensal years, and it is to that that I now turn. The earnings received by any state employee depend upon the branch of industry (or sector of the economy) in which he or she works, and upon the employee's position or status within the employing enterprise or organization. (Insofar as there are systematic differences between the wages and salaries paid out by different enterprises or in different parts of the country, earnings will depend upon these factors too.) Thus one may subdivide interpersonal disparities in earnings into two components, intrasectoral and intersectoral differentials. Although no information exists on the first of these, the second may be approached through an analysis of the way that average earnings in particular industries or sectors change through time. For some sets of these, the CSA has published annual figures since 1955 or 1960.

It is Soviet statistical practice to divide the state sector of the economy into twelve major sub-sectors, from industry, transport, and construction down to health, education, and state administration. The annual statistical handbooks contain figures on employment and average earnings for each of these sectors for 1955 and for each year since 1960. From this data it is possible to derive a number of synthetic measures of the scale of intersectoral variation in earnings. Statisticians also divide industry into a number of branches, and although the figures are neither as consistent nor as comprehensive as those for the sectors, it is possible to derive analogous measures of interbranch variations in earnings. Given the nature of the original figures, these estimates of the scale of intersectoral disparity in earnings relate to all state employees who work in particular sectors; that is, both managers and workers are included. For a limited number of sectors in material production, earnings data are given separately for manual workers, clerical staff, and managerial and supervisory personnel, but this material will not be considered here. Finally, for much the same reasons as given in the case of interrepublican disparity in per capita incomes, it seems to me that the most appropriate measure of changes in the scale of intersectoral variation in earnings is the coefficient of variation, and that is the statistic used here.

Over the period 1955-73 there was very little change in the ranking of either economic sectors or industrial branches by average earnings—at least, on the level of disaggregation for which earnings data are available. The Spearman's rank correlation coefficient for the orderings of the twelve sectors in 1960 and 1970 was 0.89, and that for the fifteen industrial branches on which there are figures in both years was 0.90. As might be expected, the correlation coefficients increase as the period between the years contracts. Most of the changes in ranking that occur can be ascribed to differences in the timing of the introduction of new wage and salary scales or to minor reversals between sectors with approximately the same average earnings. The only significant exception appears to have been a substantial and possibly permanent increase in agricultural earnings relative to those in the rest of the economy. Before 1961, agricultural earnings were lower than those in any other sector; in that year, state agriculture moved from twelfth to ninth place in the "earnings league." In 1965 it had dropped to tenth place (as a result of wage and salary increases in the nonproductive sphere). By 1968-69 it had risen to eighth place, which position it has retained ever since.

The relative stability in the ranking of sectors by average earnings has been accompanied by a contraction in the scale of differentiation, particularly since 1960. This is brought out clearly by chart 9.1, in which the coefficient of variation in average sectoral earnings is plotted against time for a number of years since 1955. The chart shows, first, that wage reorganization in industry (between 1955 and 1960-61) had very little impact upon the rest of the state sector—which suggests that in this period, there was very little tendency for earnings to rise more rapidly in those sectors that competed most closely with industry for labor. The extension of wage reorganization to the rest of the state sector in 1960-61 and 1964-65 resulted in substantial declines in intersectoral differentiation. There was a further decline in 1968. Since that time, differentials have tended to increase, although they are still some 10 to 15% lower than in 1955. The post-1968 increases can be attributed to the introduction of new pay scales in construction and other precursors of the so-called post-1972 wage round. Thus, chart 9.1 suggests that changes in the dispersion of sectoral earnings coincide with changes in rate structures decreed from the center. Although there is no information on how intrasectoral differentials changed over the period, it seems plausible to conclude that central wage policy was instrumental in bringing about the reduction in interpersonal differentiation in earnings recorded in table 9.4.

The evidence provided by interindustrial variations in earnings, however, is less clear. One problem is that I do not have a consistent set of figures covering the whole period. For 1955-68, the coefficient of variation is calculated from figures relating to ten branches of industry and accounting for 88% of industrial employment, while for 1960-74 the figures relate to fifteen branches accounting for 89% of employment.[9] Nevertheless, there seems to be sufficient agreement in the direction of changes between the two series for certain general conclusions to be drawn. First, it appears that between 1955 and 1960, interindustrial differentials increased; between 1960 and 1961 they declined sharply and in the latter year were very little different than in 1955. This pattern makes a certain sense. In its initial stages, wage reorganization was conducted on an industry-by-industry basis, and if the new wage scales resulted in substantially higher earnings for converted industries, one would expect to observe an increase in interbranch differentials. A higher-than-normal variance would also be expected after the introduction of the geographical principle if there were marked differences in the pattern of location between industrial branches. Only when reorganization was complete would the variance in average earnings return to "normal." From this, two conclusions follow. First, the wage reorganization of 1956-61 had very little impact on the scale of interindustrial differentiation, whatever may have happened to disparity in earnings within individual plants or industries. And second, that reform was not complete in industry until

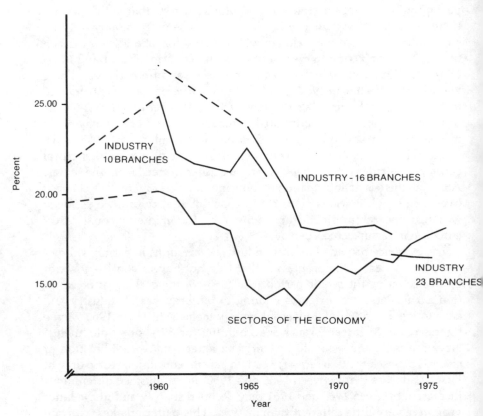

Chart 9.1. Changes in Intersectoral Differentials, 1955-75: The Coefficient of Variation in Average Sectoral Earnings, All Employees. (Hatched lines have been used where no figures are available.) Note: The three variants for industry reflect differences in the degree of detail with which the CSA has reported earnings in industry in various sources at different times in the past.

1961, in spite of Chapman's report that by 1960 "approximately thirty million workers were on new pay-scales—almost all of industry, construction and some other sectors" (Chapman, 1970, p. 24).

According to the estimates of the decile coefficient on earnings in the state sector as a whole, there was a decline of some 2-12% in inequality between 1956 and 1961. The figures in chart 9.1 indicate that, if anything, intersectoral differentials increased marginally over this period. Since interpersonal differentials are a result of intersectoral and intrasectoral differentials in earnings, these figures suggest a decline in the latter. Further, since wage reorganization was largely confined to industry and construction before 1961, it is most plausible to assume that the decline in intrasectoral differentials was greatest in these branches. Such considerations tend to support the hypothesis, mentioned in the last chapter, that reorganization resulted in a decline in effective skill differentials in earnings.

Chart 9.1 also shows that the coefficient of variation in average branch earnings increased somewhat in 1964-65 and that it declined continuously between 1965 and 1968. Since 1968 it has remained virtually constant. The increase in 1964-65 can probably be ascribed to the introduction of a new pay scale for underground miners in 1964, but the decline since 1965 is puzzling. Clearly, this decline cannot be ascribed to the introduction of the 60-ruble minimum wage in 1968; it also appears to start too soon and to end too abruptly for one to explain it as a consequence of the economic reform of 1965. (In point of fact, few enterprises were converted to the new system of management until 1967.) Perhaps it is a manifestation of incipient loss of control over earnings in 1965-67, to be discussed in chapter 10.

There is a hypothesis, first advanced by Reder, that might cast some light on the economic processes at work during this period. Reder suggested that one should expect occupational differentials to narrow in times of labor scarcity. This prediction was derived from the observation that there are two courses of action open to the employer of highly skilled (and highly paid) labor: either he can raise the wage he is prepared to pay in the hope of attracting labor away from other firms, or he can lower his standards and hire workers he would not normally employ, at existing wage rates. Insofar as this dilution attracts less-skilled (and therefore lower-paid) workers from other employment, employers of such labor will have to respond. Since the opportunities for dilution open to them are less, their response will be concentrated on the wages side. This leads to the predicted contraction in differentials.

Now, although the Reder mechanism is formally concerned with occupational differentials rather than intersectoral ones, if low-wage industries contain a higher than average proportion of low-skill workers and high-wage industries contain a higher than average proportion of high-skill workers (and such is the Soviet contention), a similar effect might be observed on the sectoral level. It is known, for instance, that the 1960s were a period of low natural increase for the Soviet labor force, which might have been expected to lead to tight labor market conditions. But this still leaves questions of timing unaccounted for. Although I think a slightly stronger case for the operation of a mechanism of this nature can be made, I do not propose to develop it here.

The primary purpose of this section has been to present the available statistical evidence about changes in the extent of earnings inequality in the state sector of the Soviet economy since the mid fifties, and to ask how far they can be attributed to the operation of the government's wage and salary policy. The figures in tables 9.4 and 9.6, for all their limitations, show that there has been a significant decline in earnings disparity since 1956. In conjunction with the results displayed in chart 9.1, they suggest that some part of this decline must have taken place within individual sectors or enterprises. Further, for the state sector as a whole, there are grounds for suggesting that reductions in inequality can be attributed to the operation of government policy. When industry is considered separately, however, the results are less clear; they may even contradict the above conclusion. It appears that much of the decline in intraindustrial differentials has occurred in periods when there have been no extensive modifications to centrally determined wage scales. Thus although industry appears to have received more than its proper share of attention from the State Committee on Labor and Wages, because of the government's ideological preconceptions, government policy seems to have been less decisive here than in other sectors. And one cannot infer that the central control of wage rates and salary scales has played a determining role. Before attempting an assessment of the way in which the Soviet authorities have achieved their basic objectives in this area, however, I propose in section 9.4 to examine more material on the pay levels of managerial and professional personnel and changes in the size of what one may call status differentials.

9.4 MANAGERIAL AND PROFESSIONAL SALARIES

The earnings of managers, teachers, doctors, and professionals in general in the USSR are much less extensively documented than are the wages of industrial workers or even collective farmers. Soviet economists have published salary scales used in education, health, and the so-called productive sphere of the economy, and there has been some discussion of the principles on which they were constructed, but there is little information about how individuals are distributed between the different grades or how scales vary within industry. However, some impression of the extent of differentiation can be gained from the material available. In this section I propose to describe, briefly, salary structures within health and education, the two most important service sectors, and to comment on the principles embodied in their construction. Other salaries in the non-productive sphere are, I believe, organized on similar lines. The rest of the section will be devoted to a discussion of the salaries and earnings of managerial and technical personnel in industry and the way in which these have changed, relative to industrial wages, since the fifties.

In general terms it is possible to identify four categories of salaried employees in the Soviet economy: there are managers of enterprises in industry, agriculture, construction, and so on; there are clerical workers in both the productive and nonproductive spheres; there are members of the professions—teachers, doctors, nurses, and so on; and there are ad-ministrators—Party officials, ministers, deputy ministers, and the senior staffs of such bodies as Gosplan. On the salaries of this last group there is no official information; it is rumored that some are the highest in the USSR. Perhaps the rumors are exaggerated, but insofar as Soviet salaries conform to the hierarchical principle, the principle that superiors must earn more than their subordinates if they are to be able to exercise authority over them (and from what is known of salaries elsewhere in the economy, the principle appears to apply), salaries at the top of the central bureauc-racy, either party or state, must be substantial.[10]

There is some information about the salaries of the other three groups listed in the last paragraph, and I propose to deal with each in turn. In the nonproductive sphere, in schools, hospitals, and clinics, etc., where indicators of personal or institutional performance are not available, where it is difficult to measure output or productivity, bonuses are not paid and earnings consist almost exclusively of basic salaries. In medi-cine, however, there are merit payments, and other sectors may provide some sort of material incentive for those employed in them; such would be in keeping with recent Soviet attitudes, but I am unaware of any sub-stantial excluded components. Thus for these sectors, although our infor-mation is entirely limited to the salary scales payable, we can come closer to earnings than, say, in industry or construction.

There are two scales for teachers in education, one for those with higher education and one for those without. There is also a double matrix of salaries for school principals, since their salaries also depend upon school size. After the 1964 revisions, teachers' salaries ranged from 80 to 137 rubles a month for those with higher education and from 65 to 111 rubles for those without.[11] For school principals, the rates range from 90 to 208 rubles a month for those with higher education, depending upon experience and size of school, and from 82 to 207 rubles for those with-out higher education. Although the basic salary structures in education are extremely simple, the computation of actual earnings is complicated by a series of special payments for teaching supplementary sessions, for marking (grading), and for various extracurricular activities. But neither these nor the scales themselves, which do not embody the principle of annual incrementation that is characteristic of salaries in the UK, can explain the steady increase in average earnings observed after 1960 (see below, chapter 10).

Salary scales for doctors established in 1964 and maintained until 1972 ranged from 90-105 rubles a month for those with less than five years' experience to 165-170 rubles a month for those with more than thirty years' experience (*Spravochnik po zarabotnoi* . . . , 1970, p. 115). There were also a number of supplementary payments for merit or for assuming added responsibility that might have increased the earnings of this group, but little purpose would be served by detailing them.

When these salary scales were established in 1964, the minimum wage was 40 rubles a month. Thus the salaries of teachers ranged from 2 to 3.4 times the minimum wage, those for medical personnel from 2.25 to 4.25 times the minimum. This suggests that the basic salaries of teachers were approximately the same as, or rather less than, the basic wages of highly skilled workers in heavy industry. (The top three grade points on the skill scale used in ferrous metallurgy after 1958 ranged from 2.43 to 3.20 times the stavka, but the minimum rate paid in the industry was somewhat greater than 40 rubles a month.) The salaries of doctors were somewhat higher, but they still overlapped the wage scales of skilled workers in industry to a surprising extent. The basic salaries of both these groups were unaffected by the introduction of the 60-ruble minimum wage in 1968, which implied a considerable narrowing in their relative advantage. After 1968, teachers' salaries ranged from 1.3 to 2.3 times the minimum wage and those of medical personnel from 1.5 to 2.8 times the minimum. Thus after no less than seven years' additional training (two at secondary and five in further education), differentials were little more than those built into the industrial skill scales of the 1956-61 wage reorganization. Although I have not seen details of the post-1972 salary structures in education or health, if one applies the reported average increases to the 1964 scales and makes use of the new 70-ruble minimum wage, it appears that this scale of differentiation has been retained.

Yet neither education nor health appears to be short of qualified personnel, although some observers have expressed doubts about its quality (Smith, 1976, pp. 72–75). It is reported that in 1965-66 the average pupil-teacher ratio in Soviet primary and secondary education was 18:1 (Basov, 1967, p. 66), and there are more doctors per head of population than in either Britain or the USA. In 1960, there were 20 doctors for every 10,000 people in the USSR, and in 1970 there were 27.4. In the USA in that year there were only 19.2 doctors per 10,000, and in the UK as few as 15.2.

Thus the Soviet experience would seem to conflict with the predictions of both human capital theorists and those who maintain, for other reasons, that substantial differentials are necessary to attract qualified people to these service occupations. It is difficult to explain how the Soviet authorities have been able to ensure a sufficient supply of labor to these occupations. I suspect that the answer will be connected with the fact that both teaching and medicine in the USSR have a much higher proportion of women than is the case of most market economies. But the significance of this will depend upon a more extensive analysis of employment opportunities for women in the USSR and the role of women in the Soviet economy. Such an analysis will not be offered here (see Dodge, 1966).

I now turn to an analysis of the salaries payable to the two remaining groups identified at the beginning of the section. In Soviet theory, the work of the manager, like the work of the lathe operator or weaver, is considered productive labor; thus in principle it can be reduced to simple labor. It should therefore be possible to integrate the pay of managers with the wage system described in chapter 8, and indeed, in the years immediately following the 1917 revolution, managers and workers shared a common scale (Kapustin, 1968, p. 322). In practice, however, the criteria according to which "reduction" should take place are not clear, and the salary system differs from the wage system.

The earnings of management in the USSR have two components: a basic salary determined by the person's official position, and bonuses which depend in some way or other upon the performance of the enterprise in which he or she is employed. Basic salaries are determined on the hierarchical principle—the greater the responsibility, the higher the salary. Bonuses are usually proportional to basic salaries. Salaries also depend upon the size of the enterprise and the industry to which the enterprise is attached, and reportedly upon personal qualifications, although it is not clear how important this component is in the "productive" sectors. Before the 1956-61 reorganization there were more than 700 different salary scales in use in industry alone. As a result of the reform, the number was reduced to 150, but the structure is still extremely involved.

The earnings of clerical staff in the productive sector also consist of a basic salary and a bonus component: in the nonproductive sector, apparently, no bonuses are paid. As for management, the basic salaries of clerical workers depend upon status (or responsibility) and upon the industrial affiliation of the employing enterprise. Before the 1956-61 reform, there were different salary scales for clerical employees in each of the industrial ministries. It is claimed that during reorganization this departmentalist, *vedomstvennyi*, approach was replaced by the industrial, *otraslevoi*, principle and that only two unified scales were specified. The higher was to be used in mining, heavy industry, construction, transport, and communications; the lower in the remaining branches of the economy (Kapustin, 1968, p. 312; Batkaev and Markov, 1964, p. 132). Other sources suggest that there were four scales in use in industry alone—although these same scales may also have been used in the rest of the economy (Kukulevich, 1966, pp. 148–51). Salaries depend upon age, experience, and qualifications and also upon the hierarchical principle; superiors earn more than their subordinates, and to some extent, the larger the unit the higher the salaries of its coordinators.

There are two sorts of data on managerial salaries available in the USSR. First, for some industries, mainly machine building and metal-working, there are published scales giving the basic salaries for specific positions in enterprises of various types. Second, for a sample of industrial branches and for certain productive sectors, there is information on average managerial earnings for a run of years, mostly since 1960. Similar data are available for other categories of industrial personnel. But the classification of these categories in the USSR differs somewhat from that used in other countries, and this material is less illuminating than might be hoped.

For any particular branch of industry, the managerial salary structure will consist of a matrix of salary bands. Along one dimension will be arrayed the twelve or so typical occupational groups into which management is commonly subdivided, ranging from director through chief engineer and section heads down to foremen, engineers, and technicians. Along the other dimension, the size or significance of the employing enterprise will be represented. In each cell of the matrix there will be two numbers denoting the range within which the salaries of persons in that classification must fall. The ranges vary from about 10% to as much as 40%. Where in the range a person falls is determined by his or her experience—and bargaining power, since the enterprise has considerable discretion in the matter. The scales make no provision for annual increments or for any other automatic increases in the salaries of managerial personnel. Thus chronological seniority is not a principle recognized in the Soviet salary system.

There is considerable variation in the basic salaries paid to managerial personnel of the same formal status, depending upon the characteristics of the enterprise in which they work. There are two factors involved here, an enterprise component and a branch one; I will consider each in turn. In machine building, for instance, about which most has been published, enterprises are classified into groups, depending upon employment and the character of production activity. For the largest enterprises in the industry or those producing the most complex output, the basic salary of the director in 1964 was between 300 and 330 rubles a month. Basic salaries of directors of enterprises in the lowest category varied from 100 to

140 rubles a month (*Spravochnik ekonomista* . . . , 1964, pp. 424–26).

At the other end of the managerial scale, the basic salary of the personnel manager, *nachalnik otdela truda i zarabotnoi platy*, one of the lowest paid of the central administrative staff, was 150-180 rubles a month in the largest plants, about half the salary of the director. In the smallest plants that had such a designated position, the salary was about 70% of that of the director. The basic salaries of other categories of personnel, grouped with management by Soviet statisticians and administrators, were on the whole lower than those of central management. In 1964, design engineers earned from 110 to 150 rubles, depending upon the complexity of the enterprise's output. Technicians earned least, with basic salaries of 70 to 80 rubles a month. The salaries of foremen depended upon the size of the shop in which they worked, as well as upon the character of production; rates ranged from 90 rubles to 145 rubles a month, almost as high as the salaries of design engineers.

In 1964, the average basic wage of industrial workers in machine building, the sector in which the above salary levels are applicable, was approximately 67 rubles a month, about one-fifth of the basic salary of the director of the largest engineering plant.[12] This difference is rather less than would be found in the UK, for example; but such comparisons are made difficult by differences in the progressivity of income tax and by the fact that the Soviet director is essentially only a plant manager; higher managerial functions lie in the central bureaucracy, on whose salaries nothing is published.

The figures quoted above relate to machine building; similar matrices of salaries exist for other branches. Matthews identifies seven different rates for directors of category I enterprises ranging from 400 rubles a month in 1960 for coal mining down to 180-250 rubles a month for the light, food-processing, and textile industries. It is to be presumed that each of these represents a full array like the one described above (Matthews, 1975, p. 136). Essentially similar scales exist in other productive branches, in construction, agriculture, and transport. Although the figures quoted refer to the period 1960-64, all the evidence suggests that there was no change in the level of basic managerial salaries until the end of the decade. The post-1972 wage round is reported to involve an 18% increase in the basic salaries of management in industry, with somewhat larger (25-35%) increases for foremen and other lower-paid groups like engineers and technicians (Kapustin, 1974, p. 269).

In addition to these basic salaries, management groups in Soviet industry receive bonuses whose size depends upon enterprise performance. In industry these bonuses depend upon performance in the preceding month, in agriculture upon performance over the preceding year. Before the economic reform of 1965, such bonuses depended upon the fulfillment of plans for output, cost reduction, and labor productivity. Since the reform, sales and profits are supposed to be the primary determinants. For foremen, shop superintendents, etc. there are also bonuses related to the performance of the sections under their control. In 1964, regulations limited bonuses to 40% of basic salary in industry; in 1970, bonuses were limited to 60% of the salaries of managerial personnel and specialists in agriculture (70% in the Virgin Lands) and 40% for other categories (*Spravochnik ekonomista sovkhoza* . . . , 1970, pp. 267–69). It is possible that similar regulations were introduced in industry during the so-called Kosygin reform of 1965, or perhaps somewhat earlier.[13] The question of how bonuses are determined and which categories of personnel are entitled to which premia is extremely involved and will not be pursued here.

So far, discussion has concentrated on basic salary scales and formal bonus entitlement rather than on the earnings of managerial groups in Soviet industry and other sectors, but it is data on the latter that are relevant for an assessment of the extent of intraplant inequality. Unfortunately, the statistics that exist on this depend upon the peculiar Soviet categorization of the industrial labor force.

Soviet labor statistics identify five categories of personnel in the productive sphere: workers, apprentices, ITR, clerical staff, and so-called junior service personnel, *MOP*.[14] Apprentices are sometimes classified with workers and sometimes with MOP; sometimes this last category is omitted from the statistics altogether. ITR, *inzhenerno-tekhnicheskiye rabotniki*, are those whose jobs involve the "technical control and management of production, and also those required to have the qualification of engineer or technician [*tekhnik*]" (Batkaev and Markov, 1964, p. 125). In Soviet practice, this is taken to include all supervisory personnel, foremen, and shop superintendents, as well as management proper. Clerical staff are those who service the productive process, as well as those who perform certain administrative and bureaucratic functions. The heads of various administrative departments—accounting, supply, personnel, and so on—are classified as ITR; most of the people employed in these departments are defined as clerical workers, *sluzhashchiye*, but those with some higher educational qualification, like economists, may be classified as ITR (Kukulevich, 1966, pp. 112—13). It is often difficult to distinguish between the two categories, since much of the managerial work in an industrial enterprise involves elements of both. The distinction is, in any case, bureaucratic rather than economic. The allocation of positions to one group or another—and thus the determination of the salary scale applicable—is made according to a set of definitions issued, surprisingly enough, by the CSA (Batkaev and Markov, 1964, p. 126). The groups are those in terms of which statistics on earnings in industry are presented; it is important to realize that ITR cannot be equated with managerial personnel in other economies.

Table 9.7
The Structure of ITR Earnings, Industry, 1961-70

	1961	1970
Average monthly earnings (rubles)	135.6	178.0
of which (%)		
Basic salary	78.7	64.9
Bonuses	11.4	25.9
Regional supplements	4.0	3.9
Long-service payments	1.6	0.8
Other	4.3	4.5

Notes and Sources: Kunelskii, 1972, p. 173; earnings data from *Trud*, 1968, p. 139, and *NK SSSR '73*, p. 586.

Holiday pay has been distributed among the other categories of receipt. Long-service awards are a category of merit payment that was discontinued in 1961; only those receiving them in that year continue to do so.

For industry as a whole, the growth of earnings is displayed in chart 9.2; some information about changes in the structure of ITR earnings is given in table 9.7, which brings out the importance of bonuses in managerial salaries at this time and the way in which they increased during the sixties. The figures in the table imply that in 1961 the average basic salary for ITR was 106.7 rubles a month and that by 1970 it had increased to 115.5 rubles, that is, by about 8% in nine years. A change of this magnitude is to be expected from changes in the structure of employment, changes in the size of enterprises, and other natural factors; thus these figures imply that there was no general change in the salary scales of ITR between the beginning and the end of the sixties. On the other hand, the table implies that average bonuses increased from 15.46 rubles a month in 1961 to 46.10 rubles a month in 1970, that is, by 198%. From chart 9.2 it appears that much of this increase occurred after the 1965 economic reform.

On the assumption that bonuses form at least as large a portion of the earnings of enterprise directors as they do of the earnings of ITR as a whole, the relationships in table 9.7 imply that the earnings of directors ranged from 130 to 420 rubles a month in 1961 and from 150 to 500 rubles a month in 1970. Given the size distribution of enterprises in Soviet industry, this suggests an average directorial earnings figure of 180 rubles a month in 1961 and 210 rubles in 1970. The average earnings of industrial workers were 93 rubles and 131 rubles a month in the two years. Thus at the beginning of the decade directors earned about twice as much as industrial workers; by 1970 they were earning some 60% more. The impression of relatively modest degrees of intraplant inequality conveyed by the rate data is reinforced by this admittedly crude earnings comparison. Further, the evidence suggests that differentials declined over the decade, and that even when allowance is made for the new salary scales

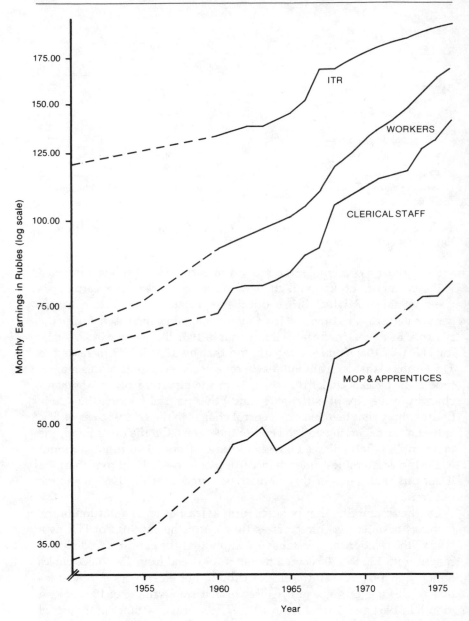

Chart 9.2. Growth in Soviet Industrial Earnings, 1950-76. (Hatched lines have been used where no figures are available.) Note: The earnings of ITR, clerical staff, and MOP and apprentices for the years 1967-69 have been interpolated on the basis of total earnings, the earnings of workers, and employment shares.

introduced in the seventies they still will be less than in 1961. Such comparisons should be treated with caution, however, since differences in institutional structure, tax-law, and the availability of fringe benefits may make them misleading.

Chart 9.2 not only contains information on the growth of the earnings of ITR and workers in industry but it also gives details for the remaining categories of industrial personnel. It permits a better idea of the scale of intraplant variation in earnings and the way in which these changed over the two decades or so covered by this study. Unfortunately, there are no figures on year-to-year changes in the earnings of particular categories of industrial personnel during the fifties; data exist for only 1950, 1955, and 1960. On the basis of these semidecadal growth figures, the chart implies that the wage reorganization of 1956-61 resulted in an increase in the annual rate of growth of workers' earnings, while leaving that of ITR (and for that matter, clerical staff) virtually unchanged. The reorganization initiated a narrowing of differentials that continued until 1964. For three years after that, differentials widened; the increase was particularly marked in 1967. In that year, average ITR earnings increased by 11.3%, while those of workers increased by 5.1%. The year 1967 was the one in which the bulk of industrial enterprises were transferred to the new system of management. The minimum wage hike of 1968 restored differentials to their 1964 level, and since that time they have continued to decline.

The chart also suggests that clerical salaries were not reorganized until 1961 and that although there was some acceleration in the growth of earnings after 1965, the 1968 wage hike was important for clerical workers. It also suggests that they are being left behind by industrial workers. Finally, since the earnings of MOP have been derived as a residual, not too much attention should be paid to their apparent decline in 1964; it is probably the result of statistical error.

The analysis of this chapter has shown that between 1956 and 1970 there was a marked reduction in earnings inequality in the state sector of the Soviet economy, and further, that this can be attributed to reductions in both intersectoral and intrasectoral differentials. Not only did differences in the average earnings of the various sectors of the economy decline, but also there was a contraction in the spread of wage rates and basic salaries within individual industries and sectors. Some part of this can be attributed to the operation of Soviet wage and salary policy described in chapter 8. A detailed examination of the timing of particular changes indicates that this was not the only factor at work, however. Market forces or the evolution of the Soviet economy appear also to have played some role. A final assessment of the relative importance of these two factors must wait until I have examined the available evidence on the growth of earnings. This is the subject of chapter 10.

10

The Growth of Earnings, 1950-74

CHAPTER 8 DESCRIBED THE INSTITUTIONS that have been responsible for wage and salary policy in the USSR since the mid fifties and the principles which have guided them. This account posed certain questions about the role of the Soviet authorities in controlling the growth and distribution of earnings in the past twenty years or so. Questions relating to earnings differentials were discussed in chapter 9; here I will concentrate on the problem of earnings growth. In particular, this chapter will attempt to resolve the paradox between the existence of an inflexible system for the determination of wage rates and salary scales and evidence of annual increases in money earnings. The analysis suggests that a key to resolving this apparent contradiction is the scope given enterprise managers in awarding bonuses paid for norm fulfillment. But this in turn raises the question of the maintenance of macrobalance, and the analysis suggests that the Soviet authorities may have lost control for a period after 1965. The chapter ends with a more general assessment of the strengths and weaknesses of Soviet wages policy.

10.1 THE EARNINGS OF STATE EMPLOYEES, 1956-73

In 1956, the average earnings of state employees were 73.40 rubles a month; in 1973 they were 134.90 rubles, an increase of 83.8%. Thus in the seventeen years since de-Stalinization, money earnings increased at an annual average rate of 3.6%; figures given below indicate that real earnings grew at the somewhat lower rate of 2.4% per annum. This represents a substantial achievement. As might be expected, gains were not recorded uniformly throughout the period; an idea of the year-to-year variations in the rate of growth of money earnings can be gained from chart 10.1. Many of the changes in year-to-year growth rates can be associated with the introduction of specific policy measures described in chapter 8. Thus the increase in 1956-57 coincides with the adoption of the 27-35 ruble minimum wage; that in 1962 coincides with the extension of wage reorganization to state agriculture and other sectors of material

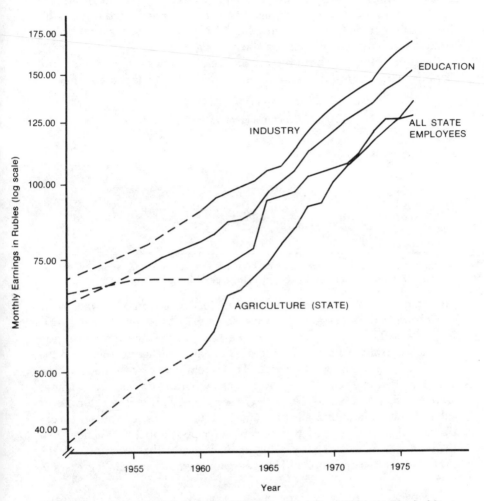

Chart 10.1. Average Monthly Earnings, USSR, Various Sectors, 1950-73. (Hatched lines have been used where no figures are available.)

production; and the impact of the 1968 increase in the minimum wage is also visible. But at this level of analysis, it is difficult to see that the three phases of wage policy described in chapter 8 had any significant impact on the growth of average earnings. It is certainly possible to discern different sub-periods from the chart, but their timing and duration do not coincide with the phases outlined above.

Rates of growth for both money and real earnings for particular sub-periods are given in table 10.1. From the figures, it is apparent that the

Table 10.1
Average Annual Growth in Earnings, USSR, State Sector

Years	Money Earnings	Real Earnings
	(% per annum)	
1950-55	2.35	6.05
1955-64	2.55	1.44
1950-64	2.48	2.94
1965-67	4.16	2.68
1967-68	7.64	5.56
1968-73	3.66	2.60

Note: Rates of growth of real earnings have been calculated by deflating the money earnings series by the Schroeder and Severin cost-of-living index.

growth of money earnings in 1955-64, the period covered by wage reorganization in the state sector as a whole, is very little higher than it was in 1950-55. This would suggest, *prima facie*, that wage reorganization (that is, centrally determined wage policy) had a negligible impact on the growth of popular living standards. This is reinforced by the observation that throughout the period 1950-64, growth rates of money earnings were less than in 1965-67, when there were no changes in wage rates or salary scales. The increase in earnings in 1967-68 was, of course, exceptional, but since that year, growth rates have been noticeably higher than in the fifties or early sixties. This again suggests that decisions of the State Committee on Labor and Wages cannot wholly explain increases in earnings.

The pattern of real wage growth differs somewhat from that of increases in nominal earnings, but care should be exercised in interpreting these figures. There were substantial reductions in the retail prices of most consumer goods between 1950 and 1955, but there are doubts about the availability of commodities at the lower prices. It is not clear how one should allow for uncertain availability in the estimation of real wages. To some extent this will have been taken into account in the derivation of the implicit price deflator used, but I suspect that the figures in table 10.1 overstate the gains accruing during this period. Taking the figures at their face value, however, they indicate that improvements were most rapid in

1950-55; during the wage reform, the rate of growth of real earnings de-clined by about three-quarters. In 1965-67 it was almost double what it had been in the preceding nine years. Again, 1967-68 stands out as an exceptional year, but growth since then (or, at least, until 1973) has been at almost the same rate as in 1965-67.

The interpretation of these figures raises certain problems. The pattern of growth in real earnings fits a certain (rather facile) political thesis: growth is high in 1950-55 when the post-Stalin leadership is consolidating its position and again in 1964-68 when the post-Khrushchev leaders as-sumed power. In each case, however, consolidation was followed by a period of slower growth. But this analysis assumes that the growth of earnings in 1950-55 was concentrated in the period after Stalin's death; it also depends upon the combination of 1965-67 with 1967-68. In this latter period the growth in earnings tended to increase as, presumably, the leaders established their positions more firmly, and this does not fit the hypothesis.

Also, it is possible to argue that a consideration of trends in real earn-ings may not be the most appropriate guide to policy intentions. As I have pointed out above, the Soviet government does not publish a proper cost-of-living index, and there is little in the statistical literature to indi-cate that one is compiled for internal circulation. It is possible, therefore, that the Soviet authorities are misled by their own economic statistics and that policy decisions may be based upon a consideration of trends in nominal rather than real incomes. If this is the case, rates of growth of money earnings would be the appropriate variable for guessing at policy intentions. (There is also some evidence, developed at greater length be-low, which implies that the growth in earnings in 1965-67 at least was higher than that intended by the authorities.)

Bearing this in mind, it might be plausible to suggest that the Soviet authorities have aimed at a rate of increase in earnings of something in the order of 2.5% per annum. In the early period, say up to 1964-65, at-tention was focused on the growth of nominal earnings. More recently, perhaps due to a growing sophistication among economic statisticians, some account may have been taken of changes in the cost of living. If this is so, the figures in table 10.1 suggest that the authorities have come close to achieving their target. But there appears to have been a period in the mid sixties when the growth of earnings was out of control. On the other hand, if no allowance has been made officially for changes in the cost of living, the record suggests that the authorities were less successful in achieving their targets after 1968 than in the period 1955-64. This might be an indirect consequence of operating with a rigid and outdated struc-ture of wage rates, which would tend to result in more frequent violations of the state's wage regulations at the enterprise level. Finally, if I am correct in assuming that, at least up to 1965, the Soviet government neglected to take account of the impact of changes in the cost of living upon the growth of earnings, the figures in table 10.1 show how important such an oversight was.

The impression that the Soviet government lost control of the growth of earnings in the mid sixties is reinforced by an analysis of changes in the level and structure of the earnings of industrial workers over the period 1957-72. This analysis involves the identification of factors which determine the growth of earnings and an attempt to assess their relative importance. It therefore helps to resolve the paradox noted at the end of chapter 8.

The rigid bureaucratic system of wage-rate determination described in chapter 8, according to which rates remain unchanged for relatively long periods of time, does not mean that earnings remain unchanged from year to year. My own calculations suggest that in the absence of specific policy changes by the authorities (and at a constant pressure of demand), industrial earnings would have increased, during the sixties, by about 1.4% per annum.[1] There are four factors which might result in the growth of average earnings, given a constant rate structure: increases in employment in high-wage sectors relative to that in low-wage sectors; the growth of employment in high-wage regions relative to the rest of the country; an increase in the numbers receiving wage supplements for working in harmful or unpleasant conditions; and finally, higher bonuses resulting from an increase in labor productivity more rapid than the increases in labor norms, or given for other reasons. Changes in average earnings caused by the first two presumably correspond to the intentions of the authorities. Those caused by the third may either reflect similar desired developments or be an unplanned response by enterprise managers to inadequate formal differentials. Changes ascribable to the last factor are most likely to be undesired and unplanned.

An analysis of the growth in industrial earnings since 1960 suggests that little if any of the increase in earnings can be ascribed to changes in the pattern of employment; indeed the tendency was for low-wage sectors to grow at the expense of high-wage ones. This is shown by the following argument. Average earnings in year t may be written as

$$\overline{w}_t = \Sigma_i a_{it} w_{it} \tag{1}$$

where a_{it} is the share of the ith industry in total employment in year t and w_{it} is average earnings in the ith industry in the same year. Then, if

$$\Delta \overline{w}_{t+k} = \overline{w}_{t+k} - \overline{w}_t,$$

$$\Delta \overline{w}_{t+k} = \Sigma_i \Delta a_{i,t+k} w_{i,t+k} + \Sigma_i a_{it} \Delta w_{i,t+k} \tag{2}$$

The first term on the RHS of (2) indicates how much of the change in average earnings is due to changes in employment, and the second shows how much is due to changes in sectoral earnings. When formula (2) was applied to data on employment and earnings both for sectors of the economy and branches of industry during the sixties, the first term was consistently small and negative. That is, changes in earnings were caused by intrasectoral factors rather than by a reallocation of the labor force between branches.

Figures in table 10.2 show that regional premia accounted for 4.4% of average monthly earnings in 1961; in 1970 they accounted for 5.4%. It is unlikely, therefore, that they explain much of the growth in average earnings over the decade. Although there are no figures available, it seems plausible to assume that little of this growth can be explained by an increase in the number of workers receiving supplements for harmful working conditions. This leaves the last two factors identified above.

Between 1962, soon after the wage reform in industry was completed, and 1972, average skill grades, whatever their interpretation, increased by about 10%.[2] This is relatively modest and suggests that illicit upgrading of workers was not a common phenomenon among enterprise managers seeking to attract or retain labor. It is, however, difficult to assess the impact of this increase in recorded skill levels upon average earnings, both because of the fact that the same skill scale is used with different wage scales and because wage scales were modified when the 60-ruble minimum wage was introduced in 1968. One method of allowing for these factors is as follows: given the wage structure outlined in chapter 8, it is possible to express the basic wage of any worker, approximately, in terms of the basic wage, stavka, applicable in his industry, the average scale coefficient, and his skill grade:

$$w_i = mq^r \tag{3}$$

where m is the stavka, r the skill grade, and q the average scale coefficient. (This formulation fails to capture the principle of increasing relative increments built in to all the postreform scales.) Since it is possible to express the stavki used in individual industries as a function of the minimum wage of the same mathematical form as (3), one may interpret m as the minimum wage, q as a composite factor reflecting "average economic significance" and an allowance for intra-industrial skill and r as the average skill attained.[3] Given data on $\overline{w}$, m, and r, the equation can be used to evaluate q in a particular year, say 1961. One can then use this value to assess the hypothetical impact of changes in average skill levels or the minimum wage upon average earnings in subsequent years. This is done in table 10.2.

Table 10.2

Structure of Earnings, Industrial Workers, USSR, 1957–73

	1957	1961	1965	1968	1970	1972
Average monthly earnings of which (rubles)	81.64	92.70	101.70	118.60	130.60	140.10
Minimum wage	27.00	40.00	40.00	60.00	60.00	60.00
Other basic wages	18.96	27.58	28.77	20.65	21.62	21.75
Incentive payments	28.33	14.37	21.69	24.40	35.27	44.62
Bonuses	4.74	7.04	13.46	10.61	20.76	29.21
Norm overfulfillment premia	23.59	7.32	8.23	13.79	14.51	15.41
Supplementary						
Regional	{ 7.35	4.45	{ 10.94	13.55	5.35	{ 13.73
Other[a]		6.30			8.36	
Average skill (VI-point scale)	—	3.0[b]	3.1	3.2[c]	3.2[c]	3.3
% norm fulfillment	169.0	119.0	121.0	130.0	131.0	133.0
Labor productivity (1960 = 100)	83	104	125	148	168	188
Skill-scale factor	—	1.19	1.19	1.10	1.10	1.10

Notes and Sources. 1957: Batkaev and Markov, 1964, p. 221. 1961, 1970: Kunelksii, 1972, p. 78. 1968, Sukharevskii, 1974, p. 241. Average Earnings (all years): Trud, 1968, p. 138; NK SSSR '73, p. 586. Other Years: minimum wage assumed; basic wages calculated using equation (3) in the text; supplementary receipts in 1965 were assumed to bear the same proportion to basic earnings as in 1961, those in 1968 and 1972 the same as in 1970. Incentive payments were then calculated as a residual; norm fulfillment was calculated according to the relation given in the text and bonuses obtained as a residual.

a. Includes holiday pay, long-service awards and other special payments.

b. 1962.

c. 1969.

The figures in the table show that skill-creep, as it may be called, was a relatively unimportant source of increase in average earnings during the sixties. In 1961, basic industrial earnings (that is, net of bonuses, other incentive payments, and regional and other supplements) amounted to 67.58 rubles a month. Had there been no change in the minimum wage or in skill-scale factors, basic wages would have been 71.21 rubles a month in 1972, an increase of less than 6% in nine years. Thus, even if enterprise managers have granted "unjustified" increases in skill grades to attract or retain labor, this has not resulted in any substantial unplanned (and therefore undesired) increase in industrial earnings.

On the other hand, the figures in table 10.2 indicate that between 1961 and 1972, incentive payments, broadly defined, increased from 14.37 rubles a month on the average to 44.62 rubles—that is, from about 15.5% of average earnings to almost 32%. This has been the major source of growth in average earnings.

Incentive payments, as recorded in the table, consist of two components: payments to pieceworkers for norm overfulfillment, and other bonuses. The figures in table 10.2 show how important the first of these components was in 1957 and also how far it had been incorporated into basic wages by 1961. Calculations show that in both 1961 and 1970, average earnings were increased by 0.57% of basic wages for each percentage point that norms were, on the average, overfulfilled. One would like further observations to confirm this relationship, but in any case, let us accept it as an "empirical law" of the Soviet labor market. It is used in the table to estimate the value of norm overfulfillment payments for other years.

Figures in table 10.2 show that although labor productivity increased by about 20% between 1961 and 1965, norm overfulfillment increased by only two percentage points. Thus, over this period, the authorities were successful in raising norms in line with productivity. In the next three years, labor productivity increased by a further 18%; norm overfulfillment increased by nine percentage points, more than half of the increase coming between 1965 and 1966. Finally, between 1968 and 1972 labor productivity increased by a further 27% and norm overfulfillment by three percentage points, thus reestablishing the relationship that held in 1961-65. This suggests that central control over norm setting was very much weaker in 1965-68, and especially in 1965-66, than during the rest of the period. Since such control forms an essential element in the maintenance of macroeconomic balance in the Soviet system, this implies that government control over the economy weakened in 1965-68.

Table 10.2 also reveals, given the "empirical law" stated above, that bonuses have, on the average, quadrupled between 1961 and 1972. Some such increase was to be expected in the wake of the Kosygin reform (which was designed to make earnings more dependent on enterprise performance), but surprisingly, half the increase occurred before 1965; and between 1965 and 1968, when new methods of control were extended to most of industry, average bonuses fell. Finally, had bonuses increased in line with labor productivity after 1968, average earnings would have been some sixteen rubles a month less than they in fact were in 1972.

These calculations suggest that throughout the post-reform period, enterprise managers continued to make use of their limited autonomy to pay wages higher than those implied by the operation of the centralized wage-rate determination system described in chapter 8. Presumably, the supplements were designed to correct for inadequacies in the rates as an allocative mechanism. These "excessive" increases have been particularly marked since 1968. Since there is no reason to suppose that such increases were built into the Kosygin system, this suggests that increases in earnings since that year have been higher than desired by the authorities. Also, as noted above, the calculations imply that there was a noticeable weakening of central control over norm setting in 1965-68. Together, these factors explain the growth of earnings recorded in chart 10.1 and table 10.1.

They imply that in the Soviet system, industrial earnings increase from year to year because of the autonomy over bonuses and norm setting enjoyed by individual enterprises. As the length of time since specific wage scales were introduced increases, as specific rate structures become obsolete, the freedom of action of enterprise managers increases and the degree of central control diminishes; the risk of macroeconomic disequilibrium grows. During the 1960s this general pattern was complicated by two special events. The accession of a new leadership and the introduction of new methods of economic administration meant that, for a time, central control was weakened. This resulted in an increase in the rate of growth of earnings. Second, for reasons largely unconnected with the labor market, the minimum wage was raised by 50% in 1968, which also led to a large increase in earnings. On the other hand, some element of slippage, of wage drift, is to be expected in any economy; and it must be admitted the unplanned increases in earnings in the USSR have been relatively small when compared with those in economies like that of the UK, the record of the early sixties being particularly good.

The discussion in the last six or seven pages has concentrated on changes in the level and structure of industrial earnings. But as the figures in table 9.1 show, industrial workers make up a minority of the labor force; it is possible that their experience is untypical. Other information given in chart 10.1 shows that this is not the case, however. The chart shows the course of earnings growth for the state sector as a whole and for three of the twelve sectors into which Soviet statisticians conventionally divide the economy. There are differences between the experience of individual sectors: the substantial relative improvement in the position of state agriculture is very clear; but the chart demonstrates that, with the possible exception of the period 1962-66, the course of industrial earnings has paralleled that of all state employees quite closely. It also shows that the wage reorganization in industry was not associated with any sudden spurt in earnings. In 1950-55, the annual average rate of growth of industrial earnings was 2.17%; in 1955-61 it was 3.18%.

On the other hand, chart 10.1 does reveal one rather puzzling anomaly. The chart provides information about the growth of average earnings in education, which has been chosen as typical of the service sectors in the Soviet economy. A very high proportion of the employees in education are salaried. Since there are no bonuses, changes in average earnings should be largely confined to years in which salary scales are changed. Certainly the effects of the 1964 revision are obvious, and there is the predicted stagnation in average earnings between 1950 and 1960. (Over the decade, earnings grew by less than 0.5% per annum.) But since 1960, and even more since 1964, average earnings have shown surprisingly large annual rates of growth that I am unable to account for satisfactorily. The same pattern characterizes other service sectors, like health, credit and insurance, and state administration.

The analysis of this section has shown three things. First, data on the growth of earnings have demonstrated that for the state sector as a whole and for industry considered separately, the wage reorganization of the late fifties and early sixties did not result in a substantially more rapid rate of growth of earnings than at other times. Thus one may infer that increases in popular living standards were not the primary objective of this policy innovation; rather, the emphasis was on rationalization (allocative efficiency) and possibly on equity. Examination of the experience of certain groups of state employees does suggest, however, that some of the increase in earnings can be attributed to the operation of state policy. This is particularly clear in the case of state agriculture in 1960-62 and of education in 1964-65. Finally, as was true of changes in earnings differentials, a consideration of the statistics relating to increases in average earnings indicates that factors other than state policy are at work. Wages and salaries are not determined exclusively by the plan or by government *diktat*, but by interactions between state policy and the decisions of other economic agents.

10.2   THE EVOLUTION OF SOVIET WAGE POLICY
The purpose of this final section is to pull together the material on the development of central wage policy in the USSR that has been presented

in the last three chapters. This should permit a final assessment of its impact in bringing about those changes in the level and structure of earnings that have been documented in previous pages. It should also cast some light on the question of how the Soviet authorities have retained effective control over the level of earnings (and of consumer demand) during the extensive transformation of labor market relationships that has occurred since 1955.

In chapter 8 I dated the beginning of a new, active, centralized, and interventionist wage policy in the Soviet Union as 1955, and suggested that it could be seen as a manifestation of increased official concern with questions of welfare and inequality. This raises a number of problems. What was this policy intended to achieve at the time, and have its objectives changed subsequently? Why was it adopted in the form it was and at the time it was? Has it contributed materially to the avoidance of overt inflation in the USSR? There are other issues that might be discussed, but I shall concentrate on these three here. But before addressing these questions, perhaps I should point out that the identification of the post-1955 policy as centralized does not imply that what went before was decentralized. In fact, wage rate determination was concentrated in the hands of some thirty or forty industrial ministries and equivalent organizations. The complexity of industrial wage scales, the inconsistencies and the irrationality were themselves the result of an earlier phase of centralized bureaucratic decision making and of the tendency towards ministerial autarchy that existed in the mature Stalinist system.

Why, then, did the Soviet authorities decide to adopt a new approach to wage determination in 1955, why did they decide to set up the State Committee on Labor and Wages and give it the powers it is vested with? It is tempting to see this as a precondition for the *sovnarkhoz* experiment. Not even Khrushchev, one might think, with all his passion for administrative innovation, would devolve responsibility for wages to one hundred or more regional economic councils. But such an explanation is wrong. There is no evidence to suggest that the abolition of the industrial ministries had even been conceived in 1955 when the new body was created.

More plausibly, the establishment of the State Committee might be seen as an administrative preparation for the relaxation of controls on the mobility of labor that had been introduced at the beginning of the Second World War. The Soviet authorities might have reasoned that if workers were to be free to move from plant to plant without the prior consent of management, the inconsistencies in relative wages generated by the ministerial system would provoke a massive increase in labor turnover. This, in turn, would entail disruption of production, loss of output, and the risk of open inflation, as managers, seeking to retain or attract labor, ignored central controls on wages and the wage fund. That is, there might be a return to the situation of the thirties. But even this conjecture suffers from certain weaknesses. It is true that legal restrictions on labor mobility were not repealed until 1956, a year after the State Committee was set up, but in practice they had been ignored since 1953 or earlier. Nor can the new policy be seen as a response to excessive labor turnover generated by the *de facto* relaxation of controls on mobility. While it is true that in the late fifties the Soviet authorities expressed some concern over the levels of labor turnover, the evidence does not suggest that turnover increased particularly rapidly in the early fifties— or that it was high by international standards. And there is no sense of urgency about the early actions of the State Committee.

The State Committee was set up to oversee the wage reorganization of 1956-65. There is little to indicate that at this time the government felt the need to supplement the existing institutions for controlling economic activity within the system, to go beyond Gosplan, Gosbank, and the Ministry of Finance. (Indeed, it was partly because it had been felt that these three institutions, together with the All-Union Central Council of the Trade Unions and the industrial ministries, gave the authorities sufficient control that Narkomtrud was disbanded.) Thus, I suggest that the State Committee was initially set up to undertake a once-and-for-all improvement in the structure of wages, particularly industrial wage rates and salary scales. It is only subsequently that the central authorities (and here I mean the Politburo, the Council of Ministers, and their advisers) have come to realize that wage structures, however carefully designed, grow obsolete and need replacement; that compliance with regulations must be monitored; that the performance of the system needs to be assessed; in short, that there is a place in the Soviet system for a ministry of labor.

The argument of the preceding paragraphs suggests that official attitudes towards labor policy in general and towards the state's regulation of wages in particular have changed since the mid fifties, that the role of the State Committee has developed. It does not indicate why the new policy took the form it did in 1955. Although it is dangerous to place too much reliance on *ex-post* justifications of Soviet policy in seeking explanations for its adoption, I believe that the material in section 8.3 contains an important insight into this question. The structure of wage rates and salary scales that existed in 1955 was complex, incomprehensible, and irrational. According to Marxist-Leninist theory, occupational differentials should be deducible, logically if not quantitatively, from elementary factors like skill and economic significance. At this time, the authorities were seeking to modernize their system, to make up for ten years of bureaucratic immobilism and a further period in which almost all other objectives had been subordinated to the war effort. At the same time, if it does not seem too paradoxical, there was a desire to return to the past, to

Leninist norms, to the socialism of the twenties. Thus, it was felt that a logical and comprehensible structure of differentials would contribute to modernization, to making the economy more efficient; but perhaps the logic should be derived from Marxist precepts. (And one should not neglect the desire for legitimation through increases in popular living standards.) I suggest, then, that the new departure in wage policy should be seen as only one element in a whole process of de-Stalinization of which the secret speech is the best known (but possibly not the most important) incident. Indeed, one might go farther and suggest that the increased concern over welfare and inequality with which this book is concerned is itself part of the same process and that this process has continued into the seventies. Major societal distortions like Stalinism cast long shadows onto the future.

Before turning to the content of the new policy, I should like to comment on the extreme centralization that characterized it. Such an approach was adopted, I think, partly because Khrushchev and other Soviet leaders realized that the only way in which innovation is likely to succeed in the Soviet system is for it to receive sufficient impetus from the political authorities. There is a lot of social inertia to be overcome. But also, I believe that the Soviet leaders felt (and feel) that innovation from above is desirable—indeed, that it is the only permissible form. Only in this way can they maintain control, can they be sure that wage reform (or anything else) does not get out of hand. The fear of *stikhiya*—uncontrolled social processes, autonomous social activity, anarchy—is very strong among Soviet politicians. And they appear to believe that *stikhiya* is very close to the surface of society.

The reorganization of wages, the modernization of systems of payment for labor and consequently the establishment of the State Committee were integral parts of the new approach to social and economic issues that emerged in the mid fifties. But what, specifically, was the new wage policy intended to achieve? Rationalization was certainly one objective, a radical simplification of existing wage and salary scales. It has been claimed that, also, the new wage scales were supposed to embody sufficient incentives for the acquisition of skills and to ensure increases in earnings for key workers, *rabochiye vedushchikh professii* (Volkov, 1974, p. 22). I interpret statements of this kind to mean that the reform was intended to produce a pattern of differentials that would allocate labor in accordance with government priorities; that is, in the terms of section 8.2, the emphasis was placed upon the allocative function of wages. But Volkov also states that the reorganization was intended to reduce differentiation by ensuring that increases in earnings went primarily to the low-paid. If differentiation were reduced, it would reduce the incentive to acquire skills, and so forth. The initial objectives of wage reform appear to have been inconsistent; certainly they were not well thought out. Thinking through Soviet wage policy has been an achievement of the academic labor economists and those who work for NIIT. And although they have continued to emphasize the allocative function of wages in their writings, they have succeeded in making both horizontal equity and distributive justice integral parts of the wage determination process.

The intentions behind the new wage policy are not clear, but neither is the record of its effects upon the distribution of earnings or the allocation of labor. The limited empirical evidence produced in chapter 8 suggested that the differentials built into the *industrial* wage scales of 1956-61 were both excessive and inadequate. It suggested that the premia for skill may have resulted in job rationing (that is, excess supply of labor), at least in certain industries; but also, both regional supplements and payments for adverse working conditions appear to have been inadequate. There is little evidence about the adequacy or inadequacy of wage and salary scales used in other sectors of the economy, but the growth of educational and medical services in the sixties does not suggest that the pay of doctors or teachers was too low, however inappropriate it might appear by international standards.

The changes introduced into industrial wage and salary scales in 1972-76 tend to confirm this analysis. Skill differentials were reduced, regional premia extended, and payments for special conditions made more sophisticated and more uniform. At the same time, increases in the basic salaries of managerial and technical personnel might suggest that there were difficulties in recruiting these categories in the wake of the 1968 increase in the minimum wage. Or possibly, the reduced scale of intraplant differentiation, *uravnitelnost,* conflicted with prior conceptions of an appropriate reward for responsibility, appropriate recognition of authority. In this connection, the evidence of chart 9.2 suggests that dissatisfaction is longer lasting. It was not the 1968 wage hike that produced differentials that were unacceptable to managers, but the 1956-61 wage reorganization. Given the opportunity, earnings disparities were increased in 1965-67. Thus post-1955 policy appears to have failed in its second objective, even if it achieved its first. But this is not surprising; it is surely unlikely that any centrally computed set of relative wages based on a theory that fails to take supply and demand into consideration would be capable of sustaining an efficient allocation of labor; and it is unrealistic to assume that the *same* set of relative wages, even if appropriate at one time, would remain optimal for as long as ten or fifteen years. However, the situation is not completely bleak. The activism of the State Committee and more particularly of NIIT means that some attempt is made to monitor the adequacy of existing differentials. Also, as far as one can tell, adjustments have been in the right direction, even if sometimes too little too late (or possibly too much too late). Finally, as I suggested in chapter 8, not all adjustments have been made with allocative efficiency in mind. It is at least probable that the 1968 increase in the minimum wage was decided upon at the expense of allocative considerations because the authorities were not prepared to adopt alternative methods of eliminating or reducing urban poverty.

The bureaucratic determination of wage rates does not by itself lead to annual improvements in earnings and living standards, particularly when new scales are introduced at infrequent intervals. Although it is possible for all the members of a system to receive annual increases in earnings even if average wages remain constant (consider the analogous case of a stable population in which all grow older, though the average age remains constant), I believe that the Soviet authorities have been committed to a policy of rising living standards and hence of continuing growth in money earnings. The material in section 10.1 suggests that they have been successful in achieving this goal without inflation, at least until the mid sixties. The analysis indicates that this was achieved through the growth of incentive payments rather than through skill creep or other rate-related mechanisms. Since the size and distribution of incentive funds are to a significant extent controlled by the enterprise or by the ministry to which it is subordinate, this implies that there is another element to the state's wage policy. (The analysis of section 10.1 referred to industrial wages, and at this stage I must admit that I do not understand the mechanism whereby continuing growth in the earnings of those employed in the services sector of the Soviet economy has been secured since 1960.)

If the enterprise exercises some degree of autonomy in deciding how much to pay its employees, how have the Soviet authorities been able, by and large, to match the growth of labor incomes to the increases in goods and services available for consumption, how have they maintained some semblance of macroeconomic equilibrium? This cannot be attributed solely to the existence of a centralized wage-rate determination mechanism; after all, there is scope for demand management in a market economy. But I believe that the activities of the State Committee on Labor and Wages have contributed to the success of the Soviet government in this sphere.

The simple answer to the question of how the growth of earnings in the Soviet economy is restricted to the increase in consumption made available through the plan is in the tight control exercised over the wage fund at the enterprise level. That is, the authorities have specified explicit and fairly rigid limits to expenditure on wages, enterprise by enterprise, and they have been successful in enforcing them. There are severe penalties for managers who transgress, and workers are not immune either. The penalties consist primarily of a prohibition on transfers to the bonus fund for enterprises that exceed their limits and a proscription on premia for the managers responsible. I believe that regulations by themselves would not be enough, however. Similar severe sanctions existed in the thirties when the wage fund was regularly and substantially overspent; and the analysis of section 10.1 suggested that there was an incipient inflation in 1965–67.

Differences in the success of wage fund controls in the period after 1947 and that before 1941 can be explained by differences in the economic environment in which managerial decision making took place. For this, centralized wage policy was partly responsible, but there were other factors. First, in the thirties, fulfillment of the output plan was regarded as paramount. If output targets were met, contraventions of the wage regulations were often condoned, at least by the industrial ministry on which the manager's job security and promotion prospects depended. *Per contra*, if output targets were not met, there was little approval for the fact that wage fund limits had not been exceeded. Although emphasis on output at the expense of other plan targets remained in the system until the 1965 reform, if it is not still there today, the pressure for plan fulfillment at any cost has been less in the postwar period. Further, it is my impression that the quality of planning improved between the thirties and the fifties. This is not to say that the efficiency of resource allocation increased; indeed, a case might be made for suggesting that it declined in the second half of the fifties and the early sixties. Rather, since the war, plans have been less taut, enterprises have found it easier to achieve their targets with the resources at their disposal. This has meant that managers have had less of an incentive (or a compulsion) to ignore limits on wage expenditure.

In all of this, the activities of the State Committee have helped. If the structure of wages is nearly right, if the pattern of differentials is approximately the one that can achieve an appropriate allocation of labor, given the plan, the adjustments introduced by managers will be minor and actual expenditure on wages will come close to planned expenditure. Now, although I have suggested that the differentials built into the 1956–61 wage reorganization in industry were inadequate in a number of respects, they were surely an improvement on the chaos that went before. And also, although the central determination of rates imposes a high degree of rigidity on the system and makes rate adjustment very slow, the continuing research activities of NIIT and the monitoring functions of the State Committee provide some assurance that adjustments will be in the right direction. Finally, the Soviet manager possesses very little information about the scarcity relationships that exist on an economy-wide scale in the USSR, information that in theoretical models is conveyed by relative prices; there can be little reason for supposing, therefore, that full decentralization of wage-rate determination to the enterprise level would generate an adequate set of shadow prices for labor unless it was accompanied by other substantive changes in the system of economic administration. Thus a central rate determination procedure has contributed to the effectiveness of wage controls.

It should also be pointed out that the operation of this system is made somewhat easier by the absence of effective trade unions, because neither managers nor the central bureaucracy has to consider the effect of their decisions upon organized labor. On the one hand, there is no collective economic response, no expression of workers' attitudes at the level of the enterprise or industry; more difficult to gauge, but perhaps equally important in practice, there is little articulation of specifically workers' interests at the political level. But this point should not be overstressed. Certainly after the removal of restrictions upon labor mobility, Soviet workers have been able to express discontent on an individual basis by changing jobs; and there are other ways in which an inappropriate structure of wages will affect adversely the supply of work effort.

It might even be argued that the emphasis on equal pay for equal work and on a national job-evaluation program, the desire the provide differential increases in the earnings of the low-paid and to reduce intraplant inequality, in short, the whole emphasis on horizontal equity, was an intuitive attempt to incorporate what it was thought the workers would want (or what they ought to want). That is, the State Committee might be thought of as a surrogate for an independent trade union movement. Insofar as it fulfills this role adequately it will increase the acceptability of Soviet wage differentials and consequently improve the workability of the system. And, of course, the central authorities would prefer such an institution to the reinvigoration of the All-Union Central Council of Trade Unions or the liberation of individual unions. The risks of *stikhiya* are much less.

I think that this interpretation of the concern for reducing earnings inequality that is apparent in post-1955 wage policy is too narrow, however. I do not think that the State Committee has attempted to articulate what it thinks are workers' attitudes on this question simply to make its wage structure more workable, more likely to generate an allocation of labor in accord with government priorities. As I have tried to suggest earlier, there was an element of philanthropy in the motives that prompted the whole de-Stalinization process, a desire to better the conditions of the mass of the Soviet people. In however tenuous a form, the post-Stalin Soviet leaders were affected by a socialist concern for equality, and this concern has been felt more strongly by those responsible for the articulation of policy. A reduction in earnings disparity has been seen as desirable in itself and as an instrument in reducing the wider inequality in living standards. The account given in the last three chapters suggests that substantial effort has been devoted to this objective and that, on the whole, it has had the desired result.

11

The Soviet Welfare State

IN THE LAST THREE CHAPTERS I have shown how the authorities have used their control over wage and salary scales to influence the distribution of earnings and incomes in the USSR. But earnings from employment are not the only source of income for Soviet households. In the USSR as in many other countries the population obtains a variety of services like education free of charge; others are available at subsidized prices; and the social security-social insurance system provides a range of transfer payments to particular population groups. Soviet economists and statisticians refer to resources committed to these uses collectively as social consumption expenditures, *obshchestvennye fondy potrebleniya*. They may be regarded conveniently, if somewhat inaccurately, as the Soviet welfare state.

The way in which social consumption programs are financed, the principles used to determine entitlement, the formulae used to calculate benefits, and the scale on which specific aspects of the programs are operated will affect both average living standards and the degree of inequality in the USSR. Since these features are all more or less under government control, the Soviet welfare state can be regarded as the authorities' second main set of instruments for influencing income distribution. In this chapter I will describe in greater detail the programs and policies included in social consumption, examine changes since the mid fifties, and attempt to assess the contribution they have made to the reduction of inequality in the USSR.

Although there are a number of unresolved conceptual difficulties and although the statistical evidence is inadequate, the materials presented here suggest that social consumption expenditures made a substantial contribution to the living standards of the average Soviet household in the late fifties and that their importance increased, if only marginally, in the following decade and a half.

The redistributive impact of the programs, however, is less clear, but is probably not as great as is assumed by many Soviet economists. The social security-social insurance system was extensively reorganized in 1955-56, but even after reorganization, coverage was incomplete, and entitlement criteria built into the new legislation resulted in a tendency for transfer payments to reinforce rather than offset the primary distribution of income. Better-off households, that is, tended to receive larger cash benefits than did the poor. In the 1960s, the only substantial modification of this system was its partial extension to collective farms. While this resulted in the provision of limited financial support to certain needy groups, it did not introduce any new principle into the administration of the system. One may therefore infer that its impact on kolkhoznik income distribution resembled its impact on the state sector. It is only in the early seventies that the system began to move away from the principles enshrined in the 1955-56 legislation but essentially inherited from the Stalin period. Before the seventies the tax structure remained effectively proportional, with relatively modest marginal rates.

The assessment in the preceding paragraph refers to the net effects of money transfers, but social consumption also includes a range of free and subsidized services. It is more difficult to assess the effect of these on the distribution of economic welfare. On the one hand there is evidence that these services were used disproportionately by the less-well-off and that for such families they constituted a substantial addition to total income. But it may also be argued that the value placed on the services by their recipients was less than that by the state and that therefore the use of national income estimates results in an understatement of perceived inequality.

On a different level, however, one may suggest that the existence of a fairly centralized bureaucratic system for the provision of such services as education or medical care has helped to integrate the various parts of the USSR and has had an important influence on the modernization of relatively backward areas. This is not a new point; Nove and Newth made it some time ago in their study of Soviet Central Asia. But it has, perhaps, a more general validity (Nove and Newth, 1967, pp. 65 ff.).

In this chapter, section 11.1 provides an overview of the level and structure of social consumption expenditure in the USSR and the way that it has changed since 1950. It also contains some limited information on sources of finance. Section 11.2 contains a brief discussion of the Soviet philosophy of social welfare, while sections 11.3-11.5 illustrate how this has been realized in specific programs. The material permits an assessment of the contribution that social consumption expenditure makes to the reduction of income inequality. This is taken up in the concluding section of the chapter.

11.1 SOCIAL CONSUMPTION

Table 11.1 contains estimates of the value and structure of social consumption expenditures in the Soviet Union for a number of postwar

Table 11.1
Social Consumption Expenditures, USSR, 1950-74

	1950	1955	1960	1965	1970	1974
Total expenditure (billion R)	13.0	16.4	27.3	41.9	63.9	83.0
of which (%)						
Holiday pay	13.1	14.0	11.7	12.2	14.2	14.0
Pensions	18.5	26.8	26.0	25.3	25.4	26.6
Allowances	9.2		9.5	8.4	9.6	8.8
Stipends	3.8	3.0	2.2	2.2	2.0	2.5
Total Cash Transfers	44.6	43.9	49.4	48.0	51.2	51.9
Education	33.8	31.7	26.7	29.4	27.1	26.8
Medical care	16.9	18.9	18.3	16.5	15.5	14.5
Social security	0.8	1.2	1.1	0.7	0.8	1.1
Housing subsidy	3.8	4.3	4.4	5.5	5.5	5.8
Expenditure per capita (R per year)	72.8	84.4	128.5	182.5	264.4	330.8

Notes and Sources: 1950, 1960-74, *NK SSSR* '70, p. 537; ibid '74, p. 578. Holiday pay and housing subsidy, 1960-70, Basov, 1967, p. 28, Kulikov, 1972, p. 98. Holiday pay, 1974, *NK SSSR* '74, p. 553, 561; housing subsidy, by residual. 1955 total expenditure, *NK SSSR* '56, p. 44; the figures in this source are consistently lower than those in later editions. The recorded entry for 1955 has been grossed up by the same percentage as that for 1950 when compared with the entry in *NK SSSR* '70—106.5%. Holiday pay, 1950-55, ratio of 1960 holiday pay to wage bill in the state sector times the wage bill. Pensions and allowances, *SSSR v tsifrakh* '58, p. 414. STipends, interpolated. Education and medical, *Gosudarstvennvi byudzhet* . . . , 1962, pp. 19, 21-23. Social security, interpolated. Housing subsidy, by residual. Columns may not sum to totals because of rounding.

years. For the most part the figures have been taken directly from Soviet official sources, but certain categories of expenditure have been estimated; details of the assumptions used are given in the notes to the table. The figures themselves refer to expenditures on the various programs, net of capital investment, from all sources. That is, they cover expenditures not only from social insurance funds and the state budget but also by enterprises and other organizations, trade unions, and collective farms. Because the estimates are taken so directly from Soviet sources, they reflect Soviet definitions and conventions rather than those more commonly encountered in the West. This results in the inclusion of certain surprising categories and the exclusion of others. Most striking, perhaps, is the inclusion of holiday pay as a transfer payment; this is usually thought of as part of earnings, but because it is not legally a payment for labor services, Soviet statisticians treat it as one of the benefits provided by the socialist state. On the other hand, while the table includes housing subsidies, it excludes subsidies on food and certain other commodities.

One Soviet economist has suggested that omitted items amount to not less than 10% of the recorded value of social consumption expenditures (Khabibi, 1975, p. 277). In strict logic this exclusion cannot be justified, since both affect living standards in the same way. But national income statistics are frequently illogical, and it would be difficult to make all the necessary adjustments. Finally, it appears that expenditures include an allowance for the depreciation of the nonproductive capital stock—that is, housing, hospital buildings, schools, and so on. This has been estimated at approximately four billion rubles in 1970 (G. Schroeder in a private communication).

Taking the figures as they stand, they record a very substantial increase in the value of social consumption expenditures over the twenty-four-year period covered by the table, both in total and on a per capita basis. Total expenditure increased by 538% and per capita expenditure by 354%. These are, of course, nominal increases; no allowance has been made for changes in costs. Given increases in the cost of living, for example, increases in the real value of expenditures on pensions would be less than that shown in table 11.1. Similarly, if allowance were made for increases in the earnings of teachers or doctors, growth in the real value of educational or medical services supplied would be less than that shown in the table. But even allowing for these factors, the figures suggest a substantial increase in the scale of provision. The figures also indicate that most of the growth occurred after 1955. Between 1950 and 1955 the average annual rate of growth of per capita social consumption was 3.0%; over the next decade, under Khrushchev, it rose to 8.0%, while in the first nine years of the Brezhnev-Kosygin period it fell back to 6.8%.

In 1960, per capita social consumption expenditures amounted to 10.70 rubles a month, or on the basis of the income estimates given in chapter 2, to 25.2% of total per capita income. By 1970, per capita expenditures had approximately doubled to 22.10 rubles a month or 28.5% of total per capita income.

Over the period as a whole, and particularly since 1955, there have also been substantial changes in the relative importance of the various components of social consumption. In 1950, cash transfers accounted for 44.6% of the total (or 36.3%, if one excludes holiday pay). By the end of the decade this had risen to 49.4% (42.7% excluding holiday pay), and in 1970 it was 51.2% (43.1%). These developments appear to have been due, in large measure, to increased expenditure on pensions after 1955 and, to a lesser extent, to the growth of holiday pay and allowances after 1965. As I point out below, a number of Soviet economists have advanced the rather superficial argument that social consumption expenditures, and particularly non-cash expenditures, are a progressive phenomenon, foreshadowing the emergence of communist distribution relationships in the

USSR. From this point of view, the developments reflected in table 11.1 are undesirable.

Increases in cash transfers have resulted in a decline in the relative importance of both education and medical care in total social consumption. This decline has been accentuated by the increased importance of housing subsidies and, after 1970, of social security. This last category relates to state spending on the maintenance of old people's homes and similar institutions.

Social insurance transfers—that is, most pensions and some allowances—are paid out of the social insurance fund, which at least formally is administered by the trade unions. The fund obtains its resources from payroll deductions, which are differentiated by industry and in principle bear some relation to the risks associated with different industrial occupations. When the social insurance—social security system was extended to the collective farm sector in 1965, a parallel fund was set up for kolkhozy which receives subsidies from general budgetary revenues, in addition to receipts from the collective farms. The general budget also provides the resources for social security transfers, for some pensions, and for most non-cash expenditures. Enterprises and other institutions also contribute to these programs, however. Some impression of the funding sources for social consumption expenditures in the Soviet Union and the way that they have changed over the past decade or so can be gained from table 11.2. Two features merit comment. The small increase in the share of ex-

Table 11.2
Social Consumption: Sources of Finance, 1960-70 (%)

	1960	1965	1970	1975
Total expenditure	100.0	100.0	100.0	100.0
of which, from				
Enterprises, organizations, etc.	17.0	17.9	20.8	20.0
Kolkhozy	1.4	3.0	3.5	4.0
Trade unions, etc.	1.5	1.5	1.7	1.6
Social insurance fund	26.4	25.4	26.6	29.1
State budget	53.7	52.4	47.4	45.3

Sources: Maier and Rakitskii, 1976, p. 198. The division between Social Insurance Fund and State Budget was calculated from NK SSSR '65, p. 786, and NK SSSR '76, pp. 488, 656.

penditures derived from enterprise funds after 1965 reflects the changes introduced by the so-called economic reform of 1965. Second, it is not clear how far expenditures from the All-Union Central Fund for Kolkhozniki (set up in 1964-65) are included under kolkhozy and how far they are reported under the state budget. On the one hand, the figures in row 3 of the table seem rather low to comprise total social security payments to collective farmers. On the other, the All-Union Fund, formally, is administratively separate from the other bodies listed in the table and should not have been combined with them. (On this subject, the figures in table 11.1 suggest that the extension of social security to the peasantry made very little difference to the system as a whole. In 1960, when kolkhozniki were effectively excluded from the system, pensions and allowances accounted for 34.5% of total social consumption; in 1970, after they had been largely integrated, pensions and allowances accounted for only 34.9% of the total. This favors the first conjecture advanced above. It also suggests that the 1965 law did not pose any additional burden on the Soviet budget; rather the extension of pensions to the peasantry was seen as an alternative to other possible developments of the social welfare system.)

The material presented in this section casts some light on the contribution that various social consumption programs have made to average living standards, to per capita money and total income. It provides very little insight into the redistributive effects of the Soviet welfare state. On this subject, the official statistics are of very little help. Analysis of semi-official and academic sample survey data in chapter 4 showed that, until the mid sixties at least, high income households received more in cash transfers than did the poor, while the poor benefitted disproportionately from other programs. From a few scattered comments by Soviet economists subsequently, it would seem that there was little change in this picture until at least 1974. My analysis has not yet shown why this is true nor indicated what would be necessary to bring about any substantial change; these questions will be taken up in sections 11.3-11.5. But first I would like to turn to a brief discussion of the Soviet philosophy of social welfare, of Soviet justifications for providing financial support to some citizens and certain services either free of charge or at subsidized prices.

11.2 THE SOVIET WELFARE STATE

In general, Soviet economists devote relatively little attention to specifying the objectives of social consumption expenditure and deriving policy prescriptions from them. There is some discussion of this in the literature, though, and it suggests reasons for the failure of the Soviet government to adopt more aggressively redistributive policies.

What may be termed the orthodox view is that social consumption represents the communist distribution principle; that is, benefits under the various social consumption programs are distributed according to need. As society moves forward into communism, distribution according to need will become more widespread at the expense of distribution according to labor. This is taken to imply an increase in social consumption relative to personal (money) incomes. But arguments of this type are rather superficial; they contain little discussion of the concept of need, nor of the relationship between need and the benefits derived from the social welfare system. They have been subjected to criticism in the Soviet Union also.

A more specific rationale for the existence and structure of present social consumption programs has been offered by Lantsev, although explicitly he is dealing only with social security:

> . . . the necessity for a social security system is derived from two groups of causes. First of all there is loss of earnings as a result of temporary or permanent loss of working capacity through sickness, old age, or injury [invalidnost]. Consequently the first task of a social security system is to provide some measure of compensation for loss of earnings in the form of a pension or allowance.
>
> The second group of causes is connected with disease, family circumstances [mnogodetnost; having many children], or other factors which impose an additional burden on the worker and his family and do not depend directly on either the level of earnings or on whether such groups are employed at all. For this reason, forms of social security connected with this group of causes, like free medical care or child allowances, have in our country from its very beginning been made available to the population as a whole. Their objective has been, by means of free services, allowances, and subsidies, to prevent the imposition of such additional expenses on the family or to reduce their burden [tyazhest] (Lantsev, 1974, p. 129).

Thus the possibility of interruptions in earnings gives rise to the development of income maintenance schemes or a system of transfer payments, while the possibility that certain households will be called upon to meet substantial and perhaps unanticipated demands upon their resources is used to justify the development of a network of free or subsidized services. Although the argument is not developed explicitly, the justification for both components is in terms of risk spreading, and also suggests a certain lack of faith in the development of decentralized mechanisms or personal provision.

For example, the above argument implies that although one can be sure that a certain number of those employed will suffer temporary or permanent incapacitation through injury or disease, ex ante one cannot say who will suffer. A priori, therefore, one would expect everyone to benefit from some sort of insurance scheme. But although incapacity may have a catastrophic effect on family finances, existing attitudes towards the likelihood of such mishaps mean that people will tend to underinsure against them. Such underinsurance not only affects the individual and members of his or her immediate family but may have wider repercussions. This justifies the development of a compulsory state system.

Similarly, possible external effects, what may be termed imperfections in forward markets, and perhaps a belief that fertility is outside the conscious control of the family, are used to justify the state's participation in the provision of educational and medical services.

The concept of need implicit in this argument of Lantsev's is similar to that to be found in the social welfare programs of many other countries. It is not lack of the means of subsistence per se that provides entitlement to assistance. Rather, the state undertakes to indemnify the household against certain extraordinary expenses (medical care, for example, or education, or part of the cost of housing) and to provide financial assistance only in specific circumstances. Lantsev in effect suggests that only those who have been employed are entitled to such support; there is no obligation to provide benefits for those who, through short-sightedness, idleness, or any other cause, are without means of subsistence. It is therefore loss of employment or working capacity and not need itself that determines entitlement. And this is in fact true of the Soviet system; there is no highly developed system of public assistance, and the family, not the state, is to a very large extent the residual source of support.[1]

Lantsev himself does not go into the justification for this state of affairs, but it has been dealt with by other authors. In part it can be explained by the historical origins of social insurance in the USSR, which grew out of the Tsarist employee insurance schemes and Lenin's criticisms of them. In part it can be derived from Marxist principles. Thus under communism there will be material abundance, and individuals will regard labor as desirable for its own sake, irrespective of material rewards. Under socialism, which is the system that exists in the Soviet Union today, neither of these conditions holds. As we have seen, this analysis is used to justify the employment of wage differentials, but it also implies that given the opportunity, people would rather be supported by the state than work for their living, and that the state is obliged to employ the threat of hunger to ensure their participation in the labor force. Lenin voiced this threat in his rather biblical slogan "He who does not work neither shall he eat"; it acquired rather more practical force in the Stalinist developments of the thirties. The belief that people would rather live in idleness at the expense of the state than seek useful employment is embodied in much current Soviet social security legislation. Most benefit programs include a wage-stop clause to the effect that cash receipts cannot exceed what a person would have earned (or did earn) when employed, and benefits are usually tied to earnings, length of employment, and the period of uninterrupted employment.

In his justification of the development of a social insurance system Lantsev does not go into the nature of the relationship between the compensation provided and the earnings lost. In his 1912 attack on the proposed Tsarist system, Lenin argued for one hundred percent compensation, implicitly claiming that the needs of highly paid workers were greater than those of the unskilled. While few Soviet programs provide for full compensation, most benefits are tied to earnings. It is because of this that high-income households receive more from the state than poor households.

Although he recognizes that ill health or children impose strains on the family budget and argues that the state has a responsibility to help the family meet those added burdens, Lantsev does not discuss why the state should respond by providing free or subsidized services rather than cash supplements and a market-oriented supply system. This question has been taken up by certain other authors. Typically, it is argued that "individuals will use their personal employment incomes primarily for the satisfaction of priority needs: food, clothing, shelter, etc. And only then will they spend anything on culture or rest. If such goods and services [as education or medical care] had to be paid for, growth in the material and cultural living standards of Soviet people would have been much slower" (Basov, 1967, p. 8; see also Kulikov, 1972, p. 81). In spite of the non-marginal nature of the allocation process described, the implication is that the marginal utility of such services as education and medical care to the average or low-income Soviet household is less than for other forms of personal consumption. If the state were to provide cash grants rather than free schools, for example, the belief is that households would spend part or all of their extra income on other things than education. By providing the services themselves, the Soviet authorities can ensure that the pattern of consumption conforms most closely to the one they desire. Such an approach, at least in the case of education, has added advantages, as we have seen.

Although they recognize certain categories of need rooted in the risks to which individuals are exposed in any society, the arguments for the existence of a social security system and more generally for the development of social consumption programs, put forward by Lantsev and other Soviet economists, do not constitute a justification for extensive income redistribution, nor are they inspired by any very strong desire for equality. But this is hardly surprising. If one accepts the claim that the structure of earnings differentials is socially desirable, or at least is appropriate to the stage of development reached, there can be no very good grounds for modifying the distribution of income it generates. Both the tax system and the structure of transfer payments will play a secondary role, their function being to supplement rather than to modify the primary distribution of income. The situation in the Soviet Union is changing, however; in the last chapter I suggested that it was the view of the State Committee on Labor and Wages (or of certain economists and sociologists in its research department, NIIT) that social security should be used to alleviate undesirable poverty. In 1968 this advice was rejected or ignored. The introduction of a family income supplement in 1974 can be seen as a step in this direction. Similarly, although there have been no changes yet, falling birth rates and increases in life expectancy, resulting in an aging population, will force a reconsideration of the pension system and particularly of old-age pensions. Indeed, one might suggest that the existence of substantial numbers of elderly collective farmers was a contributing factor in the decision to introduce pensions for collective farmers. These developments suggest the possibility of a more autonomous role for the Soviet welfare state, but as the material presented below indicates, such a role is still largely in the future.

11.3   CASH TRANSFERS

This section will outline the main cash transfers available to various groups of the population in the USSR and describe the most important changes in the regulations governing entitlement and payment in the last twenty years or so. There are two ways in which these transfers can be classified: either according to the population categories to which they refer (state employees, kolkhozniki, and so on) or according to the functions that they serve. In this chapter I adopt the second approach, which makes it possible to identify three classes of transfer: pensions paid in the case of permanent loss of working capacity; a variety of allowances available in the case of certain specific temporary interruptions in earnings; and a group of benefits that are not connected with earnings at all. I will consider each of these in turn.

PENSION PROVISION IN THE USSR

For civilian state employees and their dependents, the Pension Law of 1956 collated, codified, and rationalized the bewildering variety of industrial schemes that had grown up in the preceding quarter of a century.[2] After 1956 all civilian state employees, with the exception of certain white collar workers like teachers, were covered by the same scheme, which provided for the payment of old-age (or retirement) pensions, invalidity pensions, and survivor pensions (*pensii po sluchayu poteri kormiltsa*). According to the 1964 Law on Pension Provision for Kolkhozniki, similar benefits were made available to collective farmers and their dependents in 1965.[3] Before this, provision for the elderly, the incapaciated, and those deprived of support had been the responsibility of individual farms.

OLD-AGE PENSIONS

The 1956 law laid down that civilian state employees were entitled to an old-age pension on reaching the age of sixty, if they were men with a record of twenty-five years of state employment (*stazh*),[4] or on reaching the age of fifty-five if they were women with a stazh of twenty years. Underground workers and certain other designated categories were entitled to a pension at an earlier age, with a corresponding reduction in the necessary stazh (Zakharov and Piskov, 1972, pp. 180-81). The 1964 law laid down that male kolkhozniki were entitled to an old-age pension on reaching the age of sixty-five with a stazh of twenty-five years; kolkhoznitsy—that is, female members of collective farms—were entitled to their pensions on reaching the age of sixty with a stazh of twenty years (Zakharov, 1966, p. 7). In 1967 the age requirements for collective farmers were reduced to sixty for men and fifty-five for women (Zakharov and Piskov, 1972, p. 270).

In the 1956 law, the size of the pension was related to the value of previous earnings on a sliding scale: those earning less than thirty-five new rubles a month received 100% of previous earnings; those earning between 35 rubles and 50 rubles a month received 85% of previous earnings, but not less than 35 rubles; and so on, until those who had earned more than 100 rubles a month were awarded a pension set at 50% of earnings but not less than 55 rubles a month. Again, underground workers and some other designated categories received somewhat more favorable treatment (Zakharov and Piskov, 1972, p. 181). For the purposes of calculating the pension, earnings were defined as actual average pay in the twelve months preceding retirement (or acquisition of the right to a pension for those who continued to work), including all supplements in respect of which the employing enterprise paid social insurance premia. At the employee's choice, any five years' earnings in the preceding ten could be substituted for the last twelve months' earnings (Zakharov and Piskov, 1972, pp. 224-25).

Also according to the 1956 law, the minimum pension was set at 30 rubles a month and the maximum at 120 rubles. Within the limits of this maximum, those with an uninterrupted stazh of at least fifteen years or with a total stazh of ten years more than the requirement received a 10% supplement (Zakharov and Piskov, 1972, pp. 181-82). Pensioners with one dependent were also entitled to a 10% supplement; those with two or more received an additional 15% (but only if pension plus supplement did not exceed the maximum limit). For those living in rural areas and having some connection with agriculture, the pension was set at 85% of the value calculated by the above procedure (Piskov, 1964, pp. 129-39). In this context, "having some connection with agriculture" was subsequently specified as "living in a household that has access to a private plot of 0.15 hectares (or more, in specified republics)" (Zakharov and Piskov, 1972, pp. 217-18). In 1971, the minimum value of the pension was raised to 45 rubles a month, but there was no increase in the maximum (Zakharov and Piskov, 1972, p. 181).

The regulations governing the calculation of pensions are important, since, once specified, pensions are not changed when the minimum pension is raised (unless they fall below the new minimum). Thus in 1971, only those with pensions in the range 30-45 rubles a month received an increase; for all these people, the pension was set at 45 rubles a month, the new lower limit (Livshits, 1972, pp. 241-42).

The 1964 law on kolkhoznik pensions specified that collective farmers were to receive a pension equal to 50% of previous earnings, subject to a minimum of 12 rubles a month and a maximum of 102 rubles (Zakharov, 1966, p. 7). In 1971, the minimum was raised to 20 rubles (the maximum was left at its 1964 level), and pensions were henceforth to be calculated according to the same sliding scale as that used in the calculation of pensions for state employees (Zakharov and Piskov, 1972, p. 270). Because of the provision that adjustments to the value of pensions are not retroactive, this meant that kolkhozniki who retired between 1965 and 1971 and were earning 40-100 rubles a month from their kolkhoz when employed would be receiving lower pensions than they would have if they had retired after 1971. For example, under the 1964 law, a kolkhoznik with previous earnings of 40 rubles a month was entitled to a pension of 20 rubles; according to the sliding scale used after 1971, his pension would have been 34 rubles. In this particular case, the pension actually received is only 58.8% of the post-1971 value. Since it is to be supposed that most kolkhozniki who retired between 1965 and 1971 would have had earnings of less than 50 rubles a month, this lack of retroactivity would have resulted in some savings to the state at the expense of considerable hardship to the individuals concerned.

INVALIDITY PENSIONS

The 1956 law codified the payment of invalidity pensions to civilian state employees. The Soviet authorities recognize three classes of incapacity. Those in class I need permanent care or supervision, or can work only in specialized workshops. Those in class II are not sufficiently incapacitated to require care, *ukhod*, but cannot continue to work because to do so would lead to a deterioration in their condition. Class II also covers those who suffer significant motor defects or whose sight is seriously impaired. In class III are any who have suffered a significant loss of capacity requiring them to transfer to work of lower skill or preventing them from acquiring new skills. The extent of loss of capacity is determined by a medical-labor commission, *kommissiya vrachebno-trudovoi ekspertizy* (Babkin and Smirnova, 1975, pp. 88-89). (The commissions consist of a representative from the trade unions, a representative from the Ministry of Social Security, and three medical specialists, one of whom serves as chairman [Zakharov and Piskov, 1972, pp. 435-39].)

The regulations governing the payment of invalidity pensions are complex, since the value of the pension depends upon the individual's stazh, upon the cause of incapacity (that is, whether it was the result of an industrial accident or occupational disease or derived from more general causes), and upon the place of work. Some account is taken of current earnings, if any. Simplifying and neglecting all these special regulations, one can summarize the 1956 law by saying that it made provision for the payment of pensions within the following limits (in rubles per month):

	Minimum	Maximum
I	30	120
II	23	90
III	16	45

In 1965, the minima for classes I and II were raised to 50 rubles and 30 rubles a month respectively, and in 1973, the formulae used in the calculation of old-age pensions were substituted for the complex regulations laid down in the 1956 law. At the same time, fixed ruble supplements (as opposed to percentage additions) were introduced for dependents: 10 rubles for one dependent, 20 rubles for two, and 30 rubles for three or more (in the case of class I pensioners only) (Zakharov and Piskov, 1972, pp. 183-84; Piskov, 1964, pp. 131-32; Babkin and Smirnova, 1975, pp. 12-14).

The 1964 law on kolkhoznik pensions introduced the principle of class I and class II invalidity pensions for collective farmers; class III pensions were added in 1967 for industrial injury cases only. If incapacity resulted from an industrial accident or an occupational disease, a pension was paid irrespective of stazh. In other circumstances, the kolkhoznik was entitled to an invalidity pension only if he or she had been employed for roughly half the time since reaching the age of twenty. (That is, for example, a man between the ages of thirty-six and forty-one required a stazh of ten years to qualify for a pension; if he was over the age of sixty-one, he needed a stazh of twenty years.) These requirements were the same as for state employees (Zakharov, 1966, p. 8; Zakharov and Piskov, 1972, p. 270).

The formulae in the 1964 law relating benefits to earnings provided for a minimum pension of 15 rubles a month for class I incapacity and 12 rubles for class II; maxima were the same as for state employees in rural areas. In 1971 these formulae were replaced by the ones used to calculate invalidity pensions for state employees (which were more generous), and new minima were set at 30 rubles, 20 rubles, and 16 rubles a month for the three categories respectively (Zakharov, 1966, p. 8; Zakharov and Piskov, 1972, p. 271). The same lack of retroactivity that applies to old-age pensions applies also to the calculation and award of invalidity pensions. Thus by initially operating the invalidity pension scheme for kolkhozniki at a lower level than that for state employees, the Soviet authorities have been able to reduce the cost to themselves of providing for the backlog of incapacitated peasants, the consequence of almost forty years of discrimination and neglect. But such a tactic introduces an element of horizontal inequity into the Soviet social insurance system.

SURVIVOR PENSIONS

The 1956 law laid down that when a state employee or pensioner died, certain members of his or her family were entitled to a pension. These were the children, grandchildren, or siblings under the age of sixteen (or eighteen if in full-time education), parents or a surviving spouse, if over the age of sixty (fifty-five for women), or grandparents without other sources of support. For purposes of entitlement, adopted children and stepchildren were regarded as equivalent to offspring by blood. There were also clauses covering possible relationships for other dependents (for example, parents-in-law, foster parents, etc.). A child was entitled to such a pension even if the other parent was alive (Zakharov and Piskov, 1972, pp. 185-86).

The value of the pension paid depended on previous earnings of the decedent and on the number of dependents who were left. It was higher if death was the result of an industrial accident or occupational disease or if the deceased had been employed underground or in certain designated occupations. In 1956, minimum pensions were set at 16 rubles a month for one dependent, 23 rubles for two dependents, and 30 rubles for three or more dependents; maxima were set at 40-120 rubles (Piskov, 1964, pp. 133-35). In 1965, minima were raised to 21-50 rubles a month, and in 1973 they were raised again to 23-70 rubles a month. In the same year, the maximum for a single dependent was raised to 60 rubles. At the same time, the formulae relating earnings and pensions laid down in the 1956 law were replaced by those used in the calculation of old-age pensions with some minor modification (Zakharov and Piskov, 1972, pp. 186-87; Babkin and Smirnova, 1975, pp. 15-17).

The 1964 law on kolkhoznik pensions laid down conditions under which the dependents of collective farmers were entitled to survivor pensions. Briefly, the deceased had to have been employed for a sufficient number of years, and the survivor (or survivors) had to be dependents standing in a designated relationship to the decedent. To all intents and purposes the relationships were the same as for state employees. The value of the pension was related to the previous earnings of the deceased and was set within the range of 9-15 rubles to 34-76.5 rubles a month, depending upon the number of survivors (Zakharov, 1966, pp. 9-10). In 1967, the age of entitlement for adult dependents was lowered from sixty-five (sixty) years to sixty (fifty-five) years for men (women) at the same time that the pensionable age was reduced. In 1971, the benefit formulae used for calculating the survivor pensions of state employees were substituted for those set out in the 1964 law, and new minima were introduced, from 16 rubles to 30 rubles a month, depending on the number of survivors (Zakharov and Piskov, 1972, pp. 271-72).

LONG-SERVICE PENSIONS

For certain categories of white collar workers—teachers, medical personnel, some airline employees, certain types of agricultural specialist, and scientific research worker—the principles of pension designation differ from those laid down in the 1956 law. These groups are entitled to long-service pensions, *pensii za vyslugu let*. This type of pension dates from before the 1956 rationalization, and the various provisions were recodified in 1959 (Zakharov and Piskov, pp. 310 ff.).

Under the 1959 regulations, teachers are entitled to a long-service pension after having been employed for twenty-five years, medical personnel after having served for twenty-five years in rural areas or thirty years in urban areas. The employment requirements for other categories are similar (Zakharov and Piskov, 1972, p. 310).

The 1959 regulations specified that the pension should equal 40% of previous salary within the range 30-120 rubles a month; and the pension was to be paid irrespective of whether the individual retired or continued to work, on condition that pension and salary did not exceed 200 rubles a month (Piskov, 1964, pp. 198-200). When salary scales in health and education were raised in 1964-65, these regulations were changed. After that date, the pension was to be calculated on the basic salary of those with ten to twenty-five years' service or on actual earnings, whichever was the less, and pensions were no longer payable to those who continued in employment (Zakharov and Piskov, 1972, p. 310).

PERSONAL PENSIONS

Personal pensions are awarded to those who have performed some special service to the state or to the cause of revolution. Again, this class of transfer antedates the 1956 codification—indeed, dates back to the early years of the USSR. Personal pensions were recodified in 1956, but not in the 1956 law on state pensions.

Personal pensions can be awarded at all three levels of government in the USSR (All-Union, republican, and local); they are paid for out of the budget of the relevant government unit. The 1956 regulations stated that the maximum All-Union personal pension should be 200 rubles a month and that the maximum republican (local) pension should be 120 (60) rubles a month (Piskov, 1964, pp. 222-29). In 1970, the maximum local pension was raised to 80 rubles (Zakharov and Piskov, 1972, p. 334). In addition to their pensions, personal pensioners are entitled to extra accommodation, to purchase the services of utilities (gas, electricity, etc.) at subsidized rates, and to purchase pharmaceuticals at special prices. They may also be entitled to other privileges. Very little is known about the frequency with which these personal pensions are awarded.

There is very little information available about the distribution of pensions, their average value, or the proportion of those in various age and population groups who actually receive them. But the evidence suggests that pensions are low and that coverage is less than complete, although the situation appears to have improved since the late fifties.

It has been reported that the average value of an old-age pension in the USSR before the introduction of the 1956 pension law was as low as 21 rubles a month (Acharkan, 1971, p. 118). The 1956 law is supposed to have resulted in a more than twofold increase in the average value of an old-age pension (Acharkan, 1965, p. 48). If one assumes, in consequence, that the value of an old-age pension in 1960 was 45 rubles a month, then data on total expenditure on pensions of all types and on the number of pensioners in different classes suggest that the average value of other types of pensions in that year was little more than 21 rubles a month.[5]

Further, it has been reported that in 1970 the average value of an old-age pension was equal to 44% of average earnings, implying a value of 54 rubles a month (Sarkisyan, 1972, p. 144). On the assumption that other nonkolkhoznik pensions bore the same relation to old-age pensions in 1970 that they did in 1960, data on total expenditure on pensions and on the number of pensioners in different categories imply an average value for all kolkhoz pensions of approximately 22 rubles a month. The same data imply an average value of kolkhoznik old-age pensions of 24 rubles a month.

These estimates relate to a period before the minimum pension was raised to 45 rubles a month (20 rubles for collective farmers) and before the state-sector calculation formulae were employed for kolkhozniki. Data on total expenditure and on the number of pensioners imply that the average pension increased by about a quarter between 1970 and 1974. At a rough guess, therefore, the average old-age pension might have been as high as 33 rubles a month for kolkhozniki in the latter year and 59 rubles for state employees, and the average value of all other pensions about 30 rubles a month.

Table 11.3 contains figures on the number of pensioners of different types in the USSR in 1959 and 1970 and also estimates of the number of persons of pensionable age in these two years. The figures indicate how small a proportion of those of pensionable age in 1959 actually received a pension—something less than 20%. Of course some persons of pensionable age would have received other types of pension and others would have been kolkhozniki (and thus excluded from the system), but

Table 11.3
Pension Provision in the USSR, 1959-70 (millions)

	1959	1970		
		Total	Under Law on Kolkhoz Pensions	Under Other Laws
Numbers receiving a pension of which:	19.9	40.1	12.1	28.0
Military veterans and dependents	6.9	4.4	—	4.4
Invalids, survivors, etc.	8.6	12.0	1.6	10.4
Old-age pensioners	4.4	23.7	10.5	13.2
Persons of pensionable age	25.3	36.5	n.a	n.a

Notes and Sources: *NK SSSR* '65, p. 607; *NK SSSR* '74, p. 614; *Itogi . . .* , 1970, vol. 2, pp. 12-13. It is assumed that the proportion of old-age pensioners among all nonmilitary pensioners in 1959 was the same as in 1961.

even making allowances for these factors one might conjecture that as many as half of the state employee population over the age of sixty (fifty-five) was without financial support from the state.

By 1970, the figures in table 11.3 suggest, old-age pensioners accounted for almost two-thirds of those of pensionable age. Making some allowance for those receiving other types of pension, perhaps as many as three-quarters or four-fifths of the population over the age of sixty (fifty-five) were beneficiaries of state financial aid; a considerable improvement over eleven or so years earlier. But this still means that some six or seven million elderly Soviet citizens are completely dependent upon their savings or the earnings of their relatives for support in their old age (and this figure excludes the collective farm population).

SOCIAL INSURANCE TRANSFERS

The transfers described so far are payable as a result of permanent loss of working capacity, although in the case of old-age pensions the loss is conventional rather than real. The Soviet social insurance system also provides financial assistance in certain cases of temporary incapacitation, notably sickness and pregnancy-maternity, and under certain circumstances, grants for births and deaths. The programs are described below. The regulations governing the payment of sickness benefits to state employees date from 1955, although benefits of one form or another were available before that time. Coverage was extended to the collective farm population in the second half of the sixties.

SICKNESS BENEFITS

State employees are entitled to sickness benefits under the 1955 regulations in the case of sickness resulting in the temporary loss of working capacity, while in quarantine, if caring for a sick member of the family, during residence at a sanitorium, or during temporary reclassification occasioned by TB or an occupational disease. Benefits are payable only if the disease is contracted while the person is employed, and loss of working capacity must be attested by a physician. Employees are entitled to benefits irrespective of the length of time they have worked, with the exception of those who have been dismissed for breaking labor discipline or committing a crime. In such cases, the person must have been employed for six months in his new place of work before he acquires entitlement. (If incapacity is the result of an industrial accident or an occupational disease, sickness benefit is paid immediately.) (Zakharov and Piskov, pp. 54-59)

Benefits are payable from the first day of incapacity and are paid for as long as incapacity lasts, or until a medical-labor commission declares that it is permanent. (At this point the person is entitled to an invalidity pension.) If incapacity is the result of a domestic injury, *bytovoi travmy*, benefits are payable only from the sixth day. If incapacity is occasioned by the need to care for a sick member of the family, the 1955 regulations laid down that benefits were payable for only three days (Zakharov and Piskov, 1972, pp. 56-58).

Rates of benefit specified under the 1955 regulations depend upon the period of uninterrupted employment. In principle, this refers to employment at a particular enterprise or organization, but as might be expected, there exists a complex set of conditions and legal rulings covering justifiable interruptions in service and legitimate changes in employment. For example, maternity leave does not constitute a break in employment, nor do service in the armed forces, time spent in party or state office, and so on. Benefits also depend upon the cause of incapacity, in that industrial accidents and occupational diseases confer entitlement to 100% of previous earnings. In other cases, the 1955 regulations specified that those with less than three years' continuous service should receive 50% of previous earnings, rising by stages to 90% of earnings for those with at least twelve years in the same employment. Those under the age of eighteen were to receive 60% of previous earnings, and invalids from the Second World War 90%, irrespective of employment record. State employees who were not members of a trade union received half the above rates. The regulations also prescribed that the minimum payment should be 30 rubles a month (27 rubles in rural areas) or the equivalent per diem rate. Benefits could not exceed ten rubles a day (Piskov, 1964, pp. 43-46).

In 1967, the relationship between length of service and the value of benefits was changed: those with five to eight years' service received 80% of earnings instead of 70%, and those with more than eight years' received 100% (instead of 80-90%). Employees who are not union members still receive half the above rates. At the same date, the 1955 maximum limit was repealed, but no change was made in the minimum (Zakharov and Piskov, 1972, pp. 59-60). In 1975, it was laid down that those with three or more children under the age of sixteen (or eighteen if in full-time education) should receive 100% of previous earnings, irrespective of employment record—unless dismissed for breaking labor discipline or committing a crime *(Sobraniye postanovleniya SSSR* 1975, no. 1, p. 2).

Until 1970, members of collective farms were not entitled to sickness benefits. A 1970 law extended the state employee system to kolkhozniki, with certain modifications. Benefits are payable in the same circumstances (incapacity, quarantine, etc.) but are paid only if the kolkhoznik would have been called upon for collective work. They are, further, restricted in duration to four months' continuous incapacity or to five months' benefit in any calendar year (Zakharov and Piskov, 1972, p. 107). As in the state system, benefits are paid at 100% of previous earnings in the case of industrial accidents or occupational diseases and depend upon stazh in other cases. Those with less than three years' service receive 50% of earnings, rising to 70% for those with five to eight years' and 90% for those with more than eight. The law also lays down a minimum payment of one ruble per diem. Thus the treatment of kolkhozniki is somewhat more liberal than that of state employees who do not belong to a trade union but more restrictive than that of union members (Zakharov and Piskov, 1972, pp. 109-10).

MATERNITY ALLOWANCES

Under Soviet law, female state employees are entitled to fifty-six days' maternity leave before the birth of a child and to a further fifty-six days' after the birth. The postnatal leave period is raised to seventy days in the case of multiple or abnormal births. In addition, the 1955 regulations stated that women were entitled to a further three months' unpaid leave without loss of their continuous stazh (Piskov, 1964, p. 54). These same regulations specified that those who were not members of trade unions were entitled to two-thirds of their previous earnings, subject to a thirty-ruble minimum (in rural areas twenty-seven rubles) for the full 112 days' leave. For trade union members, the value of maternity benefits depended upon their stazh: those with less than one year's uninterrupted employment were treated like non-members; those with one to two years' received two-thirds of their pay for the first twenty days and 100% for the remainder; the provisions became progressively more generous, until those with a total stazh of at least three years' and not less than two years' uninterrupted employment received full pay throughout their leave (Piskov, 1964, pp. 55-56).

In 1968, the period of postnatal unpaid leave was raised from three months until the child's first birthday. In 1970, this privilege was extended to women who adopted children direct from maternity homes (Zakharov and Piskov, 1972, p. 70). In 1973, it was laid down that *all* women, no matter what their employment record or union membership status, were entitled to full pay throughout the 112 days of their maternity leave (Kotlyar and Shlemin, 1974, p. 118).

As far as I can tell, kolkhoznitsy were not entitled to maternity leave before 1965, although the situation is not clear; they were certainly not entitled to maternity benefits until that date. As of 1965, all kolkhoznitsy were entitled to both 112 days leave (126 days in the case of multiple or abnormal births) and maternity benefits. But the relevant legislation makes no mention of the possibility of their taking unpaid leave.[6] In 1965, the benefits were set at two-thirds of previous earnings; those with at least three years' employment received 100% of previous earnings (Zakharov, 1966, pp. 47-48). Female kolkhoz chairmen, specialists with higher education (or particular qualifications), and mechanizers[7] were treated as state employees for social security purposes. For the purpose of calculating benefits, previous earnings were defined as average earnings in the calendar year preceding the year in which application is made (Zakharov, 1966, p. 48); and the minimum payment was set at 0.4 rubles a day. It is not clear whether the 1968-73 modifications in the state employee system also apply to kolkhoznitsy.

MATERNITY GRANTS

In addition to the maternity benefits described above, the 1955 social insurance regulations contained provision for the payment of a maternity grant under certain circumstances. Such grants were payable on the birth of a child if the average monthly earnings of either parent (in the last three months preceding the birth) were less than 50 rubles, provided that the parent applying for the grant had been employed for at least three months. In 1955, the grant was set at 12 rubles, and an additional 18 rubles were payable when the child reached the age of five months. The first of these payments was meant to help the mother acquire a layette, and the second was intended to defray some of the costs associated with weaning (Piskov, 1964, p. 56). The 12-ruble grant was also payable to kolkhozniki.[8] In 1970, the earnings limit was raised from 50 to 60 rubles a month, and the 18-ruble supplement was made payable to kolkhozniki (Zakharov and Piskov, 1972, pp. 72-112). Given the changes in the minimum wage between 1955 and 1970, this adjustment in fact implied a more restrictive approach to these grants in 1970 than that of fifteen years earlier.

BURIAL GRANTS

Finally, the 1955 regulations provided for the payment of a burial grant in the case of the death of a state employee or pensioner, or a member of his or her family. Its value depended on the age and place of residence of the deceased, but ranged from 5 to 20 rubles. In 1970, burial grants were made payable to kolkhozniki at rural rates (Zakharov and Piskov, 1972, pp. 73, 112).

HOLIDAY PAY

Although not covered by the social insurance system, holiday pay is treated, both legally and statistically, as part of the social welfare system in the Soviet Union. Indeed, holiday pay accounted for some 12-14% of total social consumption expenditures in the period 1950-74. Before 1968, Soviet labor law provided that the minimum holiday for state employees should be twelve working days; in 1968 this was raised to fifteen days (Maier, 1971, p. 35). Over the period covered by this chapter, the average length of holiday rose from 18.5 days in 1958 to 20.9 days in 1968; it has presumably risen further since then (Matyukha, 1973, p. 111). The legislation does not apply to the collective farm sector, but there is evidence to suggest that paid holidays are becoming more common for kolkhozniki.[9] Holiday pay is calculated on the basis of average earnings in the preceding twelve months, inclusive of sickness benefits and other allowances (Spravochnik ekonomista . . . , 1964, p. 442).

Some indication of the relative importance of these various benefits and of the way that this has changed since 1950 can be gained from table 11.4. The table includes data on child allowances, which are described

Table 11.4
Expenditure on Allowances (Posobiya), 1950-74 (millions of rubles)

Allowance	1950	1960	1965	1970	1974
Sickness benefits	542	1329	1963	3734	4435
Maternity grants and benefits	176	509	616	866	1191
Child allowances	366	496	462	435	395
Other[a]	116	266	459	1065	1279
Total	1200	2600	3500	6100	7300

Sources: NK SSSR '65, pp. 785-86; NK SSSR '70, p. 537; NK SSSR '74, pp. 578, 760-61.
a. Residual; includes burial grants and, presumably, payments on behalf of military personnel and collective farm members.

below. The figures show that in 1950 sickness benefits accounted for 45% of total expenditure; by 1960 this had risen to 51%, and it has continued to increase since then. There was some increase in the share of maternity allowances between 1950 and 1960; since 1960 the relative importance of these has declined. The table also includes an unfortunately large residual category. This includes maternity and burial grants; it probably also includes allowances paid to or on behalf of military personnel, and possibly payments to kolkhozniki.[10] The inclusion of payments to kolkhozniki would explain the marked rise in the relative value of this residual after the mid sixties, but it also means that the table understates the cost to the Soviet authorities of both the sickness benefit and maternity allowance programs.

The benefits described so far have all depended directly or indirectly upon state employment or kolkhoz membership. I now turn to those transfers that are paid irrespective of place of employment: student stipends, child allowances, and since 1974, family income supplements.

STIPENDS

Stipends are payable to students in full-time education at institutions of higher learning (*VUZy*) and also to those in organizations providing secondary specialist training (*tekhnikumy*). Before 1972, stipends were set at 30-50 rubles a month for those in *VUZy* and 20-30 rubles for those in *tekhnikumy*; the exact value of the stipend depended upon the year and course of study (and also upon performance). In September 1972 these grants were raised to 40-60 rubles and 30-45 rubles a month, respectively, for the two types of institution (Matyukha, 1973, p. 39; Sarkisyan, 1972, p. 138). About three-quarters of those registered receive stipends, but it is not clear upon what entitlement depends; nor is it clear how those without a stipend support themselves during their studies. Sarkisyan has suggested the possibility of either supplementing or replacing the system of student stipends with a program of student loans to be repaid out of future earnings. He claims that such programs are already in operation in Poland and Yugoslavia. He also suggests that future employers (that is, particular enterprises or organizations) might like to participate in the provision of funds. This proposal does not seem to have provoked much of a response either way, but presumably it was made because its author felt that there were shortcomings in the existing system. What he thought those shortcomings were and how widely his opinions are shared it is not possible to say (Sarkisyan, 1972, pp. 138 ff.).

CHILD ALLOWANCES

There are two sets of payments included under this heading; the first is available to all women, the second to single mothers. The programs themselves date from the mid forties, and there have been no changes in the value of payments made under them since 1947. Under the first program, mothers with two children are entitled to a grant of 20 rubles on the birth of a third child; those with three children receive a grant of 65 rubles on the birth of their fourth child and a monthly allowance of 4 rubles from the child's first to its fifth birthday. The size of both the grant and the monthly allowance increases with each successive child, until mothers with ten or more children receive a grant of 250 rubles on the birth of their eleventh and subsequent children. They also receive a monthly allowance of 15 rubles from the child's first to its fifth birthday (Zakharov and Piskov, 1972, pp. 572-75).

Single mothers are entitled to an allowance of 5 rubles a month if they have one child, 7.50 rubles if they have two, and 10 rubles if they have three or more. The allowance continues until the child reaches its twelfth birthday, is placed in a home, or is adopted. It is retained by the mother if she subsequently marries, unless her husband legally adopts the child or children for whom the allowance is paid. Allowances are not paid for children whose paternity has been acknowledged, or for whom the mother receives alimony payments or a pension (Zakharov and Piskov, 1972, pp. 573, 575).

Since 1963, the wives of noncommissioned officers, privates, and ratings in the Soviet armed services on limited service enlistments, *srochnaya sluzhba*, have received the following child allowances: those living permanently in urban areas are entitled to 15 rubles a month for one child and 22 rubles for two or more; those living in rural areas receive 7.50 rubles a month for one child and 12 rubles for two or more children. The decree establishing these allowances does not state the age up to which the payments are to be made (Zakharov and Piskov, 1972, pp. 585-86).

FAMILY INCOME SUPPLEMENT

The child-allowance programs described above had become both antiquated and inadequate by the late sixties. As a result, a significant portion of the children were poor and a substantial number of the poor were children. Sarkisyan claims that two-thirds of all families with a per capita income of less than 50 rubles a month contained fewer than three children and therefore were not entitled to child allowances (Sarkisyan, 1972, p. 150).

At all events, in 1974 the Soviet authorities introduced a new income maintenance program—the family income supplement. Under it, all families with a per capita income of less than 50 rubles a month are entitled to a supplement of 12 rubles per child per month until the child's eighth birthday. For the purposes of determining entitlement, income is defined to include all receipts in cash and kind that accrue to the family in the year preceding the year in which the benefit is paid. (Presumably the benefit itself is excluded in those cases where it raises per capita family income above the cutoff level.) The family is defined as consisting of parents, children under the age of eighteen (or older, if classed as class I or II invalids), and any dependent relatives not receiving pensions, provided that there is no one else obliged by law to support them (*Sobraniye postanovlenii SSSR* 1974, no. 21, p. 123). Evidence of income must be submitted once a year.

For the purposes of calculating income, at least in Kazakhstan, a notional addition is made for access to a private plot. The rates quoted are 60 rubles a month for kolkhozniki, 50 rubles for rural state employee families, 35 rubles for those who live in workers' settlements (*poselki gorodskogo tipa*), and 5 rubles for those living in towns (Bush, 1975, p. 60). It is not clear whether the same rates are used in other republics; nor is it clear whether these rates represent an accurate estimate of the average value of domestic consumption out of private output for families of the different types or are rather a hidden subsidy to urban workers. One suspects the latter.

It was reported that 1.8 billion rubles were allocated to finance this program in its first year. This suggests that an estimated 12.5 million children will receive benefits. In 1970, there were 35.2 million children under the age of eight, and so it was calculated that one-third of all children in the relevant age group will be covered (Rutkevich, 1975, p. 18).

This completes the description of the various cash transfers available to various classes of Soviet citizens under the Soviet social insurance program and other legislation. A knowledge of the rules of entitlement and the way that these have changed in the past fifteen or twenty years is of interest for its own sake—for the light that it casts upon the equity, universality, and generosity of the system. It can also help to explain two problems that emerged from the preceding analysis of data on poverty and regional disparity in income: the regressive nature of cash transfers before 1965 and the suggestion that both cash and non-cash benefits were distributed regressively between republics in 1970. Indeed, the regional analysis suggested that the degree of inequity in the distribution of benefits had increased over the sixties. These issues will be taken up at greater length in the concluding section of this chapter, but here it is worth commenting on one or two conclusions that emerge from the consideration of the regulations themselves.

In the late fifties, most of the legislation relating to social insurance and other transfers in the USSR was recodified. One can therefore conclude that the principles embodied in the new decrees and regulations reflected current government thinking on relative priorities and the objectives of particular programs. These principles implied an increase in the equity with which state employees and their dependents would be treated, but they also revealed a narrow and somewhat instrumentalist approach to the question of financial support. Entitlement was still very clearly tied to employment; the system was intended to provide support for employees during temporary (or permanent) loss of earning capacity, and need was defined in terms of previous earning capacity, however inadequate that may have been relative to the government's own estimates of the cost of subsistence. Furthermore, the system was used to reward desirable behavior on the part of the workers, even though that behavior was irrelevant from the point of view of the consumption needs of their dependents. Higher benefits were paid to those with longer stazhy, or to those with a longer record of continuous employment; higher benefits were paid to those employed underground or in certain other designated occupations; those dismissed for infractions of labor discipline (overwhelmingly, one suspects, for being drunk on the job) or for having committed certain criminal offenses were deprived of some benefits for a certain time. But there is no reason to suppose that the needs of these people differed from those of the rest of the population. Further, under virtually all programs very little allowance was made for the number of dependents of the workers in question. On the one hand, this can be seen as a further example of insufficient regard to the question of need; on the other, one might argue that it was based on a belief that all Soviet citizens work and therefore possess few dependents. (Alternatively, one might suggest that it was part of a strategy to maintain the very high participation rates initially established under Stalin.) A final feature of the post-1955 system was that it perpetuated the two-class structure of Soviet society by continuing to exclude some of the poorest members of the population from most of the benefits available to the more affluent.

It might be suggested that the system as it was reconstructed in the mid fifties should not be interpreted as the creation of the Soviet leadership of that time. In a number of ways, Khrushchev and his colleagues had only a limited freedom of action. First, they were constrained by the past, by the Leninist and Stalinist history of the development of social insurance in Russia and the way in which it had grown out of a system of workmen's compensation. Also, they were creatures of the system that had produced them, suspicious of the aspirations of the mass of the people, of the extent that they would be prepared to work without the threat of hunger to goad them. In this the leaders had the support of Marx and Lenin, who had argued that under socialism (as opposed to communism), reward should depend upon labor contribution. Finally, resources available for the alleviation of poverty through cash transfers were limited, and politically it would have been impossible to reduce the volume of benefits paid to the working class in order to make some available to the collectivized peasantry. Therefore they were forced to continue Stalin's policy of discrimination. There is a great deal of truth in these suggestions, but at the same time they indicate limits on the new commitment to economic welfare and the attack on inequality.

As I have attempted to show, however, the new system was inadequate in 1955-60 and became more so in the ensuing decade or decade and a half. There was still substantial poverty among urban state employees, the group it was designed most specifically to benefit. With new and more liberal definitions of subsistence, the extent of this poverty increased. Nor was poverty confined to those without full support or to those in large families. Even relatively small families containing workers with earnings substantially above the minimum wage might be poor. The Soviet social insurance system had proved itself insufficiently flexible, unable to provide for the range of demographic and social situations that might cause family income to fall below subsistence. It was based on an inadequate model of the society and social relationships.

The first principle to be modified was the inequitable exclusion of kolkhozniki from the major benefits, pensions and sick pay. At first, such benefits were made available at lower rates on more stringent conditions, but increasingly, the collectivized peasantry has been incorporated into the state employee system. More recently, other principles have been challenged; the modifications in the system of maternity allowances call into question the relevance of distinguishing between union members and others and of tying benefits to stazh. The emphasis has shifted from an attempt to achieve multiple objectives with the same program to a more direct concern for income maintenance during periods of unquestioned need. Similarly, the family income supplement, if restrictive in many of its provisions, has also broken away from the link to employment and previous earnings. Finally, in many small (and what the leadership presumably hope are unnoticed) ways, attempts have been made to reduce the proportion of expenditure going to those with the higher incomes or earnings. The favored strategy here appears to be the belated upward adjustment of minimum payments and the failure to raise maxima at the same time or to the same extent. The impression created is one of a gradual transition from an earnings-related concept of benefits (and hence of need) to a concept of equal (and possibly subsistence-related) benefits for all. But the transition, if purposive rather than a consequence of budgetary stringency in the seventies, is erratic and slow. It has also been criticized as unsocialist (Khabibi, 1975, p. 274). I will return to some of these questions later in the chapter, but now I wish to consider changes in expenditure on education, health, and other services that contribute to total income but are excluded from personal income as I have defined it.

11.4 FREE AND SUBSIDIZED SERVICES

In addition to the monetary transfers considered so far, the Soviet authorities provide a range of services either free of charge or at subsidized prices. Chief among them are education, medical care, and subsidized housing. Access to such services raises the economic welfare of households who enjoy it; the government's expenditures on education, health, and housing constitute most of the difference between personal and total income calculated in chapter 2. But a study of their impact upon the distribution of income, the reduction of economic inequality, raises numerous problems, and the question can only be touched upon here.

The cost of the various programs discussed in this section is given in table 11.1 for a number of postwar years. But in order to assess the contribution that such expenditures make to the reduction of inequality, it is necessary to know more than how much of the various services is provided (and even this is only imperfectly measured by their cost); one must also know which families benefit. There is little in the Soviet literature or even in the accounting procedures of the Soviet government to provide this information.

It is a relatively straightforward matter to calculate a number of expenditure norms for the different programs. A knowledge of total spending to maintain the housing stock, along with an estimate of the amount of stock (both of which are available from the records of plan fulfillment), will give an estimate of the average cost of upkeep per square meter. Similarly, a knowledge of total spending on primary or secondary education, together with estimates of the number of pupils enrolled in schools of various types, will yield estimates of educational costs per pupil. Soviet statisticians, economists, and sociologists use these estimates and information on housing conditions or family composition to estimate the contribution that social consumption expenditure makes to the living standards of households at different levels of income.[11]

How accurate such estimates are will depend in part upon the degree of detail in which they are calculated: how many different categories of medical service are separately identified and costed, for example, or how much information is available on the use of such services at different levels of income. Given the problems of collecting and analyzing masses of data without electronic computers, and given the crudity with which more general indicators of economic welfare have been calculated in the USSR, at least until recently, I suspect that the estimates of the value of social consumption expenditures will be rather unreliable. Further, the use of such expenditure norms will understate (or overstate) the degree of difference resulting from such programs if there is a systematic relation between levels of per capita expenditure and the incomes of recipients. That is, for example, if it were the case that more was spent on the upkeep of the houses of the affluent than on the houses of the poor, the use of average expenditure norms would understate effective differentiation. The same effect would result if the affluent tended to use different hospitals or schools than the poor and if these institutions were permitted to provide higher levels of service.

Comprehensive information is lacking, but there are reasons to believe that the Soviet system suffers from some systematic inequalities of the type described above. For example, budgetary figures for the USSR as a whole and for a majority of individual republics indicate that expenditures per pupil in rural schools are less than those in urban areas. Insofar as the quantity (or quality) of education provided is reflected in its cost and insofar as rural living standards are lower than those in urban areas, this implies that there is systematic discrimination of the type mentioned above. Similarly, there is some evidence to suggest that expenditures per pupil in the various republics is positively correlated with per capita income. Furthermore, although the absence of clearly defined residential areas distinguished by the incomes of their inhabitants in most Soviet cities means that systematic discrimination in expenditure per pupil is limited, the existence of special schools (for example, those in which the medium of instruction is a foreign language) and the impression that it is predominantly the children of intellectuals who attend such establishments suggest some differentiation within urban networks. There are similar if less marked distinctions in the area of medical care. [12] While these and similar considerations indicate that the use of average expenditure norms may give biased estimates of the impact of social consumption on inequality, there is insufficient information available to permit any quantitative assessment of its scale.

So far, the discussion has centered on the effects of social consumption on the distribution of income at a specific time. But there are two further considerations, relating particularly to education but affecting to some extent other categories of spending, which imply that social consumption might over a period of time affect inequality. Both are important, but neither will be considered at length here.

The USSR is a federal state, but it is a highly centralized one. As a result, although there are differences between the republics and between urban and rural areas in the scale of educational and medical service, essentially the same system is provided in all parts of the country. An attempt is made to impose common standards, and these standards are those of an industrialized European state. As a consequence, the educational or medical facilities available in Soviet Central Asia, for example, or in the Soviet Arctic are more extensive than they would have been under a relatively decentralized system. Differences between the Soviet Central Asian republics and the countries immediately south of the Soviet border, Turkey, Iraq, Iran, and Afganistan, are particularly striking (Nove and Newth, 1967, pp. 65 ff.). On the other hand, it might be argued that the scale of provision in the more developed republics, the

Baltic states, the European RSFSR, and possibly the Ukraine, is less than it would have been under a different institutional framework. But, on balance, this is probably not the case: I have suggested that Soviet economists argue that the scale of provision is greater than the average household would choose. If one believes that education and medical services contribute to development (as does the Soviet government), then the Soviet bureaucratic system will have contributed to the development of Central Asia and thus to a reduction in regional inequality.

The second problem is concerned with access to education. In the USSR in the postwar period, higher education has become increasingly necessary for appointment to positions of responsibility. But it is these positions that carry the highest salaries, and therefore education and earnings are positively correlated. If it is also the case that the children of educated parents have a special advantage in acquiring further education—if educational selection procedures favor the children of educated parents (as seems to be the case not only in the USSR but in most other countries as well)—the educational system will contribute towards the emergence and perpetuation of an educated and affluent elite. It will thus contribute to the maintenance of economic inequality. The extent to which the Soviet system provides a vehicle for preserving income inequality from generation to generation rather than facilitating social and economic mobility is difficult to determine. It is a problem that has been studied by Soviet sociologists and discussed by a number of Western authors. Opinion seems to be divided, and I do not propose to examine the issue here. Certainly, the rapid expansion of a technical and managerial elite that has accompanied industrialization has provided for the upward movement of many peasants and workers through education. There is thus little evidence that the educational system was restrictive in the first forty or so years after the Revolution. By the late sixties, however, this phase of rapid expansion seems to have come to an end; but it is perhaps too early to tell what will happen over the next forty years (Yanowitch, 1977, pp. 88-89).

Evidence of the contribution that spending on education and medical care has made to the reduction of social and economic inequality in the USSR is limited and contradictory, but the indications are that, until the mid sixties at least, these programs were not adversely affected by bureaucratic immobilism. The same is not true of the other major programs, housing subsidy and preschool child care. However much these may have contributed to average living standards, there is evidence to suggest that their detailed administration has resulted in the perpetuation of substantial inequities.

The Soviet authorities are proud to claim that house rentals in the Soviet Union are the lowest in the world. In the late sixties such rents accounted for only 2-3% of the average urban family budget (4-5% if the cost of communal services is included). Rental income covers approximately one-third of the cost of maintaining and operating the existing housing stock (Sarkisyan, 1972, p. 140). The balance is met out of budgetary income and constitutes the housing subsidy recorded in table 11.1. Because of widespread population movement resulting from industrialization, the damage and destruction inflicted by the Second World War, and persistent underinvestment in house building, the Soviet housing stock has been grossly inadequate throughout the period considered in this book. In the 1920s, the Soviet government laid down a sanitary norm of nine square meters of living space per person; in 1967, only 27% of workers' households enjoyed accommodation on this scale.[13] Thus even if all managerial, professional, and clerical households had more living space than the norm (which is certainly not the case), more than half the urban population would still be living in substandard housing.

The existence of substantial shortages and the absence of price rationing mean that there is no housing market in the USSR; rather, there is a system of bureaucratic allocation. In principle, households are allocated space in accordance with their size. But given a certain security of tenure and the fact that household composition changes, and given also that enterprises and organizations control the allocation of some of the housing stock and use this control to attract skilled labor or management personnel, there is substantial variation in the housing awarded to different households.

Rent regulations are fairly complex and differ from republic to republic, but the system used in the RSFSR gives some indication of their structure. Rents in the RSFSR relate to earnings and space occupied, but since the earnings schedule was specified in 1928 and has not been changed since, all households pay at the top rates per square meter (Vlasova et al., 1970, chapter 7). The actual rate paid depends upon the age of the structure and the range of services provided, as well as the amount of space occupied. For accommodation of up to nine square meters per person, with full services, and with an allowance of 4.5 square meters per family, the rate paid is 16.5 kopeks per square meter per month. (If the structure was completed before January 1924, the rate is only 13.2 kopeks per square meter per month.) For additional space, the rate is three times as great—40-50 kopeks per square meter (Skripko, 1972, p. 28. The area is calculated net of kitchen, corridors, bathrooms, etc.; see Vlasova et al., 1970, p. 79). Various categories of individuals enjoy the privilege of paying the standard rate for extra accommodation—for example, personal pensioners, heroes of Soviet labor, and so forth. In the Ukraine, the allowance is ten square meters per person, and a double rate is charged for anything more. Other republics differ in similar ways.

If these rate schedules are adhered to, then, in the RSFSR, those with better-than-standard housing just about pay for the costs of its upkeep, since rental income covers approximately one-third of maintenance costs. For the typical family, the one below the norm, the larger the accommodation, the larger the subsidy received, which is surely inequitable. In a recent book, Sarkisyan proposed that households with more space than the sanitary norm should be charged at a rate three to five times the cost of maintenance (*raskhody soderzhaniya zhil'ya*). This, he claimed, would result in a redistribution of the housing stock and would also redistribute housing subsidies among households with differing housing conditions; that is, it would concentrate subsidies on the worst-housed (Sarkisyan, 1972, p. 141). It is intriguing to read of a suggestion to employ the market mechanism to solve a problem in the allocation of Soviet social consumption expenditures, but as far as I know, the suggestion has elicited no response on the part of the authorities, or any public discussion of its desirability (with the exception of an indirect rejection of the suggestion by Khabibi; 1975, p. 274).

For a number of years Soviet authors have emphasized the widespread availability of preschool child care facilities in the USSR and have suggested that they contribute to the high level of women's participation in paid employment and that they reduce inequality. Although these facilities are provided on a broader scale than in a majority of market economies and although they have become more available since the late fifties, the statistics suggest that access to day care nurseries or kindergartens is far from universal, even in urban areas.

The relevant statistics are given in table 11.5. They suggest that in 1960, somewhat less than 10% of all children under the age of eight were in preschool child care facilities. As might be expected, such facilities were much more common in urban areas than in the countryside—less than 3% of rural children were in day nurseries or kindergartens. The figures also show that although the number of children under eight in the USSR fell slightly between 1959 and 1970, the number in child care facilities more than doubled; indeed, by the end of the decade almost a quarter of Soviet preschoolers were enrolled. Improvements were particularly marked in rural areas, where the number cared for more than tripled. The figures in table 11.5 are relatively crude and perhaps understate the availability of child care for those most likely to benefit from its provision. Although, from the census, it is possible to obtain estimates of the total population by relatively fine age groupings, figures on the age structure of those in preschool child care facilities are much less plentiful. It has been claimed, however, that in 1970 some 14% of rural children between the ages of three and seven were in kindergartens and that in urban areas the proportion was more than 50% (Mamontova, 1973, p. 75). These proportions are higher than the estimates in table 11.5 and imply that the proportion of children under the age of three in day nurseries must be correspondingly lower.[14] The relatively scarcity of facilities of all types in 1960 suggests that under Stalin, the family (and in particular the grandmother) was in large measure responsible for preschool child care. Presumably she still plays that role for children under three whose parents cannot place them in day nurseries.

The figures in table 11.5 show that there is now an extensive network of preschool child care facilities in the Soviet Union, whether or not it is

Table 11.5
Availability of Preschool Child Care Facilities, 1960-70 (millions)

	1960			1970		
	Total	Urban	Rural	Total	Urban	Rural
Number of children under seven	37.56[a]	15.88[a]	21.67[a]	35.20	16.89	18.31
Numbers in kindergartens, etc.	3.12	2.55	0.56	8.10	6.40	1.70
Coverage (%)	8.3	16.1	2.6	23.0	37.9	9.3

Sources: *Itogi* . . . , 1970, vol. 2, pp. 12-13; *NK SSSR '65*, p. 686; *NK SSSR '70*, p. 634.
   a. Population figures refer to 1959.

as extensive as some Soviet commentators claim. But access is not free. Although figures on costs and charges are scarce, available evidence suggests that the average contribution of the state is in the order of 400 rubles per child per year and that this covers some 75-80% of the total.[15] The balance is paid by the parents. As with accommodation rentals, in principle the fees for preschool child care depend upon parental earnings. For day nurseries the charges range from 3.8 rubles per child to 10 rubles per month; for kindergartens, they are slightly higher, from 5 rubles to 12.50 rubles per month. But the wage scale upon which reduced fees depend was laid down in 1948 and has not been modified since. The result is that the overwhelming majority of parents pay the same fees—the maxima (Mamontova, 1973, p. 79). Thus unless priority is given to low-income parents when places are allocated, there is no reason to believe that having the care available will prove particularly beneficial to the poor.

This brief discussion suggests that the administration of the major social consumption expenditure programs in the USSR has not undergone as many modifications as has the administration of cash transfers. Indeed, the impression left is that the sixties was a period of stagnation—or rather, of relative immobility—as attention was concentrated on problems of current income. As I have tried to suggest, however, educational policy, and particularly those features of it that determine admission to higher education, may well be the most important single determinant of trends in long-term inequality, of whether or not an affluent and self-perpetuating elite, a new class in the sense that Djilas might have meant, develops in the Soviet Union. This question will be taken up again in the next chapter (although I am afraid it cannot be done conclusively), but now I will turn to a brief consideration of the third element in the Soviet government's battery of social expenditure controls, the direct taxation system.

11.5   DIRECT TAXATION[16]

Soviet citizens are subject to two types of direct taxes: the income tax and a variety of local taxes and levies. Tax rates, schedules, and exemptions for the income tax are determined in Moscow and are applied uniformly throughout the country, although part of the revenue is retained by the republics. There is more interrepublican variation in local levies, but even these are subject to detailed control by the All-Union Ministry of Finance. As the figures in chapter 2 and appendix F show, the yield from all these taxes is modest, which suggests that they can have little influence on the distribution of income, that they contribute little towards the reduction of economic inequality in the Soviet Union. There is, therefore, little to be gained from a detailed analysis of tax structure or attempts to ascertain the incidence of particular levies. As a result I shall ignore the battery of local taxes and concentrate on the income tax, *podokhodnyi nalog*, and its complement, the tax on bachelors and citizens with small families, *nalog na khlostyakov, odinokikh i malosemeinykh grazhdan SSSR*.

The regulations governing the payment of income tax in the USSR, like those in most other countries, contain many clauses detailing exemptions, modifications for special cases, redefinitions, and so on. These are the result of attempts by tax administrators to fit a relatively simple framework to a complex pattern of income accrual. They also reflect a predilection on the part of the authorities for granting tax exemption as a privilege to particularly worthy citizens or to those in certain occupations. In attempting to set out the basic structure of the Soviet income tax, much of this fine print must be ignored.

In spite of the many special cases referred to in the preceding paragraph, the impression created by the Soviet tax regulations is that they define a system in which horizontal equity (the equal treatment of equals) has been surrendered to administrative simplicity. That is, the basic model of the economy on which the tax is constructed is one in which all individuals have earned incomes from a single source; in trying to allow for the ways in which the real world differs from this ideal picture, it appears that considerations of administrative convenience have been at least as important as a sense of fairness.

The tax structure itself differs in a number of ways from the structures to be found in a majority of industrial states. In particular, the obligation to pay tax starts at a much lower relative level than is common; procedures for income aggregation and the spreading of liability are rudimentary; the system of allowances for dependents is primitive. On the other hand, effective rates of tax are much lower than those found elsewhere.

The basic structure of the tax is as follows. As of 1968, any payment for labor, *zarabotok*, received from state enterprises, institutions, or organizations is liable to income tax. Tax is also paid on certain other categories of income: receipts from the sale of privately produced agricultural products, royalties and honoraria (although a different schedule is used), various premia for performance, and sickness benefits. (Although no mention is made of it, this would presumably imply that maternity allowances are also subject to tax.) From 1968 on until the minimum wage was raised above 60 rubles a month, no tax was paid on the first 60 rubles per month received from a person's primary employment. When the minimum was raised to 70 rubles, the tax exemption limit was also raised. Thus all earnings above the minimum wage are liable to tax.

As might be expected, certain receipts are excluded in the determination of taxable income: pensions, student stipends, and various allowances, including payments for wear and tear to workers who supply their own tools. Prizes from government lotteries and interest on deposits in the State Savings Bank are also tax-exempt. With these reservations, tax liability is determined by monthly income; the Soviet law contains no provision for aggregating income over the year as a whole and calculating an annual tax bill.

Nor does Soviet tax law provide for the aggregation of the earnings of those who have more than one source of income. The 60-ruble exemption applies only to earnings from one's primary employment; earnings of more than 3 rubles from any other source are liable for tax, but in computing that tax no account is taken of what may have been received elsewhere. As a result, individuals with the same monthly earnings and the same family circumstances can pay different amounts of tax depending upon the pattern of receipts. These differences can be quite substantial, at least relatively, although ruble differences are moderate, since tax rates are generally low. For example, a single man earning 101 rubles a month (median earnings) will pay 37% more tax if his earnings come from a single source than if a quarter come from secondary employment. For those with earnings equal to the third quartile (134 rubles a month) the surcharge drops to 17%. But at the same income, if earnings come from a single source, one pays 87% more tax than if they come equally from two sources.[17]

Furthermore, the absence of detailed allowances means that those with the same income but different family circumstances may be liable for the same amount of tax. This, to my mind, is as unfair as taxing those with similar family circumstances and the same income differently. The basic tax schedule for the Soviet income tax is applied to the earnings of those who have between one and three dependents; those who have four or more dependents qualify for a 30% reduction; those with no dependents pay an additional tax, the tax on bachelors and those with small families, mentioned above. Thus, in principle, there are three tax schedules intended to take account of all the various forms of family composition and dependency that exist in the USSR. There are also a number of qualifications and modifications to the way in which this structure is applied.

First, to qualify for the 30% reduction, a taxpayer has only to show that four or more persons depend upon his or her earnings for support (are without independent means); there is no need for the dependents to be related to the taxpayer by ties of blood or marriage. But the reduction applies only to earnings at the primary place of employment; earnings from second or third jobs are taxed at the normal rate. Furthermore, it is the tax rates that are reduced by 30%, not tax liability. Any earnings over 60 rubles a month are still liable for tax, but at a lower rate.

The so-called bachelors' tax is paid by state employees, military personnel, and literary and artistic "workers" who have no children. It is not paid by single women, but upon marriage, a woman without children becomes liable from the first wage payment following registration. More precisely, it is paid by males between the ages of twenty and fifty and by females between the ages of twenty and forty-five, provided they satisfy the above criteria. Although, in principle, military personnel are liable to the tax, noncommissioned officers and enlisted men on short-service engagements are exempt, as are generals, admirals, and officers serving outside the territory of the USSR. Their wives are also exempt.

Thus the Soviet income tax contains a number of inequities; but their importance is perhaps reduced because average rates of tax are low. In 1968, on all earnings over 100 rubles a month, whether from primary or secondary employment, the marginal rate was 13% on the standard schedule, 9.1% for those who qualified for the reduced rate, and 19% for those who were liable for the bachelors' tax. These marginal rates are the asymtotic limits towards which average tax liability tends as income increases. They are generally much lower than the average rates to be found in other countries. But because the Soviet authorities have attempted to maintain this structure for all earnings of more than 100 rubles a month, while increasing the exemption limit in line with increases in the minimum wage, and because rate adjustments have been made piecemeal, there are very much higher marginal rates at lower incomes. For example, the marginal tax rate from the standard schedule for earnings from primary employment was between 25% and 30% on earnings between 61 rubles and 75 rubles a month; it then dropped to 18% until 81 rubles a month, increased to 70% on the eighty-second ruble, fell back to 12% until 100 rubles a month, and rose to 13% thereafter. There are similar oscilations in the other schedules.

If the appropriate indicator of economic welfare and equity, in terms of which the adequacy of government policy may be assessed, is disposable income per capita (and the analyses of many Soviet economists and sociologists suggest that this is accepted in the USSR), then the Soviet tax system, as outlined above, can contribute little to the attainment of the government's goals. In principle, in the Soviet Union, the incomes of most of the population are determined by their earnings. The state's control over wage rates and salary scales will ensure that the distribution of earnings is equitable, as defined by the socialist principle of distribution. Differences in family composition, in the nature and extent of the obligations incurred by different individuals, imply that an equitable distribution of earnings may be associated with an inequitable distribution of income. To resolve this problem the state enabled itself to supplement the incomes of particular groups through its social insurance and social welfare systems described earlier in the chapter. The income tax (and possibly other direct taxes) provides it with another instrument which can modify the distribution of income. Through it, the state can not only increase the incomes of deserving groups of individuals, it can reduce the incomes of those who can best afford a reduction. The revenues thus collected can be used to finance specific programs or be transferred to the relatively indigent. Because the state exercises rather more control over the determination of earnings in a planned economy of the Soviet type than in a market economy, one would not expect the income tax to be such an important instrument of redistribution. But the direct tax system as it works in the USSR fails in even the residual role allocated to it by the economic system. It is certainly not the source of any significant revenue; nor, because of its crudity, because it is primitive and inflexible, does it contribute to an increase in the equity of the system. In the early 1960s, Khrushchev promised to abolish it; nothing more has been heard of that scheme for almost fifteen years, and one wonders why not (Newth, 1960, p. 193).

11.6   THE SOVIET WELFARE STATE: AN ASSESSMENT

I suggested in chapter 8 that a majority of Soviet economists and sociologists argue that within the constraints set by the plan, incomes (or at least earnings) should be distributed according to the socialist principle of distribution—from each according to his ability, to each according to his labor. This proposition is also accepted by the Soviet government. Such an approach places primary responsibility for the character and extent of earnings differentials (and hence, indirectly, of income inequality) upon the mechanisms and institutions that determine wage and salary relativities and the allocation of labor between occupations. But even within this framework the authorities can adopt a variety of attitudes towards the role of social consumption expenditures, towards the function of transfer payments and what has recently come to be known as the social wage. It is these expenditure programs that I call the Soviet welfare state. Alternative policies towards the welfare state will result in differences in the distribution of income. In this final section I will try to show what the Soviet government's attitudes have been towards these issues and how they have contributed to the pattern of inequality described in previous chapters.

Soviet economists advance two justifications for reliance upon the "socialist distribution principle" (apart from the fact that it had been previously advocated by Lenin). First, it is claimed that until a new socialist consciousness becomes widespread, until, that is, individuals come to derive positive utility from labor, it will be necessary to employ some compulsion to ensure that all who are capable of it contribute to the good of society. The compulsion involved is the threat of hunger for those who willfully do not work. Primitive conceptions of fairness suggest that where material goods are scarce (as they are during the first stage of socialism), those who have contributed nothing should not be entitled to share in the product of collective endeavor. But such an argument implies only that consumption should be conditional upon employment; it does not of itself imply the existence of wage differentials and inequality. It is also suggested, however, that individuals in their unregenerated state will require a positive inducement to exploit their potential to the full, to acquire the skills needed by society, to work hard while on the job, to show initiative or enterprise. And the same primitive conceptions of fairness suggest that those whose contribution has been great should derive a larger benefit from available resources than those who have done little. (A more refined morality might make reward conditional upon effort rather than achievement; after all, the socialist principle does specify that each should contribute according to his *ability*.) It has also been suggested that additional compensation might be needed to encourage individual workers to undertake dangerous, monotonous, or otherwise unpleasant jobs, although as I suggested above, this may conflict with the objective basis for the reduction of labor.

The socialist principle is primarily concerned with the distribution of earnings. The distribution of income (by which I mean variations in consumption possibilities open to different individuals or groups in the population) is influenced by the distribution of earnings, but it is also affected by patterns of marriage and dependency, population structure, and participation rates—that is, by the social and demographic composition of society. In a more general framework, it will also be affected by differences in the ownership of nonhuman factors and the returns that accrue to them. Because a given distribution of earnings (even one that conforms to the socialist principle) is consistent with a variety of income distributions, the views ascribed here to Soviet economists do not completely specify attitudes or policies towards the distribution of income. There is still a degree of freedom to modify incomes without changing earnings or undermining their functions.

The fact that the distribution of income can differ from the distribution of earnings implies the existence of individuals who do not work (or rather, who are not gainfully employed), and also the existence of sources of income other than employment. The issues facing the authorities in the USSR (or in any other society) are the determination of acceptable reasons for nonemployment, the extent to which the state will provide for the support of the nonemployed, and the form that that support will take. Answers to these questions will determine the character of the Soviet welfare state. The authorities must also decide what constitutes legitimate nonemployment income. It is in this respect that socialist states differ most from market economies; in the Soviet Union, nonemployment income is confined to the returns from private subsidiary agricultural activity, the interest on savings deposits, and a few other minor sources. The extensive private ownership of productive capital in most market economies makes nonemployment income much more significant. But this question is, to a large extent, separate from the issue of an appropriate welfare state and will not be considered further.

Formally, the approach to the delimitation of areas of official concern outlined in section 11.2 (and embodied in the legislation of the second half of the fifties) has much in common with that of the rest of Europe and North America. There is the same recognition that loss of working capacity through accident, ill health, or old age merits some financial support; assistance is also given to those in full-time education; and the state accepts responsibility for some of the extra expense occasioned by sickness and the care of children. But this formal similarity can be misleading: regulations determining entitlement in many cases were (and still are) restrictive, and the level of support was niggardly. Furthermore, the third component in the welfare programs of some European states, public assistance, or minimal financial aid for those who do not fit into one of the above categories but are still without means of support, was almost

entirely lacking. It is of interest to ask how far the authorities felt themselves constrained by the socialist distribution principle in setting out
their system (or rather in reformulating it, since most programs had existed in one form or another since the twenties), and what other principles
appear to have been important. In particular, one would be interested to
know what conception they had of need and how much need influenced
their decisions.

As pointed out above, the collective farm population was largely excluded from the network of financial assistance as it existed in the late fifties. Those unable to work as a result of injury, ill-health, or old age were
forced to rely upon the resources of their own farms or families or upon
the charity of their neighbors. The only benefits that kolkhozniki received from the Soviet welfare state were access to educational and medical facilities, and for those with large families, child allowances. This
discrimination cannot be justified by an appeal to the socialist distribution principle; nor can it be claimed that resources are distributed according to need in a system where so large a proportion of the population is
excluded on principle (unless deprivation and malnutrition among the
collectivized peasantry carried little or no weight in the government's social welfare function).

In the late fifties, financial assistance for state employees was more
generous, but even then, age and infirmity did not confer an absolute
right to support. Pensions and other benefits were conditional upon employment record, and both previous earnings and the length of uninterrupted service influenced the scale of support. This might be interpreted
as an application of the socialist principle to an analogous distribution issue: those who have contributed more while working (and hence earned
more) are entitled to a greater measure of support when incapacitated or
retired. On the other hand, social insurance benefits may have been used
to reinforce the incentives built into the structure of wage and salary differentials. Or the system may reflect a belief that those who earned more
in the past need more in benefits. But this entails a relativist conception
of deprivation, and although Marx accepts the conventional nature of
subsistence, there is little evidence of such an approach elsewhere in the
Soviet Union. Given the nature of the special cases explicitly allowed for
in legislation, the benefits provided for designated occupational groups
and so on, I believe that the second explanation is the most plausible. But
even here, simple access to uniform benefits might have been used, and
still have been consistent with distribution according to labor; differential
treatment presumably implies the belief that flat-rate benefits will act as
less of a stimulus to the highly paid than graduated payments. (In point
of fact, the structure of provision enshrined in the 1956 legislation was
probably constrained to a large extent by preexisting regulations, but this

only implies that the government of the day was not prepared to adopt any radically new approach to the question—especially if it would have involved conflict with vested interests.)

But the treatment of dependents suggests that there are limits to the applicability of the socialist distribution principle. On the one hand, if differences in reward are to have the influence on behavior credited to them, presumably it must be differences in consumption possibilities that are understood; but differences in family circumstances mean that individuals with the same earnings may enjoy very different standards of living. However, in the system it developed in the 1950s, the Soviet government provided only limited assistance for the support of dependents. Even today, the family income supplement program leaves responsibility for the support of most children (and all adult dependents) upon the shoulders of the able-bodied. The meager additions to the pensions of those with dependents may have been intended to force most women into the labor force (and to penalize those who failed to take paid employment) and thus have conformed to the socialist distribution principle, but many of those who suffered were children; and it is not clear how effective retribution is (Acharkan, 1974, p. 120).

Taken as a whole, then, it is possible to see that the authorities' perception of the necessity for appropriate earnings differentials (and their unwillingness to encroach upon existing privilege) was only partly responsible for the system of financial benefits and free services they developed after Stalin's death. It is also the case that need was interpreted in a somewhat restrictive sense; the system was designed to satisfy the needs of those incapacitated for acceptable reasons, it was not intended to alleviate the condition of any and all who were in need. Indeed, it might be argued that the acceptance of demonstrable need (poverty) as a criterion for assistance would undermine the sanctions implicit in distribution according to labor. This would suggest that an extensive public assistance program is inconsistent with socialism as it is understood in the Soviet Union. But Soviet economists also stress that their social insurance scheme is noncontributory, and one may ask how far the relief of the aged or infirm who do not satisfy the employment criteria laid down in the regulations would undermine the inducement to work that the system provides for the able-bodied?

The exclusion of collective farmers from protection under the state's social insurance scheme, the link between earnings and benefits, and the rudimentary assistance in the support of dependents, particularly children, made the Soviet welfare state as constituted in 1956-65 regressive. This tendency for the distribution of social consumption expenditures to reinforce the distribution of earnings was not offset by any extensive provision of public assistance. The system did not act as residual source of aid for those in need (or rather, it acted in this role only in extreme cases for those who could demonstrate the absence of relatives obliged by law to care for them; and in these cases the aid provided was minimal). The growth of total expenditure and demographic developments during the 1960s have both tended to accentuate these undesirable features.

But as I pointed out in chapter 8, some Soviet economists and sociologists have come to question the narrow emphasis upon distribution according to labor built into the post-1956 system, and as I have shown earlier in this chapter, there are indications that the authorities have responded to these criticisms—or possibly their response has been to the continued existence of substantial urban poverty. Rabkina, Rimashev-skaya, and others have suggested that while the socialist principle must still be used to determine wage relativities, its use does not preclude the alleviation of poverty by means of social security. On the one hand, this probably implies a greater emphasis on providing financial assistance to those with children or other "legitimate" dependents—that is, extensions to the program of child allowances and the provision of pensions to the aged and infirm who do not qualify under existing programs are both thought desirable. But also, their position appears to call into question the extent to which discriminatory benefits in fact act as an effective stimulus to desirable behavior, whether the pay-off to such discrimination justifies the costs that it imposes. For example, when the value of maternity benefits depended upon union membership and stazh, did this result in substantially larger numbers of young women joining trade unions and did it result in substantially lower turnover among such workers? And even if the answers to these questions are a qualified yes, was the benefit to society, however measured, sufficient to outweigh the costs incurred in the form of greater poverty among those who did not conform? I suggest that the above-mentioned NIIT economists would answer no, and judging by their actions, so would the Soviet authorities, in the 1970s at least.

In the late fifties and early sixties, the Soviet government appeared to believe that the inducements to participate in collective labor provided by the absence of income from property and the dependence of transfer payments upon employment were dangerously weak. For this reason it introduced (or attempted to enforce) laws which made "parasitism" a criminal offence. Whatever one's attitude towards the justice of this behavior, the fact that it was undertaken surely implies that for the young at least regulations governing entitlement to benefits in thirty or forty years' time have very little influence on behavior. Indeed, this point can be put more strongly: the prospect of immediate improvements in the standard of living is a much more powerful influence on behavior than the need to insure against the future risk of indigence. Not so much has been heard of the antiparasitism laws since Khrushchev's retirement, but the discussion of the justification for the 1968 minimum wage hike in chapter 8 suggests that the authorities at that time were still unwilling to contemplate divorcing support from employment. The fact that substantial numbers of women, through family circumstances and the absence of child care facilities, were unable to enter the labor force meant that this policy was of little benefit to them. It was also of little benefit to their children. Since then, the government has taken a number of tentative steps towards the recognition of need as grounds for participation in income maintenance schemes irrespective of employment record or status. But the elderly are still treated less generously than the young.

If the analysis presented here is correct, it suggests that the greater preoccupation with questions of welfare and inequality that developed in the Soviet Union after Stalin's death did not initially entail any radically new approach to the social welfare system. Greater concern resulted in higher levels of benefit paid out and this led to a substantial improvement in the standard of living of those then dependent on the state for support. At a later stage, rejection of the view that the existence of two social classes should necessarily be associated with positive discrimination against the collectivized peasantry led to a marked reduction in rural poverty. Also, increases in earnings under the existing system led to increases in the benefits received by new entrants; but this was a consequence of wage and salary policy rather than the social insurance system per se. New attitudes to the welfare state, an emphasis on need rather than merit, became apparent only after 1968, and they have still had little impact on the way that the system is administered. There is still no evidence of innovation in either thought or deed on the question of personal taxation.

12

Economic Welfare and Inequality
in the USSR

THE ANALYSIS OF SOVIET ATTITUDES towards the welfare state and the role of social consumption expenditure in modifying the distribution of income completes this account of welfare and inequality in the USSR. All that remains is to present a general assessment of Soviet performance, and that is the subject of chapter 12. Section 2 of the chapter also includes a few comments on the relevance of the material presented here to the wider questions of inequality and social stratification in the USSR and nearer home. But first, let me review the changes in Soviet living standards and income differentiation that have taken place since the mid fifties.

12.1 ECONOMIC WELFARE AND INEQUALITY, 1955-75
At the outset I should like to make a general point. In chapter 1 it was claimed that conventional indicators of economic welfare were inappropriate for assessing the living standards of the Soviet population. The material in chapters 2 and 6, showing significant differences in the structure of incomes accruing to the households of state employees and kolkhozniki, clearly demonstrates the inadequacy of indicators like average earnings or real wages; this inadequacy is reinforced by the possibility of differences in family size or changes in participation rates over time. And although I have not stressed the point, I also believe that synthetic indicators of economic well-being like national income or gross national product per capita are potentially misleading. There can be no substitute for an explicit calculation of the incomes that accrue to households of various types. This opinion is shared by others, I am sure, but the material presented here also demonstrates that inferences based on changes in money income will be misleading, particularly for a group like kolkhozniki. Thus the best indicators of change in economic welfare in the USSR at the present time are personal and total income. Ideally such indicators should be net of direct taxes and should be deflated by an appropriate cost-of-living index, but data limitations often force us to be content with less.

The period since 1955 (or possibly 1953) has been marked by a much greater concern for popular living standards on the part of the Soviet government than the preceding quarter of a century. The authorities have also attempted to reduce some of the grossest of the disparities in incomes that were characteristic of the late Stalin period. Much of this book has been taken up with an attempt to demonstrate that the changes in welfare and inequality that have occurred since the mid fifties have been the result of government policy rather than of the evolution of the economy. It is true that policy has often been ill considered and poorly thought out, that the Soviet authorities have neither the information nor the control over economic relationships that simple models of planning and Soviet economic institutions would suggest (and that Soviet propaganda and the writings of some Western economists would have us believe). But the record as presented here surely shows that there has been a sustained attempt to alleviate poverty and to raise the standard of living of both peasants and workers over the quarter of a century since Stalin's death.

As the expression of concern for the well-being of workers, if not for the people as a whole, has been part of the rhetoric of Soviet socialist politics since the revolution, little can be inferred from the statements of intent on the part of the authorities. For this reason, scant attention has been paid to the pronouncements of leaders in justifying the claim that a new approach to questions of welfare and inequality was adopted in the mid fifties. As is often the case in politics, actions speak louder than words—or rather, reveal intentions more honestly. However, the analyses of both academics and official spokesmen, published after the event, have tended to confirm the claim made here.

The evidence of a new approach, referred to above, is of three sorts. First, by various extensions to their data-gathering activities, the authorities have sought to make themselves better informed about the extent of inequality (and even the level of welfare) in their system. Discussion of these various modifications has revealed how very limited was the information on popular living standards at the disposal of the government before 1956-58. Even had Stalin wished to act more positively in this area he would have found it difficult to do so, given the depth of official ignorance about the state of affairs in the economy at large. But, of course, that ignorance was largely a consequence of the indifference with which questions of economic welfare were regarded by the Soviet authorities. The discussion of chapters 3 and 5, however, also indicates that in the late sixties and early seventies, after substantial investment in data collection and data processing, the authorities still possessed only limited and biased information about the distribution of income in the USSR. And although evidence is incomplete, the indications are that they do not

yet take proper account of changes in the cost of living. Thus policy formulation is still carried on without adequate information.

Attempts to improve official knowledge of the incomes and earnings
of various groups in the population were complemented by a more explicit assessment of the costs of subsistence, the effectiveness of particular
policy innovations, and the adequacy of planning procedures. These
activities were feasible largely because of the renaissance of Soviet labor
economics and the emergence of empirical sociology, but they also reflect
a more general change in the political climate: the development of a more
pragmatic approach to social policy, the acceptance of what might be
called "piecemeal social engineering."

Finally, the changes in statistical and administrative procedures resulted
in (or rather were accompanied by) more direct modifications of the instruments with which the government controls the level and distribution
of income. As shown in chapters 8 and 11, in the years after 1956
the Soviet authorities recodified the legislation relating to social insurance and embarked upon a radical reorganization of wage and salary
structures. At the same time, they introduced the first modifications to
the payment systems used on collective farms.

These three types of innovation, all developing at about the same time,
seem to me to constitute convincing evidence that the authorities adopted
a new approach to questions of economic welfare and inequality in the
mid fifties. What prompted this initiative and how successful has it been?

To a large extent, the first of these questions is beyond the scope of this
book. But as I suggested in chapter 8, when discussing innovations in
wage policy, the new approach to questions of welfare should be seen as
part of a more general attempt to modernize Soviet society, to make it
both more efficient and more equitable and to overcome the consequences
of Stalinist immobilism. It might be thought of as signaling the limited
readoption of socialist, or at least humanitarian, principles. And it is also
true that the new approach to welfare and equality both benefited and
benefited from developments elsewhere in the economy and society.

The success of Soviet policies requires a consideration of the instruments at the government's disposal and of their objectives. A consideration of Soviet economic institutions suggests that, in addition to its
ownership of most productive capital, the Soviet government possesses
two broad sets of instruments with which to influence the level of economic welfare and the distribution of income: its control over wage rates
and salary scales and its control over what I have called the Soviet welfare state. Chapters 8-11 were devoted to an analysis of the use that the
Soviet government has made of these instruments since the mid fifties.
The analysis showed that until the late sixties there was little change in
the philosophy underlying the distribution of social welfare benefits or,

more generally, the principles determining the allocation of social consumption expenditures. Change, when it came, can be interpreted as a move towards the recognition of need as a sufficient entitlement for assistance from the state, as a move away from the strict application of socialist principles to the distribution of income. Although such a development had been advocated in the writing of a number of Soviet economists there are indications that the Soviet government was not persuaded to change its approach by rational argument alone. Indeed, the evidence suggests that it was extremely doubtful about the consequences of departing from what may be called the "wages route." Only the existence of substantial poverty that had remained untouched by successive increases in the minimum wage and the economic stringency of the seventies can have finally convinced it to change its ways.

On the other hand, the government has made extensive use of its power to determine wage rates and salary scales, undertaking two substantial revisions of pay scales in the last fifteen or twenty years; it has introduced the principle of national job evaluation and set up a central bureaucracy to implement its policies. However, the originality of the philosophy that has guided these initiatives is open to question. Soviet labor economists tend to portray the new policies as a return to Marxist principles and to the Leninist norms of the twenties, but this, I think, understates the contribution made by post-Stalin thinking.

An examination of the record since 1955 suggests that the Soviet authorities, in spite of an extensive and active bureaucracy, or perhaps because of it, exercise only imperfect control over the level and distribution of earnings, and that their policies have had some unintended effects. Since the Second World War, Soviet planning procedures have succeeded in maintaining some semblance of equilibrium in the market for labor and in preventing the emergence of significant overt inflation. This achievement has been facilitated by the new approach to wages and salaries, by a new spirit of equity in the determination of wage and salary differentials; but the policies pursued were necessarily temporary, implying future conflicts over the allocation of resources and the possible emergence of inflationary pressure. And, as I show below, this phase is now over. Further, even during the period 1955-70 there are indications that control was retained only with some difficulty. There were, it appears, unanticipated (and undesired) increases in earnings in 1965-67, particularly among managerial personnel. This may have been a consequence of new methods of administration and may have reflected frustration with both the relative economic stagnation and the egalitarian tendencies of the last years under Khrushchev. In any case, the evidence suggests that the system has worked less well since 1967 than in the preceding decade; increases in both earnings and prices have been higher after 1968 than before (although rates of inflation have been negligible in comparison with those in other industrialized nation).

Neither wage and salary policy nor expenditures on social consumption have been administered as consistently or as effectively as Soviet accounts would have us believe; nevertheless, there has been substantial achievement. The material in chapters 2 and 5 makes it abundantly clear that the economic welfare of both kolkhozniki and state employees improved substantially in the ten or fifteen years up to 1970. The same material, however, suggests that living standards in the USSR are still low, both by international standards (when compared to other industrial economies) and in terms of the government's own poverty level. Even in 1967-68, approximately two-fifths of the population were living in families with a per capita income of less than 50 rubles a month. In parts of Transcaucasia and much of Soviet Central Asia, a majority of the population was poor. It might be suggested that these results are a consequence of the liberal definition of poverty adopted by the authorities in 1965, that a standard which classifies more than a third of the population as poor has a very different political and economic meaning from one which identifies the bottom 10 or 15% of income recipients. There is something to be said for this argument; but some Soviet critics have argued that the MMS standard is too low. "It is important to raise wages that do not provide a minimum standard; the required amount should be determined by scientific analysis. Given contemporary requirements in modern urban conditions, I believe this minimum should be around 100 rubles [a month] for each member of the family."[1] Of course Medvedev is not an economist and he seems to be unaware of NIIT's work on the cost of living in modern urban conditions. But he is an educated and serious observer of Soviet affairs and an informed critic of conditions within the country. Although he is only a single individual, this comment suggests that the MMS budget cannot be regarded as completely utopian.

Progress, then, has been made in raising average living standards. Turning to the various dimensions of economic inequality, the material in chapters 2 and 3 also shows that, whatever the indicator used, the gap between peasants and workers (or rather, state employees) closed between 1960 and 1970. By the end of the decade, total or personal per capita income of kolkhozniki for the USSR as a whole was some 78-85% of that of state employees. This, I think, gives a better indication of the relative living standards of the two classes than money income, which suggests that peasants received about two-thirds as much as the rest of the population. In addition to the gains reflected in these specific indicators, there was a general reduction in political, social, and economic discrimination against the collectivized peasantry, and substantial strides have been made in integrating it with the monetary sector of the Soviet economy. Of course, not all these achievements can be attributed to the wage and welfare policies under review, nor can it be claimed that they are solely the result of a new concern for equity; indeed, as suggested above, they are to a considerable extent the consequence of a preoccupation with agricultural efficiency. But they represent substantial gains in welfare and equality.

Data on the personal distribution of income for either state employees or collective farmers are rather less plentiful than estimates of average incomes, but the material in chapter 3 indicates that there was a marked reduction in inequality among the nonagricultural population between 1958 and 1967, at least in the terms in which it is measured here. Income inequality for the population as a whole, in fact, was reduced during this period. It is difficult to identify the factors responsible for this reduction, but broadly similar increases in absolute income for the bulk of the Soviet population appear to have been key. Tautologically, therefore, it can be attributed to the reform of social security, reorganization of wage and salary systems, and increased expenditure on pensions and other transfers.

As pointed out above, even in 1967-68 there was substantial urban poverty in the USSR, and I have suggested that the 1968 increase in the minimum wage was an attempt to reduce deprivation without adopting radical new social welfare policies. The way the new minimum was introduced disrupted the newly established earnings differentials so laboriously imposed between 1957 and 1965. This consequence has been sharply criticized by Soviet labor economists. It may also have generated significant dissatisfaction among managerial and professional groups and skilled workers. In any case, since 1970 there has been a move away from the level of equality in the distribution of earnings attained in 1968; I suspect that this increase in inequality will have been mirrored in the distribution of income. Unfortunately, in the absence of any published information about the results of the 1972 survey of incomes (if it was ever held), it is impossible to substantiate or refute this conjecture.

Thus substantial progress has been achieved in reducing differences in the standard of living of peasants and state employees and in reducing measured inequality in the personal distribution of income. The results of attempts to reduce differences in the economic welfare of the various nationalities in the USSR must give the authorities less grounds for satisfaction. It is true, as I have suggested, that interrepublican differentials in average incomes do not measure disparities in national living standards at all adequately, but no other feasible set of data is more appropriate. Also, as the material in chapters 5-7 suggests, developments in this area may have been an accidental consequence of the interaction of policy and socioeconomic change. But to claim that because the variance in earnings per person employed, for example, has fallen, the government's policies have enjoyed a measure of success, is to fall prey to the error that

I criticized at the beginning of the chapter. It is income and not earnings (or social welfare expenditures taken in isolation) that constitutes the appropriate indicator of success or failure.

Thus the record of 1955-70 is one of considerable achievement in raising living standards and reducing inequality, and this achievement can be attributed to a large extent to government policy. But the mechanisms by which it has been attained have implied future conflict over resource allocation, have implied that progress is not sustainable in the long run. And although material about developments since 1970 is not plentiful, the evidence suggests that the momentum of earlier years has not been maintained; the drive towards equality has slackened, if not reversed, and the rise in living standards has slowed down.

Both the rise in average living standards and the successes of the sixties in reducing inequality without excessive discontent can be attributed to the fact that they were achieved through a process of "levelling up." All income groups enjoyed improvement in living standards, but increases in the minimum wage and in expenditures on social insurance meant that the incomes of the poorest increased more rapidly than those of the affluent. Such an approach may minimize dissatisfaction, but it can be extremely costly. The figures in table 2.3 show that between 1960 and 1970 the average annual rate of growth of real per capita disposable income was more than half a percentage point above that of real per capita GNP (as calculated by Western scholars). If such a situation were to continue, it would imply changes in the pattern of resource use and a reduction in the share of output available for investment, defense, and other government uses. It is not to be expected that the Soviet authorities would willingly continue to cede control over such resources. Thus unless they curb the rate of growth of incomes, there is likely to be a period of increasing inflationary pressure.

The figures in table 12.1 indicate that the authorities have successfully returned to their previous priorities, although only with the help of a dash of open inflation. In 1970-74 the rate of growth of real GNP again exceeded the rate of growth of real disposable income. The figures also indicate that the latter fell by more than 40% when compared with the preceding decade. Thus since 1970 there has been a return to a slower but perhaps more easily sustainable rate of growth of economic welfare. Whether or not the new pace can be maintained in the long run depends in part upon economic performance, but it also depends upon the rising expectations of Soviet workers, managers and peasants. During the ninth five-year plan, attempts were made to introduce a new hard line, to damp down those expectations, to establish a political climate in which slower growth would be acceptable.[2] It is not clear whether this new atmosphere can be maintained indefinitely. If it does continue, in view of

Table 12.1
Growth in Living Standards, Kolkhozniki and Others, 1970-74 (%)

Indicator (per capita)	Average Annual Rate of Growth, 1970-74		
	Total Population	State Employees	Kolkhozniki
Money income	5.44	5.19	4.95
Personal income	4.47	4.23	4.68
Total income	4.69	4.56	4.26
Disposable personal income	4.17	3.93	4.72
Real disposable personal income	2.79	2.55	3.33
Average earnings (per person employed)	4.03	3.70	3.64
Real GNP	3.24	—	—

Sources: Rows 1-5 from tables 2.1 and 2.4; row 5 uses the Schroeder-Severin index given in appendix A. Row 6 from NK SSSR '74, pp. 422, 562, and from appendix A, tables A.1 and A.2, deflated by annual average employment in the state and collective sector. Row 7 from Greenslade, 1976, p. 275, adjusted for population change.

the world economic situation one would expect the growth in living standards given in table 12.1 to be more characteristic of the next five or ten years than of 1955-70.

The feasibility of the course set out above will depend in part upon the evolution of inequality in the USSR. If incomes are to grow at only 2.5% per annum, the possibilities of "levelling up" while providing for continued increases in the earnings and incomes of the most affluent are much reduced. And, indeed, the evidence from the post-1970 wage round suggests that further reductions in intraplant differentials are not thought desirable at the present time. It is possible that further rationalization of wage and salary scales, that continued emphasis upon equity and bureaucratic rationality will make existing levels of differentiation acceptable, particularly if accompanied by selective help to clearly disadvantaged groups. Otherwise, the stage is set for conflict.

I suggest, in fact, that further reductions in inequality within the constraints of likely future rates of income growth will necessitate actual reductions in the incomes of the most affluent; that is, that they will require a revitalization of direct taxation and the adoption of a more progressive rate structure. And as pointed out in chapter 11, of this there is no sign. Of course it is unlikely that Brezhnev and Kosygin will remain in office until 1985, and it is always possible that they will be succeeded by new men more willing to espouse radical socialist principles, but of this there is as yet little sign. And anyway, one might expect managers and skilled workers to protest against a cut in their living standards in all the ways open to them. Thus the slower growth in incomes and the absence of further progress towards equality may provoke discontent among the low-paid; attempts to introduce a more egalitarian distribution of income will be similarly unpopular. The result in either case is likely to be an increase in inflationary pressure and perhaps in central control.

I have made no explicit analysis of interrepublican differentials since 1970, but nothing in the general developments of the period 1970-74 would lead me to believe that there have been significant changes in the situation revealed by the analysis of chapters 5-7. Nor do I expect substantial modifications in policy between now and 1985. Thus the analysis offered here suggests that while considerable progress was made on all fronts between 1955 and 1970, it is unlikely that the period 1970-85 will witness as great a change in the level of inequality. Reductions in economic differentiation are not easy to achieve, however great the commitment to egalitarianism or socialist ideals.

So far, I have concentrated exclusively upon the level of economic welfare of specific groups in the USSR and upon disparities in income. In conclusion, I would like to comment on the relationship between the material presented here and the wider concept of social stratification, and this is the subject of the next section.

12.2   ECONOMIC INEQUALITY AND SOCIAL STRATIFICATION

There is now an extensive and growing literature on social stratification in Western society, and there have also been a number of recent books on the nature and extent of inequality in societies like that of the Soviet Union. There have been two approaches in this latter work. First, there is the attempt to demonstrate the inadequacy of the totalitarian model made popular by such Western writers as Kornhauser[3] in the fifties, which suggested that the key distinction in the Soviet type of society, overshadowing the traditional occupational and social differences, is between the Party, or *apparat*, enjoying a monopoly over legitimate (and illegitimate, means of coercion, and the rest of the population, united by their subjection to intimidation and terror. Second, the Soviet experience is examined for the light it can shed on likely future developments in the West. Egalitarian ideals exercise a powerful influence on many, and radical political philosophers have argued that the realization of equality is impossible without the abolition of private property in productive capital. To a large extent such private ownership was eliminated in the USSR more than half a century ago, and sociologists are interested in discovering what impact such a political revolution has had upon social stratification. Has it led to the eradication of class distinction as predicted by Marxism, or has it resulted in the emergence of a "new class" as suggested by Djilas? Alternatively, is the social structure of a country like the USSR fundamentally different from that found in Western Europe and North America, or are the imperatives of an industrial economy more influential than differences in legal arrangements, as implied by the "convergence" hypothesis?

For the most part, these studies of inequality and stratification in Eastern Europe have been written from a sociological perspective, emphasizing those aspects of differentiation that interest sociologists and are most relevant to Western society. And, clearly, this is appropriate. Yet the problems of specifying and measuring the distribution of material rewards in such societies are significant, and it is my belief that existing treatments are inadequate in a number of ways. In this concluding section I would like to suggest how I think the material in this book should modify dominant views of stratification in Eastern Europe, or at least in the USSR.

Disparities in income are only one dimension of inequality as understood by the sociologist, and perhaps they are not the most important. Other dimensions are differences in political power, in social status, in honor and prestige. Income differences are determined by occupation, and it is suggested by many that in a capitalist society, rankings in terms of income, status, and power are all coherent. Furthermore, while there are more or less extended continua in all three dimensions, there is a supposed basic cleavage between manual and nonmanual occupations. Finally, the two groups are relatively closed; there is little mobility between them. The children of workers remain workers, and the children of capitalists or the bureaucratic elite retain their parents' positions of privilege and affluence. This rigidity, the absence of effective equality of opportunity for the children of low-income groups and the extensive use of political power to protect private interests, generates *anomie* and resentment at the bottom of the social hierarchy.

According to the dominant view of stratification in the USSR, Soviet social structure differs from that outlined above in a number of significant respects. There are certainly disparities in income, and these correspond to differences in occupation. They also tend to conform to and reinforce differences in political power and social status. But, it is argued, the basic cleavage does not fall between manual and nonmanual occupations; indeed, it has been suggested that there is no unique demarcation line at all. Alternatively, the line is drawn between the educated and technically qualified managerial elite on the one hand and both manual and clerical occupations on the other. This is taken to imply that the working class does not suffer from peculiar disabilities in such a society. In any event, while disparities in material welfare exist, they are not as extreme as those to be found in a market economy.

Secondly, it is claimed that as a result of the political revolution there is much greater social mobility in the Soviet system than in Western societies. Parental occupation does not determine access to the educational system, and the way is open to great economic and social advancement for the able and ambitious child. This is seen to have three consequences. The fact that there is little self-recruitment into the elite inhibits the development of cultural exclusivity; there are few differences in attitude or behavior pattern between social groups in the USSR. Evidence of substantial mobility is also thought to encourage the ambitions of parents for their children and to prevent the emergence of a counter-culture; this increases social cohesion. It is also suggested, if only implicitly, that the greater openness of the Soviet social structure means that reward is based on achievement rather than ascription; in such circumstances, disparity in income or access to consumption possibilities generates relatively little resentment or discontent.

Thirdly, it is claimed that in the Soviet Union or other countries of the Soviet type the distribution of income and the reward structure more generally are, to a large extent, controlled by the government. The nature and extent of inequality will therefore be determined by political decisions. The fact that the Soviet government is nominally socialist (and therefore endowed with an egalitarian ideology) will constrain it to use its power to reduce the more blatant forms of discrimination. It is admitted that this is not inevitable (and Stalin's policies of increased differentiation are recognized as counter-examples), but it is claimed that only exclusive political power on the Soviet model can ensure the realization of egalitarian objectives:

> . . . socialist egalitarianism is not readily compatible with a pluralist political order of the classic western type. Egalitarianism seems to require a political system in which the state is able to hold in check those social and occupational groups which . . . might otherwise attempt to stake claims to a disproportionate share of society's rewards. The most effective way of holding such groups in check is by denying them the right to organize politically, or in other ways, to undermine social equality. (Parkin, 1971, p. 183)

Thus Soviet social structure is seen to be characterized by the absence of extreme disparity in rewards and of a clearly identifiable class division and the presence of a much greater degree of social mobility than Western industrial societies, leading to greater social cohesion and less political discontent. It is seen to have the potential for achieving social equality, even if that potential has yet to be realized.

This view of Soviet society and Soviet social structure is based on the analysis of a much wider array of evidence than that considered in this book. It is unlikely, therefore, that the material presented here would lead one to question all of these conclusions. But the material on which conclusions about the reward structure of Soviet society is based seems to me to be particularly inadequate, and it is on that that I shall concentrate. One may remark, however that in considering the extent of social mobility in the USSR and comparing it with that in the mature industrial states of Western Europe, it is important to distinguish between the effects of the political revolutions of 1917 and 1928-29 and those of the industrial revolution of 1928-41, say. The enormous expansion of industrial activity led to a significant increase in the demand for managerial skills and in the number of higher administrative and professional positions available. One would therefore expect significant recruitment from outside the "bureaucratic elite." Now that the pace of economic change has slowed, it will be interesting to see how far the pattern of open recruitment is maintained into the next generation. Great stress is placed upon the educational system as a channel of social and economic advancement, and this reflects the importance of formal qualifications in determining eligibility for "elite" positions in the USSR today. Yet caution should be exercised in drawing inferences about the openness of the system from the social backgrounds of students at provincial universities like Sverdlovsk.[4] One must also determine whether such institutions are similar to the major metropolitan universities and institutes, and depending upon how broadly one defines one's elite, the extent to which different types of educational establishment provide channels of entry.

A central conclusion of what I have called the dominant view of Soviet social structure holds that disparities in reward in the USSR are more modest and reveal less of a class character than those in Western Europe. This may be true, but it is doubtful whether such an inference can be drawn from the evidence adduced in its support. There are a number of problems here. First, virtually all the statistical evidence quoted refers to earnings and not incomes (and, incidentally, seldom makes allowance for differences in the structure of direct taxation). Throughout this book I have stressed the difference between the two concepts, and I do not propose to repeat what I have already said. Whether the distinction is important in this context depends upon whether one is interested in assessing differences in consumption possibilities open to representative members of various groups, differences in their material well-being, or whether one wishes to use reward as a partial indicator of merit. In the first case, it is meaningless to consider the employed in isolation; particular occupational groups should be considered in their social context, and this involves a consideration of their family circumstances, of alternative sources of income, of differences in participation, and so on. It is not clear how much the second case contributes to an understanding of social structure.

More serious, perhaps, than the use of earnings instead of incomes is the use of data that relate only to industrial occupations. (This, at least, is true of the bulk of the Soviet figures quoted; there are indications that those relating to Eastern Europe may be more strictly comparable with statistics on differentials in the West.) Industry, as used by Soviet statisticians, corresponds more or less to what in Britain is called manufacturing (but it includes mining and quarrying). As shown in chapter 9, industry contains only a minority of those classified as workers, *rabochiye*, in the Soviet Union; indeed, the three sectors for which data on workers' earnings are given explicitly—industry, construction, and (state) agriculture—account for little more than half of the total. There are no published figures on the earnings (or the incomes) of workers in the state sector as a whole, but since earnings in other sectors like retail trade are substantially lower than those in industry or construction, it is to be presumed that the earnings of all rabochiye (and also their incomes) will be lower than those of industrial workers. It is therefore misleading to identify this latter group with manual workers or weekly wage earners in a market economy like that of the UK.

There are similar problems with the other two occupational groups for whom earnings figures are given. As I pointed out in chapter 9, ITR, often identified with managerial status, includes some junior technical, as well as supervisory, personnel. It excludes those members of the central bureaucracy who perform many of the functions undertaken by the head-office staff of a Western corporation. Similarly, the category of clerical employment excludes those who work in financial institutions, in insurance, or in state administration.

Exclusive concentration upon industrial occupations implies a bias of another kind. The second half of chapter 2 was devoted to an analysis of the extensive social and administrative discrimination against the collectivized peasantry in the USSR. Admittedly, the disabilities from which kolkhozniki suffer have been reduced since Stalin's death, but they are still present. Yet in a recent popular account of inequality in the USSR, their situation was dealt with in four or five pages, and in Parkin they are mentioned only in passing.[5] It may be that the intention of these authors was to concentrate only on those features of the Soviet social structure that had a direct analogue in Britain, but in so doing they misrepresent the nature and extent of inequality in the USSR and convey the impression that there is a great deal more equality than there in fact is.

This is true of another feature of those analyses that emphasize social stratification as the source of inequality as well. By concentrating on differences in class and occupational status they underemphasize the importance of regional, linguistic, and ethnic factors. It might be argued that such factors are relatively unimportant in the linguistically homogeneous societies of the West (Williamson's figures, quoted in chapter 5, provide prima facie evidence to the contrary), but are disparities in material welfare any the less keenly resented because the source of discrimination is nationality rather than class?

This is not to assert that the inequalities in material welfare observable in the USSR since the Second World War have in fact been greater than those found in Western Europe; indeed, I suspect that the basic conclusion suggested above is correct. But these comments do suggest that differences in the scale of inequality between the two political systems inferred from recent sociological work have been exaggerated. They also suggest that inequality in both its narrow economic sense and its wider sociological one is more pervasive, and possibly the source of greater discontent, than conventional accounts imply.

Finally, there is the question of the extent to which the distribution of income can be directly controlled by the political authorities in the USSR—and the degree to which they interpret socialism as a body of egalitarian principles. I believe that the discussion in chapters 8 and 11 calls both of these propositions into question. It is certainly true that the Soviet government, through the State Committee on Labor and Wages, possesses the legal authority to specify any set of wage rates and salary scales that it believes will conform to its ideological principles and that, in the short run, this pay structure would have a significant influence on the distribution of income. But as pointed out above, the Soviet government controls only the demand site of the labor market, and there is no guarantee that in the absence of extensive controls over labor mobility, an arbitrarily chosen set of rate differentials (for example, equal rates for all jobs) would secure the desired allocation of labor. Although workers in the USSR do not possess an effective right to strike, and although those with particular qualifications or skills cannot form independent political groups, they are not powerless. There are a number of ways in which the economy would suffer if formal differentials were inappropriate. Shortages of particular skills, high rates of labor turnover, falling participation rates, and a general unwillingness to exercise initiative would all adversely affect economic performance and plan fulfillment. And, further, as the discussion of chapter 10 pointed out, there is a degree of autonomy built into the determination of actual earnings, however rigidly the authorities control formal rates. The logic of the planned economy provides an incentive for managers to ignore the state's structure of differentials if this conflicts with the demands of plan fulfillment; it also provides some scope for improving their own positions. To ensure equality, the Soviet government would not only have to undertake the direction of labor but would also have to eliminate managerial autonomy or greatly increase supervision. And how would it confer authority on its new controllers and reward them for conformity to the state's directives? Material incentives would conflict with the policy, and it is not clear that ideological commitment is enough. This contradiction suggests that in the absence of a widespread commitment to egalitarianism, the political institutions of a system of the Soviet type are incapable of imposing it; and if such a commitment exists, is the "dictatorship of the proletariat" and the destruction of political pluralism necessary?

If the analysis of chapters 8 and 11 calls into question the ability of the

Soviet government to impose whatever reward structure it pleases upon the USSR, it also raises doubts about the extent to which the authorities are committed, by their ideology, to radical socialist egalitarianism, to the reduction or elimination of disparities in income, power, and status, whatever their source. Earlier in this chapter I suggested that actions were a better guide to intentions than political rhetoric, and the analysis of previous chapters has shown that in 1956-65 and after 1970, the Soviet authorities were and have been intent on maintaining certain differences in income, or even increasing them. The emphasis of the earlier reorganization of wages and salaries was on greater consistency, on greater fairness or the equal treatment of equals, as much as on greater equality. This is confirmed both by Galenson's observations about post-reform differentials in industry and by much of the comment from Soviet labor economists. The material in chapter 9 indicates that much of the undoubted reduction in earnings inequality that occurred between 1956 and 1968 or 1970 can be attributed to the operation of the labor market and the government's minimum wage policy. This latter, I have suggested, should be attributed to factors other than a desire to realize egalitarian socialist principles.

Although it is dangerous to rely exclusively on what is said about the objectives of Soviet social policy, it seems to me that a careful reading of the views of labor economists and those responsible for wage determination provides little support for the claim that policy is guided by (or constrained by) an egalitarian socialist ideology. Rather, what Soviet writers derive from Marx and Lenin is justification for relating reward to achievement or merit, for maintaining disparity in income, power, and status in the USSR. Further, socialism as it has been interpreted in the Soviet Union has raised objections to, if it has not precluded, the provision of assistance to those in need; after all, did not Lenin write "He who shall not work, neither shall he eat"? And although Lenin was threatening those who had previously lived off income from property, his strictures have been applied to those thought to be the idle poor as well as the idle rich. It was doubts about the consequences of introducing income supplements for those in poverty, irrespective of employment status, that prompted the minimum wage hike of 1968. Thus, paradoxically, the largest single step in the reduction of earnings disparity in the USSR was more a consequence of suspicion about what would be called radical socialist egalitarianism in the West (that is, . . . to each according to his need) than a result of the government's espousal of that philosophy. As suggested in chapter 11, the ultimate acceptance of need as a social security criterion owes less to ideological preconceptions than to the realization that previous policies were either incapable of eliminating poverty or could do so only at an unacceptable cost.

There is a strand in Soviet thinking that argues for a reduction in industrial differentials and presumably for an overall decrease in income inequality, but it is relatively muted. Political censorship may prevent open questioning of the desirability of the very high salaries and privileges enjoyed by senior members of the Party, government, and armed services, but there is little criticism of the rewards paid to the scientific and cultural intellegentsia. Even a critical Soviet Marxist like Medvedev, unconstrained by censorship, suggests that disparities of the order of 7.5-10:1 are quite acceptable: "When ordinary workers receive 200 rubles, those more highly skilled should be paid 400-600 rubles. But top specialists and administrators should never be allowed to get more than 1,500-2,000 rubles a month, no matter how many posts they hold" (Medvedev, 1975, p. 226). All of this implies that Soviet socialist ideology has more in common with the meritocratic views of a social democrat like Crosland than the egalitarianism of a thinker like Tawney.

The comments offered here do not constitute a complete and coherent alternative to what I have called the dominant view of social stratification in the USSR, but I hope that they will provoke a reexamination of certain aspects of that view. I believe that it is still too early to tell whether or not the Soviet Union will be able to maintain the relatively open pattern of elite recruitment achieved in the past. The evidence given here demonstrates that differences in reward (or rather in material consumption) are both extensive and more complex than the partial analysis referred to above might suggest, and that political monism does not confer the ability to impose an egalitarian solution on society, nor does socialist ideology prescribe its imposition.

Soviet society may be more unequal than the descriptions of many Western sociologists would have us believe, but insofar as one can measure them, disparities in income in 1970 were less than those to be found in most market economies and less than they had been in 1955. As this book has shown, both the reduction in differentiation and the increase in the material welfare of the population can be attributed, in large measure, to the government's new commitment to raising living standards and to the policies that flowed from it. These policies have not been consistent in either formulation or application; the government has been feeling its way. Nevertheless its achievements have been considerable, and the Soviet experience merits careful study. Dr. Johnson once remarked that "a decent provision for the poor is the true test of civilization"; after a quarter of a century of barbarity under Stalin, the USSR bids fair to become more civilized than the rest of Europe.

Reference Matter

Appendix A

Total, Personal, and Money Income,

USSR, 1960-74

Table A1
Total, Personal, and Money Income, USSR, 1960-74 (million rubles)

Source of Income	Total Income	Money Income	Income in Kind	Free Services	Personal Income
1960					
Earnings from state	56,830	56,830			56,830
Earnings from kolkhozy	7,422	4,602	2,820		7,422
Private activity	15,069	4,465	10,604		15,069
Social expenditures	27,300	13,467		13,833	13,467
Other	1,818	1,818			1,818
Total incomes	108,439	81,182	13,424	13,833	94,606
1965					
Earnings from state	83,956	83,956			83,956
Earnings from kolkhozy	11,500	8,855	2,645		11,500
Private activity	16,130	4,545	11,585		16,130
Social expenditures	41,900	20,112		21,788	20,112
Other	2,132	2,132			2,132
Total incomes	155,618	119,600	14,230	21,788	133,830
1970					
Earnings from state	122,958	122,958			122,958
Earnings from kolkhozy	15,000	13,950	1,050		15,000
Private activity	18,983	4,986	13,997		18,983
Social expenditure	63,900	32,674		31,226	32,674
Other	3,497	3,497			3,497
Total incomes	224,338	178,065	15,047	31,226	193,112
1974					
Earnings from state	157,353	157,353			157,353
Earnings from kolkhozy	17,100	16,245	855		17,100
Private activity	18,848	9,411	9,437		18,848
Social expenditure	83,000	42,000		41,000	42,000
Other	3,431	3,431			3,431
Total incomes	279,732	228,440	10,292	41,000	238,732

Sources: Earnings from state, 1960-70, appendix B; 1974, *NK SSSR* '74, pp. 550, 561 (net of holiday pay). Earnings from kolkhozy, 1960-70, appendix B; proportion paid out in cash, Sarkisyan, 1972, p. 173; 1974, *NK SSSR* '74, p. 422; proportion paid out in cash assumed at 95%. Private activity, 1960-70, appendix B; proportion sold, Artemeva, 1973, p. 92; 1974, tables A2, A3. Social expenditures, 1960-70, appendix B; 1974, *NK SSSR* '74, p. 578. Other, 1960-70, appendix B; 1974, *NK SSSR* '74, pp. 609, 764.

Table A2
The Value of Private Agricultural Activity, 1974

Source of Information	Derivation of Values	Value (m. rubles)
NK SSSR '74, p. 422	Total kolkhoz pay	17,100
Ibid., p. 606	But earnings account for 44.2% of total income; therefore total income is	38,687.8
Ibid.	But private receipts 26.6% of total income; therefore private receipts are	10,291.0
NK SSSR '74, p. 338	But kolkhozniki occupy 54.6% of privately farmed land; on assumption that yields per acre the same for all social groups, total private agricultural output worth	18,848.0

Table A3
Private Receipts from the Sale of Agricultural Output, 1974

Product	State Purchases (m. rubles)	Share of Population (%)	Receipts by Population (m. rubles)
Potatoes and vegetables	3,284	18	591
Cattle and poultry	24,464	13	3,180
Milk	11,418	5	571
Eggs	2,864	7	200
Wool	2,306	16	369
Total receipts from state			4,911
CFM sales			4,500
Total value of private sales			9,411

Sources: Rows 1-5, *NK SSSR* '74, pp. 320-21; row 7, ibid., p. 621.

Table A4
Social Composition of the Soviet Population, 1960-74 (millions)

Category	1960	1965	1970	1974
Total population	212.32	229.20	241.72	250.90
of which				
State employees	145.02	172.82	193.38	208.00
Kolkhozniki	67.30	56.38	48.34	42.90
Kolkhoznik households (thousands)	17.11	15.41	14.36	13.70

Sources: Row 1, *NK SSSR* '60, p. 9; ibid. '65, p. 9; ibid. '70, p. 9; ibid. 74, p. 7. Row 3, *NK SSSR* '65, p. 42; ibid. '74, p. 38. Row 2 is residual. Row 4, *NK SSSR* '60, p. 500; ibid. '65, p. 417; ibid. '70, p. 388; ibid. '74, p. 426.

Table A5
Social Composition of Republican Population, USSR, 1960-70 (thousands)

	1960			1965			1970		
	Total	State Employees	Kolkhozniki	Total	State Employees	Kolkhozniki	Total	State Employees	Kolkhozniki
USSR	212,323	145,017	67,306	229,198	172,815	56,383	241,720	193,376	48,344
RSFSR	118,930	91,824	27,106	125,768	105,080	20,688	130,079	114,015	16,064
Uk SSR	42,465	23,601	18,864	45,100	28,213	16,887	47,126	32,489	14,637
B SSR	8,144	4,634	3,510	8,533	5,497	3,036	9,002	6,511	2,491
Uz SSR	8,372	4,456	3,916	10,130	5,954	4,176	11,960	7,288	4,672
Ka SSR	9,843	7,825	2,018	11,853	10,883	970	12,849	11,940	909
G SSR	4,131	2,033	2,098	4,483	2,609	1,874	4,686	3,196	1,490
Az SSR	3,819	1,893	1,926	4,518	2,823	1,695	5,117	3,677	1,440
Li SSR	2,761	1,694	1,067	2,949	2,141	808	3,128	2,420	708
M SSR	2,970	645	2,325	3,303	1,148	2,155	3,569	1,735	1,834
La SSR	2,113	1,622	491	2,241	1,844	397	2,364	2,031	333
Ki SSR	2,139	1,307	832	2,569	1,758	811	2,933	2,083	850
Ta SSR	2,036	847	1,189	2,482	1,162	1,320	2,900	1,553	1,347
Ar SSR	1,824	957	867	2,134	1,509	625	2,492	1,948	544
Tu SSR	1,567	735	832	1,862	1,085	777	2,159	1,266	893
E SSR	1,209	944	265	1,273	1,109	164	1,356	1,224	132

Sources: Total Population, 1960, *NK SSSR* '60, p. 9; 1965, *NK SSSR* '64, p. 9; 1970, *NK SSSR* '70, p. 9. State Employees, by residual. Kolkhozniki, USSR totals derived from the class composition of the Soviet population given in *NK SSSR*, various years. Republican totals derived from estimates of average family size grossed up by the number of kolkhoznik households in each republic. Those totals were adjusted to sum to the USSR figure. Sidorova, 1969, pp. 160-61; Sidorova, 1972, pp. 108, 123, and 115; *NK SSSR* '60, p. 500; *NK SSSR* '65, p. 416; *NK SSSR* '70, p. 388. Note: Family size in Turkmenistan was assumed to be 5.3 in 1970, rather than 3.9 as given by Sidorova: in 1965 it was 5.5, and in the 1959 census rural family size in the republic was 5.0.

Table A6
Adjusted Populations, 1960 (thousands)

	Males		Females		Adjusted Total Population, 1959	Total Population, 1959	Adjusted Total Population, 1960
	0-14	15+	0-14	15+			
USSR	31,414	62,636	30,284	84,492	191,690	208,827	194,899
RSFSR	17,422	35,003	16,846	48,263	107,948	117,534	109,230
Ukraine	5,542	13,033	5,328	17,966	38,696	41,869	39,247
Byelorussia	1,235	2,346	1,189	3,285	7,384	8,056	7,465
Uzbekistan	1,574	2,323	1,506	2,716	7,339	8,119	7,568
Kazakhstan	1,683	2,732	1,624	3,256	8,440	9,295	8,938
Georgia	605	1,260	580	1,599	3,716	4,044	3,796
Azerbaijan	704	1,052	669	1,272	3,346	3,698	3,455
Lithuania	369	876	360	1,107	2,504	2,711	2,550
Moldavia	488	846	474	1,077	2,630	2,884	2,708
Latvia	234	685	226	948	1,949	2,093	1,968
Kirgizia	391	584	377	714	1,870	2,066	1,936
Tadjikistan	396	569	372	644	1,788	1,980	1,838
Armenia	334	508	317	604	1,597	1,763	1,652
Turkmenistan	296	434	284	502	1,370	1,516	1,416
Estonia	139	386	133	539	1,113	1,197	1,124

Sources: 1959 population figures from Itogi, 1970, vol. 2, pp. 12-75. These were combined with the weights given in table 6.4.

Table A7
Adjusted Population, 1970 (thousands)

	Total Population, 1970	Males		Females		Adjusted Population, 1970
		0-14	15+	0-14	15+	
USSR	241,720	35,640	75,759	34,334	95,987	222,278
RSFSR	130,079	17,542	41,783	16,917	53,837	120,176
Ukraine	47,126	5,992	15,313	5,734	20,087	43,670
Byelorussia	9,002	1,330	2,808	1,274	3,590	8,278
Uzbekistan	11,799	2,695	3,049	2,615	3,440	10,515
Kazakhstan	13,009	2,476	3,787	2,401	4,345	11,770
Georgia	4,686	729	1,473	703	1,781	4,297
Azerbaijan	5,117	1,151	1,332	1,103	1,531	4,569
Lithuania	3,128	429	1,039	416	1,244	2,889
Moldavia	3,569	582	1,080	563	1,343	3,261
Latvia	2,364	261	820	249	1,035	2,207
Kirgizia	2,933	619	783	603	928	2,631
Tadjikistan	2,900	688	738	661	812	2,576
Armenia	2,492	501	716	473	802	2,248
Turkmenistan	2,159	491	572	477	619	1,925
Estonia	1,356	152	468	146	590	1,264

Sources: 1970 population figures from Itogi, 1970, vol. 2, pp. 12-75. These were combined with the weights given in table 6.4.

Table A8
Inflation and the Cost of Living, USSR, 1950-75

Year	Official Retail Price Index	Implicit Money Income Deflator		Quinquennial Rates of Growth
1950	132.6	100.4	1950-55	−3.7% p.a.
1955	99.1	83.7	1955-60	0.9%
1960	99.6	87.4	1960-65	1.4%
1965	100.4	93.7	1965-70	1.3%
1966	99.7	94.6		
1967	99.7	96.5		
1968	99.7	98.5		
1969	99.9	98.7		
1970	100.0	100.0	1970-75	1.6%
1971	100.0	100.8		
1972	100.1	104.8		
1973	100.2	103.8		
1974	100.2	105.5		
1975	100.4	108.4		

Source: Schroeder and Severin, 1976, p. 652, table 1. The implicit price deflator was constructed by combining the relatives of a large number of volume and value series using shares in final consumption as weights. See source for a more detailed description.

Appendix B

Personal and Total Income,

USSR and Republics, 1960-70

This appendix contains estimates of personal and total income for the USSR as a whole and for each of the fifteen union republics for the three benchmark years 1960, 1965, and 1970. Personal income is defined as including benefits in cash and kind that pass through the budgets of individual households. Total income consists of personal income and an estimate of the expenditures by the state and other organizations on the provision of free educational, health, and other services available to the people. Table B1 contains estimates of the components of personal and total incomes, while the remainder of the appendix indicates the sources of the data. Most have been taken from various All-Union and republican handbooks, but there are additional estimates and calculations under almost every heading.

Table B1.
Personal and Total Income, USSR and Republics, 1960, 1965, 1970 (million rubles)

	USSR	RSFSR	Ukraine	Byelorussia	Uzbekistan	Kazakhstan
1960						
Earnings of labor	64,252	40,429	11,363	1,606	1,923	3,104
of which						
State sector	56,830	37,256	9,478	1,359	1,250	2,750
Kolkhozy	7,422	3,173	1,885	247	673	354
Receipts from social funds	13,467	9,010	2,279	279	296	536
of which						
Holiday pay and premia	3,167	2,140	499	72	66	145
Pensions and allowances	9,700	6,510	1,668	190	211	362
Stipends	600	360	112	17	19	29
Private subsidiary activity	15,069	6,497	3,928	1,018	629	449
Receipts from financial system	918	603	156	22	19	40
Other receipts	900	592	150	21	20	43
Personal income	94,606	57,131	17,876	2,946	2,887	4,172
Noncash social expenditures	13,833	8,190	2,521	495	448	650
Total income	108,439	65,321	20,397	3,441	3,335	4,822
1965						
Earnings of labor	95,456	57,478	17,943	2,729	2,977	4,782
of which						
State sector	83,956	53,045	14,327	2,239	2,147	4,541
Kolkhozy	11,500	4,433	3,616	490	830	241
Receipts from social funds	20,112	12,756	3,663	519	537	873
of which						
Holiday pay and premia	5,112	3,356	818	128	122	259
Pensions and allowances	14,100	8,900	2,663	358	378	576
Stipends	900	500	182	33	37	38
Private subsidiary activity	16,130	6,723	4,254	1,122	758	464
Receipts from financial system	796	533	130	25	12	24
Other receipts	1,336	846	227	35	34	72
Personal income	133,830	78,336	26,217	4,430	4,318	6,215
Noncash social expenditures	21,788	12,844	3,737	763	768	1,162
Total income	155,618	91,180	29,954	5,193	5,086	7,377
1970						
Earnings of labor	137,958	82,334	25,298	4,378	4,609	6,830
of which						
State sector	122,958	76,384	20,962	3,675	3,456	6,492
Kolkhozy	15,000	5,950	4,336	703	1,153	338
Receipts from social funds	32,674	20,203	6,084	928	978	1,429
of which						
Holiday pay and premia	9,074	5,903	1,434	251	236	444
Pensions and allowances	22,300	13,600	4,408	626	679	917
Stipends	1,300	700	242	51	63	68
Private subsidiary activity	18,983	7,528	4,553	1,328	1,426	566
Receipts from financial system	1,517	932	292	52	26	51
Other receipts	1,980	1,236	336	59	55	104
Personal income	193,112	112,233	36,563	6,745	7,094	8,979
Noncash social expenditures	31,226	17,397	5,716	1,156	1,312	1,855
Total income	224,338	129,630	42,279	7,901	8,406	10,834

Georgia	Azerbaijan	Lithuania	Moldavia	Latvia	Kirgizia	Tadjikistan	Armenia	Turkmenistan	Estonia
952	836	649	494	735	469	383	450	388	471
804	661	557	337	649	370	286	367	283	423
148	175	92	157	86	99	97	83	105	48
199	163	100	81	145	85	61	93	52	88
42	33	29	16	34	20	15	19	15	22
145	121	63	60	105	60	41	69	33	62
12	9	8	5	6	5	5	5	4	4
557	222	560	340	276	120	148	135	68	122
14	11	9	5	10	5	5	7	5	7
13	10	9	5	10	6	4	6	4	7
1,735	1,242	1,327	925	1,176	685	601	691	517	695
247	212	164	150	168	121	113	114	133	107
1,982	1,454	1,491	1,075	1,344	806	714	805	650	802
1,372	1,271	1,142	1,057	1,100	805	700	765	649	686
1,184	1,077	947	629	980	627	483	661	443	626
188	194	195	428	120	178	217	104	206	60
294	262	181	142	234	151	112	152	90	146
62	55	54	34	64	36	28	35	25	36
217	187	115	98	162	105	75	105	58	103
15	20	12	10	8	10	9	12	7	7
601	238	550	438	247	194	231	99	93	118
14	8	11	6	9	4	3	8	3	6
19	17	15	10	16	10	8	10	7	10
2,300	1,796	1,899	1,653	1,606	1,164	1,054	1,034	842	966
375	356	284	266	253	225	202	196	200	157
2,675	2,152	2,183	1,919	1,859	1,389	1,256	1,230	1,042	1,123
2,028	1,829	1,874	1,591	1,619	1,201	1,008	1,280	1,056	1,023
1,785	1,567	1,566	1,090	1,449	987	778	1,149	687	931
243	262	308	501	170	214	230	131	369	92
457	425	370	276	390	265	203	268	148	250
109	107	107	70	108	67	49	78	47	64
324	287	244	186	270	182	138	170	91	178
24	31	19	20	12	16	16	20	10	8
800	408	639	554	314	206	229	152	139	142
34	13	34	13	17	10	8	17	5	13
28	25	25	17	23	16	12	18	11	15
3,347	2,700	2,942	2,451	2,363	1,698	1,460	1,735	1,359	1,443
541	548	438	437	367	345	320	304	258	232
3,888	3,248	3,380	2,888	2,730	2,043	1,780	2,039	1,617	1,675

NOTES AND SOURCES

Earnings in the State Sector. Calculated as the product of average annual employment and average monthly earnings expressed on an annual basis. Holiday pay and nonwage fund premia have been subtracted from the totals obtained. Employment data from *NK SSSR* '70, p. 513. Earnings:

Average Monthly Earnings, USSR State Sector, 1960-70 (rubles)

	1960	1965	1970
USSR	80.6	96.5	122.0
RSFSR	83.1	99.0	126.1
Ukraine	78.0	94.2	115.2
Byelorussia	63.2	80.9	106.4
Uzbekistan	70.1	89.2	114.8
Kazakhstan	82.0	98.0	124.2
Georgia	75.0	87.0	106.0
Azerbaijan	77.3	90.3	109.6
Lithuania	72.4	89.6	119.6
Moldavia	67.4	81.9	102.8
Latvia	78.5	95.0	125.6
Kirgizia	74.9	89.6	112.6
Tadjikistan	78.3	96.0	117.6
Armenia	75.4	91.9	112.0
Turkmenistan	79.1	100.0	128.0
Estonia	81.9	99.9	135.3

USSR: *NK SSSR* '70, p. 519. RSFSR: *NK RSFSR* '70, p. 340. Ukraine: *UK SSR v tsifrakh* '69, p. 144, *BSE*. Byelorussia: *NK BSSR* '73, p. 154. Uzbekistan: *NK Uz. SSR* '71, p. 227. Kazakhstan: *NK Ka. SSR* '71, p. 242. Georgia: *GSSR v tsifrakh* '71, p. 127. Azerbaijan: *NK Az SSR* '70, p. 226. Lithuania: *Ek i kult. Li SSR* '72, p. 292. Latvia: *NK La SSR* '73, p. 306. Kirgizia: *NK Ki SSR* '71, p. 192. Tadjikistan: *NK Ta SSR* '71, p. 141. Armenia: *NK Ar SSR* '67, p. 20, *BSE*. Estonia: *NK ESSR* '70, p. 240. Turkmenistan: 1960-65 implied as residual; 1970, *BSE*.

Earnings from Kolkhozy. Appendix D.
Holiday Pay and Non-Wage-Fund Premia. Appendix E.
Pensions and Allowances. Appendix E.
Stipends. Appendix E.
Private Subsidiary Activity. Equated with the output of private agricultural activity. Calculated on the assumption that yields per hectare on nonkolkhoznik plots equal to those on kolkhoznik plots in each republic. Consequently kolkhoznik receipts were grossed up by the ratio of total to kolkhoznik-sown areas. See text for further discussion of this assumption. Kolkhoznik receipts from appendix D; sown areas from *NK SSSR* '59, p. 328, *NK SSSR* '64, p. 263, and *NK SSSR* '69, p. 305.

Receipts from Financial System. Consists of receipts from state loans and lotteries, All-Union total allocated according to the wage bill; loans to population, taken as equal to credits by Stroibank to housing cooperatives (*NK SSSR* '70, p. 740); interest on savings deposits, calculated as 2% of value of deposits outstanding at year-end. Deposits from *NK SSSR* '69, p. 587, and *NK SSSR* '72, p. 561.

Other receipts. Arbitrarily estimated at 1.5% of the wage bill in the state sector.

Appendix C

Personal and Total Income,

State Employees, USSR and Republics, 1960-70

Table C1
Personal and Total Income, State Employees, USSR and Republics, 1960 (million rubles)

	Earnings and Other Income	Private Activity	Social Welfare Receipts	Personal Income	Non-Cash Social Expenditures	Total Income
USSR	55,817	3,515	13,132	72,464	10,470	82,934
RSFSR	37,128	1,911	8,861	47,900	6,313	54,213
Ukraine	9,015	512	2,183	11,710	1,868	13,578
Byelorussia	1,256	278	270	1,804	379	2,183
Uzbekistan	1,182	145	276	1,603	256	1,859
Kazakhstan	2,792	207	525	3,524	529	4,053
Georgia	726	51	192	969	171	1,140
Azerbaijan	630	—	157	787	159	946
Lithuania	540	153	96	789	122	911
Moldavia	256	20	71	347	97	444
Latvia	647	69	143	859	127	986
Kirgizia	354	40	80	474	91	565
Tadjikistan	267	49	55	371	84	455
Armenia	325	45	90	460	82	542
Turkmenistan	271	—	47	318	109	427
Estonia	428	35	86	549	83	632

Sources: Appendix B and appendix D, tables D3 and D10.

Table C2
Personal and Total Income, State Employees, USSR and Republics, 1965 (million rubles)

	Earnings and Other Income	Private Activity	Social Welfare Receipts	Personal Income	Non-Cash Social Expenditures	Total Income
USSR	83,540	5,158	19,195	107,893	16,644	124,537
RSFSR	53,439	2,680	12,385	68,504	10,123	78,627
Ukraine	13,874	800	3,370	18,044	2,608	20,652
Byelorussia	2,156	406	485	3,047	575	3,622
Uzbekistan	2,076	207	472	2,755	545	3,300
Kazakhstan	4,613	348	854	5,815	951	6,766
Georgia	1,093	113	280	1,486	263	1,749
Azerbaijan	1,041	79	246	1,366	275	1,641
Lithuania	939	150	169	1,258	208	1,466
Moldavia	561	55	109	725	168	893
Latvia	980	74	227	1,281	191	1,472
Kirgizia	614	97	137	848	167	1,015
Tadjikistan	464	77	96	637	147	784
Armenia	634	33	145	812	149	961
Turkmenistan	423	—	79	502	154	656
Estonia	633	39	141	813	120	933

Sources: Appendix B and appendix D, tables D5 and D11.

Table C3
Personal and Total Income, State Employees, USSR and Republics, 1970 (million rubles)

	Earnings and Other Income	Private Activity	Social Welfare Receipts	Personal Income	Non-Cash Social Expenditures	Total Income
USSR	123,765	8,000	29,484	161,249	26,234	187,483
RSFSR	77,685	4,146	18,902	100,733	14,810	115,543
Ukraine	20,637	926	5,108	26,671	4,717	31,388
Byelorussia	3,696	593	742	5,031	979	6,010
Uzbekistan	3,361	611	791	4,763	1,049	5,812
Kazakhstan	6,620	432	1,360	8,412	1,614	10,026
Georgia	1,699	235	376	2,310	449	2,759
Azerbaijan	1,525	204	360	2,089	481	2,570
Lithuania	1,596	284	305	2,185	342	2,527
Moldavia	1,038	98	203	1,339	313	1,652
Latvia	1,464	169	356	1,989	305	2,294
Kirgizia	984	88	224	1,296	285	1,581
Tadjikistan	713	57	157	927	260	1,187
Armenia	1,134	76	244	1,454	252	1,706
Turkmenistan	662	—	121	783	187	970
Estonia	951	81	235	1,267	191	1,458

Sources: Appendix B and appendix D, tables D7 and D12.

Appendix D

Total Income, Kolkhozniki and Their Dependents,

USSR and Republics, 1960–74

THE INCOMES OF KOLKHOZNIKI, 1960-74

The estimates of kolkhoznik incomes given in this appendix are derived from Sidorova, 1969, and Sidorova, 1972. As indicated in the notes to particular tables, materials from *Narodnoye Khozyaistvo* for various years have been used to convert Sidorova's figures into ruble totals. Sidorova's figures cannot be used to generate estimates of kolkhoznik incomes in 1974. The ones given here have been obtained from official statistical sources in the manner explained.

Table D1
The Structure of Total Income,[a] Kolkhozniki and Their Dependents,
USSR, 1960–74 (million rubles)

| Year | Labor Payments from Kolkhozy | Social Welfare Expenditures | | | Private Subsidiary Activity | Wages from Socialist Sector | Other | Total |
		Total	from State	from Kolkhoz				
1960	7,422	3,698	3,264	434	11,554	2,295	536	25,505
1963	8,732	4,642	4,034	608	11,578	2,211	470	27,633
1964	10,116	5,000	4,302	698	11,337	2,180	436	29,069
1965	11,500	6,061	4,942	1,119	10,972	2,082	466	31,081
1966	12,800	6,569	5,248	1,321	11,581	2,438	474	33,862
1969	14,100	7,568	5,890	1,678	11,280	2,356	392	35,696
1970	15,000	8,182	6,302	1,880	10,983	2,322	368	36,855
1974	17,100	7,699	na	na	10,921	3,018	580	38,688

Notes and Sources: Labor payments, *NK SSSR '74*, p. 422, *NK SSSR '70*, p. 383, *NK SSSR '73*, p. 456, *NK SSSR '67*, p. 466; 1963 from Sidorova, 1972, p. 107; 1964 interpolated. 1960–70 Remaining entries derived from percentage totals given in Sidorova, 1969, p. 143, and Sidorova, 1972, p. 100. 1974. *NK SSSR '74*, p. 606.

a. Total income includes an estimate of the value of services, like education, that are provided by the state and kolkhoz without charge. It corresponds to Sidorova's *polnyi sovokupnyi dokhod* (1969) or *fond vozproizvodstva rabochei sily* (1970).

Table D2
Total Income, Kolkhozniki and Their Dependents,
USSR and Republics, 1960-70 (million rubles)

	1960	1963	1964	1965	1966	1969	1970
USSR	25,505	27,633	29,069	31,081	33,862	35,696	36,855
RSFSR	11,108	11,560	12,168	12,553	12,964	13,938	14,087
Ukraine	6,819	7,869	8,542	9,302	10,169	10,568	10,891
Byelorussia	1,258	1,399	1,450	1,571	1,749	1,929	1,891
Uzbekistan	1,476	1,590	1,571	1,786	2,194	2,274	2,594
Kazakhstan	769	560	594	611	728	783	808
Georgia	842	860	884	926	1,196	1,130	1,129
Azerbaijan	508	501	452	511	668	613	678
Lithuania	580	679	683	717	710	804	853
Moldavia	631	844	907	1,026	1,157	1,197	1,236
Latvia	358	352	355	387	386	423	436
Kirgizia	241	340	344	374	422	433	462
Tadjikistan	259	393	407	472	528	545	593
Armenia	263	250	235	269	308	312	333
Turkmenistan	223	259	297	386	494	533	647
Estonia	170	177	180	190	189	214	217

Sources: 1960, 1963, 1965–66, and 1970, from tables D3–D7; 1964 and 1969 from Sidorova, 1969, p. 160, and Sidorova, 1972, p. 108, grossed up by the number of kolkhoznik households (from table D8) and adjusted to sum to total income.

Table D3
The Structure of Total Income, Kolkhozniki and Their Dependents,
USSR and Republics, 1960 (million rubles)

	Labor Payments from Kolkhozy	Social Welfare Expenditures			Private Subsidiary Activity	Wages from the Socialist Sector	Total
		Total	from State	from Kolkhoz			
USSR	7,422	3,698	3,264	434	11,554	2,831	25,505
RSFSR	3,173	2,026	1,840	186	4,586	1,323	11,108
Ukraine	1,885	749	635	114	3,416	769	6,819
Byelorussia	247	125	119	6	740	146	1,258
Uzbekistan	673	212	157	55	484	107	1,476
Kazakhstan	354	132	117	15	242	41	769
Georgia	148	83	78	5	506	105	842
Azerbaijan	175	59	54	5	222	52	508
Lithuania	92	46	44	2	407	35	580
Moldavia	157	63	47	16	320	91	631
Latvia	86	43	39	4	207	22	358
Kirgizia	99	35	28	7	80	27	241
Tadjikistan	97	35	28	7	99	28	259
Armenia	83	35	33	2	90	55	263
Turkmenistan	105	29	21	8	68	21	223
Estonia	48	26	24	2	87	9	170

Sources: USSR totals from table D1; columns 1, 2, and 5 from table D5 and Sidorova, 1972, p. 107; column 7 from Sidorova, 1972, p. 108; column 4 from Sidorova, 1972, p. 109; columns 3 and 6 as residuals. Sidorova's figures were grossed up by the number of kolkhoznik households from table D8. Entries have been adjusted to sum to USSR totals; the basis of adjustment is explained in the text.

Table D4
The Structure of Total Income, Kolkhozniki and Their Dependents,
USSR and Republics, 1963 (million rubles)

	Labor Payments from Kolkhozy	Social Welfare Expenditures			Private Subsidiary Activity	Wages from Socialist Sector	Total
		Total	from State	from Kolkhoz			
USSR	8,732	4,642	4,034	608	11,578	2,681	27,633
RSFSR	3,358	2,462	2,207	255	4,453	1,287	11,560
Ukraine	2,891	1,064	864	200	3,517	397	7,869
Byelorussia	322	153	145	8	748	176	1,399
Uzbekistan	676	217	184	33	547	150	1,590
Kazakhstan	220	179	127	52	126	35	560
Georgia	136	84	80	4	487	153	860
Azerbaijan	140	71	67	4	213	77	501
Lithuania	112	58	56	2	461	48	679
Moldavia	266	88	67	21	365	125	844
Latvia	80	53	49	4	194	25	352
Kirgizia	153	54	45	9	89	44	340
Tadjikistan	154	51	45	6	125	63	393
Armenia	74	38	36	2	80	58	250
Turkmenistan	104	37	33	4	87	31	259
Estonia	46	33	29	4	86	12	177

Sources: USSR totals from table D1; columns 1, 2, and 5 from table D5 and Sidorova, 1972, p. 107; column 7 from Sidorova, 1972, p. 108; column 4 from Sidorova, 1969, p. 79; columns 3 and 6 as residuals. Sidorova's figures were grossed up by the number of kolkhoznik households from table D8. Entries have been adjusted to sum to USSR totals; the basis of adjustment is explained in the text.

Table D5
The Structure of Total Income, Kolkhozniki and Their Dependents,
USSR and Republics, 1965 (million rubles)

	Labor Payments from Kolkhozy	Social Welfare Expenditures			Private Subsidiary Activity	Wages from Socialist Sector	Other	Total
		Total	from State	from Kolkhoz				
USSR	11,500	6,061	4,942	1,119	10,972	2,082	466	31,081
RSFSR	4,433	3,092	2,651	441	4,043	781	204	12,553
Ukraine	3,616	1,422	1,041	381	3,454	693	117	9,302
Byelorussia	490	222	194	28	716	126	17	1,571
Uzbekistan	830	288	204	84	551	98	19	1,786
Kazakhstan	241	230	200	30	116	19	5	611
Georgia	188	126	114	12	488	77	47	926
Azerbaijan	194	97	86	11	159	45	16	511
Lithuania	195	88	76	12	400	29	5	717
Moldavia	428	131	85	46	383	72	12	1,026
Latvia	120	69	59	10	173	22	3	387
Kirgizia	178	72	52	20	97	22	5	374
Tadjikistan	217	71	52	19	154	25	5	472
Armenia	104	54	50	4	66	39	6	269
Turkmenistan	206	57	42	15	93	26	4	386
Estonia	60	42	36	6	79	8	1	190

Sources: USSR totals from table D1; column 8 from Sidorova, 1972, p. 108; other entries from Sidorova, 1969, p. 148. Sidorova's figures were grossed up by the number of kolkhoznik households from table D8. Entries were adjusted to sum to USSR totals; the basis of adjustment is explained in the text.

Table D6
The Structure of Total Income, Kolkhozniki and Their Dependents,
USSR and Republics, 1966 (million rubles)

	Labor Payments from Kolkhozy	Social Welfare Expenditures			Private Subsidiary Activity	Wages from Socialist Sector	Other	Total
		Total	from State	from Kolkhoz				
USSR	12,800	6,603	5,282	1,321	11,615	2,438	406	33,862
RSFSR	4,997	3,226	2,725	501	3,746	837	158	12,964
Ukraine	3,848	1,599	1,138	461	3,792	841	89	10,169
Byelorussia	543	251	207	44	794	149	12	1,749
Uzbekistan	888	346	249	97	783	146	31	2,194
Kazakhstan	312	249	223	26	138	22	7	728
Georgia	328	151	135	16	566	98	53	1,196
Azerbaijan	244	114	101	13	225	71	14	668
Lithuania	223	99	83	16	359	23	6	710
Moldavia	437	156	100	56	484	69	11	1,157
Latvia	130	73	60	13	158	21	4	386
Kirgizia	196	79	57	22	119	23	5	422
Tadjikistan	227	80	60	20	174	42	5	528
Armenia	107	63	56	7	84	49	5	308
Turkmenistan	252	72	51	21	127	38	5	494
Estonia	68	45	37	8	66	9	1	189

Sources: USSR totals from table D1; column 8 from Sidorova, 1969, p. 160; other entries from Sidorova, 1969, p. 149. Sidorova's figures were grossed up by the number of kolkhoznik households from table D8. Entries were adjusted to sum to USSR totals; the basis of adjustment is explained in the text.

Table D7
The Structure of Total Income, Kolkhozniki and Their Dependents,
USSR and Republics, 1970 (million rubles)

	Labor Payments from Kolkhozy	Social Welfare Expenditures			Private Subsidiary Activity	Wages from Socialist Sector	Total
		Total	from State	from Kolkhoz			
USSR	15,000	8,182	6,302	1,880	10,983	2,690	36,855
RSFSR	5,950	3,888	3,155	733	3,382	867	14,087
Ukraine	4,336	1,975	1,384	591	3,627	953	10,891
Byelorussia	703	363	258	105	735	90	1,891
Uzbekistan	1,153	450	319	131	815	176	2,594
Kazakhstan	338	310	267	43	133	27	808
Georgia	243	173	153	20	565	148	1,129
Azerbaijan	262	132	116	16	204	80	678
Lithuania	308	161	128	33	355	29	853
Moldavia	501	197	120	77	456	82	1,236
Latvia	170	96	75	21	145	25	436
Kirgizia	214	101	74	27	118	29	462
Tadjikistan	230	106	77	29	172	85	593
Armenia	131	76	67	9	76	50	333
Turkmenistan	369	98	67	31	139	41	647
Estonia	92	56	42	14	61	8	217

Sources: USSR totals from table D1; columns 1, 2, and 5 from table D5 and Sidorova, 1972, p. 107. Labor pay in Kirgizia from Sidorova, 1972, p. 109; column 7 from Sidorova, 1972, p. 108. Columns 3 and 6 as residuals. Sidorova's figures were grossed up by the number of kolkhoznik households from table D8. Entries were adjusted to sum to USSR totals; the basis of adjustment is explained in the text.

Table D8
The Number of Kolkhoznik Households, USSR and Republics, 1960-70 (thousands)

	1960	1963	1964	1965	1966	1969	1970
USSR	17,106	16,101	15,887	15,414	15,400	14,707	14,363
RSFSR	7,091	6,333	6,260	5,860	5,720	5,311	5,128
Ukraine	5,373	5,290	5,274	5,241	5,291	5,145	5,061
Byelorussia	938	907	906	885	889	873	827
Uzbekistan	677	747	749	758	793	802	812
Kazakhstan	418	225	218	207	208	201	201
Georgia	492	462	464	462	467	419	397
Azerbaijan	352	367	289	294	301	272	272
Lithuania	304	292	278	259	263	259	258
Moldavia	565	561	560	560	568	546	536
Latvia	173	163	153	153	152	142	140
Kirgizia	165	174	170	170	176	175	174
Tadjikistan	199	226	230	231	236	233	230
Armenia	154	138	120	118	117	107	105
Turkmenistan	121	136	138	141	147	153	156
Estonia	84	80	78	75	72	69	66

Sources: 1960, *NK SSSR* '60, p. 500; 1963, *NK SSSR* '63, p. 348; 1964, *NK SSSR* '64, p. 402; 1965, *NK SSSR* '65, p. 47; 1966, total from *NK SSSR* '67, p. 466, allocated between republics proportionately to numbers in 1967 from *NK SSSR* '67, p. 474; 1969, *NK SSSR* '69, p. 404, *NK SSSR* '70, p. 388.

Table D9
The Number of Kolkhozniki and Their Dependents,
USSR and Republics, 1960-70 (thousands)

	1960	1963	1964	1965	1966	1969	1970
USSR	67,306	57,335	56,335	56,383	52,606	51,588	48,344
RSFSR	27,106	21,928	21,808	20,688	18,833	17,487	16,064
Ukraine	18,864	16,690	16,769	16,887	16,055	15,352	14,637
Byelorussia	3,510	3,024	3,014	3,036	2,759	2,784	2,491
Uzbekistan	3,916	3,876	3,829	4,176	4,120	4,786	4,672
Kazakhstan	2,018	978	937	970	930	952	909
Georgia	2,098	1,807	1,776	1,874	1,774	1,638	1,490
Azerbaijan	1,926	1,857	1,424	1,695	1,457	1,511	1,440
Lithuania	1,067	913	851	808	798	746	708
Moldavia	2,325	2,032	2,022	2,155	1,994	1,966	1,834
Latvia	491	419	400	397	369	351	333
Kirgizia	832	959	765	811	803	883	850
Tadjikistan	1,189	1,210	1,201	1,320	1,285	1,438	1,347
Armenia	867	703	606	625	600	639	544
Turkmenistan	832	715	717	777	772	913	893
Estonia	265	224	216	164	147	142	132

Table D10
Personal Income, Kolkhozniki and Their Dependents,
USSR and Republics, 1960 (million rubles)

	Primary Income	Cash Receipts from Social Funds			Personal Income
		Total	Stipends	Other Cash	
USSR	21,807	335	182	153	22,142
RSFSR	9,082	149	82	67	9,231
Ukraine	6,070	96	50	46	6,166
Byelorussia	1,133	9	7	2	1,142
Uzbekistan	1,264	20	9	11	1,284
Kazakhstan	637	11	6	5	648
Georgia	759	7	6	1	766
Azerbaijan	449	6	4	2*	455
Lithuania	534	4	3	1*	538
Moldavia	568	10	4	6	578
Latvia	315	2	1	1	317
Kirgizia	206	5	2	3*	211
Tadjikistan	224	6	3	3*	230
Armenia	228	3	2	1*	231
Turkmenistan	194	5	2	3*	199
Estonia	144	2	1	1*	146

Notes and Sources: Based on the assumption that kolkhozniki and their dependents receive only stipends as cash from the state; other cash receipts are from the kolkhoz. Total kolkhoz expenditure from table D3; percent cash equated with proportion paid out as pensions and allowances in 1958-59 from Sidorova, 1969, p. 59; republics marked with an asterisk calculated by residual. Stipends, total from appendix table E1; allocated between kolkhozniki and state employees proportionally to population. Population from appendix table A5. Primary income is defined as total income less social welfare expenditures; from table D3.

Table D11
Personal Income, Kolkhozniki and Their Dependents,
USSR and Republics, 1965 (million rubles)

	Primary Income	Cash Receipts from Social Funds			Personal Income
		Total	Stipends	Other Cash	
USSR	25,020	917	221	696	25,937
RSFSR	9,461	371	82	289	9,832
Ukraine	7,880	293	68	225	8,173
Byelorussia	1,349	34	12	22	1,383
Uzbekistan	1,498	65	15	50	1,563
Kazakhstan	381	19	3	16	400
Georgia	800	14	6	8	814
Azerbaijan	414	16	8	8	430
Lithuania	629	12	3	9	641
Moldavia	895	33	7	26	928
Latvia	318	7	1	6	325
Kirgizia	302	14	3	11	316
Tadjikistan	401	16	5	11	417
Armenia	215	7	4	3	222
Turkmenistan	329	11	3	8	340
Estonia	148	5	1	4	153

Notes and Sources: Based on the assumption that kolkhozniki and their dependents receive only stipends as cash from the state; other cash receipts come from the kolkhoz. Total kolkhoz expenditure from table D5; percent cash equated with share of cash payments from kolkhoz funds in 1966 (comprising pensions, allowances, and holiday pay) given in Sidorova, 1969, p. 61. Stipends, total from appendix table E2; allocated between kolkhozniki and state employees proportionately to population. Population from appendix table A5. Primary income is defined as total income less social welfare expenditures, from table D5.

Table D12
Personal Income, Kolkhozniki and Their Dependents,
USSR and Republics, 1970 (million rubles)

| | Primary Income | Cash Receipts from Social Funds | | | Personal Income |
		Stipends	Other	Total	
USSR	28,673	259	2,931	3,190	31,863
RSFSR	10,199	86	1,215	1,301	11,500
Ukraine	8,916	76	900	976	9,892
Byelorussia	1,528	14	172	186	1,714
Uzbekistan	2,144	25	162	187	2,331
Kazakhstan	498	5	64	69	567
Georgia	956	8	73	81	1,037
Azerbaijan	546	9	56	65	611
Lithuania	692	4	61	65	757
Moldavia	1,039	9	64	73	1,112
Latvia	340	2	32	34	374
Kirgizia	361	5	36	41	402
Tadjikistan	487	7	39	46	533
Armenia	257	4	20	24	281
Turkmenistan	549	4	23	27	576
Estonia	161	1	14	15	176

Notes and Sources: Primary Income defined as total income less social welfare expenditures; appendix table D7. Stipends total from appendix table E3, allocated between social classes and republics proportionately with population. "Other" assumed to consist primarily of pensions; total value of cash receipts inferred from *NK SSSR* '74, p. 606, and appendix table D7. Allocated between republics in proportion to the number of persons receiving pensions under the Kolkhoznik Pension Scheme, *NK SSSR* '70, p. 570.

Appendix E

The Structure of Social Welfare Expenditures in the USSR

and Republics, 1960-70

Table E1
The Structure of Social Welfare Expenditures, USSR and Republics, 1960 (million rubles)

	Education		Health, etc.	Social Security	Housing Subsidies	Holiday Pay and Premia	Total	% Cash
	Total	Stipends						
USSR	7,808	600	5,078	10,019	1,228	3,167	27,300	49.3
RSFSR	4,654	360	3,034	6,734	638	2,140	17,200	52.4
Ukraine	1,394	112	952	1,725	230	499	4,800	47.5
Byelorussia	281	17	161	196	64	72	774	36.0
Uzbekistan	262	19	174	218	24	66	744	39.8
Kazakhstan	342	29	212	368	119	145	1,186	45.2
Georgia	150	12	92	146	16	42	446	44.6
Azerbaijan	120	9	83	125	14	33	375	43.5
Lithuania	101	8	57	65	12	29	264	37.9
Moldavia	84	5	62	61	8	16	231	35.1
Latvia	88	6	56	109	26	34	313	46.3
Kirgizia	74	5	43	62	7	20	206	41.3
Tadjikistan	74	5	37	42	6	15	174	35.0
Armenia	72	5	40	70	6	19	207	44.9
Turkmenistan	56	4	39	34	41	15	185	28.1
Estonia	56	4	36	64	17	22	195	45.1

Table E2
The Structure of Social Welfare Expenditures, USSR and Republics, 1965 (million rubles)

	Education		Health, etc.	Social Security	Housing Subsidies	Holiday Pay and Premia	Total	% Cash
	Total	Stipends						
USSR	13,031	900	7,039	14,414	2,304	5,112	41,900	48.0
RSFSR	7,700	500	4,000	9,100	1,444	3,356	25,600	49.8
Ukraine	2,128	182	1,417	2,723	314	818	7,400	49.6
Byelorussia	440	33	260	366	88	128	1,282	40.5
Uzbekistan	511	37	253	386	33	122	1,305	41.1
Kazakhstan	694	38	336	586	160	259	2,035	42.9
Georgia	240	15	125	219	23	62	669	43.9
Azerbaijan	229	20	113	191	30	55	618	42.4
Lithuania	187	12	83	118	23	54	465	38.9
Moldavia	169	10	90	101	14	34	408	34.8
Latvia	140	8	74	168	41	64	487	48.0
Kirgizia	139	10	68	107	26	36	376	40.2
Tadjikistan	136	9	59	77	14	28	314	35.7
Armenia	137	12	53	108	15	35	348	43.7
Turkmenistan	95	7	60	59	51	25	290	31.0
Estonia	86	7	48	105	28	36	303	48.2

Table E3
The Structure of Social Welfare Expenditures, USSR and Republics, 1970 (million rubles)

	Education		Health, etc.	Social Security	Housing Subsidies	Holiday Pay and Premia	Total	% Cash
	Total	Stipends						
USSR	18,659	1,300	9,904	22,749	3,514	9,074	63,900	51.1
RSFSR	9,900	700	5,700	14,000	2,097	5,903	37,600	53.7
Ukraine	3,493	242	1,829	4,418	626	1,434	11,800	51.6
Byelorussia	748	51	325	628	132	251	2,084	44.5
Uzbekistan	887	63	396	680	91	236	2,290	42.7
Kazakhstan	1,138	68	506	932	264	444	3,284	43.5
Georgia	355	24	173	328	33	109	998	45.8
Azerbaijan	360	31	178	288	40	107	973	43.7
Lithuania	285	19	125	245	46	107	808	45.8
Moldavia	290	20	135	190	28	70	713	38.7
Latvia	215	12	107	279	48	108	757	51.5
Kirgizia	234	16	103	183	23	67	610	43.4
Tadjikistan	223	16	93	138	20	49	523	38.8
Armenia	225	20	87	171	11	78	572	46.8
Turkmenistan	171	10	77	91	20	47	406	36.4
Estonia	135	8	70	178	35	64	482	51.9

The expenditures on social welfare reported here correspond to the Soviet category *vyplaty i lgoty iz obshchestvennykh fondov potrebleniya*. This comprises the following six categories of expenditures (*NK SSSR* '69, p. 827):

1. Free education and the raising of qualifications (excluding State expenditures on scientific research, the press, and the arts)
2. Free medical care and visits to sanitoria (excluding amounts paid by the population)
3. Pensions, allowances, and stipends
4. Expenditures by the state on the upkeep of the housing stock (insofar as this is not covered by rental payments)
5. Holiday pay
6. Other subsidies and allowances

All expenditures are reported net of capital investment, but apparently include an allowance for depreciation of the capital stock assigned to the relevant sector. These expenditures are met out of the resources of the state, enterprises, kolkhozy, trade unions, and other organizations.

SOURCES OF THE ESTIMATES

For the following republics full details of the level and structure of social welfare expenditures are given in the publications listed:

Georgia, *G SSR v tsifrakh 1971*, p. 135 (excluding stipends)

Azerbaijan (1960, 1965), *NK Az SSR v 1960*, p. 250, *Az SSR k 50-letiyu velikogo oktyabrya*, 1967, p. 163 (excluding stipends)

Latvia, *NK La SSR v 1973*, p. 310, ibid., 1972, p. 286

Tadjikistan, *NK Ta SSR v 1971*, p. 139 (excluding stipends)

Armenia (1960, 1965), *NK Ar SSR v 1967*, p. 242 (excluding stipends)

For the following republics details of expenditures on items 1-3 above are available as follows:

RSFSR (1965, 1970), *NK RSFSR v 1973*, p. 37

Uzbekistan, *NK Uz SSR v 1971*, p. 236 (excluding stipends)

Kazakhstan, *NK Ka SSR v 1971*, p. 264

Lithuania, *Ekonomika i kultura Li SSR 1972*, p. 313

Kirgizia, *NK Ki SSR v 1971*, p. 209 (excluding stipends)

Estonia, *NK E SSR v 1971*, p. 72 (excluding stipends)

For the following republics and the USSR, data on total expenditures is available as follows:

USSR, *NK SSSR v 1972*, p. 535

Ukraine, *Uk RSR v tsifrakh 1969*, p. 143, *BSE*

Byelorussia, *NK B SSR v 1973*, p. 167 (including expenditures on pensions)

Moldavia, *NK M SSR v 1970*, p. 178

RSFSR (1960), *NK RSFSR v 1970*, p. 39

Azerbaijan (1970), *NK Az SSR v 1970*, p. 225

Armenia (1970), *BSE*

Total expenditure in Turkmenistan was derived as a residual. Details on the structure of social welfare expenditures for the USSR as a whole is given in Basov, 1967, p. 28 (1960, 1965), and Kulikov, 1972, p. 97 (1970). Moldavia from *NK MSSR v 1972*, p. 131 (excluding holiday pay and housing subsidies).

Missing data were estimated as follows:

Education

    1960, 1965: Balance of unallocated expenditure distributed in proportion to state expenditures on this heading. State expenditures from *Gos Byudzhet i byudzhety soyuznykh respublik*

    1970: Azerbaijan and Armenia, education expenditures assumed to bear the same relationship to total expenditures as in 1965. For other republics as above

Health, etc., as above

Social security as above

Stipends, distributed in proportion to budgetary subventions under this heading

Holiday Pay and non-wage-fund premia:

    1960, 5.0% of wage-bill

    1965, 5.4% of wage-bill

    1970, 6.4% of wage bill; RSFSR as residual

Housing Subsidies as residuals

The cash component of social welfare expenditures comprises stipends, pensions, and allowances, holiday pay, and non-wage-fund premia. For the USSR as a whole, the cash component is given in Basov, 1967, and Kulikov, 1972. It is also given for a number of republics. For the remainder, unallocated pensions and allowances were distributed proportionally to total expenditures on social security.

Appendix F

Direct and Indirect Taxation,

USSR and Republics, 1960-70

Table F1
Direct and Indirect Taxes, USSR and Republics, 1960 (million rubles)

	Income Tax	Bachelors' Tax	Agricultural Tax	Local Tax	Total Direct Taxes	Turnover Tax
USSR	4,637	559	398	148	5,742	31,337
RSFSR	3,077	359	188	81	3,705	20,183
Ukraine	742	96	124	35	997	5,010
Byelorussia	89	11	17	4	121	972
Uzbekistan	89	12	17	6	124	880
Kazakhstan	208	29	7	7	251	1,308
Georgia	60	8	10	3	81	432
Azerbaijan	48	7	5	2	62	376
Lithuania	40	7	5	2	54	361
Moldavia	23	3	9	1	36	326
Latvia	51	9	3	2	65	432
Kirgizia	30	3	2	1	36	236
Tadjikistan	23	3	3	1	30	206
Armenia	25	3	3	1	32	219
Turkmenistan*	24	3	3	1	31	184
Estonia	35	6	2	1	44	212
unallocated	73	—	—	—	73	

Table F2
Direct and Indirect Taxes, USSR and Republics, 1965 (million rubles)

	Income Tax	Bachelors' Tax	Agricultural Tax	Local Tax	Total Direct Taxes	Turnover Tax
USSR	6,772	566	356	175	7,869	38,664
RSFSR	4,390	355	162	94	5,001	24,289
Ukraine	1,103	97	112	41	1,353	6,344
Byelorussia	151	12	15	5	183	1,278
Uzbekistan	153	15	18	7	193	1,117
Kazakhstan	346	29	7	8	390	1,654
Georgia	84	9	11	4	108	530
Azerbaijan	73	8	5	2	88	531
Lithuania	70	9	5	2	86	527
Moldavia	41	4	5	2	52	427
Latvia	79	10	3	2	94	580
Kirgizia	42	3	3	2	50	324
Tadjikistan*	36	3	4	1	44	283
Armenia	46	3	2	2	53	276
Turkmenistan	35	3	3	1	42	238
Estonia	52	6	1	2	61	266
unallocated	71				71	

Table F3
Direct and Indirect Taxes, USSR and Republics, 1970 (million rubles)

	Income Tax	Bachelors' Tax	Agricultural Tax	Local Tax	Total Direct Taxes	Turnover Tax
USSR	11,607	803	327	196	12,933	49,380
RSFSR	7,385	495	142	105	8,127	30,224
Ukraine	1,881	134	100	46	2,161	8,577
Byelorussia	310	23	14	6	353	1,765
Uzbekistan	290	24	21	6	341	1,337
Kazakhstan	578	36	7	10	631	1,963
Georgia	145	13	11	4	173	680
Azerbaijan	123	12	6	3	144	705
Lithuania	142	15	4	3	164	720
Moldavia	87	7	5	2	101	638
Latvia	140	14	2	3	159	749
Kirgizia	82	5	3	2	92	500
Tadjikistan	66	5	5	1	77	384
Armenia*	98	6	3	2	109	474
Turkmenistan*	62	5	3	1	71	284
Estonia	93	9	1	2	105	380
unallocated	125				125	

Table F4
Direct Taxes Paid by Kolkhozniki and Others, 1960-74 (million rubles)

Category	1960	1965	1970	1974
Total Population	5,742	7,869	12,933	18,580
State Employees	5,181	7,434	12,454	18,116
Kolkhozniki	561	435	479	464

Sources: Row 1, 1960-70, appendix tables F1-F3; 1974, Schroeder and Severin, 1976, p. 658. Row 2, residual. Row 3, appendix table D1, *NK SSSR '74*, p. 606, and *NK SSSR '72*, p. 563.

NOTES AND SOURCES FOR TABLES F1-F3

Income Tax. The tax paid by the residents of individual republics is assumed to be twice the amount recorded in the budgetary statistics (cf. A. G. Zverev, 1959, p. 38, and V. F. Garbuzov, 1970, p. 35). For those republics marked with an asterisk, it is assumed that recorded receipts equal total deductions.

Bachelors' Tax. Full retention by individual republics assumed.

Agricultural Tax. Full retention by individual republics assumed.

Local Taxes. These consist of the buildings tax, state fees, collections, and a residual calculated by methods suggested in Bronson and Severin, 1973, p. 396, i.e. 50% of the first two plus all of the last. For 1970 the residual is assumed to bear the same proportion to the buildings tax as in 1965.

Data on all these taxes are from *Gosudarstvennyi byudzhet* . . . , 1966, pp. 100-213, and *Gosudarstvennyi byudzhet* . . . , 1972, pp. 107-221.

Turnover Tax. The tax paid in each republic is assumed equal to the *kontingent*, adjusted for repayments which have been allocated between the republics in proportion to the kontingent. Data from *Gosudarstvennyi byudzhet* . . . , 1966, p. 15, and ibid., 1972, p. 17.

Appendix G

The Distribution of Earnings and Incomes:

Sources and Methods

THE RECONSTRUCTION OF SOVIET EARNINGS AND INCOME DISTRIBUTIONS
This appendix provides a description of the methods used to generate numerical estimates of the various earnings and income distributions to be found in chapters 4 and 10 from the limited materials to be found in Soviet publications—the so-called Wiles-Markowski method. Soviet sources provide graphs, histograms, or more often, frequency polygons, from which all numerical information has been removed and a variety of indirect statistics. The graphical material is often badly printed, but does convey valuable information about the nature and extent of dispersion around the mean, the ruble value of which is either available or can usually be inferred from other sources. In this book, I have assumed that

a. graphs have been constructed from underlying histograms by joining the mid-points of their columns;
b. the metric scale has been used in the construction of the histograms and in reduction of the figures for printing and hence, at least on the abcissa, one would expect plausible metric lengths;
c. possibly the true mode rather than the mid-point of the modal column is used as the point of inflection; and that
d. histogram columns have bases that are integral multiples of 5 rubles.

In reconstructing any particular distribution the following steps are involved:
1. Careful measurement of the printed graph to locate points of inflection in the frequency polygon
2. Determination of the number and width of the underlying histogram columns. At this stage assumptions b and c are used to account for inaccuracies caused by bad printing, and assumption d is used to infer "missing" columns
3. Measurement of the heights of points of inflection above the abcissa to determine the height of the underlying histogram columns
4. Calculation of the total area of the underlying histogram (in square millimeters)
5. Calculation of the mean of the distribution with reference to the start of the first column of the underlying histogram

6. Approximate identification of the calculated mean with the ruble mean derived from other sources. This and assumption d locate the distribution and fix the scale of the abcissa

Details of the sources of particular diagrams and the measurements involved in the construction of individual distributions are given below.

G1. INCOME DISTRIBUTIONS, NONAGRICULTURAL POPULATION

Sources: Rabkina and Rimashevskaya, 1972, p. 120, and Rimashevskaya, 1965, p. 61. The 1958 distribution was derived from a distribution of "earnings" in that year, using a set of decile ratio coefficients given in Rabkina and Rimashevskaya, 1972, p. 215. The basic characteristics of the reconstruction are

	1958 Earnings	1967 Individuals	1967 Families
Scale (= 5 rubles)	2mm	3mm	3mm
Histogram origin	20 R	20 R	20 R
Number of columns[a]	9	12(11)	12(11)
Upper limit	260 R	170 R	170 R

a. Figures in parentheses indicate the number of identified points of inflection in the printed diagram. Others have been added to make the scale fit in accordance with assumption d.

The implied ruble intervals on the abscissa are
1958 (Earnings): 4 x 10, 2 x 20, 40, 2 x 60
1967 (Both Distributions): 6 x 5, 2 x 10, 3 x 20, 40

The distributions were located by reference to earnings distributions and the set of decile ratio coefficients referred to above.

G2. INCOME DISTRIBUTIONS, KOLKHOZNIKI

Source: Rabkina and Rimashevskaya, 1972, pp. 122-23. Neither of the scales derived is particularly plausible on numerological grounds, but both are as good as possible alternatives. Location was finally determined on the basis of estimates of personal income given in chapter 3. The basic characteristics are

	1965	1968
Scale (= 5 rubles)	3mm	3mm
Histogram origin	5 R	15 R
Number of columns	12	12
Upper limit	150 R	150 R

The implied ruble intervals on the abscissa are
1965: 6 x 5, 3 x 10, 35, 2 x 25
1968: 6 x 5, 10, 15, 4 x 20

G3. EARNINGS DISTRIBUTIONS, STATE EMPLOYEES

1956-59, 1964. Source, Shvyrkov and Aidina, 1968, p. 233. Shvyrkov actually prints the histograms; reconstruction involves determination of location and scale. The basic characteristics are

	1956	1957	1959	1964
Scale (= 5 rubles)	3mm	3mm	2mm	2mm
Histogram origin	10 R	10 R	15 R	20 R
Number of columns	14	15	14	17
Upper limit	220 R	220 R	225 R	230 R

The implied ruble intervals on the abscissa are
   1956: 15, 3 x 5, 6 x 15, 3 x 20, 30
   1957: 15, 3 x 5, 7 x 15, 3 x 20, 15
   1959: 15, 3 x 5, 10, 5 x 15, 2 x 20, 25, 30
   1964: 15, 5 x 5, 6 x 10, 15, 20, 25, 30, 25

As an indication of the adequacy of these reconstructions, the parameters of a log-normal distribution fitted to my estimates may be compared with those given by Shvyrkov. The parameters of the reconstructions were estimated by the quantile method. (For details see Aitchison and Brown, 1957, pp. 40-42; quantiles were estimated on the assumption that observations were uniformly distributed within intervals.)

	Shvyrkov				Fitted			
	1956	1957	1959	1964	1956	1957	1959	1964
m	4.076	4.147	4.215	4.366	4.110	4.158	4.241	4.433
s	0.58	0.56	0.54	0.52	0.64	0.61	0.59	0.47

1966-68. Source, Rabkina and Rimashevskaya, 1972, pp. 138, 194. Only the polygons are given, so the underlying histograms had to be inferred for these years. The basic characteristics are

	1966	1968
Scale (= 10 R)	4mm	3mm
Histogram origin	30 R	40 R
Number of columns	11(9)	13
Upper limit	260 R	280 R

The implied ruble intervals on the abscissa are
   1966: 10, 20, 4 x 10, 3 x 20, 40, 60
   1968: 7 x 10, 2 x 20, 10, 40, 30, 50

Rabkina and Rimashevskaya give the following equations (p. 250) describing the mean and decile ratio as functions of time. These may be used to infer the values of these parameters in the underlying histograms, and the latter may be compared with their analogues derived from the reconstructions.

$$\bar{x}(t) = \exp(3.829 + 0.0376t)$$
$$\log K(t) = \exp(0.6742 - 0.0242t)$$

where $K(t)$ is the decile ratio in year t and $t = 0$ in 1945. Substituting, one obtains

	Rabkina and Rimashevskaya		Fitted	
	1966	1968	1966	1968
$\bar{x}$	101.40	109.27	98.7	110.9
K	3.16	2.98	3.4	2.8

1961, 1970. Derived from a log-normal distribution based on the parameters implied by the above equations.

G4.   EARNINGS DISTRIBUTIONS, INDUSTRIAL EMPLOYEES

Source: Rabkina and Rimashevskaya, 1972, pp. 79, 198, 202. The basic features of the reconstructions are

	Employees		Workers	
	1961	1964	1961	1968
Scale (= 10 rubles)	4mm	4mm	3mm	3mm
Histogram origin	30 R	20 R	20 R	50 R
Number of columns	13(12)	13(10)	14	15
Upper limit	300 R	320 R	300 R	300 R

The implied ruble scales on the abscissa are:
  1961 (Employees): 9 x 10, 2 x 20, 40, 100
  1964 (Employees): 8 x 10, 3 x 20, 40, 120
  1961 (Workers): 8 x 10, 5 x 20, 100
  1968 (Workers): 11 x 10, 2 x 20, 2 x 50

The remaining distributions given in chapter 10 were derived from those given above by using employment weights from *Trud v SSSR*, 1968, various pages.

Notes

CHAPTER 1

1 Sociologists have also contributed to this venture. In Britain, it was Titmuss's classic study *Income Distribution and Social Change* that effectively challenged the adequacy of income distribution statistics based upon tax returns prepared by the Inland Revenue. In it he questioned the widely held belief that there had been a significant reduction in inequality in Britain since the Second World War. In so doing, he prompted a number of others to construct alternative estimates of the distribution of income in the United Kingdom.

2 Soviet authors do not use the Russian word for poverty to describe the condition of the least-well-off families in the USSR. Literally, *maloobespechennost* means possessing few resources, but throughout this book I have translated it as poverty.

3 There is a brief history of the use of normative budgets in the USSR in Sarkisyan and Kuznetsova, 1967, pp. 8-18. Soviet views on the relativity of consumer preferences and tastes are discussed further in McAuley, 1979. For a more general discussion of the problems associated with a definition of poverty see Plotnick, 1975, pp. 31-46.

4 Sarkisyan and Kuznetsova, 1967, p. 66. The estimate of the cost of the MMS budget for a single worker was derived by grossing up per capita expenditures on food and clothing by the reciprocal of the adult equivalents given by Kapustin and Kuznetsova, 1972, pp. 53, 56; the average of these weights was used for other expenditures. If it is assumed that there are no economies of scale in the consumption of other services, the cost of subsistence for a single worker rises to 65 rubles a month.

5 *Nauchno-issledovatelskii Institut Truda*, the research institute of the State Committee on Labor and Wages (the Soviet equivalent of a Ministry of Labor).

CHAPTER 2

1 In fact, Khrushchev was replaced in October 1964, but system inertia allows one to ascribe the results of the 1960-65 period to his government rather than attempting to estimate the level and structure of income in 1964.

2 Sidorova, 1969, p. 148, and 1972, p. 107. See appendix D for details. Sidorova's estimates are presumably based on unpublished family budget survey data.

357

There is reason to believe that the family budget survey suffers from significant upward bias (see below, pp. 51–53, for details), but since this is the source used by Soviet official statisticians for estimates of private agricultural output, there is apparently no way of eliminating the bias. See Matyukha, 1973, p. 72.

3 Some evidence in support of the suggestion that kolkhoznik private plots are more productive than those of other groups (or at least are used more intensively) is given by the notional allowances made for the ownership of a private plot in the computation of family income for the purposes of determining entitlement to the family income supplement. It has been reported in a German-language newspaper in Kazakhstan that income from a private plot will be assessed on the following scale: kolkhozniki, 60 rubles a month; state employees in rural areas, 50 rubles a month; state employees in worker settlements, 35 rubles a month; state employees in urban areas, 5 rubles a month. *Freundschaft*, 31 October 1974, quoted by Bush, 1975, p. 60. Of course these differentials may only reflect the traditional pro-urban bias of the Soviet government.

4 Because, legally, kolkhozniki are members of cooperatives and are thus owners of the means of production, they are not considered part of the working class.

5 Figures in the next chapter suggest that the monthly money income of nonagricultural state employees in 1958 was 48.4 rubles. This is substantially higher than the 40 rubles a month in 1960 implied by table 2.4 for all state employees. Similarly, the 62.6 rubles a month for nonagricultural state employees in 1967 is much higher than the 50 rubles implied by table 2.4 for 1965. It is unlikely that the exclusion of sovkhozniki and their dependents would make such a difference. See below, chapter 3, p. 57, for details of the derivation; the difference may be in part a result of an upward bias in the estimates of chapter 3 due to the fact that they are derived from a sample survey rather than from national income accounts.

6 *Itogi*, 1970, vol. 7, p. 252. In Tadjikistan it was as high as 34.5%, while in Estonia it was only 30.4%; in other Baltic republics it was even lower. On the other hand, it is reported that in a survey of schoolchildren in Estonia, those coming from mixed (father-worker, mother-specialist) families were twice as numerous in first grade as in the graduating class. Those from another type (father-worker, mother-clerical) were 30% more common in the former group. This is taken to imply increasing heterogeneity in the Soviet working class. See Filippov, 1975, p. 20.

7 It is reported (in an article not otherwise distinguished for methodological sophistication and clarity) that of a sample drawn from the artistic intelligentsia in Sverdlovsk and Chelyabinsk, one-third were married to workers (male or female) and a further 13% to kolkhozniki/kolkhoznitsy. See Kopyrin, 1975, p. 77.

8 Inferred from *NK SSSR* '74, p. 605. Personal income is defined as total income less expenditure on health, education, etc., from social consumption funds.

9 *Itogi*, 1970, vol. 7, p. 252, and Sarkisyan, 1972, p. 190. Pure families are those in which all employed persons are in the same occupational group. It is not possible to calculate family size allowing for nonresident members. Of course,

Sarkisyan's comment may not provide independent confirmation: he himself may have assumed that urban and industrial workers were the same.

10 Earnings data inferred from table 1 and *NK SSSR* '72, p. 562, ibid. '74, p. 605. Wage data from *NK SSSR* '65, p. 566, ibid. '70, p. 518, and ibid. '74, p. 561. For 1960 it was assumed that holiday pay bore the proportion to annual earnings as in 1965. The structure figures relate to income per family, but of course for any given year they apply equally to total income or income per capita.

11 Cf. *NK SSSR* '65, p. 566, ibid. '74, p. 561. The numbers of workers supposedly rose from 1.6 per family to 1.8; these figures relate to the state sector as a whole and not just to industrial workers.

12 Calculated from data in *Trud*, 1968, and *NK SSSR*, various years. In 1960-65 industrial wages grew at an annual average rate of 2.5%; in 1965-70 the rate was 5.1%.

CHAPTER 3

1 Much of the material in this chapter is taken from McAuley, 1977.

2 A detailed history of family budget studies in the Soviet Union is given in Matyukha, 1967. The author has been director of the section of the CSA responsible for the family budget survey for a number of years. Details of sample sizes are taken from Matyukha, 1973, p. 72.

3 Sidorova, 1969, p. 140. The actual comparison was carried out by V. V. Shvyrkov and reported in *Zakonomernosti potrebleniya promyshlennykh i prodovolstvennykh tovarov*, Moscow, 1965, p. 28.

4 Matyukha, 1973, p. 78. If this suggestion is correct, the practice differs from that used in the computation of gross agricultural output, where average realization prices are used. This makes it difficult to compare estimates of subsistence consumption for income purposes with those constructed from the production point of view. Since state retail prices differ from realization prices (a combination of state purchase and collective farm market prices) it also means that measured income, particularly for kolkhozniki, will depend upon whether output is sold or consumed by the family.

5 Zhutkovskaya, 1966, p. 108, claims that an allowance for the imputed rent of free accommodation is included in income, but there is no mention of accommodation in the copy of the survey questionnaire given in Matyukha, 1960, and this claim should be treated with caution.

6 This figure is taken from *Trud v SSSR*, Moscow, 1968, p. 137; according to *Narkhoz SSSR* '73, pp. 586-87, the increase was 34.6%. No explanation has been given for differences between the two series.

7 The 1965 distribution given here differs from that in McAuley, 1977; the whole distribution has been shifted approximately 5 rubles to the left.

8 Komarov and Chernyavskii, 1973, p. 71. The figures given refer only to workers (*rabochiye*), but I assume that those for all nonagricultural state employees would not have been too different.

9 Wiles, 1974, p. 48, gives the following estimates of decile ratios: Poland 3.1; Hungary 3.0; Czechoslovakia 3.1; Bulgaria 2.7; United Kingdom (1969) 3.4; Italy (1969) 5.9; USA (1968) 6.7. For the USSR, his estimate is 3.5-3.7.

10 Matthews, 1975, gives examples of the salaries that certain members of the Soviet elite are reported to receive. They range from about 300 rubles a month for junior officials of the Central Committee up to 900 rubles for the first secretary—to which should be added various allowances.

CHAPTER 4

1 When allowance is made for changes in the cost of living, the number with an income below 30 rubles a month (32.75, in 1965 rubles) declined by 24.4 million, 59.6% of the 1958 total, while the number with incomes below 50 rubles (45.8, in 1958 prices) fell by 18.4 million, 23.2% of the total.

2 The figures given in table 4.3 were derived from data on the proportion of individuals in households of different sizes in each income class and in the sample as a whole. These were adjusted to take account of the number of single persons. This calculation gave the proportions 0.188 : 0.654 : 0.158 for groups I-III. These appear consistent with other cross-classifications. The weights differ from the relative shares in table 4.3, since they refer to individuals rather than households.

3 Midpoints of the intervals were chosen to ensure that the average given in table 4.3 coincided with that in table 3.2.

4 A poverty level of 25-30 rubles per month per capita is given some support by early analyses of time budgets; one of these used the intervals (-30), (30-50), (75-100), and (100-) rubles. See G. S. Petrosyan, *Vnerabochee vremya trudyashchikhsya v SSSR* (Moscow, 1965), pp. 62, 110. The surveys themselves were conducted in 1959-62.

5 In 1970, 44.8% of urban workers, 44.3% of rural workers, and 44.6% of workers in the USSR as a whole were women. (In each case workers = *rabochiye*.) See *Itogi*, 1970, vol. 5, p. 26.

6 The Worsted Mill at Pavlovskii Posad was used by Vasil'eva in her study of changes in the standard of living since the revolution. She chose it because it had previously been studied and described by tsarist factory inspectors and by its medical officer (*sanitarnyi vrach*). See Vasil'eva, 1965.

7 The midpoints were 38.6 rubles and 94.0 rubles for the first and third classes respectively.

8 Gordon and Klopov define income to consist of *regular* receipts—wages, pensions, stipends, maintenance payments (*alimenty*), and other allowances. The 1958 survey defined income to consist of money received in the month preceding interview. Gordon and Klopov claim that regular receipts make up more than 90% of income (1972, p. 35).

9 In a recent legal text, the minimum wage was defined as "that limit of remuneration below which the labor of workers who conscientiously fulfill their obligations cannot fall" (Livshits, 1972, p. 228). I think it unlikely that an individual who regularly failed to fulfill his norms or whatever would retain his job.

10 On the other hand, Rabkina and Rimashevskaya claim that "research has shown that low-paid workers are primarily women engaged in unskilled or

low-skill occupations." Women tend to predominate in such occupations because "they have not yet been able to overcome the contradiction between
woman-as-mother and woman-as-worker" (1972, p. 47). It is to be expected
that the single mother would suffer from this contradiction in a peculiarly
acute form. But this also implies that such women would have benefited significantly from successive increases in the minimum wage. Thus there may
have been a real reduction in the incidence of poverty among incomplete
families.

11 Rabkina and Rimashevskaya do not give ruble intervals for either the wage
classes or the income classes in terms of which they present their data, nor do
they give the marginal totals. The figures in table 4.9 were derived as follows.
It was assumed that both the ruble intervals and the marginal totals for per
capita incomes were the same as in the Gordon and Klopov large-town sample.
This yields marginal totals for the wage distribution, which were used to calculate quantiles from the distribution of industrial workers by earnings in
1968 (see table 9.6). The wage class boundaries given in table 4.9 correspond
to the following percentiles: 90 R, 30.1%; 150 R, 75.7%; 160 R, 85.1%. Since
the minimum wage was raised from 40-45 rubles to 60 rubles a month in 1968
and since the sample refers to 1967-68, it would seem to follow that the wage
classes are, if anything, too high.

12 Social welfare expenditures consist of transfer payments (pensions, sick pay,
etc.) and state expenditures on health, education, and so on. See below, chapter 11 and appendix E, for more details.

13 Maslov and most of those who quote him refer only to "Enterprise I" and
"Enterprise II" or to "Food Industry" and "Heavy Industry"; the identities of
the plants involved are given in Pisarev, 1966, pp. 99-100.

14 See, for example, Mstislavskii, 1961, p. 94; Ozeran, 1962, p. 44; Kapustin,
1962, p. 194; Ekonomicheskaya gazeta, no. 1, 1964, p. 27; Maslov, 1965, p.
31; Krylov, 1966, p. 135; Pisarev, 1966, pp. 99-100; and Gubareva, 1968, p.
124. It is probably also the source of figures quoted in Burova, 1963, p. 79,
and Kruk and Chertkov, 1964, p. 28.

15 Wiles and Markowski, 1971, p. 509. In 1961 the ruble was converted so that
one new ruble equalled ten old ones.

16 Average earnings in the sample were 82.3 rubles per employed person per
month. In 1960, average earnings in the textile industry for the USSR as a
whole were 70.5 rubles a month, and those for workers (rabochiye) were
71.2 rubles. In the same year, average industrial earnings were 91.3 rubles a
month (workers, 89.8 rubles), and average earnings in the state sector were
80.1 rubles (Trud v SSSR, pp. 137-43). Thus the sample was relatively poor in
comparison with other industrial personnel but about as well-off as other state
employees.

17 Writing in 1973, T. I. Mamontova claims that non-cash benefits go primarily
to the less-well-off, cash benefits go rather more to the better-off, and social
welfare benefits in total, per capita, are higher in more affluent families
(Mamontova, 1973, p. 80).

CHAPTER 5

1 For an account of the methods used in the compilation of both versions, see Gosplan SSSR, *Metodicheskiye ukazaniya* . . . , 1969, pp. 524-46. For a critical evaluation of the BMIEP and its compilation, see Arouca, 1974.

2 Karapetyan and Rimashevskaya, 1969, p. 124. My own calculations suggest that in the mid sixties, for Latvia, expenditures calculated in this way may have exceeded incomes by as much as 20%.

3 From table 5.1 it can be seen that the poorest republics do rather better in terms of total income than in terms of personal income. This might be taken to imply that social consumption expenditures act as an equalizing force, contrary to the conclusion reached below. The apparent inconsistency depends upon the interpretation given to the concept of equalization.

4 For a discussion of some of the issues involved, see Atkinson, 1975, pp. 42ff. Soviet approaches to this question are dealt with in McAuley, 1978.

5 Clayton, 1975, p. 40. The figures themselves were produced by J. Williamson in "Regional Inequality and the Process of National Development," in L. Needleman, ed., *Regional Analysis* (1968), pp. 99-158. Williamson reports that the coefficients of variation were Australia 5.8%, New Zealand 6.3%, United Kingdom 14.1%, USA 18.2%, Japan 24.4%, and France 28.3%. Clayton's figures show that for the USSR the analogous figure was 12.4%.

6 Soviet rental payments were calculated on the assumption that the family of four occupied the "sanitary minimum" of 36 square meters and paid a rent of 13 kopeks per square meter per month. See Kapustin and Kuznetsova, 1972, p. 56. For the United Kingdom expenditure patterns, see *Economic Trends*, September 1975, p. 10.

7 There is a brief history of this topic in Batkaev and Markov, 1964, pp. 179-80.

8 For a detailed list of raiony, see Spravochnik ekonomista . . . , 1970, pp. 269-70. See also Batkaev and Markov, 1964, p. 184.

CHAPTER 6

1 Sidorova, 1969 and 1972. Some of this material has been used by Gertrude Schroeder in her studies of republican differences in living standards. See Schroeder, 1973 and 1974.

2 That is, for example, all the entries for kolkhoz labor payments in 1960 were increased by 2.18% (= 100/97.87), and so on.

3 Using population weights, the coefficient of variation of total income per capita was 15.8% in 1960 and 20.8% in 1970, showing the same rising trend as the figures in table 6.3.

4 As a consequence of the way in which the figures were derived, state employee earnings include receipts from the financial system. They were not large for the republics as a whole, some 2-3% of total income. Kolkhoznik earnings refer to payments by collective farms; the earnings of dependents in state employment and receipts from the financial system are included in other sources of income. These inadequacies should not result in a rejection of the conclusion given above.

5 The comparison is based on the Soviet concept of real income, which differs from the ones used here. It is also not clear whether the figures refer to income per capita or income per person employed. See Drank, 1972, p. 81.

CHAPTER 7

1 As pointed out in chapter 1, Atkinson's results call the use of this statistic into question. But these problems will be ignored here.

2 Of course, policies which increase mean incomes while leaving the variance unchanged in ruble terms will also reduce the coefficient of variation. Some of these policies were considered in chapter 2. No further attention will be paid to this point here.

3 The discussion in sections 7.2–7.6 is more heavily statistical than that in the rest of the book. Readers interested only in the conclusions and not in the evidence on which they are based should turn to section 7.7, where the argument of the chapter is summarized.

4 This is not quite the case. The relationship described in the text is derived from the regression equation. Errors, and possibly, omitted variables, meant that some republics with a per capita primary income below 400 rubles a year had negative net receipts in 1965, and also that some of those with an average primary income above 400 rubles had positive receipts.

CHAPTER 8

1 Schroeder and Severin, 1976, p. 652. There was some rise in the rate of inflation in the seventies, but this can surely be attributed to other causes. Such price stability is a postwar phenomenon in the USSR; between 1928 and 1940 the official retail price index rose by 637%, and there was an 86% rise between 1940 and 1950 (A. N. Malafeyev, *Istoriya tsenoobrazovaniya v SSSR 1917-1963* [Moscow, 1964], p. 407). I believe that the difference in the behavior of prices in the two periods 1928-50 and 1950-75 reflects a real difference in the level of excess demand in the system, brought about by improvements in control techniques.

2 The issues raised in this section are discussed at greater length in Bergson, 1944, pp. 8-25. In this section I use *wages* to refer to both wages and salaries. From a theoretical point of view, administrative distinctions in the form in which employment income is distributed are unimportant, and the use of a single word rather than a clumsy circumlocution is clearer.

3 The analysis in the text abstracts from the problem of money illusion that may in practice be extremely important. Also, it is possible that high wages are taken as an indicator of power or prestige. If so, wages will be sought by those interested in these goals irrespective of the way that goods and services are distributed. Further, if certain jobs carry fringe benefits or perquisites of office, nominal wages will determine occupational choice only in part, provided the applicant knows of those benefits. The analysis given above is clearly a simplification.

4 Marx referred to the lower and higher stages of socialism. His views on the

question of earnings differentials are most adequately set out in the *Critique of the Gotha Program*. The International Publishers edition (New York, 1966) also contains Lenin's marginal notes. See, especially, pp. 59 ff.

5 This, at least, was the formal position. Because very few workers were employed on jobs classified into the lowest skill grades, effective differentials were less than formal ones. See Kirsch, 1972, pp. 94 ff.

6 For an instance of this *ex-post* justification of the Soviet wage structure see Batkaev and Markov, 1964, pp. 110-24.

7 Maier, 1968, pp. 33 ff. For a fuller discussion of Maier's ideas, see Kirsch, 1972, pp. 112-17. The ideas themselves echo some of Strumilin's work in the twenties.

8 There is an extended discussion of the Soviet approach to job evaluation in Batkaev and Markov, 1964, pp. 71-91; see also Kirsch, 1972, pp. 81 ff.

9 Kapustin, 1968, p. 311. In practice, the situation is rather more complex: individuals transferred temporarily to less-skilled work are usually paid at the higher rate. For details see "O vyplate mezhrazryadnoi raznitsy" in *Spravochnik ekonomista i planovika promyshlennogo predpriyatiya* (Moscow, 1964), pp. 416-17.

10 See Kirsch, 1972, p. 104, and the references cited there. On the other hand, I. Kaplan ("Ucheba i kvalifikatsiya," *Trud*, 11 April 1966) states that the number of workers in the highest skill grades that the enterprise is permitted to employ is strictly limited by the plan, and on the basis of a sample of 3,500 workers in engineering plants in Leningrad (conducted in 1965), Blyakhman reports that only 40% of grade VI work was undertaken by workers with that level of skill. This suggests that financial control might be the cause of the observed queue for high-skill, high-wage jobs. See Blyakhman, Sochilin, and Shkaratan, 1968, p. 39.

11 Commenting on this situation in 1962-64, Batkaev and Markov remarked that differences between the sectors "could scarcely be explained by the characteristics of the branches in question" (Batkaev and Markov, 1964, p. 106). See also Kirsch, 1972, p. 35.

12 Batkaev and Markov, 1964, p. 100. Under this heading they include unpleasant or monotonous work, dirty work, and jobs without prospects.

13 Kapustin, 1974, p. 271, states that the three-tier system was extended to the leather, light, food, and paper-cellulose industries, and possibly to others.

14 There is an extended discussion of the role of piecework and various bonus systems in Soviet industry in Kirsch, 1972, pp. 31-43.

15 Blyakhman et al., 1965, p. 72. The sample, however, should not be thought of as representative of either Leningrad industry or of industry in the USSR as a whole; it is probably representative of separations in Leningrad and it may be representative of separations in the USSR as a whole.

16 Hoeffding quotes the example of machine tool production, which was by no means unique. The relevant ministry was responsible for only 55 of the 171 plants primarily engaged in the industry in 1957; the remainder were distributed among nineteen other ministries, each with its own wage scale or scales. Hoeffding, 1959, p. 72. See also Kirsch, 1972, pp. 2-4.

17 In Russian, *povysheniye zarabotnoi platy nizkooplachivaemykh rabochikh i*

sluzhashchikh (Volkov, 1974, p. 23). Soviet commentators do not always distinguish clearly between wage rates and earnings, although context can sometimes help. In view of the difficulty in deciding whether intra-industrial differentials were reduced or increased in 1956-61, this ambiguity is unfortunate.

18 Blyakhman reports that labor turnover in Soviet industry increased from 15% to 19% per annum between 1950 and 1960; in Leningrad itself, turnover went up from 15.8% in 1958-59 to 18% in 1961. He suggests that this increase can be explained by the removal of administrative restrictions on mobility, and claims that the reform itself led to a decline in turnover in such industries as coal mining. Since the restrictions were lifted in 1956, the Leningrad increase certainly occurred rather late to be ascribed to this cause. See Blyakhman et al., 1965, pp. 15-16.

19 When salaries in education and health were raised in 1964-65, the differential was abolished in these sectors. Maier, 1968, p. 100.

20 The sectors covered were engineering, light industry, sugar refining, and canning. They accounted for slightly more than half of industrial employment at the time. See Danilov, 1973, p. 189.

21 Danilov, 1973, p. 144. The Russian terms for these two categories are *slesari* and *elektromontery*; their relative wages gave rise to continuing problems throughout the sixties. See Kirsch, 1972, pp. 138-42.

22 Kapustin, 1974, p. 266, claims that "for a period of time [after 1968] there developed a certain equalization [*uravnitelnost*] of wages and salaries." Sukharevskii, 1974, p. 226, states that the 1968 wage hike "led to excessive narrowing [*sblizheniye*] in the wages of certain groups of state employees, which to a large extent will be eliminated with the introduction of a minimum wage of 70 rubles a month and when the wages and salaries of the middle-paid are increased during the ninth five-year plan."

23 For an assessment of attitudes among Soviet workers based on underground and emigré sources, see Holubenko, 1975. In my opinion, this account relies too heavily upon rumors of what happened in Novocherkask and Rostov in 1962.

CHAPTER 9

1 The crude participation rates given above may be misleading, since the occupied population includes those who are gainfully employed but are above retirement age.

2 The figures in table 9.1 exclude "moonlighting," as well as most of the employment in the grey areas of the so-called second economy that has received a good deal of attention recently.

3 *Industry* here refers to the Soviet definition, which corresponds approximately to manufacturing, mining, and quarrying.

4 Each year in the first list is mentioned in at least two of the following sources: Karapetyan and Rimashevskaya, 1969, p. 92; Krushevskii, 1968, p. 87; Matyukha, 1973, p. 77; and Rimashevskaya, 1965, p. 46. Krushevskii also mentions 1957, and there is a histogram for that year in Shvyrkov and Aidina, 1968, p. 234. Matyukha also refers to 1972. No explicit mention of 1968 or 1970 has been found, but there is a frequency polygon for the first year in

Rabkina and Rimashevskaya, 1972, p. 194, and statistics relating to the second year are given in Sarkisyan, 1972, pp. 132-33.

5 With the exception of the figures for 1961 and 1970, the distributions in table 9.2 are the same as those given in McAuley, 1977.

6 There is also a substantial deviation, in table 9.4, between the two series on average earnings for 1970; but I suspect that this is due to the way in which the distribution for this year has been derived.

7 Actually, this is misleading. The earnings figures presumably relate to March or possibly April 1964, while the new wage and salary scales were not introduced in education and health, etc., until May of that year. The reduction in inequality should therefore be attributed to reform in other sectors—unless, of course, the wage census was held late in that year.

8 The best estimate of the ninety-fifth percentile of the earnings distribution of the state sector as a whole is 243.7 rubles. This is based on the assumption that the frequencies in the top two income classes are the average of those in 1959 and 1964.

9 The first set are taken from *Trud*, 1968, pp. 140 ff., and the second from *Vestnik Statistiki*, no. 4, 1971, pp. 87-88, no. 11, 1972, pp. 93-94, no. 9, 1974, pp. 93-95, and no. 9, 1975, pp. 92-94. Coverage figures relate to 1965 in both instances.

10 Matthews, 1975, pp. 135-39, provides estimates of the salaries of top officials, based to some extent on rumors circulating within the USSR.

11 The scale provides for increments after five, ten, and twenty-five years' experience. See *Spravochnik po zarabotnoi . . .* , 1970, p. 115.

12 The figure for basic wages was calculated by applying the basic-wage earnings relationship for industry as a whole (derived in the next chapter) to average earnings in machine building.

13 Kukulevich quotes a regulation of the State Committee on Labor and Wages and the VTsSPS of 1963 relating to the lumber industry (no. 124, p. 11, of 6 May 1963) which sets 60% of basic wages as the upper limit for the premia of any employee (*rabotnik*). See Kukulevich, 1966, p. 164.

14 *Mladshii obsluzhivayushchii personal:* sweepers, cleaners, wardrobe attendants, doormen, lift operators, night watchmen, and so on.

CHAPTER 10

1 This coincides with Soviet estimates for the state sector as a whole. "Even with unchanged conditions for the payment of labor, as a result of increases in labor productivity, productive efficiency, and labor skills, average earnings of state employees increase by 1-1.5% per annum." Sukharevskii, 1974, p. 208.

2 For industry as a whole, the changes in skill grades were as follows:

Skill Scale	% of Labor Force Covered		Average Skill Grade	
	1962	1972	1962	1972
VI	72	74	3.0	3.3
VII	7	10	4.1	4.4
VIII	10	5	4.9	5.4
X	2	1	5.9	6.2
No Scale	9	10	—	—

Source: *Vestnik statistiki*, no. 10, 1970, pp. 76-77, and no. 11, 1973, pp. 78-79.

3 The approach used here is based on a model developed in Karapetyan, 1968, pp. 7-14. To keep the calculations simple it was assumed that average skill levels for industry as a whole were adequately represented by those on the VI-point scale.

CHAPTER 11

1 For a discussion of the role of the family in the Soviet welfare system and the way it has changed since the revolution, see Madison, 1968, pp. 147-77. See also Madison, 1972, pp. 836-39.

2 There is an account of the history of pension provision in the USSR before 1955 in Acharkan, 1965, pp. 29-48.

3 The 1956 law, *zakon*, its associated decree, *polozheniye*, and most of the relevant subsequent amendments and regulations are reprinted in Zakharov and Piskov, 1972; the same volume also contains most of the documents on pension provision for collective farmers.

4 Employment record and uninterrupted employment record in particular enterprises play an important role in determining both entitlement and the value of benefits in the Soviet system. Because the Russian word is relatively simple and because the concept can only be expressed by a clumsy circumlocution in English, I shall use *stazh* frequently for the rest of this chapter.

5 In 1960, total expenditures on pensions amounted to 7.1 billion rubles; there were 5.4 million old-age pensioners and 21.9 million pensioners in all, implying a total of 4.2 billion rubles divided among 16.5 million recipients. If it is assumed that the average old-age pension was 42 rubles a month, the average value of other pensions rises to 22 rubles. See tables 11.1 and 11.3.

6 There is no mention of kolkhoznitsy in the 1955 *Polozheniye*. See Zakharov, 1966, p. 11.

7 Mechanizers cover tractor drivers, chauffeurs, maintenance mechanics, electricians, etc. See Zakharov and Piskov, 1972, p. 302.

8 Or rather, "if the child's mother lives in a rural area and is a member of a kolkhoz, then only the grant for the layette is provided." Piskov, 1964, p. 56.

9 In 1966, only 30% of kolkhozniki received paid holidays. See Mamontova, 1973, p. 72.

10 The first two rows of the table are taken from a Soviet table recording expenditure from the state social insurance budget, and the final row refers to the total value of allowances, *posobiya*, in social consumption. According to Soviet convention, transfers to military or collective farm households are not part of *state* social insurance but are part of social security. See Akhromenko, 1967, pp. 5–9.

11 Such calculations underlie Vasilieva's estimates of the contribution that free services made to the living standards of textile workers in Pavlovskii Posad in 1960, for example, or Zemlyanskii's estimates of the contribution of social consumption to income for families of different sizes referred to in chapter 4 above.

12 For example, it is claimed that although 40–45% of the population live in rural areas, only 11% of doctors are to be found there. NIIT claims that after allowing for the use of urban facilities, rural consumption of medical services is only 89% of that of the urban population. See Taichinova, 1974, p. 57.

13 According to a 1967 survey (presumably the survey of incomes, family composition, and housing conditions) 27% of worker households in towns and urban settlements and 28% of worker households in rural areas possessed more than nine square meters of housing space per person; see Sarkisyan, 1972, p. 140. Although both Soviet and Western analysts use the figure of nine square meters as the norm, in fact the sanitary norm differs between republics.

14 On the basis of a fairly crude subdivision of the population age groups given in the census, and using Mamontova's figures, one obtains the estimate of 35,000 rural children under the age of three in preschool care facilities and 913,000 urban children in the same category. These figures imply that approximately 0.5% of rural children and 15.4% of urban children under the age of three are provided for by the state in this way.

15 The figure for the cost to the state is given by Lantsev, 1974, p. 129. Basov, 1967, p. 65, suggests that parental contributions cover some 22% of the total cost, and Rzhanitsyna, 1973, p. 79, claims that the state meets more than 75% of the cost of preschool child care facilities.

16 The account of the Soviet tax system given in this section is based on Pashkevich and Gilitskii, 1968, pp. 220–59. Although increases in the minimum wage have entailed some changes in exemption limits and tax rates on lower levels of income, there has been no change in the basic structure of the system.

17 The figures given in this and subsequent examples refer, of course, to the situation as it was in 1968.

CHAPTER 12

1 Medvedev, 1975, p. 225. This book was originally published in Russian in Amsterdam in 1972 and probably written in 1969-71. The above passage is from the English translation.

2 For example, Brezhnev is reported to have written in 1972, "To care about the welfare of the workers does not mean that we have to play Santa Claus [*byt dobrymi dyadyushkami*] to all state employees irrespective of the contribution they make to social production. Wages should be *earned* by all." Cited in Volkov, 1974, p. 34 (emphasis in the original).

3 See W. Kornhauser, *The Politics of Mass Society*, London, 1959.

4 See, for example, Lane, 1971, table 19, p. 113. Even in Sverdlovsk, according to this table, nonmanual workers and their children make up more than three-quarters of the students at the university proper; they also predominate in the Law Institute, the Teachers' Institute, and the Conservatory.

5 See Lane, 1971, pp. 55-59. There is no mention of peasants or anything similar in the index to Parkin, 1971.

Glossary

alimenty: maintenance payments
apparat: party; machinery of state
bytovaya travma: domestic injury
dacha: summer residence in resort area
dotatsiya: state grant or subsidy
diapazon, pl. *diapazony*: maximum spread
Edinyi tarifno-kvalifikatsionnyi spravochnik skvoznykh professii: *Comprehensive Guide to Skill Rates in All Professions.*
fond vosproizvodstva rabochei sily: fund for the reproduction of labor power
invalidnost: injury, disability
ITR (inzhenerno-tekhnicheskiye rabotniki): those whose jobs involve technical control and management of production; also qualified engineers, technicians, and supervisory personnel (e.g., foremen)
izba, pl. *izby*: traditional peasant huts in rural areas
kolkhoz, pl. *kolkhozy*: collective farm
kolkhoznik, pl. *kolkhozniki*: collective farmer
kolkhoznitsy: female collective farmers
kommissiya vrachebno-trudovoi ekspertizy: medical-labor commission which determines loss of capacity of invalids.

komplektovaniye: recruitment, hiring of personnel
maloobespechennost: Soviet definition of poverty
minimum materialnoi obespechennosti: minimum of material well-being
mnogodetnost: having many children
mobilnyi dokhod: personal income
MOP: junior service personnel
nachalnik otdela truda i zarabotnoi platy: personnel manager
nachislennaya zarabotnaya plata: gross earnings
nalichnye kolkhoznye dvory: kolkhoznik households
nalog na kholostyakov, odinokikh i malosemeinnikh grazhdan SSSR: tax on bachelors and citizens with small families
Narkomtrud: People's Commisariat of Labor
naseleniye imeyushchee zanyatiya: total occupied population
naseleniye v trudosposobnom vozraste: population of working age
neprivlekatelnost: unattractiveness (of work)
oblast, pl. *oblasti*: administrative division of USSR; province
obshchestvennye fondy potrebleniya: social consumption expenditures
oformlen, inf. *oformlyat*: to register,

371

arrange with authorities (as with housing)

otchet, pl. *otchety:* accounting after census

pensii po sluchayu poteri kormiltsa: survivor pensions

pensii za vyslugu let: long-service pensions

podokhodnyi nalog: income tax

polnyi sovokupnyi dokhod: full gross income

poselki gorodskogo tipa: workers' settlements

posobiya: allowances

pozhilye: elderly

rabochii, pl. *rabochiye*: worker

rabochiye promyshlennosti: industrial workers

rabochiye vedushchikh professii: key workers

rabotnik: employee

rabotniki prostogo truda: unskilled laborers

raion, pl. *raiony*: smallest administrative unit; district

raskhody soderzhaniya zhil'ya: cost of maintenance of accommodation

sad i ogorod: private plot, garden

samizdat: unofficial or underground publication

samodeyatelnoye naseleniye: gainfully employed population

sluzhashchiye: clerical workers

sovkhoz, pl. *sovkhozy*: state farm

sovkhoznik, pl. *sovkhozniki*: worker on state farm

sovmestitelstvo: holding more than one position

sovnarkhoz, pl. *sovnarkhozy*: regional economic council

sovokupnyi dokhod: total income

spravochnik, pl. *spravochniki*: handbook, guide

srochnaya sluzhba: limited service enlistment

stavka, pl. *stavki*: basic wage rate

stazh: record of state employment

stikhiya: uncontrolled social process

tarifnye poyasy: wage bands

tarifnye setki: skill scales

tekhnikum, pl. *tekhnikumy*: organizations providing secondary specialist training

trudyashchiyesya: workers

tyazhest: arduousness (of work)

tipovye perechni rabot: lists of typical work environments

ukhod: care of disabled

uravnitelnost (also *uravnilovka*): egalitarianism

VUZ, pl. *VUZy*: institutions of higher learning

vzroslye trudosposobnye chleny semya: able-bodied adult family members

zanyatoe naseleniye: population in employment

zarabotok: payment for labor, wage

Bibliography

Acharkan, V. A. *Obespecheniye veteranov truda v SSSR*. Moscow, 1965.
_____. "Pensionnoye zakonodatelstvo i problema zanyatosti." *Sotsialisticheskii trud*, 1971, no. 1, pp. 117-25.
_____. "Sotsialisticheskii printsip raspredeleniya po trudu i sotsialnoye obespecheniye." *Sotsialisticheskii trud*, 1974, no. 11, pp. 119-29.
Agenbegyan, A. G., N. K. Zemlyanskii, L. S. Meshchaninov, and M. A. Mozhina. "Osobennosti deistviya zakona raspredeleniya po trudu v period razvernutogo stroitelstva kommunisticheskogo obshchestva." *Nauchnye trudy novosibirskogo universiteta* (seriya ekonomicheskaya), no. 1, 1964, pp. 111-49.
Aitchison, J., and J. A. C. Brown. *The Lognormal Distribution*. Cambridge: Cambridge University Press, 1957.
Akhromenko, F. *Spravochnik po gosudarstvennomu sotsialnomu strakhovaniyu*. Moscow, 1967.
Aleksandrov, A. "Nekotorye dannye o zhiznennom standarte naseleniya SSSR." *Posev*, 1975, no. 9, pp. 52-58.
Arouca, L. *On the Balance of Money Incomes and Expenditures in the USSR*. Ph.D. dissertation, London University, 1974.
Artem'eva, I. I. "Struktura dokhodov naseleniya." In G. S. Sarkisyan, ed., *Dokhody trudyashchikhsya i sotsialnye problemy urovnya zhizni naseleniya SSSR*, pp. 82-89. Moscow, 1973.
Atkinson, A. B. "On the Measurement of Inequality," *Journal of Economic Theory* 2 (September 1970), 244-63.
_____. *The Economics of Inequality*. Oxford: Oxford University Press, 1975.
Babkin, V. A., and G. B. Smirnova. *Kommentarii k polozheniyu o poryadke naznacheniya i vyplate gosudarstvennykh pensii*. Moscow, 1975.
Bandera, V. N., and Z. L. Melnyk, eds. *The Soviet Economy in Regional Perspective*. New York: Praeger, 1973.
Basov, V. I. *Obshchestvennye fondy potrebleniya i byudzhet*. Moscow, 1967.
Batkaev, R. A., and V. I. Markov. *Differentsiatsiya zarabotnoi platy v promyshlennosti SSSR*. Moscow, 1964.
Batkaev, R. A., and N. A. Safronov. "Trud i zarabotnaya plata v promyshlennosti." In A. P. Volkov, ed., *Trud i zarabotnaya plata v SSSR*, 2d ed., rev., pp. 373-401. Moscow, 1974.

Bergson, A., *The Structure of Soviet Wages*. Cambridge, Mass.: Harvard University Press, 1944.

Berkov, N. T. *Migratsiya deneg i metody eye izucheniya*. Moscow, 1966.

Berzkaln, O. Ya. "O differentsiatsii rabochikh, sluzhashchikh i kolkhoznikov Latviiskoi SSR po urovnyu dokhoda i potrebleniya." In *Statistika i elektronno-vychislitelnaya tekhnika v ekonomike*, no. 4, pp. 64-79. Moscow, 1971.

――――. "Voprosy prognozirovaniya raspredeleniya naseleniya po urovnyu dokhoda." *Statistika i elektronno-vychislitelnaya tekhnika v ekonomike*, no. 6, pp. 208-14. Moscow, 1973.

Blyakhman, L. S., A. G. Zdravomyslov, and O. I. Shkaratan. *Dvizheniye rabochei sily na promyshlennykh predpriyatiyakh*. Moscow, 1965.

Blyakhman, L. S., B. G. Sochilin, and O. I. Shkaratan. *Podbor i rasstanovka kadrov na predpriyatii*. Moscow, 1968.

Bornstein, M. "Soviet Price Statistics." In V. Treml and J. P. Hardt, eds., *Soviet Economic Statistics*, pp. 355-76. Durham, N.C.: Duke University Press, 1972.

Boyarskii, A. Ya., ed. *Vyborochnoye nablyudeniye v SSSR*. Moscow, 1966.

Bronson, D., and B. Severin. "Soviet Consumers' Welfare: The Brezhnev Era." In Joint Economic Committee, *Soviet Economic Prospects for the Seventies*, pp. 376-403. Washington, D.C., 1973.

Burova, L. P. *Rost bogatstva i blagosostoyaniya naroda*. Moscow, 1963.

Bush, K. "Soviet Living Standards: Some Salient Data." In *Economic Aspects of Life in the USSR*, pp. 49-64. Brussels, 1975.

Chapman, J. *Real Wages in Soviet Russia since 1928*. Cambridge, Mass.: Harvard University Press, 1963.

――――. *Wage Variations in Soviet Industry*. Rand (RM 6076-PR), 1970.

――――. "Soviet Wages under Socialism" In A. Abouchar, ed., *The Socialist Price Mechanism*. Durham, N.C.: Duke University Press, 1977

Clayton, E. M. "Regional Consumption Expenditures in the Soviet Union." *ACES Bulletin* 17, nos. 2-3 (Winter 1975).

Danilevich, V. G. *Spravochnik po zarabotnoi plate*. 2d ed. Minsk, 1969.

Danilov, L. M. *Dvizheniye rabochikh kadrov v promyshlennosti*. Moscow, 1973.

Dodge, N. *Women in the Soviet Economy*. Baltimore: Johns Hopkins University Press, 1966.

Drank, L. Ya. "Dinamika balansa denezhnykh dokhodov i raskhodov naseleniya Latviiskoi SSR." In *Voprosy urovnya zhizni naroda*, sec. 1, pp. 80-83. Riga, 1972.

Economic Aspects of Life in the USSR. Brussels: NATO, 1975.

Fearn, R. M. *An Evaluation of the Soviet Wage-Reform, 1956-1962*. Washington, D.C.: CIA/RRER, 1963.

Filippov, F. R. "Sotsialnye peremeshcheniya v sovetskom obshchestve." *Sotsiologicheskiye issledovaniya*, 1975, no. 4, pp. 14-21.

Galenson, W. "Wage Structure and Administration in Soviet Industry." In J. L. Meij, *Internal Wage Structure*. Amsterdam, 1963.

Goodman, L. A. "On the Exact Variance of Products." *Journal of the American Statistical Association* 55 (1960), 708-13.

Gordon, L. A., and E. V. Klopov. *Chelovek posle raboty*. Moscow, 1972.

Gordon, L. A., E. V. Klopov, V. Ya. Neigoldberg, and T. B. Petrov. "Razvitoi sotsializm: blagosostoyaniye rabochikh." *Rabochii klass i sovremennyi mir,* 1974, nos. 2-3, pp. 53-72.

Gosplan SSSR. *Metodicheskiye ukazaniya k sostavleniyu gosudarstvennogo plana razvitiya narodnogo khozyaistva SSSR.* Moscow, 1969.

_____. *Gosudarstvennyi pyatiletnii plan razvitiya narodnogo khozyaistva SSSR na 1971-75 gody.* Moscow, 1972.

Greenslade, R. "The Real National Product of the USSR, 1955-1975." In Joint Economic Committee, *Soviet Economy in a New Perspective,* pp. 269-300. Washington, D.C., 1976.

Gubareva, O. E. *Istochniki rosta narodnogo blagosostoyaniya.* Moscow, 1968.

Hanson, P. *The Consumer in Soviet Society.* Evanston: Northwestern University Press, 1968.

Hoeffding, O. "The Soviet Industrial Reorganisation of 1957." *American Economic Review* 39 (May 1959), 65-78.

Holubenko, B. "The Soviet Working Class." *Critique,* no. 4 (spring 1975), pp. 5-26.

Joint Economic Committee. *New Directions in the Soviet Economy.* Washington, D.C., 1966.

_____. *Soviet Economic Prospects for the 'Seventies.* Washington, D.C., 1973.

_____. *Soviet Economy in a New Perspective.* Washington, D.C., 1976.

Kapustin, E. I., ed. *Obshchestvennye fondy i rost blagosostoyaniya naroda v SSSR.* Moscow, 1962.

_____. "Tarifnaya sistema i eye rol v organizatsii i regulirovanii zarabotnoi platy." In A. P. Volkov, *Trud i zarabotnaya plata v SSSR,* pp. 309-36. Moscow, 1968.

_____. "Tarifnaya sistema i eye rol v organizatsii i regulirovanii zarabotnoi platy." in Volkov, *Trud i zarabotnaya plata,* 2d ed., pp. 247-73. (1974)

_____, and N. M. Rimashevskaya, eds. *Matematicheskiye metody v ekonomike truda.* Moscow, 1966.

_____, and N. P. Kuznetsova. "Regionalnye osobennosti povysheniya zhiznennogo urovnya naseleniya." *Ekonomicheskiye nauki,* 1972, no. 1, pp. 49-59.

Karapetyan, A. Kh., ed. *Dokhody i pokupatelskii spros naseleniya.* Moscow, 1968.

_____. "Analiticheskaya model raspredeleniya rabochikh po razmeram zarabotnoi platy." In his *Dokhody i pokupatelskii spros naseleniya,* pp. 7-14. (1968)

_____, and N. M. Rimashevskaya, eds. *Balansy dokhodov i potrebleniya naseleniya.* Moscow, 1969.

Karcz, J. "Seven Years on the Farm." In Joint Economic Committee, *New Directions in the Soviet Economy,* pp. 383-450. Washington, D.C., 1966.

Katsenellenboigen, A. I. "Disguised Inflation in the USSR." In *Economic Aspects of Life in the USSR,* pp. 101-9. (1975)

Khabibi, R. I. "Sootnosheniye oplaty po trudu i obshchestvennye fondy potrebleniya: sotsialno-ekonomicheskii aspekt." In A. P. Shvetsov, ed., *Sotsialisticheskii obraz zhizni i narodnoye blagosostoyaniye,* pp. 272-87. Saratov, 1975.

Khanelis, Ya. N., ed. *Zhiznennyi uroven.* Moscow, 1966.

Kirsch, L. *Soviet Wages.* Cambridge, Mass.: MIT Press, 1972.

Komarov, V. E., and U. G. Chernyavskii. *Dokhody i potrebleniye naseleniya SSSR*. Moscow, 1973.

Kopyrin, V. A. "Sotsiologicheskoye issledovaniye khudozhestvennoi intelligentsii." *Sotsiologicheskiye issledovaniya*, 1975, no. 2, pp. 74-81.

Korzhenevskii, I. I. *Osnovnye zakonomernosti razvitiya sprosa v SSSR*. Moscow, 1971.

Kotlyar, A., and A. Shlemin. "Problemy ratsionalnoi zanyatosti zhenshchin." *Sotsialisticheskii trud*, 1974, no. 7, pp. 110-19.

Kotov, G., and V. Kvachev. "Vyravnivaniye ekonomicheskikh uslovii khozyaist-vovaniya." *Ekonomika selskogo khozyaistva*, 1976, no. 7, pp. 86-90.

Kruk, D. G., and D. G. Chertkov. *Ot chego zavisit uroven zhizni trudyashchikhsya v SSSR?* Moscow, 1964.

Krushevskii, A. V. "Prognozirovaniye zarabotnoi platy s planovymi ogranicheni-yami." In Karapetyan, *Dokhody i pokupatelskii spros naseleniya*, pp. 15-23. (1968)

Krylov, P. "Zadachi perspektivnogo planirovaniya i statisticheskogo analiza zhiznennogo urovnya." In Khanelis, *Zhiznennyi uroven*, pp. 131-36. (1966)

Kukulevich, N. I. *Zarabotnaya plata v voprosakh i otvetakh*. 2d ed. Moscow, 1966.

Kulikov, V. S. *Rol finansov v povyshenii blagosostoyaniya sovetskogo naroda*. Moscow, 1972.

Kunelskii, L. E. "Glavnoye napravleniye rosta dokhodov trudyashchikhsya." *Sotsialisticheskii trud*, 1968, no. 1. pp. 81-90.

————. "Sotsialno-ekonomicheskoye znacheniye povysheniya minimalnykh raz-merov zarabotnoi platy." *Sotsialisticheskii trud*, 1968, no. 12, pp. 14-22.

————. *Sotsialno-ekonomicheskiye problemy zarabotnoi platy*. Moscow, 1972.

————. "Sotsialno-ekonomicheskiye problemy zarabotnoi platy." In Sarkisyan, *Dokhody trudyashchikhsya*, pp. 16-32. (1973)

Labok, P. I. "Vyborochnoye obsledovaniye zarabotnoi platy rabochikh, ITR i sluzhashchikh v promyshlennosti i stroitelstve." In Boyarskii, *Vyborochnoye nablyudeniye v SSSR*, pp. 270-80. (1966)

Lagutin, N. S. *Problemy sblizheniya urovnei zhizni rabochikh i kolkhoznikov*. Moscow, 1965.

Lailiev, D. S. *Proizvoditelnost truda i rentabelnost proizvodstva v selskom khozyaistve Kirgizskoi SSR*. Frunze, 1973.

Lancaster, K. *Consumer Demand: A New Approach*. New York, 1971.

Lane, D. *The End of Inequality? Stratification under State Socialism*. London: Penguin, 1971.

Lantsev, M. "Sovershenstvovaniye sistemy sotsialnogo obespecheniya v usloviyakh razvitogo sotsializma." *Sotsialisticheskii trud*, 1974, no. 9, pp. 128-36.

Levin, A. I. *Sotsialno-ekonomicheskiye problemy razvitiya sprosa naseleniya v SSSR*. Moscow, 1969.

Lion, V. A. "O raspredelenii obshchestvennykh fondov potrebleniya i ikh vliyanii na semeinyi byudzhet." *Vestnik moskovskogo universiteta*, series 8, 1965, no. 2, pp. 11-20.

Litvyakova, P. P., ed. *Demograficheskiye problemy zanyatosti*. Moscow, 1969.

Livshits, R. Z. *Zarabotnaya plata v SSSR*. Moscow, 1972.

Loznevaya, M. I. "Matematicheskiye metody v planirovanii zarabotnoi platy." *Sotsialisticheskii trud*, 1968, no. 10, pp. 126-35.

_____. "Ispolzovaniye metoda naimenshikh kvadratov dlya otsenki slozhnosti rabot." *Ekonomika i matematicheskiye metody*, 1969, no. 2, pp. 271-75.

McAuley, A. "The Distribution of Earnings and Incomes in the Soviet Union." *Soviet Studies* 29, no. 2 (April 1977) pp. 214-37.

_____. "The Empirical Study of Demand in the Soviet Union." *Ost Europa Wirtschaft Jahrbuch*, forthcoming, 1979.

_____. "Wage Determination in Soviet Industry." In S. Markowski, ed., title unknown, forthcoming.

Madison, B. *Social Welfare in the Soviet Union*. Stanford: Stanford University Press, 1968.

_____. "Social Services for Families and Children in the Soviet Union since 1967." *Slavic Review* 31 (Autumn 1972), pp. 831-52.

Maier, V. F. *Zarabotnaya plata v period perekhoda k kommunizmu*. Moscow, 1963.

_____. "Zarabotnaya plata v period perekhoda k kommunizmu." *Nauchnye trudy*, Seriya ekonomicheskaya, no. 1, pp. 20-31. Novosibirsk, 1964.

_____. *Planirovaniye realnykh dokhodov naseleniya*. Moscow, 1966.

_____. "Differentsirovannyi balans dokhodov i potrebleniya naseleniya kak instrument perspektivnogo planirovaniya." *Vestnik moskovskogo universiteta*, series 7, 1967, no. 2, pp. 31–37.

_____. *Dokhody naseleniya i rost blagosostoyaniya naroda*. Moscow, 1968.

_____. *Uroven zhizni trudyashchikhsya*. Moscow, 1971.

Maier, V. F., and B. V. Rakitskii. "Obshchestvennye fondy potrebleniya i rost blagosostoyaniya naroda." In *Oplata truda pri sotsializme: voprosy teorii i praktiki*, pp. 190–206. Moscow and Warsaw, 1976.

Mamontova, T. I. "Povysheniye roli obshchestvennykh fondov potrebleniya v reshenii sotsialnykh problem." In Sarkisyan, *Dokhody trudyashchikhsya*, pp. 56-81. (1973)

_____. "Vliyaniye obshchestvennykh fondov potrebleniya na differentsiatsiyu v urovne zhizni rabochikh i sluzhashchikh." In Shvetsov, *Sotsialisticheskii obraz*, pp. 294-302. (1975)

Markovskaya, K., and A. Voronov. "Balans denezhnykh dokhodov i raskhodov gorodskogo i selskogo naseleniya." *Dengi i kredit*, 1971, no. 5, pp. 28-34.

Maslov, P. P. "Sotsialno-kulturnye meropriyatiya gosudarstva i ikh otrazheniye na byudzhete rabochei semi." In I. Ya Pisarev, ed., *Voprosy povysheniya urovnya zhizni trudyashchikhsya*, pp. 27-51. Moscow, 1959.

_____. "Dopolnitelnye dokhody trudyashchikhsya." In I. Ya. Pisarev, ed., *Metodologicheskiye voprosy izucheniya urovnya zhizni trudyashchikhsya*, pp. 113-39. Moscow, 1959.

_____. *Dokhod sovetskoi semi*. Moscow, 1965.

Matthews, M. *Class and Society in Soviet Russia*. London: Allen Lane, 1972.

_____. "Top Incomes in the USSR." In *Economic Aspects of Life in the USSR*. pp. 131-58. (1975)

Matyukha, I. Ya. "Iz opyta primeneniya vyborochnogo metoda pri izuchenii zhiznennogo urovnya naseleniya." *Vestnik statistiki*, 1960, no. 9, pp. 14-26.

————. *Statistika byudzhetov naseleniya*. Moscow, 1967.

————. "Povysheniye zhiznennogo urovnya trudyashchikhsya SSSR." *Vestnik statistiki*, 1972, no. 12, pp. 44-50.

————. *Statistika zhiznennogo urovnya naseleniya*. Moscow, 1973.

Matyukha, I. Ya., and T. Chernisheva. "Vnedreniye matematiko-statisticheskikh metodov v issledovanii zhiznennogo urovnya naseleniya." *Vestnik statistiki*, 1975, no. 1, pp. 15-25.

Mazurenko, I., and P. Stremskii. "O metodike razrabotke balansa denezhnykh dokhodov i raskhodov naseleniya v administrativnykh raionakh." *Dengi i kredit*, 1972, no. 10, pp. 12-20.

Medvedev, R. *On Socialist Democracy*. Translated by Ellen deKadt. New York: Norton, 1975.

Mints, L. E. "Statisticheskiye metody perspektivnogo planirovaniya potrebleniya." In V. V. Shvyrkov, ed., *Opyt primeneniya matematicheskikh metodov i EVM v ekonomiko-matematicheskom modelirovanii potrebleniya*, pp. 9-20. Moscow, 1968.

Morton, H. W. "What Have the Soviet Leaders Done about the Housing Crisis?" In H. W. Morton and R. L. Tokes, eds., *Soviet Politics and Society in the 1970's*, pp. 163-200. New York: Free Press, 1974.

Mozhina, M. A. "Izmeneniya v raspredelenii promyshlennykh rabochikh SSSR po razmeram zarabotnoi platy." *Biulleten nauchnoi informatsii: trud i zarabotnaya plata*, 1961, no. 10, pp. 18-25.

Mstislavskii, P. S. *Narodnoye potrebleniye pri sotsializme*. Moscow, 1961.

Nemchinova, I. I. "Differentsiyatsiya dokhodov i potrebleniya semei rabochikh i sluzhashchikh." In Shvetsov, *Sotsialisticheskii obraz*, pp. 385-91. (1975)

Newth, J. A. N. "Income Distribution in the USSR." *Soviet Studies* 12, no. 2 (1960), pp. 193-96.

Nicholson, J. L. "Variations in working-class family expenditures." *Journal of the Royal Statistical Society*, series A, vol. 112, no. 4 (1949), pp. 359-411.

Nove, A., and J. A. N. Newth. *The Soviet Middle East: A Model for Development?* London: Allen & Unwin, 1967.

Ozeran, L. G. *Rost blagosostoyaniya trudyashchikhsya SSSR*. Moscow, 1962.

Parkin, F. *Class, Inequality and the Political Order*. London: McGibbon & Kee, 1971.

Pashkevich, B., and F. Gilitskii. *Spravochnik raschetshchika po zarabotnoi plate*. Minsk, 1968.

Pisarev, I. Yu., ed. *Voprosy povysheniya urovnya zhizni trudyashchikhsya*. Moscow, 1959.

————, ed. *Metodologicheskiye voprosy izucheniya urovnya zhizni trudyashchikhsya*. Moscow, no. 1, 1959; no. 2, 1962.

————, *Naseleniye i trud v SSSR*. Moscow, 1966.

Piskov, V. M., ed. *Sotsialnoye obespecheniye i strakhovaniye v SSSR*. Moscow, 1964.

Plotnick, R., and F. Skidmore. *Progress against Poverty.* New York: Academic Press, 1975.

Portes, R. *Macroeconomic Equilibrium under Central Planning.* Institute for International Economic Studies of the University of Stockholm, Seminar Paper 40 (1974).

―――. *Macroeconomic Equilibrium and Disequilibrium in Centrally Planned Economies: A Model for Empirical Implementation.* Discussion Paper no. 45 in Economics. London: Birkbeck College, 1976.

―――. "The Control of Inflation: Lessons from East European Experience." *Economica* 44, no. 2 (May 1977), pp. 109-30.

Portes, R., and D. Winter. "The Demand for Money, and for Consumption Goods in Centrally Planned Economies." *Review of Economics and Statistics.* Forthcoming

Rabkina, N. E., and N. M. Rimashevskaya. *Osnovy differentsiatsii zarabotnoi platy i dokhodov naseleniya.* Moscow, 1972.

Rakitskii, B. V. *Obshchestvennye fondy potrebleniya kak ekonomicheskaya kategoriya.* Moscow, 1966.

Rasulev, F. *Denezhnye dokhody i raskhody naseleniya Uzbekistana.* Tashkent, 1969.

Reder, M. "The Theory of Occupational Wage Differentials." *American Economic Review,* 1955.

Resheniya partii i pravitelstva po khozyaistvennym voprosam (1917-1967g). 6 vols. Moscow, 1968.

Rimashevskaya, N. M. *Ekonomicheskii analiz dokhodov rabochikh i sluzhashchikh.* Moscow, 1965.

Rutkevich, M. N. "Sotsialnoye planirovaniye v usloviyakh razvitogo sotsializma." *Sotsiologicheskiye issledovaniya,* 1975, no. 3.

Rzhanitsyna, L. "Obshchestvennye fondy potrebleniya—vazhnyi istochnik rosta blagosostoyaniya sovetskikh lyudei." *Sotsialisticheskii trud,* 1973, no. 7, pp. 78-85.

Sarkisyan, G. S. "Vazhnoye sredstvo povysheniya zhiznennogo urovnya naroda." *Politicheskoye samoobrazovaniye,* 1963, no. 11, pp. 19-26.

―――. *Uroven, tempy i proportsii rosta realnykh dokhodov pri sotsializme.* Moscow, 1972.

―――, ed. *Dokhody trudyashchikhsya i sotsialnye problemy urovnya zhizni naseleniya SSSR.* Moscow, 1973.

―――. "Obshchestvennye fondy potrebleniya." In Volkov, *Trud i zarabotnaya plata v SSSR,* 2d ed., pp. 297-320. (1974)

―――, and N. P. Kuznetsova. *Potrebnosti i dokhod semi.* Moscow, 1967.

Schroeder, G. "Regional Differences in Incomes and Levels of Living in the USSR." In Bandera and Melnyk, *Soviet Economy,* pp. 167-95. (1973)

Schroeder, G. "Soviet Wage and Income Policies in Regional Perspective." *ACES Bulletin* 16, no. 2 (fall 1974), pp. 3-19.

Schroeder, G., and B. Severin. "Soviet Consumption and Income Policies in Perspective." In Joint Economic Committee, *New Perspective*, pp. 620-660. (1976)

Senyavskii, S. L. *Izmeneniya v sotsialnoi strukture sovetskogo obshchestva 1938-70*. Moscow, 1973.

Shvetsov, A. P., ed. *Sotsialisticheskii obraz zhizni i narodnoye blagosostoyaniye*. Saratov: Saratovskogo Universiteta, 1975.

Shvyrkov, V. V. "Shkaly potrebleniya tovarov i uslug." In Pisarev, *Metolodologicheskiye voprosy*, pp. 228-58. (1959)

————, ed. *Opyt primeneniya matematicheskikh metodov i EVM v ekonomiko-matematicheskom modelirovanii potrebleniya*. Moscow, 1968.

————. "Ekonomiko-matematicheskiye metody postroyeniya spetsialnykh shkal raskhodov na pokupku tovarov po dannym byudzhetnykh obsledovanii." In his *Opyt primeneniya*, pp. 324-40.

Shvyrkov, V. V., and L. K. Aidina. "Model raspredeleniya naseleniya po dokhodu." In his *Opyt primeneniya*, pp. 230-44.

Sidorova, M. I. *Obshchestvennye fondy potrebleniya i dokhody kolkhozov*. Moscow, 1969.

————. *Vozmeshcheniye neobkhodimykh zatrat i formirovaniye fonda vosproizvodstva rabochei sily v kolkhozakh*. Moscow, 1972.

Simons, H. *Personal Income Taxation*. Chicago: University of Chicago Press, 1938.

Skripko, V. R. *Zhilishchnye prava grazhdan*. Moscow, 1972.

Smith, H. *The Russians*. New York: Quadrangle Press, 1976.

Spravochnik ekonomista i planovika promyshlennogo predpriyatiya. Moscow, 1964.

Spravochnik ekonomista kolkhoza i sovkhoza. Moscow, 1970.

Sukharevskii, B. M. "Zarabotnaya plata i materialnaya zainteresovannost." In Volkov, *Trud i zarabotnaya plata v SSSR*, pp. 267-308. (1968)

————. "Zarabotnaya plata v SSSR." In Volkov, *Trud i zarabotnaya plata v SSSR*, 2d ed., pp. 201-46. (1974)

Taichinova, K. "Povysheniye zhiznennogo urovnya selskogo naseleniya." *Voprosy ekonomiki*, 1974, no. 6, pp. 50-60.

Treml, V., and J. P. Hardt, eds. *Soviet Economic Statistics*. Durham, N.C.: Duke University Press, 1972.

Urlanis, E. B. "Vliyaniye demograficheskikh sdvigov v strukture semei rabochikh i sluzhashchikh na uroven materialnogo obespechennosti." In Kapustin and Rimashevskaya, *Matematicheskiye metody*, pp. 135–46. (1966)

Vasil'eva, V. A. *Byudzhety rabochikh prezhde i teper*. Moscow, 1965.

Vinokur, A. *Surveys of Family Budgets in the USSR: A Review*. Mimeographed. The Hebrew University of Jerusalem, 1975.

Vlasova, A. G., V. I. Zamyatin, and V. R. Skripko. *Zhilishchnoye zakonodatelstvo*. Moscow, 1970.

Vogel, H. "Social Security and Medicare." In *Economic Aspects of Life in the USSR.*, pp. 207-34. (1975)

Volkov, A. P., ed. *Trud i zarabotnaya plata v SSSR*. Moscow, 1968.

————. "Trud, zarabotnaya plata i narodnoye blagosostoyaniye v SSSR." In his *Trud i zarabotnaya plata v SSSR*, pp. 3-46. (1968)

_____, ed. *Trud i zarabotnaya plata v SSSR*. 2d edition, revised. Moscow, 1974.

_____. "Trud, zarabotnaya plata i narodnoye blagosostoyaniye v SSSR." In his *Trud i zarabotnaya plata v SSSR*, 2d ed., pp. 3-52. (1974)

Voprosy urovnya zhizni naroda "Problemy povysheniya blagosostoyaniya naseleniya i izucheniya sprosa na tovary narodnogo potrebleniya i uslugi" (materialy respublikanskoi nauchnoi konferentsii). Secs. 1–3. Riga, 1972.

Wiles, P. *Distribution of Income: East and West*. Amsterdam: North Holland, 1974.

_____. "Recent Data on Soviet Income Distribution." In *Economic Aspects of Life in the USSR*, pp. 113-30. (1975)

Wiles, P., and S. Markowski. "Income Distribution under Communism and Capitalism. "*Soviet Studies* 22, no. 4 (April, 1971), pp. 487–511.

Yanowitch, M. *Social and Economic Inequality in the Soviet Union: Six Studies.* London: Martin Robertson, 1977.

Zakharov, M. L., ed. *Sotsialnoye strakhovaniye i pensionnoye obespecheniye v kolkhozakh*. Moscow, 1966.

Zakharov, M. L., and V. M. Piskov. *Sotsialnoye obespecheniye i strakhovaniye v SSSR*. Moscow, 1972.

Zhutovskaya, M. L. "Edinovremennoye vyborochnoye obsledovaniye sostava semei, dokhodov i zhilishchnykh uslovii rabochikh i sluzhashchikh nesel-skokhozyaistvennykh otraslei narodnogo khozyaistva." In Boyarskii *Vyborochnoye nablyudeniye v SSSR*, pp. 96-114.

STATISTICAL SOURCES

Az SSR k 50-letiyu velikogo oktyabrya. Baku, 1967.

Bolshaya sovetskaya entsiklopediya (ezhegodnik). Various years.

Ekonomika i kultura Li SSR v 1972. Vilnyus.

Garbuzov, V. F. *O gosudarstvennom byudzhete na   god i ob ispolnenii gosudarstvennogo byudzheta za   god*. Moscow, various years.

Gosudarstvennyi byudzhet SSSR i byudzhety soyuznykh respublik. Moscow, 1962, 1966, 1972.

GSSR v tsifrakh v 1971. Tbilisi.

Itogi vsesoyuznoi perepisi naseleniya za 1959 godu. 16 volumes. Moscow, 1962-63.

Itogi vsesoyuznoi perepisi naseleniya za 1970 godu. 7 volumes. Moscow, 1971-73.

Narodnoye khozyaistvo Ar SSR v 1967. Erevan.

Narodnoye khozyaistvo Az SSR v 1960. Baku.

Narodnoye khozyaistvo Az SSR v 1970. Baku.

Narodnoye khozyaistvo BSSR v 1973. Minsk.

Narodnoye khozyaistvo ESSR v 1970. Tallin.

Narodnoye khozyaistvo ESSR v 1971. Tallin.

Narodnoye khozyaistvo Ka SSR v 1971. Alma Ata.

Narodnoye khozyaistvo Ki SSR v 1971. Frunze.

Narodnoye khozyaistvo La SSR v 1972. Riga.

Narodnoye khozyaistvo La SSR v 1973. Riga.

Narodnoye khozyaistvo MSSR v 1970. Kishinev.

Narodnoye khozyaistvo MSSR v 1972. Kishinev.

Narodnoye khozyaistvo RSFSR. Moscow: 1970, 1973.

Narodnoye khozyaistvo SSSR. Moscow: 1956, 1959-65, 1967-70, 1972-74.

Narodnoye khozyaistvo Ta SSR v 1971. Dushanbe.

Narodnoye khozyaistvo Uz SSR v 1971. Tashkent.

Trud v SSSR. Moscow, 1968.

Uk SSR v tsifrakh and *Uk RSR v tsifrakh* (in Ukranian). Kiev, 1969.

Zverev, A. G. *O gosudarstvennom byudzhete SSSR na 1960 god i ob ispolnenii gosudarstvennogo byudzheta za 1959*. Moscow, 1959.

Index

383

JACKET DESIGNED BY IRVING PERKINS
COMPOSED BY FOCUS / TYPOGRAPHERS, ST. LOUIS, MISSOURI
MANUFACTURED BY McNAUGHTON & GUNN, ANN ARBOR, MICHIGAN
TEXT AND DISPLAY LINES SET IN PALATINO

Library of Congress Cataloging in Publication Data
McAuley, Alastair, 1938–
Economic welfare in the Soviet Union.
Bibliography: p.
Includes index.
1. Income distribution—Russia. 2. Poor—Russia.
I. Title.

HC340.I5M2   339.2′0947   78-53290
ISBN 0-299-07640-7

British Library Cataloging in Publication Data
McAuley, Alastair
Economic Welfare in the Soviet Union.
1. Income distribution—Russia
I. Title

339.2′0947   HC340.15
ISBN 0-04-335038-0